The
Financial Risk
Manual

RISK
management

The Financial Risk Manual

A Systematic Guide to Identifying and Managing Financial Risk

JOHN HOLLIWELL

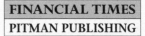

FINANCIAL TIMES
PITMAN PUBLISHING

FINANCIAL TIMES
MANAGEMENT

LONDON · SAN FRANCISCO
KUALA LUMPUR · JOHANNESBURG

Financial Times Management delivers the knowledge,
skills and understanding that enable students,
managers and organisations to achieve their ambitions,
whatever their needs, wherever they are.

London Office:
128 Long Acre, London WC2E 9AN
Tel: +44 (0)171 447 2000
Fax: +44 (0)171 240 5771
Website: www.ftmanagement.com

A Division of Financial Times Professional Limited

First published in Great Britain in 1997

The right of John Holliwell to be identified as author
of this work has been asserted by him in accordance
with the Copyright, Designs, and Patents Act 1988.

ISBN 0 273 62418 0

British Library Cataloguing in Publication Data
A CIP catalogue record for this book can be obtained from the British Library.

10 9 8 7 6 5 4 3 2

Typeset by Northern Phototypesetting Co. Ltd, Bolton
Printed and bound in Great Britain by Bell and Bain Ltd, Glasgow

The Publishers' policy is to use paper manufactured from sustainable forests.

About the author

John Holliwell has over 30 years' experience across a wide range of activities in the financial sector. He is currently the Managing Director of Smith & Williamson Consultancy, specializing in risk management, and acts as a banking expert witness.

John was a director of merchant bankers Henry Ansbacher & Co. and a Business Centre Manager for Barclays Bank. His experience in the UK and overseas has included company turnarounds, lending, international trade, commercial property, trusts, training and consultancy. He is a Member of the Securities Institute and a Fellow of The Chartered Institute of Bankers.

Contents

About this book   xi

How to use this book   xiii

Acknowledgements   xv

SECTION ❶ **BUSINESS RISK**   1

The fundamentals of risk management   3

SECTION ❷ **COUNTERPARTY RISK (including credit risk)**   21

Due diligence   24

The numbers (key ratios)   27

Lending   52

Credit insurance   62

Trade payments   65

   Open account   65

   Payment in advance/on delivery   66

   Documentary letters of credit   68

   Incoterms   85

   Collections   87

   Bills of exchange/drafts   93

   Bonds/contract guarantees   95

   Avalising   105

   Countertrade   105

   Medium- and long-term finance for
exporters   109

SECTION ❸ FUNDING RISK 111

Business plans 114

Cash flow forecasts 116

Profit and loss forecasts 119

Types of funding 120

    Equity 120

    Borrowing from banks and elsewhere 123

    Mergers and acquisitions 124

    Bond markets 127

    Rating agencies 128

    Project finance 136

Borrowing 138

    The documentation (loan agreements) 138

Asset-based financing 160

    Confidential invoice discounting 161

    Factoring 163

Forfaiting 170

Acceptance credits 179

Negotiating a bill of exchange/draft 180

Advances against collections (bill advances) 182

SECTION ❹ DERIVATIVES: THE BASICS 183

Exchange traded derivatives 186

Over-the-counter (OTC) derivatives 188

Risks 189

Futures 190

Options 191

Swaps 194

Equity/index derivatives   194
Commodity derivatives   196
Credit derivatives   196

SECTION **5** **INTEREST RATE RISK**   199

Variable rate facilities   204
Fixed rate facilities   205
Forward rate agreements (FRAs)   205
Interest rate futures   212
Interest rate options   219
Interest rate caps, collars and floors   224
Interest rate swaps   229

SECTION **6** **CURRENCY RISK**   237

Spot   242
Invoicing in foreign currency   243
Currency borrowing   244
Forward contracts   246
Currency options   249
Currency collars   255
Currency futures   256
Currency swaps   257

Glossary   263
Index   329

About this book

For our purposes *financial risk* falls conveniently into four categories:

- counterparty risk
- funding risk
- interest rate risk
- currency risk.

To understand and be able to manage these exposures is critical for
business success, and an essential skill for financiers and advisers.
This book explains the nature of these financial risks, and the techniques used in their management.

How to use this book

Either:

use the 'route maps' at the beginning of each section to find the topics you need

or:

look up a reference in the *Glossary* and use the index to guide you to the relevant text.

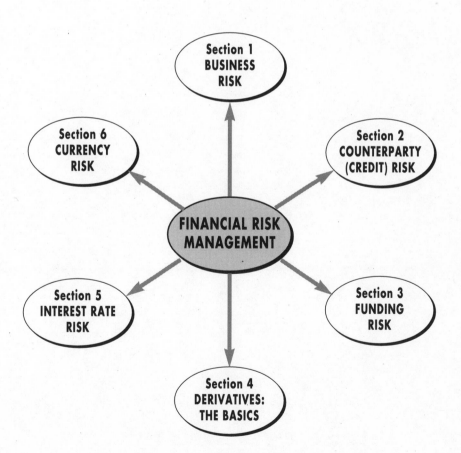

Acknowledgements

I am deeply indebted to all those who have so kindly given of their time and skills in helping me to write this book. My particular thanks to:

John Burge	Dresdner Kleinwort Benson
Ian Burns	Smith & Williamson
Jane Bush	Clifford Chance
John Clegg	London Forfaiting Company UK Limited
Phil Cook	London Forfaiting Company UK Limited
Glenn Cooper	Apax Partners
David Double	Merita Bank Limited
John Eaton	Eaton & Co.
Peter Frankl	SBC Warburg
Philip Gauntlett	SBC Warburg
Barry Hancock	Standard & Poor's
John Hubbard	Consultant
Peter Manning	Moscow Narodny Bank Ltd
Ron Merrett	Consultant
Brent Osborne	BNY Financial Limited
Stephen Osmond	Merrill Lynch
John Price	NCM Credit Insurance Limited
Mike Symes	BNY Financial Limited
Francesca Taylor	Taylor Associates
Maurice Withall	Grant Thornton

It has been a pleasure to work with Richard Stagg and his team at Pitman Publishing, who have provided invaluable advice and support.

My heartfelt thanks to Sue, who typed and re-typed this work through its many revisions.

Business Risk

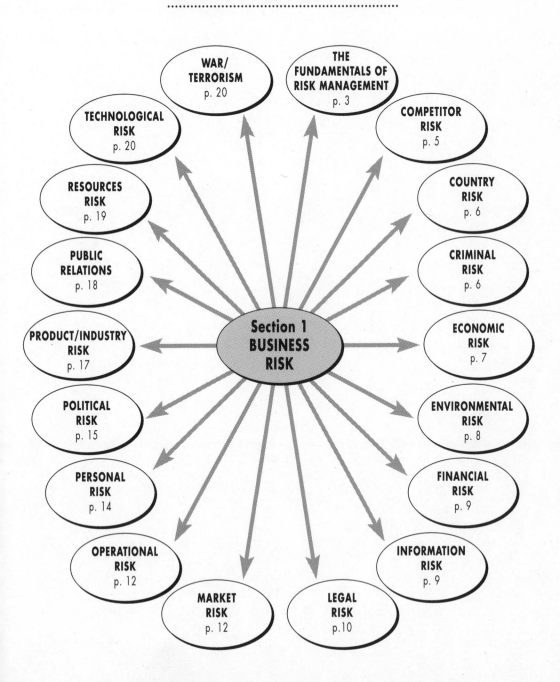

WAR/
TERRORISM
p. 20

THE
FUNDAMENTALS OF
RISK MANAGEMENT
p. 3

TECHNOLOGICAL
RISK
p. 20

COMPETITOR
RISK
p. 5

RESOURCES
RISK
p. 19

COUNTRY
RISK
p. 6

PUBLIC
RELATIONS
p. 18

CRIMINAL
RISK
p. 6

PRODUCT/INDUSTRY
RISK
p. 17

Section 1
BUSINESS
RISK

ECONOMIC
RISK
p. 7

POLITICAL
RISK
p. 15

ENVIRONMENTAL
RISK
p. 8

PERSONAL
RISK
p. 14

FINANCIAL
RISK
p. 9

OPERATIONAL
RISK
p. 12

INFORMATION
RISK
p. 9

MARKET
RISK
p. 12

LEGAL
RISK
p.10

The fundamentals of risk management

To be in business you must make decisions, each of which involves risk. Taking a particular gamble may have turned out to be the best thing you ever did, but to repeatedly 'bet the business' is asking for trouble.

However sophisticated the tools at your disposal, you can never hope to provide for every contingency, but unpleasant surprises can be kept to a minimum.

The secret is to know:

- *the risks to which you are exposed*
- *if they are big enough to worry about*
- *if there is anything you can do to protect against them*
- *what it will cost to reduce or to hedge your risks.*

Then, if action is needed, *do something about it*!
Ask yourself the following questions.

- Are the risks to your business clearly understood – particularly if you have a portfolio of different activities?
- Do you grade the risks faced by your business in a structured way?
- Do you know the maximum potential liability of each exposure?
- Are the risks large in relation to the turnover of your business? What impact could they have on your profits and balance sheet?
- Over what time periods do the risks exist? Are they one-offs or recurring?
- Do you know enough about the ways in which your exposures can be reduced or hedged? What would it cost, including the potential loss of any upside profits?
- Is there an effective risk management policy with responsibility at board or senior executive level? Do you differentiate between hedging your risks and speculating for profit?
- Is this policy regularly reviewed to identify new and changing exposures, as on even a single transaction the risk profile can change over time? Effective risk management requires thinking that the unthinkable might happen and anticipating the consequences.
- Are there adequate risk monitoring processes, including those for contingent liabilities?

- Are your colleagues and staff 'risk-conscious'? They probably attend marketing and customer care meetings, but what about risk management meetings? Is there a forum where issues of risk can be constructively considered by everyone concerned? A single sale rarely changes the future of the business, but one mismanaged risk can destroy the hard work of years.
- Are decisions being made on the basis of reliable and timely information? How quickly can you react?
- Is there an adequate division of duties, and have trading 'front office' and risk management or administrative 'back office' functions been clearly separated?
- Are the rewards of your business matched to the risks?
- Are the owners of the business happy at the level of exposure, or might they prefer a lower-risk profile with a potentially reduced return? What is their appetite for risk?
- What motivates individuals – is pressure on management and staff or the way they are remunerated encouraging them to take unauthorized risks or to cover up their mistakes?
- Can management and staff ask questions or admit they do not understand without fear of the consequences?
- Do you have regularly updated disaster recovery plans for a range of contingencies?
- Are the ethics of your business something of which you are proud – or does the culture leave much to be desired?
- Do you learn from your mistakes?

Many major problems have resulted from simple errors or omissions that could have been avoided by common sense or more information.

Financial exposure can only be considered in context of the generic risks faced by every business (see box).

Principal business risks

- Competitors
- Country
- Criminal/fraud
- Economic
- Environmental
- Financial:
  - counterparty
  - funding
  - currency
  - interest rate
- Information

- Legal
- Market
- Operational
- Personal
- Political
- Product/industry
- Public relations
- Resources
- Technological
- War/terrorism

The categories in the box, which are considered in detail on the following pages, may not all agree with the textbook classifications of risk – but are relevant to the problems that businesses throughout the world face every day.

See also *Due Diligence*, page 24.

Competitor risk

The harsh realities of competition are well-known and understood by anyone in business – from the pricing and marketing of products or services to the speed at which others copy your new ideas.

But with:

- *national frontiers ever less of a barrier*
- *the impetus of technology*
- *strategic alliances changing overnight*

do you know where your competition is going to come from?

Information on known or established rivals is invaluable, but all too often the challenge derives from an unexpected quarter.

For example, in some countries, leading retailers offer a range of personal financial services, including insurance, investment and consumer credit. This has encouraged the banks and other institutions faced with such competition to seek strategic alliances with the retailers, that, as a consequence, can now provide an even wider product range.

Who will *you* be competing with tomorrow?`

Country risk

This is an amalgam of many factors, but essentially refers to the additional risks inherent in dealing with a State ('sovereign risk') or any overseas business.

For each country you may need to consider:

- political risk, including exchange controls and other restrictions on the repatriation/remittance of profits, capital or other payments
- social and economic stability
- the costs and time incurred in visiting the overseas territory, and of employing local or expatriate staff
- finding, where necessary, a trustworthy local agent or representative and the extent to which they can commit you under local law – dispensing with their services if they prove unsuitable can also be difficult or costly
- trading practices, customs and ethics
- commercial law and the effectiveness of its application, including insolvency situations
- restrictions on foreign ownership and/or management
- delays in money transmission
- the basic problems of controlling anything at a distance.

Just as you set limits on your exposure to every other business or individual with which you deal ('counterparty risk'), so there should be a predetermined limit to the amount of exposure you will accept relating to any single country. These limits should be reviewed regularly, and immediately in the light of changing events.

Criminal risk (including fraud)

Theft, criminal damage, computer 'hacking' and arson are all risks to which businesses are accustomed or can relate, and for which insurance may be available, but consider in addition the following.

- Fraud, including the actions of employees under pressure to produce results. A great deal of damage can be done to a business by the falsification of figures, even when the employee responsible derives no direct personal financial benefit. Less measurable, but potentially no less harmful over time, can be the impact of 'shrinkage' of stock through staff pilfering, 'fiddling' of expense accounts and other similar practices. These very much depend upon the culture of a business, which is set by senior management, but can be hard to change once established. Does the way you reward staff encourage them to take risks with your money?

- When an employee resigns or is dismissed, what do they take with them to help in their next job? This has been made very much simpler by the advent of computers, where so much information can be stored on a disk that drops into a pocket. Do you have password protection at different levels? The more notice an employee has of their departure, the greater the time available for such activities; and do not overlook the ill-will that can result from a dismissal. If an employee knows or suspects that they may be asked to leave, they might destroy records, or plant a 'virus' in your computer system. It is not unknown for them to intentionally enter into contractual or trading commitments on terms harmful to their employer. Grievance procedures often require considerable advance warning, which can make it harder to fully protect your business. But if you allow a dismissed employee working in a sensitive area to return to their desk, even if supervised, the risks are considerable.

- Industrial espionage is a major problem in some sectors, whether through corrupt employees or sophisticated electronic 'snooping' devices. Businesses susceptible to this risk are usually well aware of the dangers and take appropriate action. It can, however, affect *anyone* involved in negotiating a major contract or other business transaction. Obvious advice is to shred confidential papers, only discuss the deal with those who must be in the know and not talk loudly to colleagues in public. In some parts of the world, particularly where everybody seems to know all that is going on, taxi drivers can earn good money by passing on what they overhear on the way from the airport or while taking business people around town. Similarly, sit in any first-class section of a plane or train, and there is a good chance you will hear conversations that should have been confidential.

- In some territories corruption and criminal control of business are endemic. If you decide to operate in such countries, take advice from those who know the area, and be prepared to get on the next plane home if things turn unpleasant. Do you have an agreed procedure, insurance cover or contingency arrangements if a member of your staff is taken hostage?

How often do you review the defences against fraud and other criminal acts?
See also *Character and ability*, page 52.

Economic risk

Economies are inherently cyclical, with potentially wide fluctuations in activity levels and asset values. However long-predicted, the transition from a bull to a bear market usually happens with a speed that catches people out and leaves them to count their losses.

Although governments are generally getting better at managing economies, the cycle is such a powerful combination of upside greed and downside fear that to some extent it will always be with us. Accordingly, the onus is on every business to arrange its financial, counterparty and other activities so as to achieve the desired level of protection.

Why is it that so many are wrong-footed when the music stops? Lending banks provide a useful object lesson, because you would think the cumulative experience of that industry, coupled with the resources and information at their disposal, might help protect them from the risks. That has rarely been the case.

At the start of an economic upturn, the banks are bruised from the difficulties suffered during the recession that is just ending, and are probably still trying to sort out their residual problem loans. Equally important, the staff who survived and have risen to senior positions are likely to be of a more cautious disposition, whilst their subordinates will be imbued with the wisdom of saying 'no'. Inquests carried out into what went wrong will have addressed the lessons to be learned, and suggested ways 'to prevent such mistakes ever occurring again'. The combined effect will encourage banks to exercise caution in lending to those businesses which, having survived the downturn, now need help in funding working capital and investment.

Gradually confidence will return and competitive pressures increasingly encourage banks to lend more, with less security at lower interest margins. It is now the turn of those members of staff who are best at business development to rise through the ranks, being assessed and rewarded on the volume rather than quality of the lending they achieve. They will be welcomed with open arms by those businesses that are chasing turnover and need to fund their overtrading.

By the time the latest 'boom' is coming to an end, most of the lessons from the last recession will have been forgotten, setting the scene for yet another crisis. Many banks recognize this scenario and make great efforts to avoid falling victim to the pattern, but it is hard to change human nature.

On a different timescale, there is the economic risk that adverse movement in the competitive international position of the country in which you are based or operate will impact upon an ability to trade profitably. This frequently results from a change in the international strength of your domestic currency, which may be linked to the rate of domestic inflation. Unless arising from some dramatic event, the change is likely to be gradual. Even if identified, there may be little that can be done to protect your business, unless you are able to re-locate or outsource in another country.

Environmental risk

This occurs in many ways, including:

● the need to comply with environmental or safety legislation, the costs of which can be considerable – it may not even be economically viable to continue your operations

- higher costs, or shortages, of raw materials if your supplier(s) are hit by these problems

- damage to the public image of your business if targeted as environmentally unsound by pressure groups – however seemingly unfair

- the costs and disruptions that can result from the need to clean up historic pollution – this can be of a magnitude to severely damage or even destroy your business, though the cause may lie long in the past or have been inherited on acquiring a property or business

- litigation by plaintiffs claiming redress for damage to property or health, particularly if you are considered a 'deep pocket', (i.e., of sufficient financial or insured strength to be worth suing; *banks are especially wary of situations where, if they realize a charge on a property or other asset as security, they might be deemed liable for any pollution – indeed, many mortgagees insist on a site inspection or 'environmental audit' before either taking a charge or taking possession of assets where this risk exists, and some facility agreements require the borrower to warrant that they will not carry out activities on the site that might cause pollution)*

- diminution in the value of an asset when pollution is found.

Financial risk

For our purposes, financial risk falls into four main categories, each of which is considered in detail elsewhere in this book:

- **counterparty**   (pages 21–109)
- **funding**   (pages 111–182)
- **interest rate**   (pages 199–235)
- **currency**   (pages 237–261)

Information risk

Your business will only be as good as the information on which decisions are based, including:

- **costs** – at each stage of every process
- **liabilities** – actual and contingent
- **risks** – exposures, maximum potential liabilities and available protection
- **markets** – volumes and prices
- **competitors** – who they are, their positioning and intentions – present and future
- **resources** – costs and availability, including human resources
- **technology** – using what you have and knowing what you need

● **financial** – cash flow, profits and balance sheet.

If you do not know what is going on you cannot manage effectively.

The importance of obtaining, processing and circulating information through a 'value network' is now widely recognized.

Legal risk

This takes many forms, including the following.

Documentation risk

Documentation risk results from errors or omissions in documents. These can arise from a misunderstanding or ignorance as to the meaning or significance of terms and expressions, or not taking the time and trouble to check a document thoroughly before signing. If, subsequently, something goes wrong such mistakes can prove very costly.

Most everyday contracts are reasonably simple, or take a standard form, but how long is it since you read yours through to remind yourself of the detailed terms and conditions? For example, are you happy with procedures to be followed in the event of a dispute?

If the document is out of the ordinary, and especially if it involves overseas jurisdictions or counterparties, then be prepared to consult a lawyer – their fee might be the best investment you ever made. But remember that responsibility for negotiating the terms of any deal is yours.

Who in your business is authorized to sign documents or otherwise enter into commitments? Are all staff aware of the risks to which they may be exposing the business by seemingly innocent statements or acts?

If something goes wrong with a transaction, read the background documents *before* taking action. It is easy to forget their detailed terms and conditions, and you can make matters worse by doing or saying something contrary to an agreement or earlier statement.

Jurisdiction risk

Which country's laws regulate any individual contract and the arbitration of disputes? Could a plaintiff take action against you in an overseas court where their prospects of success or of higher damages were greater? Even though a contract is governed by the laws of one country it *may* be that the parties could take legal action against each other in a different country. Do you fully understand the implications, including the costs and time commitment that might be incurred if it became necessary to resort to the courts?

Security risk

If you take security in support of a lending or other transaction make sure:

- it can be enforced against the appropriate party(s) in the relevant jurisdiction(s) without incurring disproportionate costs or liabilities
- where it is necessary for the security to be 'registered', that this is done within the time period allowed for that purpose
- the security documents themselves are put in a safe place with copies available for ease of reference.

Litigation

The costs of litigation, both financial and in time, can be so great that even the most frivolous claim may seriously damage your business. Is arbitration an option? When studying the statutory report and accounts or other communications of a business, look to see if any reference is made to legal actions.

Ensure variations to contracts, and any problems outside your control, are recorded in writing with counterparties and consider the legal and other implications before accepting responsibility for anything.

Where insurance is available to cover the business and/or its officers and employees this should always be considered. The problem is that premiums are often at a level where many cannot afford them, or might take out inadequate cover.

There is a widespread belief that, whatever goes wrong, someone else must pay. This 'compensation culture' approach, whatever its justification or causes, is becoming a major problem for many businesses.

'Discovery'

It is not widely appreciated that, under many legal jurisdictions, the 'other side' in a legal action can have the right to see your internal files and records – a process known as 'discovery'. Ironically, the more disciplined the way you run your business, with notes of meetings and decisions, the greater the possibility that you may provide ammunition to your opponent(s). Those memoranda in which every fact, consideration and contingency are carefully recorded are grist to a lawyer's mill. There are legally sound, commonsense ways to protect your interests and some documents can be 'privileged', and thereby not available for inspection, provided you act correctly at the appropriate time. If discovery might potentially become a problem it is worth taking legal advice at an early stage.

Market risk

In its simplest form this is the exposure to an adverse change in the price or value of something in which you trade or are holding as an investment.

An important discipline, where market risk is a factor, is the practice of 'marking to market' on a regular basis. This involves using current market prices to calculate any profit or loss that has arisen from price movements since the last time you calculated the value of your assets or the cost of meeting your liabilities.

Traders and dealers should admit their mistakes, enabling unsatisfactory positions to be closed out where appropriate, rather than 'running' them in the hope that the market will turn in their favour. The danger is that, unless discovered, a 'rogue' dealer on a losing streak will need to keep increasing the volume or speculative nature of their 'trades' if they are to have any chance of wiping out an ever-mounting deficit. After all, it is not their money.

- 'Inventory risk' is a variant of market risk, an example of which would be exposure to a fall in the value of securities held by a bank or other financial institution for trading purposes.

- 'Liquidity risk' arises when a market does not have the capacity to handle the volume of whatever you are trying to buy or sell at the time you want to deal.

- 'Hedging risk' occurs when you fail to achieve a satisfactory hedge, either because it could not be arranged in the market or as the result of an error. You may also be exposed to 'basis risk', where the available hedging instrument closely matches but does not exactly mirror or track the risk being hedged.

Operational risk

Murphy's Law says that if something can go wrong, it will. Many operational risk managers think Murphy was an optimist.

Operational risk includes:

- IT, interface, information and other system failures and deficiencies, including viruses
- confidentiality or security breaches
- human error
- fraud and theft
- weaknesses in internal controls/supervision
- physical disasters involving people, premises or equipment, whether natural (e.g., storm/earthquake) or man-made (e.g., fire/bombs)
- manufacturing and other core business failures

- product liability
- delivery failures
- health and safety/regulatory/compliance requirements
- human resource deficiencies
- dependency on third party contractors or outsourcing.

The corporate culture of your business will be a critical factor in its exposure to operational risk, for which responsibility starts at the top.

If you are thinking of changing your IT or other systems, ask the following questions.

- Is there anything wrong with your present system?
- What are the *certain* benefits of any change?
- Will you lose anything which is currently available?
- Are the gains worth the cost and disruption?
- Is it better to wait for the 'next generation'?
- What are the minimum requirements of any new system? These must be **guaranteed deliverables**.
- Are any added 'bells and whistles' likely to be of real value or simply increase the cost and problems whilst delaying installation?
- Can you modify or add to the system at a later date?
- Do you have to disband your present system before the new one has been tried and tested, or can they initially be run in tandem?
- From the outset have you involved everyone likely to be concerned with the new system? Their comments may be invaluable, and could focus on aspects overlooked by others. You might need their help if things go wrong, which is anyway less likely if everyone is working together.
- Is the system you are buying tried and tested? What has been the experience of other users?

Many otherwise successful businesses have been brought to their knees by the late delivery or failure of new systems.

Whatever your systems, have you considered the disaster scenario?

If, for example, your premises were destroyed by fire tonight, how would you function tomorrow? In many businesses, such as financial trading, even a few hours out of action could result in massive disruption and potential losses.

For businesses reliant upon computers, there is no excuse for failing to 'back-up' and safely store data. Depending on the time-critical nature of your business, you might also need to maintain back-up hardware, or to contract with a company offering disaster support.

But what if your records are paper-based, and how are you protecting original contracts and key correspondence? After a fire, would you know who owed you money and how much? Essential documents and records can be stored at the bank or in a fireproof safe, with copies kept at another location. Even if not admissible in court, such duplicates would be an invaluable point of reference. Executives should keep at home a copy of the business's disaster procedures manual and the names and phone numbers of key customers and suppliers, so that they can be contacted in an emergency.

The whole area is another one where the time to act is before the problem occurs. Decide upon the steps needed to ensure the survival of your business, including insurance cover, and then do something about it – *now!!*

Personal risk

Whilst this book is principally concerned with business, the risks of personal liability must not be overlooked.

This will largely depend upon:

● the legal form of the business

● relevant legislation and commercial practice.

In principle, and subject to applicable law, the *shareholders* are not liable (unless they have given a specific guarantee) for the debts of a company which has been incorporated with limited liability. Nor, unless they have acted negligently, or are guilty of 'wrongfully trading' when the business was insolvent, are the *directors* liable for the debts of a company.

However, courts appear increasingly to seek out the 'directing mind' behind the corporate shield – whether an individual or parent company – and to hold them responsible for the acts and deficiencies of the company. This may be particularly relevant where a holding company has overseas subsidiaries, as the courts in those countries might be more inclined to pierce the veil of incorporation.

A recent introduction in some jurisdictions is the concept of 'shadow directors' – being those other than the directors of a company who in the event of wrongful trading may be held liable for third party losses (and possibly disqualified from acting as directors) on the grounds that they are deemed to have influenced or controlled the actions of that business. Given the nature of the roles they are sometimes called upon to perform it is important for bankers to exercise particular care in this respect.

For companies with *unlimited or restricted liability* it is necessary to check the applicable law as to the personal liability of shareholders.

Sole traders are normally personally liable for all debts of the business.

Partnerships spread the risks amongst the individuals concerned, but usually on a 'joint and several basis'. This means that every partner is *personally liable* for the **entire** partnership debt. A creditor may choose to pursue just one partner, known or believed to be able to pay, leaving it to them to recover any proportion of the monies from their other partners. Before joining any partnership, ask yourself if you want to be personally liable for all partnership debts that may be incurred by your fellow partners, and if the partnership is solvent?

The legal form of any enterprise is of especial concern to those with whom it does business. For example, the knowledge that a sole trader is personally liable can be of greater comfort to a creditor than being owed money by a limited liability company, as bankruptcy remains a daunting prospect for most people, who will usually do whatever they can to avoid it. Banks lending to small and medium-sized companies often ask for the guarantees of the controlling shareholders/directors – to ensure their personal commitment and to get behind the protective shield of corporate limited liability so as to be able to pursue individuals for the debt.

Political risk

Never underestimate the potential impact on a business of decisions taken by national and supra-national governments, government agencies and the numerous regulatory bodies empowered to control trade or set prices and industry standards.

Their extensive armoury includes the following.

Taxation

The level and targeting of taxes is infinitely variable, and potentially changeable at short notice; while legislation may be drafted so that it is only in retrospect, and perhaps after testing in the courts, that the basis of assessment can be reliably determined. Uncertainty over taxes, allowances and dividend control can be a serious problem for businesses trying to plan for the future, and may be sufficient to see the cancellation or postponement of otherwise potentially viable projects. Multinationals are particularly careful to take local taxes into consideration, and are frequently accused of using transfer pricing to move profits intra group so as to reduce overall taxes.

Quotas, tariffs and other trade barriers

Any exporter fighting to win an order in the face of these obstacles knows the problems they can present. Such barriers take many forms, including prohibitions on the export of materials or technology that might be of help to another power. It may be possible to legally circumvent these difficulties by entering into local partnerships, but check the position carefully to avoid any risk of criminal charges.

Employment

Legislation on employment terms, remuneration and conditions of work, however well-intentioned, can impact on the ability of a business to trade profitably or to compete internationally. This sometimes encourages previously home-based businesses to relocate part or all of their activities or sourcing to other countries, with potentially harmful consequences for their own domestic economies.

Currency exchange controls/inconvertibility

These can:

● make it difficult or even impossible for businesses to buy from overseas, if they cannot easily exchange their local currency into the foreign currency needed to pay for the imports

● inhibit or prevent a business from operating in, or selling to, another country which operates exchange controls, when sale proceeds or profits cannot be repatriated/remitted.

Interest rates

Governments rely in large measure on using interest rates to manage their economies and to control the level of inflation. The problems come with the length of time before the effects may be experienced and the impact on the international strength of a country's currency.

Grants and subsidies

Many businesses are unaware of the help available from regional, national government and supra-national bodies. This can be considerable, and well worth the time spent making enquiries. Government officials are usually only too happy to help with advice, but exercise care with 'middlemen', particularly if they ask for an upfront fee. There are many highly reputable consultants who can genuinely assist in obtaining grants and other assistance, but think twice before you risk parting with your money, unless they are known or come highly recommended.

Licences/monopolies

It is often within the gift of a government to grant the rights to develop or exploit a natural resource or business opportunity.

Unless selected for the award of a contract or some other participation, or if the government decides to exercise the monopoly itself, you may be totally excluded from that activity.

If you win the concession, remember that a government can subsequently change the rules. Make too much profit and you invite withdrawal of licences, expropriation or additional taxes.

Environmental/health and safety

Legislation controlling industrial zoning, manufacturing processes, emissions, pollution, recycling and health and safety at work can be of considerable impact. Many projects that had looked perfectly viable have come to grief over the costs of complying with subsequently introduced legislation.

Even something as seemingly straightforward as providing fire exits to meet new safety standards in business premises can be cripplingly expensive. There is not only the capital cost of fire escapes, alarms, sprinkler systems etc., but it may be necessary to change the usage of space in a way that reduces income-earning capacity. Often the likelihood of new legislation is predictable even if its timing may be uncertain, and you can help to protect against the consequences by planning long-term. If faced with unexpected costs, ask if grants or other assistance are available.

Nationalization/expropriation

Although the trend over recent years has been to privatize previously State-run industries, do not overlook the risk of nationalization or expropriation – particularly if you are involved overseas in locally sensitive industries or the exploitation of national resources. The temptation to take over foreign-owned businesses can sometimes prove irresistible to governments and powerful local politicians. It may only take the passing of laws restricting foreign ownership to leave you with little choice but to accept whatever local offers may be forthcoming for your interests.

Restitution

In some countries, the former owners of assets that have been historically expropriated by the State are entitled to ask for its return or for compensation. If, whether directly or indirectly, you are thinking of investing in assets that might be subject to such claims, check the position thoroughly before parting with your money.

Product/industry risk

Many of the risks associated with products and services are considered elsewhere in this section, for example, under 'Environmental risk', 'Operational risk',

'Public relations risk', 'Resources risk' and 'Technological risk'.

But what if your product simply goes out of fashion, or demand declines for other reasons?

Often the change takes place gradually, or on a conventional 'product life-cycle' pattern, giving time to downsize or switch into other areas. Or you may have known from the outset that interest would be short-lived, as with a youth-targeted product which they all 'must have' until the next fashion comes along.

But occasionally the unexpected happens, and the bottom falls out of your world overnight.

The European industry for beef and its derivatives has provided a classic example. The sector was already undergoing change, with some customers moving away from 'red meat' on health or moral grounds, and many small butchers' shops closing as supermarkets increasingly dominated the market. Then fears over BSE ('mad cow' disease) being transmitted to humans hit the headlines and in many countries the market for beef crashed.

It was not just the farmers who were hit, but also their suppliers, meat wholesalers and retailers, and the manufacturers of many other products as shoppers looked at the list of ingredients printed on the wrappings of a wide range of processed food items to find, or suspect, that they contained beef extracts in various forms.

To take another example: in October 1995 the UK's Committee on Safety of Medicines wrote to doctors and pharmacists with the warning that certain brands of contraceptive pill were associated with a higher risk of a type of thrombosis. It was estimated that resultant fatalities might occur in 1 out of every 2–3 million users, which was double that for other types of pill. The higher-risk pills were not withdrawn from sale, and users were advised to finish their current course. However, many stopped taking them immediately and those who, as a result, became pregnant potentially doubled their risk of thrombosis.

The frequency of such 'scares', however legitimate, is disturbing as you cannot know which products or industry sectors will be hit next.

There is often little any individual business can do to protect against such problems, but it is a different matter for banks and other lenders. To contain the risks, they must mark limits for their exposure to each industry sector. Customers may be upset that an otherwise valid borrowing request is turned down solely because it would take the total facilities provided by a bank to that sector above a set limit, but for them to do otherwise would be highly negligent.

Public relations

The power of media, environmental and other pressure groups is now a very real issue for many businesses. It is important to be seen to be acting 'correctly', and easy to innocently fall victim to criticism.

You may, for example, have for many years been importing raw material from overseas, in all good faith. Then you open your newspaper to read an article on the alleged exploitation of the local people or damage done to the environment of that region – with reference to your business by name.

It may be necessary to show compassion and to evidence genuine sincerity whilst not admitting liability, with its potential legal and insurance ramifications.

The time to think about your response to such problems is before they happen, including consideration of the appointment of a public relations adviser. Do you have a policy on who is to speak for the business, of which all staff are aware? It can be very damaging for unauthorized employees to feel they must talk to the media – who are skilled at obtaining quotable comments. Can senior employees be contacted in an emergency?

'Reputational risk' is now taken very seriously, particularly by financial institutions subject to criticism from their regulators.

Resources risk

Every business uses resources – from the sole trader providing their time and energy to the multinational needing raw materials, water, power, labor, plant and machinery or transportation.

The key issues are:

● is what you need available:
  – when required?
  – in sufficient quantity?
  – of the right quality?
  – at an acceptable price?
● will it continue to be available?
● what are the threats to supply?
● is the price likely to change?
● are there suitable alternatives?

If your critical resource is an intellectual asset, have you taken the necessary steps to protect it?

It may be possible to enter into term contracts for the supply of goods and services, but what if your counterparty defaults, or is prevented from honoring its obligations.

Technological risk

Whilst the person who builds a better mouse trap can take out a patent, this is of little help if a way is found of eliminating all mice.

Technological risk is the threat that new ways of doing things will reduce or destroy the demand for existing products, however well-established, or make you uncompetitive.

Just 20 years ago, offices were filled with typewriters – how many do you have in your business today?

War/terrorism

Whether you are a buyer or a seller, the risks and opportunities occasioned by war or other hostile acts are self-apparent.

Are you too dependent on sales or purchases involving territories of high risk, and do you know where your suppliers are obtaining their resources?

The widespread use of 'terrorism' in different forms can, by its very nature, present particular problems for business. Whilst there may be a risk to life or property, the target is often disruption of normal commercial activity. A few strategically placed and well-reported bombs, even if they do not explode, can have a significant effect.

If terrorists take foreign tourists hostage, they guarantee media coverage, with potential damage to the holiday industry on which individual businesses, or even the local economy may be dependent.

● Do you have 'disaster recovery' plans covering a wide range of contingencies?

● Should your executives have kidnap insurance?

Recent years have seen a number of 'localized engagements', many of which occurred in territories or circumstances where such hostilities were endemic or foreseeable.

Careful consideration of 'country' and 'counterparty' exposure, coupled with insurance cover and appropriate trade finance protection where available, can do much to help reduce the risks.

Counterparty Risk

(including credit risk)

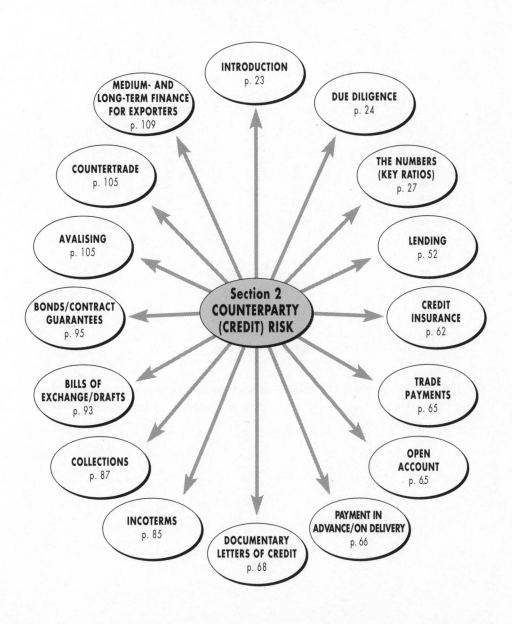

INTRODUCTION
p. 23

DUE DILIGENCE
p. 24

MEDIUM- AND
LONG-TERM FINANCE
FOR EXPORTERS
p. 109

THE NUMBERS
(KEY RATIOS)
p. 27

COUNTERTRADE
p. 105

LENDING
p. 52

AVALISING
p. 105

Section 2
COUNTERPARTY
(CREDIT) RISK

CREDIT
INSURANCE
p. 62

BONDS/CONTRACT
GUARANTEES
p. 95

TRADE
PAYMENTS
p. 65

BILLS OF
EXCHANGE/DRAFTS
p. 93

OPEN
ACCOUNT
p. 65

COLLECTIONS
p. 87

INCOTERMS
p. 85

DOCUMENTARY
LETTERS OF CREDIT
p. 68

PAYMENT IN
ADVANCE/ON DELIVERY
p. 66

Introduction

....

The risk faced by all businesses is that others may not honor their obligations – whether the failure is to pay for, or deliver, goods and services or to repay a borrowing.

If you have fulfilled your side of a transaction, it is probably not the intention of your counterparty to default, but perhaps they:

- have themselves been let down by a third party
- cannot obtain the resources necessary to complete the transaction
- are prohibited from making payments (e.g., foreign exchange controls) or from meeting their obligations (e.g., the introduction of a ban on transfer of technology)
- have become insolvent.

Think of the effort put into winning orders that produce a profit margin very much less than the potential total loss on a default, and then do the following.

- Be careful with whom you deal – have sensible rules and stick to them whatever the temptations.
- Undertake an appropriate level of due diligence.
- Remember that circumstances change. A business you have dealt with for many years without problems could now be in trouble – how quickly would you know? Be constantly alert to any factors that might affect the ability of your counterparty(s) to honour their obligations.
- Know your counterparty. Are they a company, partnership or sole trader? Will a parent company simply walk away when difficulties arise? Should you be considering guarantees or supporting security? Is the counterparty acting *ultra vires* in entering into the transaction with you, in which event you may be unable to enforce the contract.
- Do not over commit to any single or group of connected counterparties or to any sector – set limits and wherever possible spread your risks.
- Know the extent of your exposures at all times.
- Review limits and credit approval procedures regularly.
- Act immediately in the event of a default, or its likelihood. Where would you rank for repayment against other creditors?

● Even when dealing with a low credit-rated counterparty, it may be possible to structure the transaction so that the risks are acceptable. Perhaps credit insurance, performance guarantees or financial instruments can be used to minimize the exposure until your counterparty has met some or all of its obligations?

In the financial sector, the danger that a counterparty will not make a settlement payment on the due date (for example, in completion of a foreign exchange transaction) or deliver financial instruments is known as '**settlement**' or '**delivery risk**'. It can be particularly damaging when you have already fulfilled your side of the transaction by irrevocably paying away monies or delivering financial instruments before becoming aware of the default.

The two sides of a transaction may not be due to settle on the same business day, or you might not be able to know of a default until the following day ('**overnight risk**'). Even with intra-day settlement, the two sides of a transaction may not complete at the same time ('**daylight exposure**').

There is also '**systemic risk**', where problems in one financial institution or market may cross over to others and to other countries in a domino effect, potentially threatening chaos in global financial markets.

Due diligence

If you are thinking of:

● buying a business

● a merger

● committing to a joint venture

● entering into a major contract

● lending money or providing other financial facilities

then to undertake 'due diligence' on your counterparty will probably be an essential part of the evaluation. The process is analogous to a medical check-up, where all matters critical to the subject's health are thoroughly examined. Above all, it relies on facts not suppositions.

Due diligence is often undertaken by merchant bankers, accountants and lawyers, whose reputations and clients depend upon the efficiency with which they perform this task. It is also a core skill for lending bankers and venture capitalists needing to know about the businesses they may be financing.

The extent to which due diligence is appropriate will depend upon individual circumstances. You may already know the counterparty, or have reason to consider them undoubted for the amount and nature of the transaction.

Would an in-depth enquiry be cost-effective? Can all or part of it be undertaken in-house, or will it be necessary to instruct third parties to act on your behalf? If you employ providers of specialist services then have them enter into 'engagement letters.' These set out their responsibilities, scope of the work to be undertaken, reporting dates and fees.

Common sense will usually tell you which are the 'critical dependencies', being those factors that make the difference between success and failure of a business. But are there any 'hidden dependencies', such as reliance on a member of staff whose vital contribution is not understood or recognized. You may need to consider all or some of the following:

- strategic plans and vision
- nature and diversification of products and services
- market potential and industry risks
- product lifecycles
- technological risk
- research and development programme and costs
- market shares and the order book
- competitors, positionings and differentiations
- spread of client base and dependencies/continuity
- customer care policy and practice
- public relations
- trends (e.g., turnover) and costs
- benchmarking of key factors
- whether growth has been generic or by acquisition
- changes in the nature of the business
- intra-group trading and exposures
- management style
- ethics and culture
- historic and management accounts
- financial strengths and weaknesses
- key financial ratios
- basis of funding and terms of borrowings
- accounting, depreciation and dividend policies
- off-balance-sheet transactions
- control of treasury functions (are the exposures and risks understood?)

- economic risks
- terms of trade
- debtors and creditors, their spread and collection/payment periods
- currency exchange rate exposures
- interest rate exposures
- lease and hire-purchase agreements
- security given and available
- borrowing covenants
- bases of valuations, including property, stock and intellectual assets
- insurance, including assets, key man and loss of profits
- human resources, including spread and depth of skills and experience, continuity and succession planning
- board and organizational structures
- executives' contracts, remuneration and benefits
- subcontracting and outsourcing
- resources, including dependencies and threats to supplies
- stock levels
- operational and IT risks
- system costs and useful life
- property, plant and equipment
- environmental issues
- licences, goodwill, intellectual assets, franchises
- capital and contractual commitments
- contingent liabilities, including warranties and guarantees
- pension, health and welfare commitments
- group structure
- equity structure and holders, including warrants, options and conversion rights
- legal entity and jurisdiction of business
- legal issues, including ownership of assets
- litigation
- regulatory issues
- management information systems and knowledge management
- country risks
- political risks
- risk management culture, policy and risk aversion

- sensitivity analysis

- disaster scenarios.

You will need to differentiate between those factors that are 'quantitative' (e.g., measurable factors such as financial ratios) and those that are 'qualitative' (e.g., subjective factors such as ethics and culture).

Do not be rushed into a deal before there has been time to complete an adequate due diligence and, if appropriate, ask a vendor or other counterparty to provide you with warranties or indemnities. As it is notoriously difficult to succeed with warranty claims consider making a retention to cover them.

See also *The lending process*, page 57.

The numbers (key ratios)

Statutory and management accounts record the past performance of a business, which may be a valuable guide to the future. But, you need to know what to look for, or can end up more confused than when you started.

There are many computer software programs that will calculate the various analysis ratios, but even then it is necessary to understand what the figures mean.

The following pages show some of the key ratios, but before we begin it is worth remembering the following points.

- There is no 'right number' for any ratio.

- The 'notes' to the accounts, and any statements of the principles or assumptions on which they have been prepared, are vital to your understanding. You should read these *before* attempting any extract.

- Be particularly alert to changes of accounting policy. For example, lengthening the term over which items are depreciated reduces the deduction from profit in each individual accounting period, as does reducing any provision for warranty claims. Other 'creative accounting' techniques worth looking for are the treatment of deferred taxation, the length of time over which goodwill is written off, the bases and dates for valuations of tangible and intangible assets (and who provided these valuations), and changes in the way overseas assets and liabilities are converted into the currency in which the accounts are prepared.

- Look for any reference to significant 'post-balance-sheet events' that might alter your analysis or opinion of the business.

- If the accounts have been prepared in accordance with the requirements of a country other than your own, do not assume that the basis or principles are the same. If in doubt, ask!

- It pays to be cynical, as the following examples illustrate.

  - When property values are rising, directors often include an upward revaluation of any such assets in the accounts, but seldom seem to think it a worthwhile exercise when values are falling (although in some countries they may be required to confirm their belief that the values shown in the accounts reflect the current position).

  - Where interest payments, research and development or marketing costs are being 'capitalized' instead of deducted from profits, on whatever grounds, ask yourself if that appears reasonable.

  - It is not unknown for a business to improve its financial appearance by selling an asset to a third party for cash just before balance sheet date, but with an undertaking to buy it back shortly thereafter.

- If the assumptions used in preparing the accounts seem unreasonable or questionable, then bear this in mind when reviewing the figures and ratios that result. You can always re-work your calculations on a basis with which you feel more comfortable. Similarly, where the local accountancy rules or guidelines permit the use of 'extraordinary' or 'exceptional' items in a way you consider distorts the reality, there is nothing to stop you treating these differently for the purposes of your analysis, to see the effect. Ask yourself if any costs shown 'below the line' really belong there, and if profits from the sale of non-trading assets have been shown as revenue rather than as capital gains.

- Read any accompanying reports or letters to shareholders issued by the directors or executives. When your analysis is complete, refer back to these to see if their statements and forecasts still seem reasonable. What have they said or promised in the past? Media and rating agency comment on sectors and individual businesses can be of great value, often putting your analysis into context.

- Most accounts are prepared on a 'going concern basis' – which assumes that the business will continue to trade. This may or may not be appropriate. If there are questions as to its on-going viability, then re-work the calculations using figures more likely to apply on a 'break-up'. Key points to consider are usually the forced sale value of assets, including stock or work in progress, the nature of long-term commitments such as property leases or equipment financing, the costs of unwinding 'treasury' positions, the likelihood of payments from debtors (who may refuse to pay on grounds such as failure to complete contractual obligations or provide on-going product support) and redundancy costs.

- Wherever possible analyze and compare sets of accounts for the business covering several consecutive periods, or on a rolling basis. It may help to produce these in a graphical format, so that trends are more easily identified. The changes over time are likely to be as revealing as the figures for any single period in isolation. Indeed, many of the ratios are difficult to calculate or of limited value unless such comparisons are made. It can also help you in identifying any 'income recognition' policies designed to favour short-term results. If, for example, you are a contract-based business where the work is spread over a period, how is the income recognized? Is it taken into the profit and loss account upfront or over time, and do the accounts specify the policy that has been adopted? Be on the look-out for situations – such as borrowing in foreign rather than local currency solely because the interest rate is lower – which enhance the profit and loss account for the period but could have detrimental longer-term or balance sheet effects.

- Do the latest figures contain any 'prior year' adjustments? If so, then why, and remember to adjust any ratios or figures you may have prepared for such earlier periods.

- If the accounts have been prepared in a foreign currency, it is often best to work in it rather than convert everything into your local currency, to avoid becoming confused by exchange rate variations. Where conversion of figures is appropriate, decide upon the rate you are going to use (e.g., today's exchange rate, an average for the accounting period, or that applicable on the last date in the accounts) and be consistent. If balance sheets show long-term currency liabilities, these deserve particular attention.

- How recent is the period to which the accounts relate? Are they so old as to be of little value? Have they taken longer to prepare than usual? Does any undue delay indicate problems? As long as they can be relied upon, management accounts may be of greater interest than the more historic audited accounts, which are often received too late to be of any real value.

- If the accounts have been audited, is the auditors' report 'clean', or has it been 'qualified' by reference to any divergences from normal local accounting practice or to other reservations of the auditors.

- Where the accounts have been prepared for an overseas business, do you know if the accounting and taxation principles applied are similar to your own, and if not how they differ? Is the auditor known?

- If the business is operating in areas of high inflation, has sufficient allowance been made for its impact, for example, as regards the costs of replacing assets or providing adequate working capital, and is the growth in turnover keeping pace?

- A balance sheet shows the assets and liabilities of a business as at the date on which it is prepared (the 'balance sheet date'), whereas a profit and loss account records the trading and other financial activities of a business over a specified period of time (the 'accounting period') ending on the balance sheet date. When looking at the figures and ratios, remember they may be very different at any other time of the year and that, for example, cash is easily spent.

- The business may well have chosen the date on which its accounts are prepared to coincide with the time when it will look best. For example, in seasonal industries, one business might select the end of Christmas retail sales, whilst another might prefer the peak summer holiday period. If the accounting dates are changed from one year to another, then ask yourself if any given explanation for this is reasonable, and remember to adjust for the altered length of the accounting periods when extracting or comparing different sets of figures. A change of dates is sometimes made to hide the results of a disappointing period (whether it has already happened or is predicted for the near future). If interim accounts are available, they can provide valuable insight into the performance of a seasonal business.

- Where the information is disclosed consider separately the size and movements of each of the principal assets, for example stocks (inventory) and property.

- What values, if any, have been attributed to brands and patents, and do these appear reasonable in light of the businesses' market positioning, future development potential and the time until expiry of these and other such rights?

- Is there reference to the business having given security to support its borrowings? If so, where would you 'rank' in seniority for recovery of any debts if the business was wound up? It may be that you are last in line for payment.

- The notes to some accounts state whether or not the business has complied with any financial covenants imposed upon it under the terms for borrowings. Are there indications that these are likely to be breached?

- If unclear as to whether an asset falls into the 'current' or 'fixed' categories, it is worth remembering that normally only fixed assets are depreciated.

- Is the level of dividends reasonable, taking into consideration the potentially conflicting needs of a business to fund itself whilst meeting the income expectations of shareholders? How much is left in the business after paying dividends and interest on borrowings?

- If contributions are made by the business to pension or healthcare schemes is the cost of these likely to increase in future? Such commitments can be a very onerous financial burden. Alternatively, has the business been enjoying the benefit of a pension fund 'holiday', resulting from excess historic contributions, that may now be coming to an end?

- The figures you use for directors' remuneration should include pension contributions and any other benefits.

- Pay particular attention when there is any reference to 'contingent liabilities', including legal actions – which all too often become very real indeed. For example, a business might have made an acquisition on a deferred consideration basis, with all or part of the payment to the vendors being due at a later date. Such deals are often structured so as to incentivize key personnel of the purchased enterprise to stay on for a minimum period of time, by offering them the 'golden handcuffs' of staged or final purchase payments linked to future profits. The amount of these 'earn outs' can be considerable, and may be particularly damaging if they fall due when the acquired business has hit a low point following a period of high profits. Similar considerations apply whenever hostages to future fortune are given, such as debt issues with potentially onerous conversion terms.

● Look out for 'off-balance-sheet transactions'. Depending on local accounting practice, these may be straightforward leasing or hire purchase commitments, but could also refer to anything, for example, a property development, undertaken in the name of another entity (normally a company incorporated solely for that purpose), but structured so that any resultant benefits flow to the business that devised the scheme. Where the finance for such ventures is provided on the security of the project assets, without recourse to the business behind the arrangement, off-balance-sheet transactions may not impact negatively on that business's important gearing ratios. In many countries there are now 'substance over form' guidelines as to whether these schemes are eligible for such accountancy treatment, but be sensitive to anything that might rebound financially on the business you are analyzing.

● When the business is part of a larger group it can be difficult to find your way through the maze of 'inter-company' trading and debt. The only solution may be to analyze the entire group, but do not assume that connected companies will come to the rescue of any individual business that gets into difficulties, unless they are legally obligated.

● Have the prices at which products and services are sold between members of a group (the 'transfer price') been artificially adjusted to move profits from one enterprise or country to another? Whilst this can be attractive for the group, especially those cross-border operations seeking to minimize tax, the impact on the results of any individual business unit can be considerable. Subject to the applicable accounting standards, the allocation of profits may be changed at short notice.

● Are the profits from some areas of activity within the business hiding losses elsewhere?

● Particular care is needed when the accounts cover a period during which another business was acquired. Depending on the governing legislation this can provide a wonderful opportunity for using 'fair value adjustments' to:

  – bring in the assets of the purchased business at less than their previous book value and to

  – write off current and future costs under the heading of 'reorganization',

thereby artificially inflating the post-acquisition performance and profits of the merged business. To what extent have any pre-acquisition turnover and profits of the purchased business been incorporated into the results of the purchaser?

- At the other extreme, termination of a business activity can provide the opportunity to hide a multitude of costs and losses under the heading 'discontinued operations'.

- Allowance may need to be made for any 'minority interests' (the share in a business held by a third party other than the parent company).

- It can be very useful to compare the performance and ratios for an individual business with the 'benchmark' figures for the industry(s) and territory(s) within which it operates. Those for manufacturing will be very different from retailing or service industries. Such benchmarks are commercially published and readily available in many countries.

- Always probe the 'sensitivity' of the business to change. For example, if the average number of days that debtors take to pay increased, then how would the resultant cash shortfall be financed? Apply 'stress testing' and consider the 'worst case scenario'.

- Never forget that many of the key factors for the success of a business will be non-financial.

Current ratio

$$\frac{\text{Current assets}}{\text{Current liabilities}}$$

Also known as the 'working capital ratio', the current ratio gives an indication of the solvency of a business, by showing the extent to which current liabilities are covered by cash or by assets that *should be* capable of early conversion into cash for payment of liabilities.

An increased ratio compared with that for previous periods *may* indicate that:

- debtors (receivables) are taking longer to collect or are uncollectable
- stocks (inventory) are excessive (or unsaleable)
- fixed assets have been sold to produce debtors or cash
- stocks are being built up ready for an anticipated increase in sales
- a higher profit margin is being achieved.

A reduced ratio compared with that seen for previous accounting periods may be the result of:

- creditors being deferred or not paid

- bad debts being written off
- stock being written down
- investment of cash or short-term borrowings in fixed assets
- losses or falling profit margins.

Low ratios often lead to:

- pressure on debtors to pay early
- delay in paying creditors
- increased borrowing.

Liquid surplus/deficit

Liquid surplus/deficit is current assets less current liabilities. In sectors such as supermarket retailing, where goods are obtained on extended credit but sold for cash with a rapid turnover, this figure may be negative (i.e., liquid deficit). These businesses are in the fortunate position of being able to use creditors' monies to help finance expansion or increased sales, but risk problems if, for example, such funds are directed into fixed assets or used to cover losses and a downturn in trade is then experienced. But for most businesses a liquid deficit is a warning sign.

Current assets include:

- cash and short-term bank deposits, including those in foreign currency
- debtors and other accounts receivable where payment is due within 12 months, excluding any known bad or doubtful debts
- amounts due from directors or from other group companies (often omitted)
- quoted investments where they are held ready for short-term conversion into cash, excluding investments intended to be held long-term
- stock (finished goods and raw materials) and work-in-progress (less any up-front or stage payments for which an invoice has been issued or payment received).

Current liabilities are all debts that fall due within a year, and normally include:

- creditors, bank borrowings and other accounts payable where payment is due within 12 months including:
  - any amounts payable over the next 12 months on debts not fully repayable within that time
  - value added tax and similar sales taxes

- – remuneration and taxation liabilities relating to employees
- amounts due to directors or to other group companies
- amounts due to be paid within the next 12 months under hire purchase agreements or finance leases
- dividends that have been declared but not yet paid
- taxes on the profits of the business that are due for payment within 12 months
- deferred income (e.g., provision of computer maintenance, where the business receives the income upfront but is liable to provide its services to customers throughout the term of the contract without further charge).

Liquid ratio

$$\frac{\text{Quick assets}}{\text{Current liabilities}}$$

The liquid ratio, also known as 'acid test' or 'quick ratio', differs from the current ratio in excluding stock and work-in-progress, for which time might be needed before they can be sold and converted into cash. Thus this key *liquidity* ratio indicates the extent to which a business could pay its creditors provided it was paid by its debtors.

Quick asset surplus/deficit (net working assets) is quick assets less current liabilities.

Key points

Quick assets are the current assets as used for calculating the current ratio (see page 32) but excluding stock (finished goods and raw materials) and work-in-progress.

Current liabilities are the same as those used for calculating the current ratio.

Average credit given

$$\frac{\text{Average trade debtors for accounting period x Number of days in period}}{\text{Sales}}$$

Average credit given (collection period) shows the average number of days it has taken a business to collect its trade debts (debtors/receivables).

If the average number of days has increased since the last accounting period it will have had a negative effect on cash flow and *may* indicate:

● bad debts or other problems in obtaining payment from debtors

● the giving of extended credit terms to win sales.

Be particularly aware of businesses where you would expect most sales to be for cash but where a significant collection period is seen.

If the average number of days has decreased since the last accounting period, the effect on cash flow will have been positive, but *may* be the result of:

● pressure on creditors (or offering discounts for prompt payment) by a business needing to gather in cash to pay its debts

● invoice discounting or factoring of debtors (see pages 161–3 and 163–70).

See also *Average credit taken* (page 36) – if this has lengthened when average credit given has reduced, it *may* indicate a problem (or simply a business very good at protecting its cash flow).

The typical collection period differs from one industry to another, and you should compare with different businesses in the same sector.

Key points

The figure for 'average trade debtors for accounting period' is obtained by adding together the figure for trade debtors shown on the latest balance sheet you are examining (known as 'closing debtors', as they come at the end of the most recent accounting period) and the figure for closing debtors shown on the immediately preceding balance sheet (which became the 'opening debtors' for the next accounting period as they were the amount carried forward to its start) and then dividing this total by 2.

Where the figures for consecutive accounting periods are not available, use the closing debtors in the accounts being analyzed, without dividing by 2.

For a fast-growing business you may need to work on a shorter period, if the figures are available, as the average for an entire accounting period may give a false picture.

Such ratios are often calculated excluding value added tax, or similar sales taxes, and sales to other businesses within the same group.

Average credit taken

....

Average trade creditors for accounting period x Number of days in period
Cost of goods sold

Average credit taken shows the average number of days it has taken a business to pay its debts.

If the average number of days has increased since the last accounting period, it will have had a positive effect on cash flow, but *may* be the result of delay in paying suppliers (creditors) by a business short of cash (possibly with a resultant loss of discounts). The business is using creditors to help fund its operations. See also *Average credit given* (page 34).

If the average number of days has decreased since the last accounting period, it *may* reflect pressure by creditors anxious to obtain payment, which is often an early warning sign to banks and other lenders that may not have the 'inside' industry knowledge sometimes available to trade creditors.

The typical terms of trade will differ from industry to industry, and you should compare the number of days' credit taken with that for other businesses in the sector.

The accounts are unlikely to reveal the 'spread' of debt between different creditors (e.g., preferential creditors), which is a key requirement for anyone undertaking a detailed due diligence analysis.

Key points

The figure for 'average trade creditors for accounting period' is obtained by adding together the figure for trade creditors shown on the latest balance sheet you are examining (known as 'closing creditors' as they come at the end of the most recent accounting period) and the figure for closing creditors shown on the immediately preceding balance sheet (which became the 'opening creditors for the next accounting period as they were the amount carried forward to its start) and then dividing this total by 2.

Where the figures for consecutive accounting periods are not available, use the closing creditors in the accounts being analyzed, without dividing by 2.

For a fast-growing business you may need to work on a shorter period, if the figures are available, as the average for an entire accounting period may give a false picture.

If 'cost of goods sold' is not given in the accounts, there may be a reference to 'purchases', or you can deduct from the figure for 'sales' the total of 'profit before interest and tax' (PBIT), plus 'depreciation', plus payroll to give a rough but useable number. As a final measure you could use 'gross sales', to provide a comparison between one accounting period and another.

Stock turnover

....

Average stock for accounting period x Number of days in accounting period
Cost of goods sold

Shows the number of days of stock that has been held which, unless there are good reasons to the contrary (e.g., problems in obtaining supplies on time or imminent price increases), most businesses try to keep at the minimum to reduce funding and storage costs and increase cash flow. For many seasonal operations, stock levels will vary considerably, depending on the time of year. As the turnover ratio differs from industry to industry, it should be compared with other businesses in the sector.

If the number of days of stock held is increasing, it *may* indicate obsolete inventory, a slow down in sales, a change in the product mix or imminent launch of a new range.

A very low figure *might* indicate that stock levels are at a point where customer demand cannot be met.

How much 'stock' is finished goods ready for sale, as distinct from raw materials or partly processed work?

Who valued the stock, and on what basis?

Key points

The figure for 'average stock for accounting period' is obtained by adding together the figures for stock (finished goods and raw materials) and work-in-progress (less any progress payments) as shown on the latest balance sheet you are examining (known as 'closing stock' as they come at the end of the most recent accounting period) and the same figures as shown on the immediately preceding balance sheet (which became the 'opening stock' for the next accounting period as they were the amounts carried forward to its start) and then dividing this total by 2.

Where the figures for consecutive accounting periods are not available use the closing stock in the accounts being analyzed, without dividing by 2.

If stock turnover is particularly important, for example the business is a distributor, it may be appropriate to work on the figures for a shorter period where they are available. Those for an entire accounting period may give a false picture if the business is undergoing rapid change.

For 'cost of goods sold', see *Average credit taken* (left).

Current liability to stock

> **Current liabilities**
> ――――――――
> **Stock**

An alternative ratio is trade creditors to stock. Can the business fund an increase of stock to match a growth in sales?

Working capital turnover

> **Sales**
> ――――――――
> **Working capital**

A measure of the efficiency of working capital management and a pointer to the additional *working capital* a business might need to fund any increase in turnover (over and above any capital investment in fixed assets).

If the ratio is increasing, there is the risk the business may be overtrading, leading to pressure from creditors and a possible need for increased borrowings or equity monies (although increased sales should ultimately generate cash).

Multiply any projected level of increased turnover by the reciprocal of the working capital turnover ratio to see what working capital would be needed if the ratio of sales to working capital remained unchanged, e.g., if there were no economies of scale.

Key points

> Working capital is often considered to be the same as net current assets, i.e., current assets less current liabilities. A definition preferred by many is net current assets tied up directly in the cash conversion cycle, which will differ from net current assets in excluding non-operational assets and liabilities.

Gearing/leverage

The definitions of gearing and leverage differ from country to country, and it is important to know which is being used.

The following are possible definitions, but you need to check that there is no confusion as to the interpretation of these terms.

A highly geared business is in principle more dependent on borrowings/debt than a low-geared business which relies to a greater extent on equity.

Whatever the level of gearing, it needs to be interpreted taking into consideration the nature of the business and its asset base, and whether the borrowing/debt is being used to create future growth.

Total gearing/leverage

$$\frac{\text{Total liabilities}}{\text{Net tangible assets}}$$

Total gearing shows the ratio of 'total liabilities' to shareholders'/owners' funds. If the ratio is increasing, the business may be undercapitalized and might find it hard to raise additional borrowings, particularly if the *Net gearing* (page 40) is high.

Net tangible assets/tangible net worth is commonly considered to be the same as net worth/shareholders' funds (the value of the 'owners' equity stake in a business), but the latter might also be calculated including intangible items such as goodwill that are excluded from the former.

Key points

The figure for 'total liabilities' is current liabilities (see pages 33–4) plus term/deferred liabilities.

'Term liabilities' normally include:

● borrowings (or any part thereof) due for repayment after 12 months, including any subordinated or group debt and whether or not secured

● hire purchase/finance lease commitments after 12 months

● deferred and future taxation payable after 12 months.

Where liabilities are in a foreign currency you need to bear in mind the potential implications of any future changes in exchange rates.

'Net tangible assets' comprise:

● net current assets (liquid surplus/deficit), see *Current ratio*, page 32)

- fixed and other assets less term liabilities

  fixed and other assets include:

  - land and buildings (both freehold and leasehold) plus plant plus fixtures and fittings plus machinery, less depreciation on all these items
  - capitalized leases
  - investments in associates and subsidiaries
  - long-term investments
  - amounts due from other businesses within a group unless these are short-term and have already been included under current assets.

Depending on the accounting treatment, any substantial intangible assets (e.g., magazine titles) funded by debt can distort the picture.

If the figure for current liabilities is substituted for total liabilities you can see the difference that the burden of term debt is making to the business.

Net gearing/capital gearing

$$\frac{\textbf{Net borrowing}}{\textbf{Net tangible assets}}$$

Net gearing/capital gearing shows the ratio of net borrowings (being total borrowings less available cash and quoted investments held ready for short-term sale) to shareholders'/owners' funds.

Key points

Total borrowings include:

- short-term loans/borrowing (repayable within 12 months)
- term loans/borrowing/debt issues (repayable after 12 months)
- hire purchase/finance leases
- amounts due to group businesses (often omitted)
- amounts due to directors (often omitted).

If you suspect that the borrowing figure in the balance sheet is lower than that usually seen in the business, perhaps because of seasonality or 'year-end' window dressing, then divide the amount of interest shown as paid during the accounting period by the annual interest rate a business would probably have been paying to its bank and multiply the result by 100. If the accounting period is not 365 days, then you also need to divide by the number of days in the accounting period and multiply by 365. The final figure is an indication of the *possible* average borrowing for the accounting period. An alternative is that the business has been borrowing in a foreign currency where the interest rate is lower, but at a possible capital risk if exchange rates moved adversely.

Gross gearing/leverage

$$\frac{\text{Total borrowings}}{\text{Net tangible assets}}$$

Gross gearing/leverage shows the ratio between total borrowings and shareholders'/owners' funds. For 'total borrowings', see below left.

Operational gearing

Highlights the importance of fixed costs within the total costs of a business and the likely effect on trading profit from changes in the level of turnover (sales).

$$\frac{\text{Sales less variable costs}}{\text{Trading profit}}$$

or
(as trading profit = sales less fixed and variable costs)

$$\frac{\text{Trading profit plus fixed costs}}{\text{Trading profit}}$$

The higher the operational gearing, the higher the breakeven as a percentage of sales.

Key points

'Variable costs' are those costs which vary with the level of business activity, whereas 'fixed costs' do not vary with the level of business activity.

Breakeven

....

Breakeven is achieved when sales revenues equal costs.

The extent to which a business is operating above breakeven is a measure of its margin of safety (i.e., margin of safety = actual sales less sales needed to breakeven), and indicates how far performance can decline before losses are incurred.

The lower the fixed costs, being those that do not vary with reasonable changes in the level of sales, the greater the margin of safety (lower operational gearing). This is one of the reasons why businesses make such efforts to reduce non-variable costs to the effective minimum.

In any business there also will be areas of variable expenditure (i.e., costs that vary with changes in the level of sales) that it is essential to control if maximum profits are to be made. It can be very revealing to calculate these as a ratio of sales (or other appropriate denominator) and consider both the trends and comparison with industry benchmarks.

Net profit margin

....

Profit before interest and tax (PBIT) x100
Sales

In common with the 'gross profit margin' (see right), the net profit margin will differ from industry to industry.

If the margin is unusually high for that industry, it could be the result of good management, or of a protected position within the sector. Competitors may be attracted who force down the margin.

Key points

The figure for 'profit before interest and tax' (PBIT), also known as trading/operating profit and as earnings before interest and tax (EBIT), is the profit of the business from all sources as shown in the accounts after deducting depreciation and any exceptional or extraordinary items but *before* deducting:

● gross interest payable for the accounting period
● taxes based on the profits of the business for the accounting period
● any share of the profits of associated group businesses.

Profits (and the taxes thereon) and losses from the sale or revaluation of assets (including goodwill and intellectual assets) or deriving from other than normal trading activities, and the costs of closure of any activities, are excluded from the calculation (gains on revaluation of fixed assets are usually shown as an unrealized profit in reserves).

If the net profit margin decreases as turnover increases, then, unless volume is being bought by means of lower prices, costs may not be under control.

Is a variation in margin the result of a change of activities or product mix? This ratio differs from 'gross profit margin' (see below), because it includes all the overheads and other costs of running the business, not just the costs of producing the goods or services sold.

Gross profit margin

Gross profit x 100

Sales

Gross profit margin is a guide to management performance which, as it differs from industry to industry, can usefully be 'benchmarked' against similar businesses in the same sector. If the margin changes, it is important to understand why. Perhaps a reduction in the margin has occurred because a business has reduced its prices in the hope of greater profits from increased sales. Has there been a change in activities or product mix?

This ratio differs from 'net profit margin' (see left) as it only incorporates the cost of producing what is sold, not the overheads and other costs of running the business.

The figure for 'gross profit' is sales less the cost of producing the goods or services sold.

Key points

Return on capital employed

Profit before interest paid and tax* x 100

Average capital employed

* PBIT or EBIT (earnings before interest paid and tax)

Return on capital employed is an indicator of management performance, showing the return on the funds used in a business.

It can also be applied to compare different operations within a business.

If the return is low it might be sensible to look for other products or businesses in which to invest, and could indicate potential liquidity problems.

The figure for 'average capital employed' is calculated by adding together the 'capital employed' shown in the most recent accounts you are examining and those for the immediately preceding accounting period and dividing the total by 2. Where the figures for consecutive accounting periods are not available, use the capital employed in the accounts being analyzed, without dividing by 2.

'Capital employed' may be defined in different ways, but is conveniently calculated by adding together:

● net tangible assets (see pages 39–40)

● short-term borrowings, provided they are regarded as part of the longer-term funding of the business

● term and other liabilities not payable within 12 months

● obligations under hire purchase/finance leases

● amounts due to directors (often omitted)

● amounts due to other businesses within a group (often omitted).

The normal convention is that this calculation uses 'interest paid', even though the actual payment of interest that accrues during one accounting period might not be due or made until another period. If the information is available you can instead use the figures for 'interest accrued' or 'interest due and payable'.

Return on equity (return to shareholders)

$$\frac{\text{Profit before tax}}{\text{Net tangible assets*}}$$

* for definition see *Total gearing*, page 39.

Return on equity shows whether a business is achieving an adequate return on the capital put into it by the owners, when compared with other investment opportunities.

Return on assets

· ·

> **Profit before interest and tax**
> **Total assets**

When compared with that for other businesses in the same sector, this ratio shows how efficiently the available assets are being used to produce profits.

> 'Total assets' is everything shown as an asset in the balance sheet, including 'intangibles'.

Key points

Fixed assets to net tangible assets

· ·

> **Fixed assets**
> **Net tangible assets**

The greater the fixed assets, the larger the amount of depreciation normally to be deducted from profits.

Different industries require a different level of investment in fixed assets.

If this ratio is high for the sector in which the business operates you need to find out why, and the nature of the fixed assets.

> 'Fixed assets' are:
> ● land
> ● buildings
> ● fixtures and fittings
>
> less the depreciation thereon.

Key points

Sales to assets

$$\frac{\text{Sales}}{\text{Total assets}}$$

A low ratio when compared to other businesses in that sector may mean that the available assets are not being used effectively to produce optimum sales.

A high ratio may suggest the business is overtrading against the available level of assets.

For 'total assets' see *Return on assets* on page 45.

Sales per employee

$$\frac{\text{Sales}}{\text{Number of employees}}$$

This ratio will vary from industry to industry, but gives an indication of the efficiency of employees when compared with other businesses in the same sector.

Profit per employee

$$\frac{\text{Profit before interest and tax}}{\text{Number of employees}}$$

This ratio is a measure of how productively employees are being used.

The possible effect of increased remuneration on profits is indicated by the following ratio.

$$\frac{\text{Profit}}{\text{Total remuneration}}$$

Average remuneration per employee

> **Total employee remuneration**
> ——————————————
> **Number of employees**

When compared with similar businesses in a sector, this ratio indicates the level of control over staff costs.

Cash flow

The ways in which a business has in the past used its cash tells you a lot about its objectives and financial prudence.

When the known or likely expenditure by the business on acquiring assets, paying interest and dividends, repaying debt and funding increased working capital are taken into consideration, is sufficient cash being generated to meet the financing needs of the business without increased borrowings, additional equity, or sale of assets?

Is the business investing enough in plant and equipment, etc., to provide for future needs? Alternatively, is it investing too much without the prospect of adequate return? (See *Return on capital employed*, page 43.) The picture may be confused by leasing or hire purchase arrangements.

Where the accounts contain a cash flow statement, of money in and out of the business, it should provide the detail needed for your evaluation.

See also *Cash flow forecasts*, page 116 and *Interest cover – cash*, page 48.

From a cash flow perspective (although not necessarily strategically) it can sometimes be better to increase prices at the cost of a decline in sales, rather than chasing turnover by reducing prices and selling more. This is particularly relevant if you are already overtrading. The 'rule' is that, when necessary and possible, sales volume should only be controlled by increasing prices.

EXAMPLE

A business's goods have a unit price of $1,000 and cost $750 to produce and it has been achieving annual sales of 2000 units. From experience, this business knows that for every 1% increase in unit price there is a 2% fall in sales, whilst for every 1% decrease in unit price there is a 2% increase in sales.

Table 2.1 shows the effect on gross margin of both increasing and decreasing unit prices by 10%.

Table 2.1 Effect of 10% price increase and decrease

	Now	10% price increase	10% price decrease
Unit price	$1,000	$1,100	$900
Cost per unit	$750	$750	$750
Gross profit per unit	$250	$350	$150
Gross margin (%)	25%	31.82%	16.67%
Number of units sold	2,000	1,600	2,400
Gross profit	$500,000	$560,000	$360,000

Although sales volume falls by 20% with a 10% price increase, the gross profit is up by $60,000, whereas the 20% increase in sales volume on a 10% reduction in price resulted in a decrease of $140,000 in gross profit.

For the purposes of this example, it is assumed that the cost per unit does not alter with a change in volume. In practice, it probably will vary and this would need to be taken into consideration when making a calculation such as that in the table.

Interest cover – profits

$$\frac{\text{Profit before interest and tax}}{\text{Interest}}$$

If cover is too low, the business will be at risk from any fall in profits or increase in interest rates, and have limited ability to fund growth or reduce its borrowing by making repayments of capital, but see *Interest cover – cash* below.

Interest cover – cash

$$\frac{\text{Cash flow*}}{\text{Interest paid}}$$

* Before interest and dividends.

As interest has to be paid from cash, not profits, this is a useful additional ratio to that for *Interest cover – profits* above. As during any individual accounting period the cash flow may be affected by many factors, such as investment in future growth, a supplementary calculation often used is based on the combined figures of several years.

If, for example, the accounts for the past three years were available, then the calculation would be:

$$\frac{\text{Cash flow for 3 years}}{\text{Interest paid for 3 years}}$$

Adding capital repayments to the figure for interest shows total debt service to cash flow.

The figure for 'cash flow' is obtained from the cash flow statement in the accounts, if available. Otherwise you will need to calculate it from whatever information is available. It comprises:

- profit or loss before interest paid, and dividends but usually after tax paid
- plus depreciation
- plus decrease in stocks and work-in-progress
- less increase in stocks and work-in-progress
- plus increase in creditors (excluding tax liabilities as appropriate)
- less decrease in creditors
- plus decrease in debtors
- less increase in debtors
- plus/less any other items that affected the profit figure but did not involve cash movements.

The above is known by accountants as 'operating cash flow'.

It is common practice, when calculating 'interest cover – cash', to use a figure for cash flow that also:

- adds/deducts the proceeds of sale or costs of fixed assets
- adds or deducts any other 'one-off' transactions that are not part of normal trading but have resulted in a cash movement.

Remember that such additional transactions may not occur again.

Key points

Debt repayment

$$\frac{\text{Debt}}{\text{Operating cash flow}}$$

This ratio is an important indicator, showing how long it might take for a business to repay its debts.

Key points | For operating cash flow see *Interest cover – cash*, page 48.

Price to earnings ratio (P/E ratio)

$$\frac{\text{Middle market price of an ordinary share (stock)}}{\text{Earnings per share}}$$

The price to earnings ratio shows the number of years it would take for the earnings per share of the company at their current level to repay the cost of buying an ordinary share, and facilitates comparison between companies.

The ratio will be affected by the state of the market in general and that of the particular sector(s) in which the business operates; by the performance and market perception of the company; and by the number of shares in issue.

To deserve a high P/E ratio, a company should offer the prospect of substantial earnings growth.

'Earnings per share' is:

$$\frac{\text{Profit after tax and preference dividends}}{\text{Number of ordinary shares in issue}}$$

The 'earnings yield' is:

$$\frac{\text{Earnings per share} \times 100}{\text{Middle market price of an ordinary share}}$$

It can be seen that a rising share price reduces the yield.

Depreciation

Depreciation is the reduction in the value of an asset in the books of a business to reflect its reduced worth over a period of time. It is not a cash flow item.

The figure for *cost less depreciation* is the 'net book value' of the asset. Although the detailed accounting treatment of depreciation may differ from country to country, it is usually shown as a deduction from profits in the profit and loss account, with the balance sheet recording the residual net book value. The intention should be to show the current value of the business's assets, but it is often a subjective judgement as to the extent, if any, that assets should be depreciated.

The ratio of capital expenditure to depreciation is an indication of whether fixed assets are being replaced on an on-going basis.

There are many ways of calculating depreciation, but the most common are the straight-line method and the reducing-balance method.

(Adjustment would need to be made if at any time the accounting period was other than one year.)

Straight-line method

Here the annual depreciation is the initial cost of an asset less its estimated residual value at the end of its forecast useful life, divided by the number of years of its forecast useful life. Once the annual depreciation has been calculated in this way, it remains a constant.

Reducing-balance method

The annual depreciation is a constant *percentage* of the net book value of an asset at the start of each accounting period. The actual *amount* of depreciation therefore reduces each year, as the net book value on which the percentage is calculated is itself getting smaller as a result of each previous year's depreciation.

Lending

The canons of lending
·····································

From their collective experience over many years, bankers worldwide have come to recognize certain principles, called the 'canons of lending', as being fundamental to good lending. They are not formulated in any strict sense, and no two bankers would give exactly the same definitions, but the principles are well known, understood and observed by prudent bankers.

The following is written from a lender's perspective, but if you are a borrower wondering why a bank behaves as it does, read on.

Character and ability

Are the borrower and/or its principals known, competent, and trustworthy?

Who introduced them, or what otherwise led them to your door? Are there banks or other parties of repute whom you can approach for references? If the prospective borrower has banked elsewhere you can ask to see the original statements of account, together with any facility agreements or correspondence. If a prospective borrower says that their bank 'does not understand them', or they cannot get along with their present bank manager, it may well be true. They might indeed have sound business skills and potential, and good reason to be unhappy with their bank. But remember that the present bankers have had the benefit of a business relationship and may be in a better position than you to make a judgement. Every case must be decided upon its individual merits.

It always helps if the prospective borrower is based locally to the lender, as you are more likely to have some idea of their reputation and the regard in which they are held by the business community. If they are located some distance from the lender, the question must be asked as to why they have made the approach.

Many failed businesses are found to have had common directors or owners. Have you made enquiries or searches on the principals behind a prospective borrower?

A golden rule is that if you find someone has lied or intentionally misled you, no matter how small or seemingly trivial the matter involved, do not lend – and if they owe you money, then try and get it back as soon as possible!

Whatever the underlying transaction, the success of the venture and a borrower's ability to repay may ultimately depend upon their key personnel. Do they have the depth and spread of skills and experience for the job in hand? This will differ from business to business, and depends very much upon the scale of the operation. The entrepreneur running a one-man business must combine any essential technical skills with the ability to sell their products or services, whilst looking after the paperwork and finance. As the business grows, so will the team, with the need to acquire management and human resource competencies. If there are gaps in the skills portfolio, then the venture could be put at risk.

A lender needs to meet the key individuals, and be satisfied as to the balance and integrity of the whole team. Painful as it may be, there can be occasions when a loan cannot be made because of a single perceived weakness. Whether the banker discloses the reason for their reservations is a matter for careful consideration in light of the circumstances. Even when acting in good faith, and taking into account the impact on all concerned, it is a delicate matter, complicated with the potential risk of legal action by any individual who considers themselves to have been harmed.

It is essential to visit a borrower's premises and to meet as many executives and employees as may be necessary to form a judgement. Walking round an office or factory will give you a better idea of how it is run than the most beautifully written business plan. There can be no excuse for failing to see things at first hand. If distance is a problem it may be possible to ask local colleagues to act on your behalf, but remember where the buck stops.

Purpose

To what use will the monies be put?

When lending to a larger corporate, your facility may form part of their overall funding, without reference to any specific transaction. Normally, however, the purpose of the borrowing is known and can be factored into your lending decision.

- Is the borrower in a sector, for example, property, where you have concerns, or your bank's total exposure is already sufficient?

- Would the lending be subject to country, currency, environmental, resources, technological or other inherent risks?

- Is the project one that you are happy with on ethical or moral grounds? Would it cause embarrassment if known that you were supporting this particular transaction?

- Can you monitor or control the application of your advance, to ensure that the monies are correctly applied?

Many lenders have been surprised to discover the use to which their monies have actually been put, often by otherwise respectable businessmen facing cash flow problems. The diversion of funds might be intended as a temporary expedient, but the opportunity to put matters right may never arise.

Amount

Is the amount to be borrowed reasonable, taking into consideration the stated purpose and the adequacy of any contribution by the borrower? Who stands to lose most if it goes wrong?

It is in no-one's interest to lend less than is needed. This can result in excessive cash flow pressure on the borrower so that, even if the business does not have to stop trading, the management may lack the resources to run the business effectively. They can also find themselves too preoccupied with creditors and with day-to-day concerns about funding, to have time for customers.

All too often a banker advances a reduced amount because it falls within their personal lending discretion. Perhaps they lack confidence that the proposal would receive support from those to whom they report, or simply want to avoid having to write a report.

Bankers should not discount the possibility that a borrower already knows how much they can lend without reference to a higher authority, and has shaded the requirements accordingly. A lender must be satisfied that, after taking into account all costs and contingencies, the amount is adequate.

If the borrower needs to come back for more, a bank may either have to put up the extra money or see its existing exposure at risk.

Prospective borrowers tend to be unduly optimistic as to the amount of money they need to borrow and the time required to pay it back. It is the lender's responsibility to inject a note of realism.

There are no universal hard and fast rules as to the percentages of any transaction to be provided by the bank and customer respectively. This must depend upon the nature of the proposal, covenant and track record of the customer, available security and other relevant factors. Given the competitive nature of lending institutions, the percentage that will be lent also changes from time to time, dependent upon the state of the economy and markets. However, the contribution by the borrower should be sufficient to put beyond doubt their commitment to doing everything possible to ensure the success of the transaction. If the borrower can walk away without pain, leaving the lender to sort out any problems, then they might be tempted to do so. The borrower's contribution may also provide a comfort zone, allowing for a margin of error or loss before the lender suffers.

Equally important can be the order in which the respective funds are contributed. Is the borrower's money going in first, last or *pro rata* with that of the lender?

Repayment

Can the borrower service and repay the debt when due?

Funds for this purpose may come directly from the activities financed by the lending, or derive from other sources.

Some or all of the interest or fees charged by the bank may be capitalized and added to the principal debt.

The debt may be due for repayment:

- on demand
- in instalments (tranches) over a specified period (term)
- in a single payment (bullet) at the end of a specified period.

Whatever the arrangement there should be a reasonable expectation that the bank will be repaid on time. The factors influencing this must inevitably vary from transaction to transaction, but how certain is the source of repayment, and is it within the control of the borrower or bank? A lender will be more comfortable where they, or the borrower, can take steps to realize the necessary funds than when repayment depends upon the actions of a third party. What margin of safety has been built into the projections and assumptions?

Security

Security is taken by lenders as an insurance against things going wrong. It is not an excuse for otherwise bad lending. Given the chance, a lender rarely turns down the opportunity to enhance its position with security.

There should be a reasonable expectation that the borrower will be able to service and repay a debt without the lender needing to sell any security. For that reason, the lender must always endeavour to consider all factors, including those outside of the control of the bank or borrower, that could put the advance at risk. To lend solely against the security is 'pawnbroking'.

The decision as to what, if any, security is taken in support of a lending is dependent upon:

- the nature of the transaction underlying the borrowing
- the covenant of the borrower (i.e., their overall creditworthiness)
- market circumstances – whether security is sought often depends upon the comparative negotiating strengths of the lender and borrower in the market at the time the deal is structured
- what security is available: if the only available asset has a value disproportionately greater than the debt, the borrower may be unwilling to allow the bank to have a charge; or there may be other borrowings and the most desirable assets are already charged elsewhere.

Banks often gain by taking security at an early stage in a business's development which they never subsequently release, but could not have obtained once their customer was stronger. Subject to any documentation limiting the bank's right of recourse against such security to a specific borrowing (or other liability), the bank sits comfortably.

It is usually necessary to have an appreciation of the amount likely to be raised if the security had to be realized. Sometimes the lender can determine this themselves, or be comfortable in relying upon information provided by the borrower.

In other instances, the lender will need to consult a third party expert as to the realizable value of any security, in which event they must exercise great care when instructing the valuer as to the basis upon which they are to work, explain why the opinion is needed (e.g., that the bank will be relying upon it for lending purposes) and ensure that the valuation itself is addressed to and states that it can be relied upon by the lender. Whatever the valuation, it does not relieve the banker of all responsibility. It is an opinion of what something may be worth which can only be tested in the market at a future date. If the valuation appears inconsistent with the banker's own knowledge, understanding or perceptions, it must be treated with particular caution and questioned with the vendor.

There is no point in asking for security and then failing to perfect the charge. Whether it is the practice of a lender for this to be done by their own employees or to instruct solicitors for that purpose, it is essential to follow set procedures.

All too often a lender's records indicate that security is available for any indebtedness, when, in fact, recourse against it can only be had for specific liabilities.

Lending officers must always query any uncertainties with their legal departments or lawyers at the earliest possible date. It is usually too late when the debt has turned bad.

It must be within the ability of the lender to cost-effectively realize the security if necessary. There is little point in having assets charged that cannot be sold if things go wrong, or where the cost of so doing is disproportionate to any benefit. This can, for example, happen where before the asset can be sold it has to come into the legal ownership of the lender or his agents, and this immediately gives rise to taxation, environmental, warranty or other liabilities. These are very real concerns, and in the case of environmental liability the cost to the lender could outweigh any potential benefit. Such factors must be fully considered at the time the lending is made, not when things go wrong.

Risk vs reward

Lenders are in business to make a profit. It has been the experience of some banks that, over any given term of years, the income from business lending has not covered the total costs of providing the funds, the relationship/support personnel and bad debts. But the bank has felt obliged to commit to such transactions rather than lose customers and market share. Often the losses result from imprudent lending decisions, but, even in the best-regulated houses, some losses are inevitable and this needs to be recognized and built into the pricing models.

The lending process

It is important that a banker or other professional lender remains objective, avoiding the temptation to become emotionally committed to other than providing a quality service.

Take the time necessary to reach a lending decision. The borrower may well have been planning the project over a long period, but expects an immediate response from a financier unfamiliar with the facts. It is not in the interests of either party to get it wrong.

If in doubt, or under unreasonable pressure, the answer must be no!

Occasionally, you instinctively know there is something wrong, but cannot put your finger on the reason. If the prospective borrower is a good customer, they deserve to be told that you have reservations, and a frank and open discussion may resolve matters to mutual satisfaction. *Never lend if you feel uncomfortable about it.*

In theory a lending officer views every transaction dispassionately, but all too often this is not the case. The more a lender gets emotionally involved and tries to help, the greater the risks of a bad decision. It is not for the lender to formulate and structure the borrower's proposition. In practice, and with the best of intentions, lenders often find themselves putting the proposal together from the barest of information, and then going over the top to try and get it sanctioned.

It can be very hard to say 'no' to a customer, and all too frequently a bank's credit culture fails to take adequately into account the emotional pressure on their lending officers.

The extent to which a lending is trouble free often depends on the thoroughness of the 'due diligence' process undertaken before a decision is reached. This may only require a simple discussion with the prospective borrower, which provides enough information for the lender to make up its mind. At the other extreme, weeks can be spent studying documents, attending meetings and undertaking research into the proposition.

No lender can know everything about every sector, and it might be necessary to obtain external input. This may mean consulting a specialist, but information can often be inexpensively obtained from trade journals and newspaper articles (made very much easier by the electronic databases now available).

There is no substitute for personal visits before and during a lending. If funding stock or work-in-progress, has anyone actually seen these items, or is the warehouse empty?

Many bad decisions are made because the lender is simply too busy to complete a thorough due diligence, and it can be tempting to cut corners and hope all will be well. If the loan is fundamentally sound you can get away with this, but all too often it is the lending officer's customer, employer and career that suffer.

The information resulting from the due diligence can be summarized and an authorized representative(s) of the borrower asked to sign a statement to the effect that it is accurate. This makes the borrower think carefully as to whether the lender's understanding of the facts is correct, as there can be perfectly innocent misunderstandings. If the lender has got it wrong, this is the borrower's opportunity to set the record straight. Unless the borrower is fraudulent, they will be reluctant to sign an incorrect statement, with all the implications that might result. Such a document also constitutes an invaluable point of reference, should the transaction need to be revisited at a later date.

Too few lenders ask their borrower to sign such a confirmation, yet this simple action can prevent many problems.

The secret of due diligence is that every statement should be *capable* of verification (whether or not it is appropriate to do so), and that all assumptions are clearly specified.

The time to consider the ways in which a lending can be monitored is when undertaking the initial due diligence. It is then that the transaction is best understood, attentions are focused and covenants can be agreed with the borrower. At any later stage, the available time may be limited or circumstances and personnel have changed, and it can be harder to isolate the critical issues upon which repayment depends. All too often the lending officers receiving management accounts or other information from a customer after the start of a lending have little idea what is important. It should be mandatory for every lending submission or sanction to contain a clear statement of the critical factors to be subsequently monitored. A note should be made of the key figures contained in any forecasts upon which the lending decision has been based, so that they can be compared against actuals. It can be very effective for this to be shown visually, by means of a graph or chart, so that trends are clearly illustrated.

Often a seemingly simple request for information can create major problems or workload for the borrower, which could be avoided if the bank explained in advance what it needed and why. There is usually a simple solution once the problem is known. When management accounts or other information are received from a borrower, look at them without delay, so that any action needed to protect the bank can be taken in good time. Bad debts are often unnecessarily incurred because the warning signs had been left sitting in a pending file.

If the lender is a bank, do not overlook the wealth of information to be gained from the transactions seen on the customer's account. Unless multi-banked, these are especially valuable when compared with the financial projections, management accounts and other information provided by customers. For example, if a borrower claims a level of turnover that is not supported by the bank account, you need to ask why. Most banks now have sophisticated computer programs providing valuable analysis and identifying significant trends. The secret is to make use of all the information available.

See also, *Due diligence*, page 24.

Problem accounts

For lenders with eyes to see, there can be many warning signs of impending trouble. Banks, in particular, are likely to have a steady flow of valuable information on the health of a borrower's business, including unauthorized excesses over agreed limits or urgent requests for increased facilities.

Most monitoring procedures start with the premise that a borrower is honest, which makes fraudsters a particular danger. Protective measures against fraud start with the checks made during the initial relationship or account opening process. This stage is frequently treated as a formality, but once past this 'firewall', a fraudster is often home and away.

Listen to what others have to say, particularly if they have done business with the prospective borrower. Visit the borrower's place of business, to see for yourself and talk to any employees. It is surprising how much can be learnt by asking a few well-targeted questions.

A failure by the borrower to provide financial information when due is often the first indicator of problems, particularly when coupled with evasive management who do not return calls. There is always a good excuse for a borrower's failure to get in touch or to produce promised figures, and a lender needs to understand the business and its key individuals well enough to know when to start worrying. All too often the lender delays taking action until it is too late to prevent loss.

Once you think there may be reason for concern as to the safety of a debt, do not delay taking action.

- Find out the extent and nature of your exposure, including contingent liabilities.
- Check the facility documentation and any security for weaknesses, instructing legal advisers to report as necessary.
- Do any charged assets actually exist, and should they be revalued?
- Have insurance premiums been paid?
- Is money owed by the borrower to other lenders who might take action detrimental to your interests?
- What has caused the problems?
- Is it necessary to appoint investigating accountants or other advisers to discover the true picture? Should the account manager be changed?

Once you have the facts, decide upon a course of action and prepare an action plan. This will vary from one jurisdiction to another, depending on the enforceable rights of the lender and any options open to the borrower to frustrate or delay action. Time may not be on the lender's side, particularly if suppliers or customers of the borrower become aware of its problems.

The choices might be:

- liquidation or other insolvency routes
- to support existing management
- to enforce changes to the business or management.

Is there a realistic exit route?

If the business is potentially viable, a lender might decide to help it with a restructuring programme. This may depend, in part, on the character and skills of the management and the state of the market.

How much money would be needed to keep the business alive, and would such additional funding be recoverable in the longer term?

It may be necessary to enter into discussions with other lenders. How do their exposure and security positions compare with yours? Is their corporate culture aggressive or accommodating, and would it be in your interests to cooperate? Are there potential benefits in buying out another lender to gain their security?

It can be surprisingly hard to negotiate any rescue package with the owners and management of a defaulting business. They are likely to be in a stressed emotional state and may be highly irrational, particularly where a lender holds their personal guarantees.

A lender's options may, in any event, be limited by legal requirements and the rights of an insolvent business or of other creditors in the governing jurisdiction.

If the decision is to try and achieve a 'workout' of the problems, remember that this can absorb considerable amounts of the lender's time and money. Will the position get worse before it can get better? Might other creditors or lenders pull the business down despite your best efforts, and if they did so, would you lose more than the initial debt? All too often, the correct response when in a hole is to stop digging.

Changes at board or management level may be needed, together with the immediate imposition of firm financial controls. Unnecessary assets can be sold to reduce debts, and those parts of the business that cannot contribute to the turnaround closed or otherwise disposed of.

It may be necessary for a new chief executive to be appointed, but be sure the right person is chosen. A mistake can be very expensive. What is their track record, especially in turnaround situations, and why do you think they can succeed where others have failed? Would a new broom do any better than the existing team (if they had the same level of support from the bank), or is a change necessary to revitalize the business and set fresh goals?

A restructuring may require a rescheduling of debt payments, and possible conversion of some debt into equity. Interest on the debt may have to be deferred or written off.

Most banks maintain a 'watch list' of accounts giving cause for concern. Entry to the list may depend on scoring an unsatisfactory 'grading', being in arrears of interest or capital repayments or because there are known to be problems.

Each bank will have its own grading procedures to assess the safety of loans and other facilities. Poor-quality advances may be classified as 'doubtful', 'sub-standard', 'special mention', etc., or identified by a numerical or alphabetical coding. It is common to have up to ten such categories of classification.

There should be minimum levels of action to be taken by the responsible loan officers for each grading level. A typical grading system allocates 'scores' to a range of factors. These may be 'weighted' for importance, and the total scores used to allocate the loan classification.

The categories might include:

- borrower's financial strength (i.e., balance sheet)
- payment ability (i.e., profits and cash flows)
- strengths/weaknesses of the industry sector
- management team ability
- realizable security.

Within each category, points will be awarded, from (say) 5 points for the best possible score to 1 for the worst. It is important that this scoring is based on standard definitions.

Payment ability

EXAMPLE

5 points	a very profitable business with cash flow substantially surplus to that needed for all debt servicing.
4 points	a profitable company with cash flow greater than that needed for all debt servicing.
3 points	cash flow and profits adequate to repay or service the bank debt but with no margin to spare.
2 points	doubts as to ability to service the bank debt.
1 point	borrower cannot service the bank debt.

A borrower might score, say:

Financial strength	3
Payment ability	2
Industry sector	2
Management team	3
Realizable security	4

i.e., 14 out of a maximum of 25 points.

Assuming that the categories were not weighted (for example, to give emphasis to 'payment ability'), the total points scored would be compared against a gradings table.

	Points score
Vulnerable	5–8
Substandard	9–13
Acceptable	14–18
Good	19–22
High quality	23–25

Anything scoring less than the minimum for an 'acceptable' grade would be put on a 'watch/problem account' list for regular reports by the loan officer to those responsible for bad and doubtful debts.

Also on the watch list would be any facilities that could not be scored because the necessary information was not available, and those for which concern was felt, despite achieving scores for grades 'acceptable' or above.

It may be necessary to decide whether all or part of any debt should be 'provided for', i.e., an amount set aside from the profits of the bank to cover the likely level of loss. This provision might include the suspension of interest. Whilst interest would normally still be debited to the borrower's account, so as to establish the amount of total indebtedness, it would not be taken to profit ('non-accrual' – on the grounds that it was unlikely either to be paid to the bank by the customer or be recovered from realization of security).

The level of provisioning depends on many factors, and will need to be regularly reviewed as circumstances change. It can be helpful to indicate against each watch/problem account whether the credit risk is expected to change over time.

Credit insurance

Competitively priced credit insurance covering the sale of goods and services is available in many countries, and can offer:

- protection against bad debts, usually up to a maximum of two years; the level of cover will be subject to negotiation, but 90% is common; you can usually decide the risk you want to keep, and what percentage to insure
- cover for all, or only a selection, of your buyers
- insurance of either your domestic or international trade, or both
- cover for 'country risk', including delays in transferring money from the buyer's country, the actions of governments which prevent delivery or payment (even of those countries through which the goods or monies have to pass), and war

- international debt recovery services; the insurer may be prepared to contribute towards the costs of recovery, and will have access to specialist lawyers and debt collectors in different countries
- the benefit of the credit insurer's skills and experience, based upon their extensive exposure in the markets
- 'pre-credit risk' insurance, for the costs incurred during the manufacturing period before shipment
- cover for your costs and expenses, and for contractual interest due from the buyer
- the opportunity to win business by offering attractive terms because credit risk is no longer a significant factor
- an argument for cheaper finance from your bank, as the potential negative impact of any bad debts on your business has been reduced; because your business is therefore a better credit risk the reduction in the interest margin you have to pay a lender may cover the costs of the insurance premium
- cover for the losses in meeting forward exchange commitments, where your buyer has defaulted.

The benefits gained from supplementing the in-house risk management skills of your business with those of the insurer can make credit insurance attractive to even the largest of companies. The insurer is more likely to know if a potential buyer is a slow payer or that circumstances have changed for an individual buyer or market, and be far better placed to assess the risks of overseas trading. They will have a database showing payment histories, and can buy in additional information as needed.

Speed is often the essence in winning business, and orders can be lost if you delay while checking credit references. This is where an insurer can be of particular value. For example, NCM, an international insurer providing cover exceeding £75 billion annually, can offer on-line credit decisions for most buyers based on a database of around 6 million businesses worldwide. Their average premiums currently are under 0.5% for exports, including country risk, and less than 0.2% for domestic sales.

The sound disciplines that an insurer brings to credit control will be reinforced by an occasional 'audit' of your systems, which can be invaluable in highlighting areas of risk.

In reaching their credit decisions, insurers principally take into consideration:

- industry sector
- country risk (if any)
- types of goods or services you are providing
- terms of trade

- track record of your buyers: this is usually of more interest to an insurer than the statutory accounts of a business.

The time allowed before an insurer will reimburse bad debts varies, but will typically be immediately on a buyer's insolvency or otherwise six months after payment was due (or after the due date of bills of exchange or promissory notes). If your terms of trade offer two months' credit then the insurance would not be payable for, say, eight months. Before making any payment for bad debts, an insurer will wish to be satisfied that:

- the goods or services have been delivered or otherwise provided
- the debt is valid, and that the buyer actually exists; the insurer's credit checks are usually based on searching for negative factors, so that if a buyer was fictitious this would not necessarily be revealed at an early stage; it is for your business to satisfy itself that a buyer is genuine
- the buyer is not disputing payment; check your policy document to find out what happens if a buyer disputes; what, if anything, can you do, and will the insurer pay a reduced amount; are you required to re-sell any goods the buyer has refused to accept before the insurer will contribute to the loss?
- credit limits have been respected; there is usually provision for the business to set discretionary limits for individual buyers, up to a maximum detailed in the credit insurance policy document
- insurance premiums have been paid; these normally comprise a basic fee plus a premium based on the level of activity.

A business that has taken out credit insurance must be careful:

- not to extend the due date for payment by a buyer unless this is permitted by the policy or has been agreed by the insurer
- to promptly notify the insurer of any event likely to cause a loss, or if payment is overdue (subject to the policy terms)
- not to 'do a deal' with the buyer for reduced payment without the insurer's consent
- not to continue trading with a buyer in default, unless this is permitted by the insurance policy
- if a group, to trade in the names of the companies that have the insurance cover
- to observe all laws and regulations that might affect the contracts with buyers, including exchange controls
- to obtain any import/export licences or other necessary authorizations
- to observe any special requirements of the insurer for trading with individual buyers, including reservation (retention) of title

- where making part shipments, to withhold the next delivery until the last has been paid for, unless the insurance cover is adequate – businesses often overlook that the total cost of an order may be outside the policy limit, and then despatch more than is covered at any one time.

Trade payments

Open account

....

The seller despatches goods or supplies services on the basis of trust that the buyer will subsequently pay for what is received.

Definition

Buyer   The recipient of the goods or services who makes payment to the seller.

Seller   The provider of the goods or services who receives the payment from the buyer.

PARTIES

A seller enters into a contract for the supply of goods to a buyer. When they are despatched, the seller sends an invoice (together with any other relevant documents) to the buyer for the amount due, including any costs or taxes to be paid by the buyer. The invoice should specify when payment is due, and might state that there is a charge for late payment and/or a discount for prompt payment. The buyer then makes payment to the seller in settlement of the account (or accepts a tenor draft).

EXAMPLE

Buyer

- Does not need to pay until the goods or services have been received and found to be satisfactory.
- Its cash flow is enhanced by delayed payment.
- Where the invoice is in a foreign currency the buyer can gain from any favourable movement of exchange rates prior to the date of payment.

BENEFITS
including risks
avoided

Seller

- A straightforward, low-cost, way of selling that is normal between businesses where there are no particular concerns as to creditworthiness or other payment risks. Unwillingness to trade on open account terms, where that is the accepted industry practice, may result in loss of business.

Buyer

- If payment is to be made in a foreign currency, then the exchange rate could move against the buyer before the date when payment is made.
- The seller may not deliver the goods or services on time or of the quality needed for the buyer to meet obligations to its own customers.

Seller

- That the buyer will not pay or is prevented (e.g., exchange controls) from paying for the goods or services, or delays making payment. Although it may be possible to claim 'reservation (retention) of title' to the goods, the seller could find itself without either goods or cash. Further, the buyer might dispute quality or claim that there are deficiencies (whether or not this is justified) as grounds for a reduced payment, whilst holding on to, selling or otherwise using the goods. Credit insurance may be worth considering, or asking the buyer to provide a standby letter of credit.
- Have the goods been adequately insured? Even where the buyer was supposed to arrange and pay for insurance cover during transportation, it may be worth the seller taking out inexpensive 'transit insurance' in its own name – giving protection to the seller if the buyer has failed to do so.
- If the invoice is in foreign currency, the exchange rate may move against the seller before payment is received from the buyer.
- Where the invoice is accompanied by the transport documents it may be appropriate to obtain ships' waybills rather than bills of lading as with the former the buyer has to identify itself to collect the goods, whereas possession of the bill of lading can be sufficient to give title to the goods.
- Businesses selling on open account terms incur the costs of credit control and collection.
  See also *Collections*, page 87.

Payment in advance/on delivery

See also *Collections*, page 87.

Definition

> *The buyer of goods or services pays for them, in whole or part, in advance or at the time of the seller delivering the goods or providing the service.*

PARTIES

Buyer The recipient of the goods or services who makes the payment to the seller.

Seller The provider of the goods or services who receives the payment from the buyer.

EXAMPLE

A manufacturer of furniture is asked to supply items to a buyer with whom he has not previously done business, or who has failed to pay for past shipments. Rather than take a credit risk, the seller of the furniture asks for payment upfront. Often the seller will send the buyer a pro forma invoice, which is effectively a quotation inviting the buyer to place an order. A pro forma invoice may be required where the buyer needs evidence of the terms of an intended purchase to obtain exchange control or import licences. The buyer sends the payment, and on its receipt, the manufacturer despatches the goods.

Buyer

BENEFITS
including risks
avoided

- Is able to obtain goods or services when the seller might otherwise be unwilling to do business.

- In return for an advance or on-delivery payment, the buyer may be able to negotiate a favourable price from the seller.

- When the payment is made in advance, the buyer knows the cost in its own currency of any payment in foreign currency, and is not exposed to future adverse changes in exchange rates.

Seller

- Where payment is received in advance, there is no risk of default by the buyer.

- There may be a saving in administration and credit control costs.

- Has use of the monies received from the buyer for a longer period, which helps the seller's cash flow.

- If, when selling in foreign currency, payments received are converted immediately into the seller's own currency, any further exchange rate risk is removed.

Buyer

RISKS
REMAINING

- That the seller may not deliver the goods or supply the services, or these may be unsatisfactory, after payment has been made in advance. It may be possible to obtain an advance payment or performance bond, or some other form of guarantee, from the seller's bank.

- Has adequate transit and other insurance been put in place? If the seller was responsible for arranging and paying for this cover did it do so, or should the buyer take out inexpensive back-up 'transit insurance' in its own name?

- The negative effect on the buyer's cash flow by paying in advance may result in it experiencing financial pressure. This would be made all the worse if the goods or services supplied by the seller were delayed or defective, preventing the buyer from using them to generate cash flow and profits.

Seller

- If the buyer does not pay on or before delivery, the seller may be left with goods that are hard to sell elsewhere and (if already shipped) with the costs of insurance, storage and possible re-shipment.

Documentary letters of credit

Definition

> *An undertaking issued by a bank at the request of its customer, to pay a third party against presentation to the bank of specified documents evidencing compliance with the terms and conditions set out in the documentary credit.*

A documentary letter of credit (letter of credit/documentary credit) enables a buyer of goods or services to provide the seller with reasonable assurance that they will be paid provided the terms and conditions specified in the credit are met.

The *Uniform Customs and Practice for Documentary Credits* (current edition *UCP 500*) published by the International Chamber of Commerce are accepted as the principles to be observed by users of documentary credits ('credits').

Payment to the seller on presentation of the documents may be as follows.

- Immediate (i.e., by negotiation or sight payment). 'Negotiation' is the sale of a sight or tenor draft (bill of exchange) for an immediate cash payment.

- Deferred to a specified future date (the issuing bank undertakes that payment will be made at that time, provided the terms of the credit have been met).

- By 'acceptance' of drafts drawn by the beneficiary on the issuing or accepting bank. 'Acceptance' under a credit is the process whereby a tenor ('usance' or 'term') draft is drawn by the beneficiary on a bank (i.e., the bank is the named 'drawee'). The bank 'accepts' the draft and thereby becomes the 'acceptor' (see *Bills of exchange/drafts*, page 93). The draft is subsequently presented to the acceptor at its maturity date for payment. The acceptor must pay the draft at maturity, even if it cannot recover the money from the applicant or any other party.

  Although, strictly speaking, 'tenor' refers to any period of time for which a draft is drawn to run before it matures and could, therefore, apply to a draft payable at sight, the word 'tenor' is used here to denote a term/usance draft.

PARTIES   **Applicant**   The buyer/importer of the goods or services who asks the issuing bank to set up the credit, and is liable for payments made under it by the bank to the seller.

Beneficiary The seller/exporter of the goods or services who is the named beneficiary under the credit and entitled to payment, or acceptance of a tenor draft, on presentation to a nominated bank of the specified documents in good order.

Issuing bank The bank instructed by the applicant to issue the credit in favour of the beneficiary.

Advising bank The bank asked by the issuing bank to advise the beneficiary of the issue and terms of the credit.

Confirming bank At the request of the issuing bank, a confirming bank undertakes that, on presentation to it or another nominated bank of the specified documents in good order, the beneficiary will be paid (either immediately or at a later date). The beneficiary does not, therefore, have to depend upon the monies being sent by the issuing bank, which is normally situated in another country.

The undertaking of the confirming bank is in addition to, not in substitution of, the undertaking of the issuing bank.

The confirming bank is normally, but not necessarily, the advising bank. For example, the advising bank may already have entered into other financial exposures with the issuing bank, using up the credit limit it marks for transactions with the issuing bank and leaving insufficient room for an additional credit. In such event another bank, with sufficient limit available for this credit exposure on the issuing bank, may be asked to confirm the credit. In practice, it is unusual for the confirming bank to be other than the advising bank.

Nominated bank The confirming bank or any other bank nominated to pay the beneficiary, or accept or negotiate drafts, or incur a deferred payment liability under the credit, provided the documents specified therein have been presented to it in good order.

Reference is sometimes made instead to the 'paying bank' or to the 'accepting bank'.

An example of a letter of credit is shown in Figure 2.1 and an example of a confirmation of a letter of credit is shown in Figure 2.2.

- A buyer (applicant) and a seller (beneficiary) of goods or services agree a transaction. **EXAMPLE**

- One of the terms of their agreement is that the beneficiary requires the applicant to arrange for a credit to be issued in its favour, and stipulates whether or not it is to be 'confirmed'.

- The applicant goes to its bank (issuing bank) and, if they are prepared to accept the credit risk on the applicant for providing this service, they will issue a credit in accordance with the terms and conditions advised to them by the applicant (which should, in turn, conform to the terms the applicant agreed with the beneficiary).

- The issuing bank selects as the advising bank a correspondent or other bank, usually located in or near the country of the seller, and sends them the credit asking that it be advised to the beneficiary. A correspondent bank is one with which another bank has an established relationship and with which it often, although not always, maintains accounts enabling each to debit the other without waiting for funds to be transmitted in settlement of every transaction. A bank which pays away money to the debit of an inadequately funded account maintained with it by another bank is

---

TEXT OF LETTER OF CREDIT SENT FROM ISSUING BANK TO ADVISING BANK BY TESTED TELEX

TO: SBC WARBURG
               A DIVISION OF SWISS BANK CORPORATION,
               LONDON

WE BUYER'S BANK, CALCUTTA HEREBY OPEN OUR IRREVOCABLE DOCUMENTARY LETTER OF CREDIT NO: 36319 FOR AN AMOUNT OF USD 59,280.00 (UNITED STATES DOLLARS FIFTY NINE THOUSAND TWO HUNDRED AND EIGHTY) BY ORDER OF INDIAN BUYER LTD, CALCUTTA IN FAVOUR OF UK SELLERS LTD, LONDON, VALID UNTIL 21ST NOVEMBER 1996 AND AVAILABLE BY SIGHT PAYMENT AT YOUR COUNTERS, AGAINST PRESENTATION OF BENEFICIARY'S DRAFT DRAWN AT SIGHT ON YOURSELVES FOR 100 PERCENT INVOICE VALUE AND ACCOMPANIED BY THE UNDER-MENTIONED DOCUMENTS.

1.   BENEFICIARY'S SIGNED INVOICE IN ONE ORIGINAL AND TWO COPIES.

2.   FULL SET OF ORIGINAL CLEAN ON BOARD MARINE BILLS OF LADING ISSUED TO OUR ORDER, MARKED FREIGHT PAID AND NOTIFY INDIAN BUYER LTD, CALCUTTA.

3.   CERTIFICATE OF ORIGIN ISSUED BY A CHAMBER OF COMMERCE IN COUNTRY OF ORIGIN IN ONE ORIGINAL AND ONE COPY.

4.   PACKING LIST IN ONE ORIGINAL

5.   BENEFICIARY'S CERTIFICATE STATING THAT THEY HAVE SENT ONE SET OF COPY DOCUMENTS DIRECTLY TO THE APPLICANT THREE DAYS AFTER SHIPMENT.

COVERING:

60 CASES PHARMACEUTICAL PRODUCTS EACH CONTAINING 100 PACKS.
UNIT PRICE: USD 9.88 PER PACK CFR CALCUTTA
SHIPMENT FROM UK PORT TO CALCUTTA PORT BY LATEST 31ST OCTOBER 1996.

OTHER CONDITIONS:

1.   ALL YOUR CHARGES ARE FOR BENEFICIARY'S ACCOUNT.

2.   PART SHIPMENTS NOT ALLOWED. TRANSHIPMENT NOT ALLOWED.

3.   DOCUMENTS MUST BE PRESENTED NO LATER THAN 21 DAYS AFTER DATE OF SHIPMENT DATE.

PLEASE ADVISE BENEFICIARY AND ADD YOUR CONFIRMATION.

REIMBURSEMENT INSTRUCTIONS TO CONFIRMING BANK
UPON RECEIPT OF YOUR TESTED TELEX CONFIRMING THAT YOU HAVE RECEIVED DOCUMENTS PRESENTED IN CONFORMITY WITH L/C TERMS AND CONDITIONS, AND THAT THEY HAVE BEEN FORWARDED TO OURSELVES IN ONE LOT BY COURIER, WE WILL COVER YOU IN ACCORDANCE WITH YOUR INSTRUCTIONS VALUE TWO WORKING DAYS.

THIS CREDIT IS SUBJECT TO UNIFORM CUSTOMS AND PRACTICE FOR DOCUMENTARY CREDITS (1993 REVISION) INTERNATIONAL CHAMBER OF COMMERCE PUBLICATION NO. 500.

REGARDS
BUYER'S BANK, CALCUTTA
DATE: 30TH SEPTEMBER, 1996

Fig. 2.1 Example of a letter of credit (source: courtesy of SBC Warburg)

dependent upon reimbursement from that bank in due course. Similarly, a bank which leaves funds on its account with another bank is taking the risk of default by that bank. The maintenance of such accounts therefore involves the banks marking appropriate credit limits.

● If required by the beneficiary, and provided the relationship and credit limit between the issuing bank and the advising bank permits, then the advising bank may be

---

SBC Warburg
A DIVISION OF SWISS BANK CORPORATION

SWISS BANK CORPORATION

1 High Timber Street
London EC4V 3SB
Tel: 0171-329 0329
Telex: 887434 SBCO G
SWIFT address: SBCO GB 22

Global Trade Finance/PG

Date: 2nd October, 1996

UK Sellers Ltd
London
Attention Export Dept

Dear Sirs,

Letter of Credit No. 36319 issued by Buyer's Bank, Calcutta.
Our reference: L/C 78466.

We enclose the operative copy of an authenticated telex issuing the above letter of credit in your favour.

This letter of credit is confirmed by SBC Warburg, a division of Swiss Bank Corporation, and we hereby undertake that payment will be effected by us with value two working days after receipt of documents presented at our counters in London in conformity with the terms of this credit.

All bank charges outside India are for beneficiary's account, please therefore remit the sum of £......... being our confirmation commission in this connection. Any charges remaining outstanding will be deducted from any payment effected by us hereunder, as will our payment commission.

This letter of credit is subject to the *Uniform Customs and Practice for Documentary Credits* (1993 Revision) International Chamber of Commerce Publication No.500.

Please acknowledge receipt by signing and returning the attached copy of this letter.

Yours faithfully
SBC Warburg
A division of Swiss Bank Corporation

Fig. 2.2 Example of confirmation of a letter of credit (source: courtesy of SBC Warburg)

asked by the issuing bank to add to the credit their confirmation that the beneficiary will be paid on presentation to them of the specified documents in good order. The advising bank thereby becomes the 'confirming bank'. Should the advising bank be unable or unwilling to add its confirmation, another bank prepared to do so could become the confirming bank.

● In due course the beneficiary will present to the nominated bank the documents specified as being those against which payment will be made.

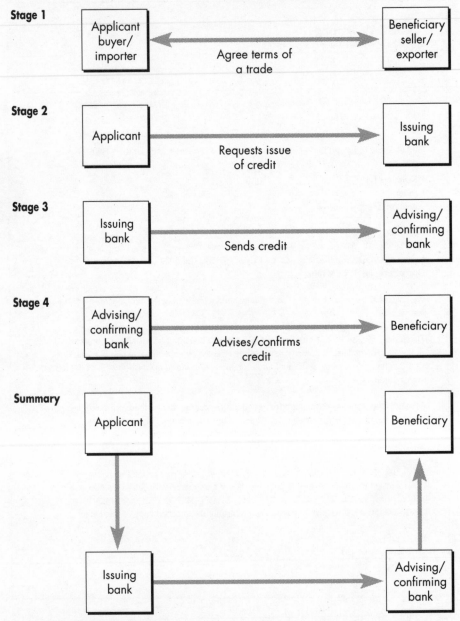

Fig. 2.3 Issue of a letter of credit

- The nominated bank checks that the documents are in accordance with the credit and then does one of the following.

  - If it is a confirming bank and the documents are in order it either pays the beneficiary immediately, undertakes to pay at a deferred date or accepts drafts, and sends the documents to the issuing bank. Where a draft is accepted by a bank it may be possible to have it 'discounted' by the accepting or some other bank. The beneficiary thereby obtains immediate payment for the face value of the draft less a charge for interest up to the maturity date. The applicant still has the benefit of not paying until the maturity date, and sometimes agrees in advance to bear the beneficiary's discounting costs.

  - If it is a bank other than an issuing or confirming bank, it sends the documents to the issuing bank for acceptance and/or payment. When subsequently authorized by the issuing bank, it:
    (i)   pays the beneficiary, *or*
    (ii)   undertakes to pay at a deferred date (but see *Note*), *or*
    (iii) accepts drafts (but see *Note*).
    Under a credit available by negotiation, the nominated bank could agree to negotiate with recourse any drafts and/or documents drawn under the credit.

    Note: Before doing any of the above an advising or other nominated bank would want either to have received the necessary funds from the issuing bank, or be satisfied with any credit risk it takes on that bank. It is unusual for a bank that is not an issuing or confirming bank to accept a draft or undertake to make a deferred payment.

  - If there are discrepancies in the documents presented by the beneficiary, the nominated bank can send either the documents or an explanatory communication to the issuing bank asking if the applicant will waive the discrepancies. If the beneficiary is a good customer of the nominated bank, and considered creditworthy (or if another bank is prepared to indemnify the nominated bank on behalf of the beneficiary), then the bank might meanwhile pay the beneficiary under the credit on a recourse basis, i.e., the monies are to be repaid to the bank by the beneficiary if the discrepancies are not waived by the applicant.

The credit may call for the documents to be sent direct to the issuing bank by the beneficiary (i.e., it is 'payable at the issuing bank's counters'), but that is unusual.

- On receiving the documents the issuing bank uses 'reasonable care' in checking them to see if 'on their face' they conform to those specified in the credit and, if in order, it delivers them to the applicant. If there are discrepancies, these will normally be referred to the applicant to see if they can be waived. The decision as to whether to ask the applicant if it wishes to waive a discrepancy, or to simply reject and return the documents can be made by the issuing bank. The issuing, confirming or other

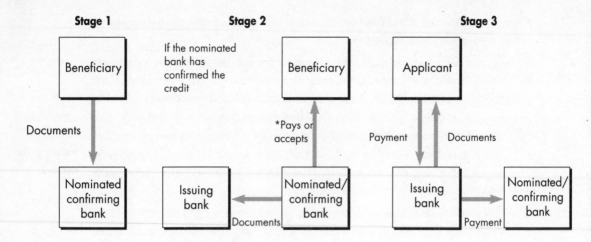

Stage 1   **Stage 2**   **Stage 3**

If the nominated bank has confirmed the credit

*If the nominated bank had not confirmed the credit then payment to the beneficiary (or acceptance) would normally be deferred until authorization is received from the issuing bank.

Summary (if documents are in order)

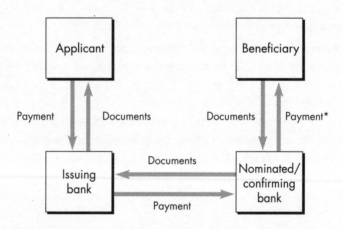

*If the documents are in order and the nominated bank has confirmed the credit, it must make payment to the beneficiary, or accept drafts, without waiting until approval or funds are received from the issuing bank.

Fig. 2.4 Presentation under letter of credit (assuming documents are in order)

nominated bank is not required to check any documents presented unless those documents are specifically called for in the credit.

- When all is in order, the applicant's account will be debited with the amount paid to the beneficiary – either immediately or at maturity of any deferred payment period.

Applicant

BENEFITS
including risks
avoided

- By substituting the creditworthiness of a bank for its own, the applicant gives comfort to the beneficiary that it will be paid provided the terms of the credit are met, thereby reducing the likelihood of the beneficiary declining to do business because of credit risk.
- To be paid the beneficiary must have submitted to the nominated bank documents evidencing 'on their face' compliance with the terms of the credit.
- There are cash flow advantages if the beneficiary agrees to payment being made on a 'term' basis, i.e., a specified number of days after shipment or some other event of compliance with the terms of the credit, against an accepted draft or bank undertaking to make a deferred payment.

Beneficiary

- Has greater comfort under a credit than with trading on an open account basis or a documentary collection as the credit risk on the applicant has been reduced by bank undertakings.
- If the credit has been confirmed then it means that a bank, usually in the same country as the beneficiary (or if not, then situated in a nearby territory) and probably known to the beneficiary, will have undertaken to make payment on presentation of the specified documents.
- All the beneficiary has to do to be entitled to payment under the credit is to comply with its terms and submit to a nominated bank the documents specified therein in good order. There is no need to wait for the applicant to accept the goods or documents.
- If, in order to win the business, the beneficiary needs to give the applicant time to pay, then the credit can provide for delayed payment against acceptance by a bank of a tenor draft (or a bank's undertaking to pay at a deferred date). The beneficiary can then take the accepted draft to its own, or another, bank to be discounted so as to receive an immediate payment.

Issuing bank

- Earns income from issuing the credit and from any associated foreign exchange or other transactions.
- Helps its customer, the applicant, to develop business, which may make the account of greater value to the bank.

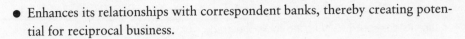

- Enhances its relationships with correspondent banks, thereby creating potential for reciprocal business.

Advising/nominated/confirming bank

- Earns income from the credit and any associated foreign exchange or other transactions.
- Unless the beneficiary is already a customer of the bank, it provides an opportunity to establish a relationship that may lead to other business.
- Enhances its relationship with its correspondent (issuing) bank.

RISKS REMAINING In practice, it is a frequent occurrence for there to be discrepancies in the documents, although these are often waived by the applicant. However, if a bank exposes itself by paying away funds before any discrepancies have been resolved, then the applicant may have no incentive to help out by waiving even the most minor of irregularities, nor the beneficiary any reason to help resolve matters.

Documents, including shipping documents giving possession of the goods, may go astray in transit.

Banks run the risk that they will incorrectly communicate, or fail to comply with, the terms of the credit.

In addition, there are the following risks for the various parties involved.

Applicant

- Payment by the banks to the beneficiary is made against only the documents presented, *not* against inspection of goods or satisfaction as to the supply of services. The banks are not liable for the genuineness or accuracy of the documents, nor for the quantity and quality of goods or services. A fraudulent beneficiary could, therefore, claim and receive payment from the nominated bank on submission of forged or otherwise fraudulent documents, and there is no guarantee that the goods or services are actually as ordered or undamaged. In such an event the applicant is still obligated to fully reimburse the issuing bank with the monies paid to the beneficiary.

- Changes to the contract terms agreed between the applicant and beneficiary must, where necessary, be covered by the issue of amendments to the credit.

- Has adequate transit and other insurance been put in place, and has the beneficiary paid the premiums for any 'seller's insurance' for which it is responsible under the credit? It may sometimes be worth while the applicant taking out inexpensive 'transit insurance' in its own name, to cover the risk that the beneficiary has not arranged such cover.

- The confirming or other nominated bank could make a mistake and pay away monies against incorrect documents. If that bank then debits the account with it of the issuing bank (assuming it is a correspondent bank with whom an account relationship is maintained), the issuing bank may, dependent upon the terms of the indemnity an applicant is usually required to provide to the issuing bank, be entitled to claim reimbursement from the applicant (even where the issuing bank had selected the nominated bank which made the mistake). Although the nominated bank should, in such circumstances, refund the monies to the issuing bank, there is always the risk that it will decline to do so. A refusal to effect restitution is far from unknown when dealing with banks in certain countries, where the banks' relationships with local businesses may outweigh their wider duties and responsibilities. Even if the payment is eventually reimbursed, it can take many months of correspondence and argument, during which time the applicant could be out of its money.

- Where the transaction is in a foreign currency, the exchange rate may move against the applicant before the date of payment.

- The documentation submitted under the credit by the beneficiary may not be received by the applicant until after the goods have arrived. If, for example, these include bills of lading without which delivery cannot be taken then, where the applicant needs to obtain possession of the goods, it may have to arrange for the issue of a bank guarantee to the shipping line indemnifying them for handing over the goods without presentation of a bill of lading (for which a fee is payable to the bank). Alternatively, demurrage may be incurred (the cost of storage until collection is possible). However, the terms of credits are normally such that the applicant should receive the documents in good time. For example, the applicant could insert a clause in the credit specifying the maximum number of days after shipment date that are allowed for presentation of documents by the beneficiary at the counters of a nominated bank.

- That a third party may be able to obtain goods for which the applicant is paying. For example, unless the credit specifies a *full* set of bills of lading, then someone in possession of a single part could possibly collect the goods.

Beneficiary

- Changes to the contract terms agreed between the applicant and beneficiary must, where necessary, be covered by the issue of amendments to the credit.

- A revocable credit can be altered or cancelled by the issuing bank at any time prior to presentation thereunder of documents by the beneficiary, without the beneficiary's consent.

- If the beneficiary submits documents that do not comply with the credit, then payment/acceptance may be refused and the beneficiary will need to locate and store the goods until the problem(s) can be resolved or the goods re-shipped or re-sold. There is the cost of demurrage, whether adequate transit and other insurance have been put in place and whether the applicant has already obtained possession of the goods whilst refusing payment on the grounds of discrepancies.

- Where the transaction is in a foreign currency, the exchange rate may move against the beneficiary before the date payment is received.

- That the confirming bank fails to pay on presentation of the specified documents in good order, or the acceptor of a tenor draft fails to honour its payment at maturity. Is there any reason for the beneficiary to doubt the creditworthiness of these banks, or of the issuing bank against which ultimate recourse would be sought? Unless the credit is confirmed by a first-class local bank, the beneficiary runs a risk on the creditworthiness of the issuing bank, together with the 'political risk' of deferred or non-payment because of exchange control or other reasons.

- If a beneficiary receives a credit purporting to come direct from an issuing bank, it might be a forgery. The beneficiary could either have it confirmed by a local bank or ask its bank to authenticate that it is genuine.

Issuing bank

- The issuing bank must honour its obligation to pay out under the credit in favour of the beneficiary, even if its customer, the applicant, is unwilling or unable to reimburse the issuing bank. For this reason, the credit risk on issuing a credit is very real and, before making this facility available to its customer, the bank has to make an exposure decision similar to that for a loan.

- Amongst the factors to be considered by the issuing bank is whether, should the applicant default, the bank could get back any of its money by selling the goods. Will the applicant already have taken possession of the goods? Are the goods of reasonable quality and saleable? Are they perishable or subject to market price fluctuations? Have they been damaged in transit, and if so were they insured and does the bank have any right to the insurance monies? Was there a fraud between the applicant and beneficiary, and the goods were never shipped in the first place? Are there any restrictions (e.g., licences) on sale of the goods by other than the applicant?

- Where the credit was not confirmed the issuing bank may very occasionally be requested to approve payment to the beneficiary without having seen the documents presented under the credit. Unless the issuing bank obtains an indemnity from its customer, the applicant, for authorizing payment on such basis then it runs the risk that the documents are incorrect and it will be unable to claim reimbursement from the applicant, although the issuing bank should still have recourse to the paying bank for paying against documents that did not comply with the credit terms.

- If the issuing bank pays, or commits to make a future payment, without having exercised reasonable care in checking that the documents presented 'appear on their face' to comply with the credit, then it may be unable to obtain reimbursement from the applicant.

Advising bank

- The advising bank is required to have taken reasonable care to satisfy itself that the credit is genuine, including authenticating the signatures of the issuing bank, before advising the beneficiary.

Nominated bank

- Unless it is also the confirming bank, there is no obligation on the advising bank to make any payment to the beneficiary before funds are received from the issuing bank. However, they may sometimes do so on a 'with recourse' basis to help the beneficiary, and thereby expose themselves to a credit risk on the issuing bank or the beneficiary. The risk is obviously greater if the documents presented by the beneficiary do not conform to the terms of the credit.

Confirming bank

- If the documents are in order, then the confirming bank must effect payment to the beneficiary, irrespective of whether or not it expects to be able to recover the monies from the issuing bank. There is, therefore, a credit and country (including exchange controls) risk on the issuing bank.

- If the confirming bank pays or commits to make a future payment without having exercised reasonable care in checking that the documents presented 'appear on their face' to comply with the credit, then it may be unable to obtain reimbursement from the issuing bank.

Types of letters of credit

Irrevocable The credit cannot be altered or cancelled by the applicant without the agreement of the beneficiary, the issuing bank and any confirming bank. Banks will only confirm irrevocable credits.

Revocable The credit can be altered or cancelled by the issuing bank without the agreement of the beneficiary, at any time prior to a payment or commitment to the beneficiary under the terms of the credit. Unless stated to be revocable, a credit is taken to be irrevocable. Banks will not confirm revocable credits.

Confirmed Where a bank, usually in the country of the beneficiary, adds to the credit its confirmation that the beneficiary will be paid on presenting to the confirming bank the specified documents in good order.

Transferable The benefit of a transferable credit can be transferred in whole or in part by the beneficiary named therein (first beneficiary) to another beneficiary, who is usually the actual supplier of the goods. Although the credit can only be transferred once (i.e., unless specifically stated in the credit the second beneficiary cannot, in turn, transfer to other beneficiaries), it can be divided by the first beneficiary into a number of separate portions with different second beneficiaries. It is essential that the original credit specifies that it is 'transferable'. The transfer can specify shorter dates for shipment, document presentation and expiry than those in the original credit, and be for a lesser amount. The first beneficiary normally replaces the invoices of the second beneficiary with its own, and retains the difference between the amount paid to the second beneficiary and the amount that can be drawn under the original credit.

Although the credit may not be designated 'transferable', there is nothing to stop a beneficiary assigning all or part of the proceeds it is due to receive under it. The beneficiary can give the nominated bank an irrevocable instruction assigning a specified amount of the credit proceeds to a third party, normally either a supplier to the beneficiary or the beneficiary's bank. If the nominated bank accepts the instruction, which it is not obliged to do, it notifies the assignee, but does not thereby guarantee payment. Despite this inherent uncertainty, the beneficiary's supplier or banker may derive sufficient comfort from the assignment to grant credit facilities to the beneficiary. When payment is made under the credit, the nominated bank remits the specified amount to any assignee in accordance with the instruction it had received from the beneficiary. The risk to any supplier or banker relying on an assignment for repayment of credit given to a beneficiary is that the terms of the credit may not be complied with, as a result of which payment under the credit is refused.

Back-to-back   The beneficiary uses the credit to obtain the goods or services needed to complete its contract with the applicant. The beneficiary does this by asking its bank to issue a separate credit in favour of its subcontractors, relying on the original credit to produce the monies necessary to cover the payment(s) to them when due. There is no authority for, or reference to, the back-to-back transaction in the original credit, and they are generally disliked by banks because the terms of the two credits rarely match, and this often leads to problems. Their most common use is in the commodity markets.

Standby   In countries where there are restrictions on banks issuing guarantees (often for overseas beneficiaries), including those defined as bid and performance bonds, they may, instead, be able to provide standby letters of credit, undertaking to pay the beneficiary if the applicant defaults in respect of specified obligations. When used as performance bonds, standby letters of credit are provided on behalf of the seller to the buyer, unlike documentary letters of credit which are provided by the buyer to the seller.

A key difference between ordinary letters of credit and standby letters of credit is that the former are issued in the expectation that the beneficiary will claim against them for payment on supplying goods or services, whilst the usual hope is that there will be no cause or occasion for the beneficiary to claim under the latter. To claim under a standby letter of credit, the beneficiary would, typically, submit to the issuing bank a simple statement giving reasons for the claim.

Revolving   These are credits that remain available for repeated re-use over a specified period of time, although normally subject to a maximum amount during any set period. They are used to cut down on the administration and costs of repeatedly issuing credits where the applicant and beneficiary enter into a regular series of similar transactions.

Red clause   These allow the beneficiary to draw a percentage of the value of the credit from the confirming or other nominated bank in advance of any shipment, against an undertaking to use the monies for the underlying purposes of the credit. It is a way for the applicant to help the beneficiary fund the transaction.

Documents

The principal documents presented under credits are as follows.

Shipping documents

These include the following.

Bills of lading   These evidence the contract of carriage and receipt for goods between the exporter and the carrier (a ship, shipping line or its agents) (see Figure 2.5). A 'clean' bill of lading is where the ship or shipping line has received the goods from the exporter in apparent good order, i.e., without any obvious sign of damage. Bills of lading are usually issued in several original copies, *any one of which* is normally sufficient to give title to the goods.

A bill of lading is a 'negotiable' document giving title to the goods to the transferee (endorsee) provided the transferor (endorser) had good title. Because of this limitation they are sometimes referred to as being 'quasi-negotiable' documents.

Most bills of lading contain the words 'to the order of' in the consignee box, which means that when the exporter endorses the bill of lading in blank it becomes a 'bearer' document, i.e., the goods will be released to whoever presents an original bill of lading to the shipping company (as distinct from an endorsement in favour of a named party, i.e., a specific endorsement, when only that named party is entitled to collect the goods).

Ship's (sea) waybill   An alternative to bills of lading, these are not negotiable and not a document of title. The named importer must identify itself to obtain release of the goods. An added advantage of waybills is that, where the shipment time is short, the buyer can collect the goods without waiting for arrival of the bills of lading.

Air waybill   The contract of air transport carriage and receipt issued by a carrier to the exporter. They are non-negotiable and do not give title to the goods. The importer obtains release of the goods by identifying itself.

Commercial documents

These include the following.

Invoice   The statement of goods or services provided, prepared by the seller and addressed and sent to the buyer, specifying the amount to be paid in settlement

Shipper: UK SELLERS LTD LONDON		Page 2 B.L. No. 1 **LINER BILL OF LADING** Reference No.	
Consignee: TO THE ORDER OF BUYER'S BANK CALCUTTA		Carrier: XYZ SHIPPING COMPANY	
Notify Address: INDIAN BUYER LTD CALCUTTA			
Pre-carriage by*	Place of receipt by pre-carrier*		
Vessel: SOPHIE	Port of loading: SOUTHAMPTON		
Port of discharge: CALCUTTA	Place of delivery by on-carrier:		

Marks and Nos.	Number and kind of packages; description of goods	Gross weight	Measurement
◇ GW 429 CALCUTTA 1–60	ONE 20 FOOT CONTAINER No. 456789 S.T.C.:- 60 CASES PHARMACEUTICAL PRODUCTS EACH CONTAINING 100 PACKS	660 KILOS	

ORIGINAL

Particulars furnished by the merchant

Freight details, charges etc.	
FREIGHT PAID	SHIPPED on board in apparent good order and condition; weight, measure, marks, numbers, quality, contents, and value unknown, for carriage to the Port of Discharge or so near thereunto as the Vessel may safely get and lie always afloat, to be delivered in the like good order and condition at the aforesaid Port unto Consignees or their Assigns, they paying freight as indicated to the left plus other charges incurred in accordance with the provisions contained in this Bill of Lading. In accepting this Bill of Lading the Merchant expressly accepts and agrees to all its stipulations on both pages, whether written, printed, stamped or otherwise incorporated, as fully as if they were all signed by the Merchant. One original Bill of Lading must be surrendered duly endorsed in exchange for the goods or delivery order. IN WITNESS whereof the number of original Bills of Lading stated below have been signed, all of this tenor and date, one of which being accomplished, the others to stand void.
*Applicable only when document used as a Through Bill of Lading	Freight payable at: SOUTHAMPTON / Place and date of issue: SOUTHAMPTON 31\10\96
	Number of original Bs L: 3 / Signature: ABC TRANSPORTS LTD

Fig. 2.5 Example of a bill of lading (source: courtesy of SBC Warburg)

and usually the date by which payment is to be made. If presented under a credit the description of the goods must comply *exactly* with the specified terms.

INVOICE

ORIGINAL

UK SELLERS LTD	INVOICE NUMBER:	23
LONDON	INVOICE DATE:	31.10.96

Sold to:
INDIAN BUYER LTD
CALCUTTA

Description of Goods	Unit Price:	Amount:
60 CASES OF PHARMACEUTICAL PRODUCT EACH CONTAINING 100 PACKS	US$9.88 PER PACK	US$59,280 CFR CALCUTTA

GOODS ARE OF UNITED KINGDOM ORIGIN SHIPPED FROM SOUTHAMPTON TO CALCUTTA PER SOPHIE ON 31ST OCTOBER 1996.

DRAWN AGAINST BUYER'S BANK, CALCUTTA LETTER OF CREDIT NO. 36319.

....
Signed
for UK SELLERS LTD

Fig. 2.6 Example invoice (source: courtesy of SBC Warburg)

1. Consignor UK SELLERS LTD LONDON	No. DA 061451	ORIGINAL
	31/10/96	
2 Consignee INDIAN BUYER LTD CALCUTTA	**CERTIFICATE OF ORIGIN**	
	3. Country of Origin UNITED KINGDOM	
4 Transport details (Optional) SOPHIE SOUTHAMPTON TO CALCUTTA	5. Remarks L/C NO 36319	
6. Item number: marks: numbers: number and kind of packages: description of goods		7. Quantity 660 KILOS

GW 429

60 CASES PHARMACEUTICAL PRODUCTS EACH CONTAINING 100 PACKS

CALCUTTA 1–60

8. THE UNDERSIGNED AUTHORITY CERTIFIES THAT THE GOODS DESCRIBED ABOVE ORIGINATE IN THE COUNTRY SHOWN IN BOX 3

UNITED KINGDOM CHAMBER OF COMMERCE

Fig. 2.7 Example certificate of origin (source: courtesy of SBC Warburg)

Certificate of origin   A statement evidencing the place of origin of goods, usually issued by the exporter or a local Chamber of Commerce.

Insurance certificate   This may need to be endorsed by the exporter in favour of the importer, so that they can claim against the policy if necessary.

Inspection certificate That the goods conform to specification, usually issued by an independent inspector or government body.

Financial documents
These include the following.

Bill(s) of exchange (drafts) See Figure 2.8.

Promissory note(s) A written and signed unconditional undertaking to pay a specified amount at a specified date, effectively an IOU.

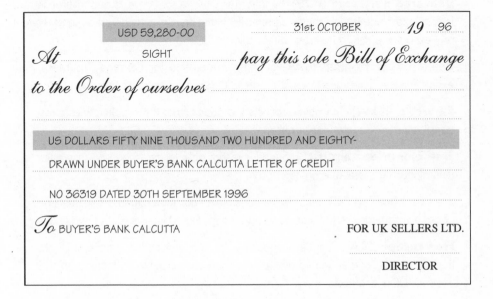

USD 59,280-00

31st OCTOBER   *19* 96

At   SIGHT   *pay this sole Bill of Exchange*

to the Order of ourselves

US DOLLARS FIFTY NINE THOUSAND TWO HUNDRED AND EIGHTY-

DRAWN UNDER BUYER'S BANK CALCUTTA LETTER OF CREDIT

NO 36319 DATED 30TH SEPTEMBER 1996

To BUYER'S BANK CALCUTTA   FOR UK SELLERS LTD.

DIRECTOR

Fig. 2.8 Example of a 'sight' draft (bill of exchange) (source: courtesy of SBC Warburg)

Incoterms

Incoterms are standard contract terms published by the International Chamber of Commerce which set out the respective transit responsibilities of a buyer and of a seller for trade transactions.

Those in most common usage are summarized in the box.

SOME COMMONLY USED INCOTERMS

Cost and freight (CFR) Supplier responsible for the cost of carriage to a named port of destination, export licence, duties and taxes and for insurance until loaded on board the vessel at the port of shipment.

Cost insurance and freight (CIF) Supplier responsible for the cost of carriage to a named port of destination, delivery on board the vessel, export licence, duties and taxes and insurance during the carriage.

Delivered duty paid (DDP) Supplier responsible for carriage and insurance to a named place (usually buyer's premises) in the country of importation, and for any export and import licences, duties and taxes.

Delivered at frontier (DAF) Supplier responsible for carriage, insurance, export licence, duties and taxes to a named place at a named frontier.

Ex works (EXW) The buyer collects the goods from the supplier and is responsible for carriage and insurance.

Free alongside ship (FAS) Supplier responsible for carriage and insurance until alongside vessel at a named port.

Free on board (FOB) Supplier responsible for carriage and insurance until on board a specified vessel at a named port, and for export licence, duties and taxes.

Free carrier (FCA) Supplier responsible for carriage and insurance until into the custody of a carrier named by the buyer at a named point, and for any export licence, duties and taxes.

Carriage and insurance paid (CIP) Supplier responsible for carriage to a named place of destination, delivery into the custody of a carrier, export licence, duties and taxes and insurance during the carriage.

Carriage paid to (CPT) Supplier responsible for carriage to a named place of destination into the custody of a carrier, export licence, duties and taxes and insurance until delivered to the carrier.

Where it is the responsibility of the buyer to insure the goods whilst in transit, it may be worth while the seller arranging (relatively inexpensive) supplemental 'transit' insurance in its own name (sometimes known as 'seller's interest insurance'). If the goods are damaged or lost in transit and the buyer had, in fact, failed to take out adequate cover, the seller then has an alternative to what might otherwise prove a protracted action for recourse from the buyer.

Collections

·······················

> *The sending, on behalf of a seller of goods or services, of documents to a bank for them to be presented to a buyer of those goods or services for either payment or the acceptance of a tenor bill of exchange (draft).*

The *Uniform Rules for Collections* (URC 522) published by the International Chamber of Commerce are accepted as the principles governing collections.

There are two types of collection.

- **Clean** Where the only documents are financial documents, e.g., drafts (bills of exchange) or promissory notes. There are no commercial documents.

- **Documentary** Where the documents are commercial documents, e.g., bills of lading and other transport or title documents, with or without accompanying financial documents.

Banks are not required to 'examine' the documents, although in practice they often check for deficiencies.

Principal ('drawer') The seller of the goods or services who asks the remitting bank to handle the collection. A clean collection is often used for settlement of open account trading.

Drawee The buyer of the goods or services to whom presentation of the documents is made by the presenting bank.

Remitting bank The bank which, at the principal's request, forwards the documents to a bank (collecting/presenting bank) located conveniently near to the drawee.

Collecting bank Any bank (whether nominated by the principal or selected by the remitting bank) involved in the collection chain other than the remitting bank. Usually it is the presenting bank.

Presenting bank The bank which receives the documents and contacts the drawee. The principal may require payment or acceptance (of a draft), or alternatively specify that other terms and conditions are to be met, before the documents can be released to the drawee.

The instructions to be followed by the banks are set out in the 'collection instruction' (collection order) that accompanies the documents.

You may come across references to '*inward*' and '*outward*' collections.

- **Inward collections** are where a bank receives from an overseas bank a collection for presentation to a local buyer (importer).
- **Outward collections** are where a bank receives from a seller (exporter) in its own country a collection to be sent to a presenting bank for presentation to the buyer (importer).

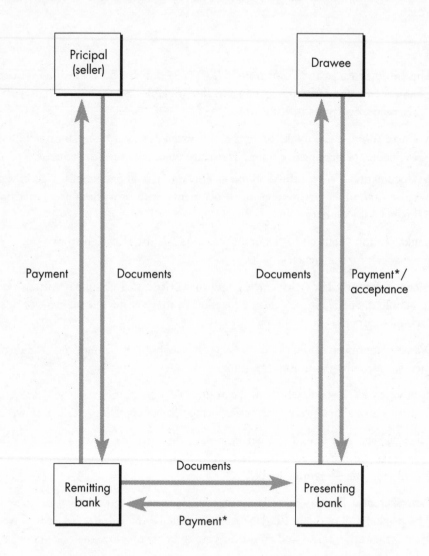

*Payment will be at the maturity date where the drawee accepted a draft or issued a promissory note.

Fig. 2.9 Example of documentary collection

Documentary collection

The principal (seller) forwards the shipping and other documents to its bank (remitting bank). To be helpful, that bank may look through the documents to see if they appear to be in order, but they do *not* thereby accept liability for any errors or omissions in the documents. The remitting bank then sends the documents (possibly via a collecting bank) to a presenting bank located conveniently near to the drawee with instructions that the documents are to be handed over to the drawee against either payment or the acceptance of a tenor bill of exchange, issue of a promissory note, or some other condition(s). When the drawee has paid, accepted or otherwise met the terms and conditions specified by the principal, then the documents are released to the drawee. Unless instructed to send any accepted bill of exchange, or promissory note, to the remitting bank, it will be retained by the presenting bank and presented to the drawee for payment at maturity. Any payments from the drawee are sent by the presenting bank to the remitting bank for the account of the principal.

The collection instruction should say whether a draft is to be 'protested', if it is not paid or accepted on presentation.

It is important where payment is at a future date, e.g., against an accepted tenor bill of exchange, that the principal specifies whether the commercial documents are to be released to the drawee against such acceptance (documents against acceptance, 'D/A'), or only released against payment (documents against payment, 'D/P'). Unless otherwise specified the presenting bank will only release the commercial documents to the drawee against payment.

You sometimes come across an 'acceptance D/P' basis, where the drawee is required to accept the draft, but the documents are not released until they make payment at maturity. A typical example would be where the maturity date is timed to coincide with the delivery of the goods after a lengthy period of transportation.

With 'documents against payment' (i.e., payable at sight) there is no need for a bill of exchange, as payment can be against an invoice, although sight drafts are often called for.

Whereas for a documentary letter of credit, any tenor draft can *only* be accepted by a bank, not the drawee, in the case of a tenor draft under a documentary collection (whether clean or documentary), acceptance will be by the drawee.

Principal

● The principal has the comfort that the documents are only to be released to the drawee against payment or acceptance.

● It will normally be possible to sue a drawee who has accepted a tenor draft or issued a promissory note solely on the grounds of failure to honor the draft/note at maturity, without the principal having to prove that it has fulfilled the terms of the underlying commercial transaction.

● A representative may be named in the country of the drawee who is authorized to act on behalf of the principal if the drawee refuses to pay or accept. The powers of any such representative should be clearly specified.

Drawee

- Although, theoretically, the drawee should make payment or accept drafts on presentation of the documents without examining them, in practice they commonly have the opportunity to first examine the documents at the presenting bank.

- If the documents are released to the drawee against acceptance of a draft or issue of a promissory note the goods can be used or on-sold before the date when payment has to be made at maturity.

Remitting bank

- Earns income from the collection and from any associated foreign exchange or other transactions.

- Enhances the relationship with the collecting/presenting banks, thereby creating potential for reciprocal business.

Collecting/presenting bank

- Earns income from the collection and from any associated foreign exchange or other transactions.

- Unless the drawee is already a customer of the collecting/presenting bank it provides an opportunity to establish a relationship that may lead to other business.

- Enhances the relationship with the remitting bank thereby creating potential for reciprocal business.

RISKS
REMAINING

Principal

- That, contrary to instructions, the presenting bank releases the commercial documents to the drawee prior to their payment or acceptance. This is a possibility in some countries where greater importance is attached by banks to the relationship with local businesses than to their wider duties and responsibilities, and it may be of little comfort to the principal that they could try to claim against the presenting bank.

- The signature on an acceptance might be a forgery, or *ultra vires* the authority of the drawee or the signatories.

- Remitting banks usually insist that if the collecting/presenting bank fails to carry out their instructions any resultant loss is borne by the principal, even if the principal had no part in selecting the collecting/presenting bank.

- That all or some of the documents may go astray, e.g., are the whereabouts of the *full* set of original bills of lading known. Where the presenting bank agrees you can consider having the goods consigned to them as named consignee. The drawee is thereby hindered in obtaining release of the goods until the presenting bank gives its consent (i.e., after payment or acceptance).

- The goods to which the documents relate should only be sent to, or to the order of, a bank with its prior consent. Otherwise that bank has no responsibility for the storage, insurance, delivery or release of the goods.

- Where a bank acts to protect the goods, for example by arranging storage, they are not liable for any loss or damage that may result.

- The principal will usually be responsible usually for any costs which a bank incurs for the protection of goods, even if they were not asked to do so.

- The drawee pays the presenting bank in return for the documents but the bank fails to transfer these funds to the remitting bank for benefit of the principal. This may, for example, result from the presenting bank being subject to exchange controls that prohibit or delay the transfer of funds overseas. When this happens, the principal can find itself permanently out of the money, or have to wait a long time for payment. Where there are restrictions on the presenting bank remitting funds overseas, then the presenting bank should not in theory release the document to the drawee until payment can be released – but it happens! When exchange controls require the presenting bank to pay in its local currency, they can only do so (and thereby legitimately release the documents) if that is authorized in the collection instrument.

- The presenting bank sends the money to the remitting bank, who fail to pay it to the principal.

- The drawee declines to pay or accept, but the goods have long ago been shipped. Even if the principal can take legal action against the drawee under any contract, this will take time and, meanwhile, the goods have to be located and stored or re-shipped by the principal. It may not be possible to sell them to someone else. Where the principal is unwilling to take a risk on an acceptor paying at maturity of a tenor draft, it can either ask that the collection be on an 'acceptance D/P' basis (if appropriate to the nature of the underlying transaction) or that the acceptor's bank add their aval (see page 105).

- Is there adequate transit and other insurance, and would the principal be able to claim against it for loss or damage?

- Banks are not liable for any lost or delayed documents.

- Unless the transaction is in the principal's local currency, there is an exchange rate exposure until payment is received.

- Where any collection costs and expenses, or interest charges, are specified as being for the account of the drawee/acceptor, but the drawee/acceptor refuses to pay them, the presenting bank can release the documents as instructed in the collection order, provided the drawee meets the other amounts due under the collection. In such event, the presenting bank can deduct the amount of any collection costs due to it from the amount paid by the drawee. The exception is where the collection specifically instructs that the documents must not be handed over unless the drawee/acceptor pays such costs and interest charges.

Drawee/acceptor

- Although there will normally have been an opportunity to examine the documents before payment or acceptance, the goods themselves will not have been inspected and may not conform or have been delivered or insured as specified. The drawee is also exposed to the risk of the seller presenting forged or otherwise fraudulent or inaccurate documents. Is there a full set of original bills of lading, or could someone else be using one part to obtain release of the goods? The banks have no liability either in respect of forged or otherwise fraudulent or inaccurate documents, or for the failure of the goods or transportation to conform to the documents.

- Having accepted the draft, or issued the promissory note, the drawee/issuer can be sued by the principal if payment is not made at maturity. Even if the drawee/issuer believes there are grounds for non-payment because, for example, the goods supplied by the principal were defective, that will not serve as a defence. Once the draft is accepted or note issued the principal can sue them for non-payment without having to prove that it had honoured its obligations under any contract with the drawee. To dishonour a bill or note is extremely damaging to the defaulter's commercial reputation.

- Unless the transaction is in local currency, there is an exchange rate exposure until payment.

Remitting bank

- Unless in some way failing to comply with its responsibilities, the remitting bank is only at risk if it pays the principal, or lends to it in expectation of receipt of the proceeds of the collection, before they are received from the presenting bank. If the monies are not received, then the remitting bank has a credit risk for repayment by the principal.

Presenting bank

- Is not required to examine the documents, but is at risk if it sends funds to the remitting bank before payment has been made by the drawee/acceptor. In such event, or if it lends the money to the drawee/acceptor to make the payment, the presenting bank has a credit risk on the drawee/acceptor.

- Is required to check that the documents it receives are those listed as having been sent to it, and if not then to advise the bank from whom they were received.

- The remitting bank may request that, if the drawee does not pay or accept, then the presenting bank arranges for the goods to be 'stored and insured' until re-sold or re-shipped. If it does so, the presenting bank should be satisfied that it will be able to recover the costs thereby incurred. This would also apply if, as sometimes happens, the presenting bank acted to protect the goods even when they had not received a specific instruction to that effect (although they usually require instructions before taking any action).

Bills of exchange/drafts

> *An unconditional order in writing signed by the party which prepares it (drawer) requiring the party to whom it is addressed (drawee) to pay a stated amount to, or to the order of, a specified party or to bearer, either on demand or at a fixed or determinable future date (the 'maturity' date).*

Drawer   The seller of goods or services who prepares the draft (bill of exchange) drawn on the drawee.

Drawee   The buyer or other party to whom the draft is addressed.

Payee   The party to be paid by the drawee.

Acceptor   A drawee who signs the draft, thereby committing to honour its payment in full at the maturity date.

Drafts can be either:

- sight drafts – payable on demand (see Figure 2.8).
- tenor (term/usance/time) drafts – payable at a future 'maturity' ('due') date (see Figure 2.10).

The tenor draft can be 'accepted' by a drawee signing it and usually adding the word 'accepted'. An acceptor is legally bound to pay the full ('face') value of the draft if it is presented to it on the maturity date.

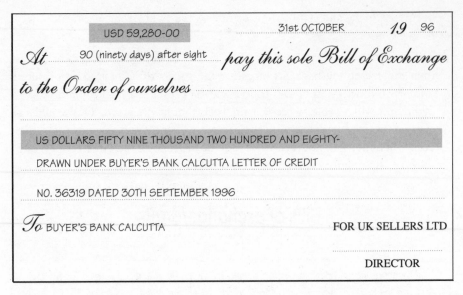

USD 59,280-00   31st OCTOBER   *19* 96

At   90 (ninety days) after sight   *pay this sole Bill of Exchange*

to the Order of ourselves

US DOLLARS FIFTY NINE THOUSAND TWO HUNDRED AND EIGHTY-

DRAWN UNDER BUYER'S BANK CALCUTTA LETTER OF CREDIT

NO. 36319 DATED 30TH SEPTEMBER 1996

To BUYER'S BANK CALCUTTA   FOR UK SELLERS LTD

                                            DIRECTOR

Fig. 2.10 Example of a tenor draft (bill of exchange) (source: courtesy of SBC Warburg)

EXAMPLE Under a letter of credit, the documents presented by the beneficiary usually include a sight or tenor draft drawn on either the confirming or the issuing bank (*not* on the buyer). By accepting the tenor draft, the bank undertakes that the seller will be paid on the due date.

EXAMPLE Under a documentary collection, a draft is drawn on and accepted by the buyer of the goods or services. The seller can gain extra comfort in those territories, for example continental Europe, where it is the commercial practice for a bank to be able to add its 'aval' to an accepted draft, whereby the bank accepts liability for payment should the acceptor default. See *Avalising*, page 105.

If, when drawing up a tenor draft, the drawer inserts the maturity date, then technically it need not be accepted by the drawee, although in that event there would be no acceptor who could be sued on the draft. Usually a tenor draft specifies payment 'xx days after sight' (or after the date of a bill of lading or some specified date), and when the acceptor signs and dates the draft by way of acceptance, the maturity date is thereby fixed.

Bonds/contract guarantees

Definition

> *A written undertaking normally given on behalf of a seller in favour of a buyer, usually by a bank or insurance company, to make a payment under specified circumstances.*

The bond or contract guarantee is a separate (usually non-assignable) document from the trade or other contract it supports, and should state:

- name of principal
- name of beneficiary
- maximum amount of liability
- the transaction to which it relates
- currency in which payable
- date liability commences
- expiry date or termination event
- terms on which demand can be made
- where any claim must be made
- basis of any reductions in the amount of liability
- the legal jurisdiction to which it is subject.

In some countries, bonds/guarantees cannot be issued by banks, and instead they offer 'standby letters of credit' ('standby credits') undertaking to pay the beneficiary against presentation of specific documents. These are provided at the request of a seller in favour of a buyer, unlike documentary letters of credit which are provided by the buyer to the seller. A key difference between documentary letters of credit and standby letters of credit is that the former are issued in the expectation that the beneficiary will claim against them for payment on supplying goods or services, whilst normally the hope is that there will be no cause or occasion for the beneficiary to claim under the latter.

Strictly speaking, standby letters of credit are demand guarantees, but their special characteristics and wider applications result in them being principally covered by the *Uniform Customs and Practice for Documentary Credits* (currently publication *UCP 500*) issued by the International Chamber of Commerce.

For all practical purposes, a standby letter of credit is a guarantee.

Principal (the seller/exporter)   Who asks the bank or insurance company to issue the bond/guarantee.

Beneficiary (the buyer/importer)   In favour of whom the bond/guarantee is issued, and who cannot usually assign the benefit to any third party.

Guarantor   The bank, insurance company or other party issuing the bond/contract guarantee in favour of the beneficiary at the request of the principal.

EXAMPLE   A UK company competing for a construction contract in the Middle East is required to submit with its tender a bond ('tender' bond) under which a bank guarantees to pay (say) 5% of the contract value to the party which invited the tender, if the principal is offered the work but refuses to enter into a contract. This is intended to prevent submission of tenders by parties who are 'frivolous' or might, for whatever reason, withdraw if offered the work, causing potential delay and expense to the party which invited the tender. The UK company might, at the same time, have to submit confirmation from its bank that if awarded the contract, a performance bond would be available. As the contract terms often call for provision of a performance bond, the failure by a business to provide this if awarded the contract is, in any event, likely to be a breach for which a claim could be made under the tender bond).

If the UK company is successful in its tender and enters into a contract, then the guarantor will probably be asked to provide a performance bond for, say, 10% of the contract value and the tender bond will be returned to the guarantor for cancellation. Further bonds might be required to cover advance payments made to the principal, early release of retention monies at completion of the contract and on-going maintenance/warranty.

There are two types of bond/contract guarantee issued by banks:

- **on demand** – where the beneficiary has only to make demand (accompanied by any specified documents) on the guarantor under the bond/guarantee to be entitled to payment
- **conditional** – where the beneficiary is required to claim a default by the principal, and may have to support this with specified documents.

Where the bond has been issued by an insurance company, payment is commonly subject to proof of default, which often results in arbitration. As this takes time, they may be less attractive to beneficiaries than bonds or contract guarantees issued by banks.

Bonds/guarantees are principally issued to cover the following.

Bid/tender

- That if awarded the work a tenderer will enter into a formal contract with the beneficiary of the bond, being the party to whom the tender is being submitted (the bond is usually for less than 10% of the contract value, and 2.5% would be typical). An example of a bid bond is shown in Figure 2.11.

Performance

- That the principal will honour its commitment to provide the goods or services as specified in a separate contract with the beneficiary of the bond (the bond is usually for less than 20% of the contract value, and 10% would be typical).

Some insurance companies offer cover that provides for arrangements to be made for completion of the contract by a third party in the event of the default of the original principal (normally bank bonds/contract guarantees only provide for a cash payment). An example of a performance guarantee is shown in Figure 2.12.

Advance payment

- That advance and progress payments made by the beneficiary of the bond to the principal will be refunded if the principal fails to comply with its contractual obligations under a separate contract with the beneficiary. An example of an advance payment guarantee is shown in Figure 2.13.

Retention

- That if the beneficiary of the bond releases retention monies to the principal, these will be refunded to the beneficiary if the principal fails to meet its post-contract completion obligations.

Payment

- Guarantee claims by the seller against the buyer for payment of the contract price by the due date. An example of a payment guarantee is shown in Figure 2.14.

Warranty and/or maintenance

- That the principal will provide the beneficiary of the bond with on-going warranty or maintenance support for a specified period of time. An example of a warranty guarantee is shown in Figure 2.15.

Principal Unless able to provide bonds the principal may not be considered for contracts.

Beneficiary The beneficiary is wholly or partially safeguarded against defaults by the principal, depending on the wording of the bond.

Guarantor The bank, insurance company or other party issuing the bond is paid a fee, enhances the relationship with its customer and may be able to earn revenue from foreign exchange or other associated transactions.

BENEFITS including risks avoided

Schweizerischer Bankverein
Société de Banque Suisse
Società di Banca Svizzera
Swiss Bank Corporation

...
(beneficiary = buyer)

Bid Bond No. ...

We have been informed that Messrs ... (supplier) have submitted to you on ... under your tender No. ... of ... their bid for the supply of ... at a total price of .... According to your tender conditions, Messrs ... (supplier) are required to provide you with a bid bond in the amount of ....

This being stated, we, **Swiss Bank Corporation**, ... (address), irrespective of the validity and the legal effects of the above-mentioned contract and waiving all rights of objection and defence arising from the principal debt, hereby irrevocably undertake to pay immediately to you, upon your first demand, any amount up to

(currency / maximum amount) (in full letters: ...)

upon receipt of your written request for payment and your written confirmation stating that you have accepted, in whole or in part, the above-mentioned bid and that Messrs ... (supplier) have failed to sign the contract in due time or in accordance with the tender conditions.

For the purpose of identification, your request for payment and your confirmation have to be presented through the intermediary of a first-rate bank confirming that the signatures are legally binding upon your firm. If, in this respect, such bank will make use of tested telex, SWIFT or tested cable, it will have to transmit in any case the full wording of your request for payment and of your above-mentioned written confirmation and to confirm at the same time that the originals of these documents, legally binding upon your firm, have been forwarded to us.

Our guarantee is valid until
...

and expires in full and automatically, irrespective of whether the present document is returned to us or not, should your written request for payment and your above-mentioned written confirmation or the above-described tested telex, SWIFT or tested cable sent by the bank not be in our possession by that date at our counters in ....

With each payment under this guarantee our obligation will be reduced *pro rata*.

...   **SWISS BANK CORPORATION**
(Place, date)

Fig. 2.11 Example of a bid bond (source: courtesy of SBC Warburg)

Schweizerischer Bankverein
Société de Banque Suisse
Società di Banca Svizzera
Swiss Bank Corporation

...
(beneficiary = buyer)

<u>Performance Guarantee No. ...</u>

We have been informed that you have concluded on ... a contract No. ... with Messrs ... (supplier) for the supply of ... at a total price of .... According to this contract, Messrs ... (supplier) are required to provide you with a performance guarantee in the amount of ... (... % of the total price).

This being stated, we, **Swiss Bank Corporation**, ... (address), irrespective of the validity and the legal effects of the above-mentioned contract and waiving all rights of objection and defence arising from the principal debt, hereby irrevocably undertake to pay immediately to you, upon your first demand, any amount up to

<u>(currency / maximum amount)</u> (in full letters: ...)

upon receipt of your written request for payment and your written confirmation stating that Messrs ... (supplier) have not fulfilled their obligations in conformity with the terms of the above-mentioned contract.

For the purpose of identification, your request for payment and your confirmation have to be presented through the intermediary of a first-rate bank confirming that the signatures are legally binding upon your firm. If, in this respect, such bank will make use of tested telex, SWIFT or tested cable, it will have to transmit in any case the full wording of your request for payment and of your above-mentioned written confirmation and to confirm at the same time that the originals of these documents, legally binding upon your firm, have been forwarded to us.

Our guarantee is valid until

...

and expires in full and automatically, irrespective of whether the present document is returned to us or not, should your written request for payment and your above-mentioned written confirmation or the above-described tested telex, SWIFT or tested cable sent by the bank not be in our possession by that date at our counters in ....

With each payment under this guarantee our obligation will be reduced *pro rata*.

                                                SWISS BANK CORPORATION
...
(Place, date)

Fig. 2.12 Example of a performance guarantee (source: courtesy of SBC Warburg)

Schweizerischer Bankverein
Société de Banque Suisse
Società di Banca Svizzera
Swiss Bank Corporation

...
(beneficiary = buyer)

Advance Payment Guarantee No. ...

We have been informed that you have concluded on ... a contract No. ... with Messrs ... (supplier) for the supply of ... at a total price of .... According to this contract, you are required to make an advance payment to Messrs ... (supplier) of ... (... % of the total price). Your claim for reimbursement of this amount, should Messrs ... (supplier) fail to supply the goods in conformity with the terms of the contract, is to be secured by a bank guarantee.

This being stated, we, **Swiss Bank Corporation**, ... (address), irrespective of the validity and the legal effects of the above-mentioned contract and waiving all rights of objection and defence arising from the principal debt, hereby irrevocably undertake to pay immediately to you, upon your first demand, any amount up to

(currency / maximum amount) (in full letters: ...)

upon receipt of your written request for payment and your written confirmation stating that Messrs ... (supplier) have failed to supply the goods in conformity with the terms of the above-mentioned contract and that, as a result thereof, you are entitled to claim reimbursement of your advance payment.

The present indemnity will enter into force only after receipt of the above-mentioned advance payment by Messrs ... (supplier).

For the purpose of identification, your request for payment and your confirmation have to be presented through the intermediary of a first-rate bank confirming that the signatures are legally binding upon your firm. If, in this respect, such bank will make use of tested telex, SWIFT or tested cable, it will have to transmit in any case the full wording of your request for payment and of your above-mentioned written confirmation and to confirm at the same time that the originals of these documents, legally binding upon your firm, have been forwarded to us.

Our guarantee is valid until
...

and expires in full and automatically, irrespective of whether the present document is returned to us or not, should your written request for payment and your above-mentioned written confirmation or the above-described tested telex, SWIFT or tested cable sent by the bank not be in our possession by that date at our counters in ....

With each payment under this guarantee our obligation will be reduced *pro rata*.

...   **SWISS BANK CORPORATION**
(Place, date)

Fig. 2.13 Example of an advance payment guarantee (source: courtesy of SBC Warburg)

Schweizerischer Bankverein
Société de Banque Suisse
Società di Banca Svizzera
Swiss Bank Corporation

...
(beneficiary = buyer)

<u>**Payment Guarantee No. ...**</u>

We have been informed that you have concluded on ... a contract No. ... with Messrs ... (buyer) for the supply of ... at a total price of .... According to this contract, payment of the goods supplied, up to ... (...% of the total price), shall be secured by a bank guarantee.

This being stated, we, **Swiss Bank Corporation**, ... (address), irrespective of the validity and the legal effects of the above-mentioned contract and waiving all rights of objection and defence arising from the principal debt, hereby irrevocably undertake to pay immediately to you, upon your first demand, any amount up to

<u>**(currency / maximum amount)**</u> (in full letters: ...)

upon receipt of your written request for payment and your written confirmation stating that:

– you have supplied Messrs ... (buyer) with the goods ordered in conformity with the terms of the contract

and

– you have not received payment from Messrs ... (buyer), at the due date, in the amount claimed under this guarantee.

For the purpose of identification, your request for payment and your confirmation have to be presented through the intermediary of a first-rate bank confirming that the signatures are legally binding upon your firm. If, in this respect, such bank will make use of tested telex, SWIFT or tested cable, it will have to transmit in any case the full wording of your request for payment and of your above-mentioned written confirmation and to confirm at the same time that the originals of these documents, legally binding upon your firm, have been forwarded to us.

Our guarantee is valid until
...

and expires in full and automatically, irrespective of whether the present document is returned to us or not, should your written request for payment and your above-mentioned written confirmation or the above-described tested telex, SWIFT or tested cable sent by the bank not be in our possession by that date at our counters in ....

With each payment under this guarantee our obligation will be reduced *pro rata.*

...
(Place, date)

SWISS BANK CORPORATION

Fig 2.14 Example of a payment guarantee (source: courtesy of SBC Warburg)

Schweizerischer Bankverein
Société de Banque Suisse
Società di Banca Svizzera
Swiss Bank Corporation

...
(beneficiary = buyer)

Guarantee for Warranty Obligations No. ...

We have been informed that you have concluded on ... a contract No. ... with Messrs ... (supplier) for the supply of ... at a total price of .... According to this contract, Messrs ... (supplier) are required to provide you with a guarantee for warranty obligations in the amount of ... (...% of the total price).

This being stated, we, **Swiss Bank Corporation**, ... (address), irrespective of the validity and the legal effects of the above-mentioned contract and waiving all rights of objection and defence arising from the principal debt, hereby irrevocably undertake to pay immediately to you, upon your first demand, any amount up to

(currency / maximum amount)   (in full letters: ...)

upon receipt of your written request for payment and your written confirmation stating that Messrs ... (supplier) have not fulfilled their warranty obligations in conformity with the terms of the above-mentioned contract.

For the purpose of identification, your request for payment and your confirmation have to be presented through the intermediary of a first-rate bank confirming that the signatures are legally binding upon your firm. If, in this respect, such bank will make use of tested telex, SWIFT or tested cable, it will have to transmit in any case the full wording of your request for payment and of your above-mentioned written confirmation and to confirm at the same time that the originals of these documents, legally binding upon your firm, have been forwarded to us.

Our guarantee is valid until
...

and expires in full and automatically, irrespective of whether the present document is returned to us or not, should your written request for payment and your above-mentioned written confirmation or the above-described tested telex, SWIFT or tested cable sent by the bank not be in our possession by that date at our counters in ....

With each payment under this guarantee our obligation will be reduced *pro rata*.

...   **SWISS BANK CORPORATION**
(Place, date)

Fig. 2.15 Example of a warranty guarantee (source: courtesy of SBC Warburg)

Principal

- The beneficiary may make an unfair demand which the guarantor has to pay (unless, for example, it is an insurance bond potentially subject to arbitration). The guarantor, in turn, demands reimbursement of the money from the principal under the counter-indemnity it will have taken from the principal. It would then be up to the principal to try and recover from the beneficiary any monies paid against an unfair claim. Insurance against 'unfair calling' under the bond may be obtainable.

- Are the terms of the underlying trade or other contract with the beneficiary clearly understood, and particularly the circumstances in which a default is likely to occur or demand be made under the bond?

- In some countries, irrespective of international convention, the bond may by law or practice be subject to legal extension of its term after the specified expiry date, until such time as the beneficiary agrees to its cancellation. Even where local laws do not permit such extension, the beneficiary can threaten to make (however unfairly) a claim unless the term of the bond is extended. This ties up the principal's credit limit with its guarantor and usually incurs on-going fees.

- Be clear as to the jurisdiction governing the bond and any disputes, and the implications of this (it is often the place of business of the guarantor, but other courts may claim jurisdiction).

- If the bond has been issued in a foreign currency, it is hard to protect against exchange rate changes when you do not know when, or if, a claim will be made. To remove or reduce this risk, try quoting for a contract in your own currency, or on a base linked to appropriate exchange rate movements, where this is allowed. A currency option derivative contract may sometimes be appropriate.

- Demand may be made under an advance payment or retention bond, even though the principal never received payment under the contract from the beneficiary. If in doubt, the principal's bank should be instructed that the bond may only be delivered to the beneficiary against payment. Similarly, if the principal is to receive payment under the contract by means of a documentary letter of credit, then a bond might be worded so that it only becomes valid once the letter of credit is effective.

- The beneficiary might hold on to the tender bond even after the contract is signed and a performance bond issued, with the risk that an unfair claim can still be made under it. Tender bonds are usually valid for only a short time, but may be subject to extension under local laws or custom.

- However careful the principal might be, a claim might be triggered by the default of a subcontractor or other party.

From the above, it can be seen that a principal needs to exercise great care before asking a guarantor to issue a bond, and providing it with a counter-indemnity and any security in support. It may be possible to obtain insurance cover against unjustified claims (unfair calling). What has been the experience of others trading with this beneficiary or its country?

Beneficiary

- If the guarantor has its own financial problems, or is subject to exchange control or other constraints, the beneficiary's claims may not be met. This risk can be reduced by the beneficiary requiring the bond to be confirmed by a local bank or insurer of good repute.

- The bond/guarantee may be a forgery. If in doubt, ask for it to be confirmed, or otherwise authenticated, by a local bank.

- Be clear as to the jurisdiction governing the bond/guarantee and disputes, and the implications of this.

- If the beneficiary has purchased foreign currency to make advance payments or released retention monies early, then the exchange rate could have moved adversely by the time a claim is made and payment received under the bond/guarantee.

- The beneficiary must claim before the expiry date, subject to any provisions for extension.

Guarantor

- If a claim is made, the guarantor has to pay, whether or not reimbursement can be obtained under the counter-indemnity from the principal.

- When the guarantor is the lead bank in a syndicate issuing the bond or guarantee, which is not uncommon for large amounts, can it recover from the other banks?

- Is the principal capable of meeting the contractual obligations covered by the bond/guarantee?

- Given the 'on demand' nature of many bonds/guarantees, is the underlying contract between the principal and beneficiary genuine, or money laundering?

Bonds/guarantees and standby letters of credit are a very real potential liability requiring a credit decision similar to that for a loan (and making capital adequacy demands on the bank). Whilst a claim may never be made the potential can exist for a very long period of time.

Avalising

> *Avalising (an 'aval') is the guarantee by a bank, or other financial institution or government department (the 'avalor'), that a bill of exchange (draft), promissory note or other instrument will be paid at maturity. Avalising is also known as 'acceptance pour aval'.*

After the drawee has accepted the draft or issued the promisory note, the avalor signs its face or reverse with the addition of the words 'pour aval'.

An aval provides exporters with the comfort of a payment guarantee, and is often the basis of forfaiting (see page 170).

The avalor has to be satisfied with the credit risk on the drawee/acceptor, to whom it must have legal recourse. In some countries, the practice of avalising may not be formally recognized, and it can then be necessary to obtain a separate guarantee from an acceptable guarantor to make payment in the event that the drawee/acceptor fails to pay.

Collections (see page 87) are sometimes on a 'documents against acceptance pour aval' basis rather than simply 'documents against acceptance' – as a bill accepted only by the drawee (or their promissory note) whilst being proof of debt often offers little more certainty of payment than trading on open account.

Countertrade

> *The direct or indirect exchange of goods or services for other goods or services.*

Countertrade is of particular interest to governments in less-developed and newly industrialized countries needing to stimulate their export trade or to generate additional 'hard' currency to pay for imports.

Non-governmental transactions play an important role in the commodity sector, enabling different types of goods to be exchanged or raw materials processed and returned in a refined state.

Countertrade deals are seldom straightforward.

At best, a government will issue clear regulations about what it expects from foreign suppliers. In these cases it is usually possible to engage the services of a trading house or financial institution experienced in this type of trade, which will take over the transaction for a fee.

Where there are no regulations in existence it can take a great deal of time and effort to try and establish what is legally acceptable, and the majority of such transactions come to grief.

Countertrade takes many different forms, including the following:

Barter

Barter is the direct exchange of goods or services for other goods or services. The arrangement is regulated by a single contract with equal values passing in each direction (see Figure 2.16).

Although there is no movement of convertible funds out of a country, the Central Bank, or its equivalent, will still normally need to approve the deal because the goods to be exchanged would, if able to be sold for cash on the world market, have contributed directly to its foreign currency reserves.

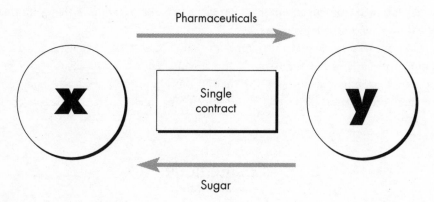

Fig. 2.16 Example of barter

Counterpurchase

Unlike barter which is regulated by one contract, counterpurchase needs to be seen in the context of two separate parallel contracts (see Figure 2.17). The first contract governs the sale of goods or equipment by a foreign supplier, usually to a public-sector buyer in another country. The second contract commits the supplier to purchase (or 'counterpurchase') goods or services from that country from a preferred list and for an agreed percentage of the value of the first contract. Each contract is settled in cash or on credit terms.

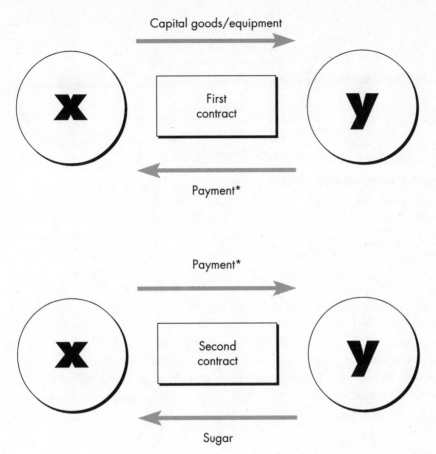

*Payment – either in full under first contract with reimbursement in whole or part under second contract – or only for the difference in value between the first and second contracts.

Fig. 2.17 Example of counterpurchase

Buy-back

Foreign suppliers, typically of manufacturing or mining equipment, are sometimes requested to accept payment in the shape of the product that forms the output of the factory, plant or mine, at some time in the future (see Figure 2.18). A popular idea at one time amongst importers of capital plant, the concept is now generally seen to be inflexible and high-risk.

Buy-back deals can be structured in the form of barter, in which no money passes, or counterpurchase, in which money passes.

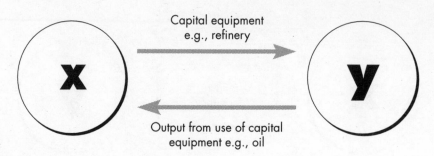

Fig. 2.18 Example of buy-back (barter structure)

Offset

More widely practised than any other form of countertrade, offset is an increasingly important element of contracts for military equipment. Originally, the importer would insist on 'direct offset' (co-production), for example, making components to be incorporated in imported aircraft. In recent times there has been a tendency for importing countries to opt for 'indirect offset'. This can take the form of provision to the importer of new technology, a production role unrelated to the equipment being imported or even investment by the exporter in job or wealth creation schemes.

Switch

Switch trading refers to the use that third party traders were able to make of bilateral trading accounts which were out of balance (because the parties were unable or unwilling to buy from or supply to each other in equal quantities). As bilateral trading agreements are now rare, switch trading has become virtually extinct.

BENEFITS

- Possibly the only way for two countries lacking hard currency to do business together.

- A means of generating additional exports and the foreign exchange needed to pay for purchases from abroad, and of opening up new markets.

- Can maintain or even enhance job opportunities in a less developed country.

- By imposing the need for 'additionality', the countertrade products are introduced into new overseas markets.

- Offset deals in particular enhance the development of technology and related skills.

- Far from always being a burden, countertraded goods can be a valuable new or alternative source of supply of raw materials or components.

- Buy-back deals, in particular, may risk a failure to deliver as contracted (timing, quantity, quality).

- Political.

- Products offered in countertrade may be of lower or unmerchantable quality.

- Foreign suppliers may be unable to find reliable trading house partners to take the products offered.

- Products taken in countertrade may have to be 'dumped' on a domestic market, potentially undermining the price of the locally produced version and possibly damaging the reputation and future trading prospects of the supplying country.

Medium- and long-term finance for exporters

Many countries have government-backed export credit agencies, offering support to their exporters. Their services typically comprise advice, insurance for credit or country risk and preferential financing. Recent years have seen a trend towards emphasis on medium- and longer-term projects, with the shorter end of the market being covered by commercial operations such as those of NCM.

The extent and nature of the support varies enormously, and you should find out what is available to importers and exporters in your own and your trading counterparty's country.

Make your enquiries at the earliest possible date. It can take time to complete any arrangements, and you will, for example, be better placed to win an order if preferential terms are available to the buyer.

Funding Risk

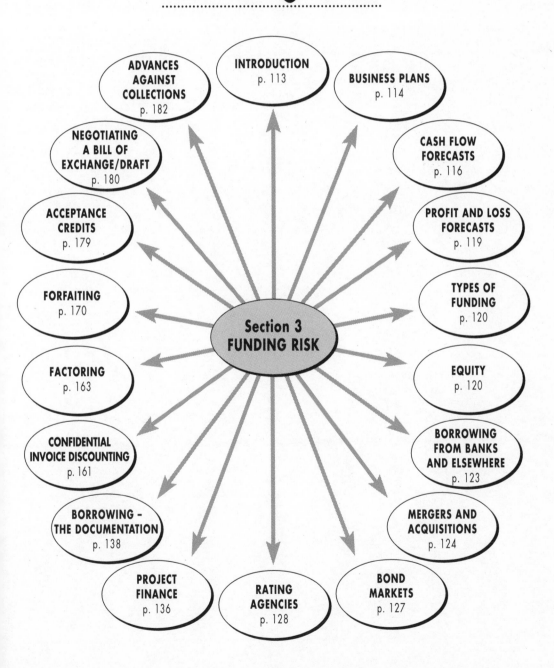

ADVANCES AGAINST COLLECTIONS p. 182

INTRODUCTION p. 113

BUSINESS PLANS p. 114

NEGOTIATING A BILL OF EXCHANGE/DRAFT p. 180

CASH FLOW FORECASTS p. 116

ACCEPTANCE CREDITS p. 179

PROFIT AND LOSS FORECASTS p. 119

FORFAITING p. 170

TYPES OF FUNDING p. 120

Section 3 FUNDING RISK

FACTORING p. 163

EQUITY p. 120

CONFIDENTIAL INVOICE DISCOUNTING p. 161

BORROWING FROM BANKS AND ELSEWHERE p. 123

BORROWING – THE DOCUMENTATION p. 138

MERGERS AND ACQUISITIONS p. 124

PROJECT FINANCE p. 136

RATING AGENCIES p. 128

BOND MARKETS p. 127

Introduction

·····················

Businesses principally obtain their funding from:

- **equity** – the capital provided by the owners of the business
- **borrowing** – in its many forms, including debt issues
- **trading** – generating cash from your business activities.

'Trading' includes factoring or invoice discounting and obtaining goods or services on credit and using them to produce something that can be sold with payment being received from your debtors before you pay your creditors. In countries where overdue trade accounts do not incur 'statutory' interest penalties it is usually to the financial benefit of a business to defer paying creditors for as long as possible (but not necessarily good for supplier relationships).

Depending on local regulations and taxation, a business may also be able to obtain the assets it needs on attractive terms through leasing and hire purchase agreements, rather than having to find the cash to pay for them outright.

Debt and equity is traded in the 'capital markets'. These include:

- **money markets** – for short-term debt (usually considered to be not more than one year)
- **bond markets** – for medium- and longer-term debt
- **stock (equity) markets** – investment of risk capital without a redemption date, usually by the 'owners' of a business.

Never confuse profits with cash. Profits, as shown in the profit and loss account of a business, are not a record or forecast of the availability of cash, and can owe as much to creative accounting skills as to successful trading.

You can sell your products or services at a profit and still be in trouble if you run out of cash. When the bills are not being paid your business must sooner or later stop trading. The first consideration of every business should be its cash flow, hence the bankers mantra 'Cash is King'.

A problem common to many businesses is that of **overtrading**, where your level of sales cannot be supported by the available working capital. Amongst other factors this will depend on how long your debtors take to pay you, and how long before you have to pay your creditors.

The effect of overtrading is illustrated by the following simplified example.

EXAMPLE Assume that you have been trading satisfactorily for several years with an annual turnover of around £300,000 and a borrowing facility from your bank of up to £50,000. It takes four months to complete and deliver any order.

Your margin of profit on costs is 25%, with your expenditure incurred 20% upfront and the remaining 80% spread evenly over the next 4 months.

The terms of trade for your debtors calls for payment at 30 days.

If you win a £125,000 order, that will take your turnover to £425,000, the champagne corks will pop and you will think of ways to spend the £25,000 profit on the costs of £100,000.

But consider the cash flow implications, ignoring the costs of borrowing.

£000	Day 1	30 days	60 days	90 days	120 days	150 days
Expenditure	(20)	(20)	(20)	(20)	(20)	
Income						125
Net cash	(20)	(40)	(60)	(80)	(100)	25

Unless the necessary finance has been arranged in advance, or your customer is making upfront or stage payments, you may be unable to pay your debts as they fall due or the patience of your creditors wears out. And your bank may not feel comfortable increasing its lending from £50,000 to £150,000 to finance the sale. Indeed, your overtrading may be the last straw if they are already worried about recovering their debt. A business that has been struggling to survive seldom appreciates the reasons for its banker's unwillingness to help when it has just won new orders.

The above example assumes that everything goes according to plan, but what if you are late in making the delivery or your customer delays paying? Everyone in business knows that things go wrong, and that deadlines are missed, but all too often fail to make allowance for this when preparing business plans and cash flows.

Business plans

Before starting work on a business plan, ask yourself the following.

● Why is it being written, e.g., to persuade bankers or investors to provide finance, or to record and quantify objectives?

● At whom is it targeted, e.g., your board of directors or your bankers?

- How will you measure its success, if on the strength of the plan, your board approves a new project or an investor provides funds, for example?

If the business plan is confidential then number each copy and keep a record of the recipients. State clearly on the front page that the document cannot be given to third parties or copied other than by the recipient for their own use, and that all copies must be returned at your request. In exceptional circumstances, where the information is highly confidential or sensitive, you may even need to stipulate that the document can only be inspected by third parties at your own or your solicitor's premises.

Make sure you are not breaching any statutory or regulatory requirements. If you are asking people to invest in the business, is the document a 'prospectus' that may be subject to specific rules? You might need to take legal advice on this issue, particularly if the intended recipients are domiciled outside of your own jurisdiction. Do you need to include any disclaimers, or to recommend that potential investors take independent professional advice?

The onus is on the issuer of the business plan to ensure its accuracy, and there may be severe penalties for businesses or individuals who make misleading statements. Always specify the assumptions on which the plan has been based, and never express opinions as if they were facts. As you write the plan, keep asking yourself: 'What evidence is available if someone asks me to prove the truth of what I have said?'

Every business plan should be written in a way that best suits its objectives and target audiences, but most include the following:

- **brief introduction** – why the document has been prepared
- **index/contents** – with page or section references
- **summary of conclusions ('executive summary')** – usually no more than one page
- **background** – the 'story' of the existing or proposed business and, if relevant, its promoters
- **products/services** – the business activities underlying the plan – include copies of marketing material, possibly as an appendix
- **market** – the size and nature of the present and prospective market(s) for the underlying products or services, and the existing or projected customer base – include any relevant extracts from newspaper and trade magazines, possibly as an appendix
- **competitors** – including their market shares and strengths/weaknesses
- **sales projections** – be realistic, as your competitors are unlikely to stand idly by while you capture the market
- **organizational** – the production, delivery, administration and 'after sales' for your products or services

- **resources** – property, plant and equipment, copyrights, patents, personnel, etc.; include an organization chart and CVs for executives and other key employees

- **financial** – for an existing business the audited accounts for normally the greater of the past three years or since commencement of trading, plus interim management accounts and cash flow, balance sheet and profit and loss projections (for as far into the future as is realistic, but for no longer than has any meaning). Detail the assumptions on which any forecasts are based, and show how the business is currently funded. A banker will want to know what security is available, and what has been provided to third parties. Comment on past trading, possibly using bar charts or graphs to illustrate trends. Provide the key ratios for assessment of the business. Where appropriate provide 'base', 'best' and 'worst' cases.

- **the proposal** – unless the plan is intended as a record of decisions already made you may need to say what is wanted or needs to be decided, why and when, and for what projected return or benefit (either make specific recommendations or detail the options)

- **SWOT analysis** – which provides an honest summary of the strengths, weaknesses, opportunities and threats of and to the business and the proposal

- **strategy** – the strategic vision behind the plan.

Check the document for errors that would damage its creditability, bind it suitably for the intended recipients and, if appropriate, provide a point of contact for responses.

Cash flow forecasts

If you cannot pay your debts you will go out of business and, therefore, need to know how much cash you will have or want, and when.

In preparing a cash flow forecast it is important to be honest with yourself. If the average time your debtors take to pay is 60 days there is no point in working on 30 days just because that is in your published 'terms of trade'. Be realistic not optimistic.

Before starting work on the cash flow you should list the assumptions on which it will be based (e.g., the level of future sales, anticipated price or cost increases, outcome of rent reviews and, where relevant, currency exchange and interest rates). Are the assumptions used in the cash flow the same as those in your business plan or profit and loss forecast?

Without these assumptions, which should be spelt out in detail in the final cash flow document, any projection is of only limited value. And when circumstances change it is easier to amend the projections if the original assumptions are there for reference. You should keep working papers showing how you arrived at any figures.

EXAMPLE

	Month 1		Month 2		Month 3		Month 4		Month 5	
	Budget	Actual	Budget	Actual	Budget	Actual	Budget	Actual	Budget	Actual
Receipts (a)	100	50	150	100	100	100	200	200		
Payments (b)	50	25	125	150	150	100	150	125		
Net cash flow (a - b)	50	25	25	(50)	(50)	–	50	75		
Opening cash balance	–	–	50	25	75	(25)	25	(25)		
Closing cash balance	50	25	75	(25)	25	(25)	75	50		

Fig. 3.1 Example of a cash flow forecast

A cash flow forecast (see Figure 3.1), as the name implies, is only concerned with 'cash', meaning any money that changes hands, whether as notes and coins or in the form of paper/electronic transfers. If time is required before paper or electronic receipts can be regarded as 'cleared funds' (i.e., as cash available for you to spend) then allow for any such delay in your projections. It may, however, be that the spread of your receipts or the covenant of the remitters is such that your bank will allow you to draw against 'uncleared funds'. For example, where you pay into your bank account cheques (checks) received from debtors then these will be uncleared until they have been presented to and paid by the drawer's bank. If your bank permits you to spend the money before they receive the cash from the drawer's bank then they are taking a risk that the items will be dishonoured. Where you are allowed to draw against uncleared items the bank will normally charge interest on the amounts involved, as it is effectively a loan by the bank until they receive payment.

The 'opening cash balance' and 'closing cash balance' are usually those at your bank, unless you keep your money in notes and coins in your safe.

Receipts would typically include:

● proceeds of sales (actual cash received, not the issue of invoices), which would include any 'sales taxes' you collect for subsequent payment to the government, and receipts from factoring or invoice discounting

● borrowings

● equity capital

● interest earned on deposits.

Payments would typically include:

- payments to creditors (actual cash payments not the receipt of their invoices)
- staff costs (including any taxes, which may need to be shown for payment at a different date to the day the employees are paid)
- rental/premises costs (if these are only paid, say, every three months then you only show the payment when it will actually be paid, not an 'average' figure in each of the months)
- lease and hire purchase payments
- travel and entertainment costs
- insurance premiums
- professional fees
- heat, light and power
- maintenance and repairs
- communications costs
- interest paid on borrowings (not the interest that has accrued at any time, but only when it will actually be paid)
- taxes, including the sales taxes you collected from customers
- capital expenditure (the full cash outlay, unlike profit and loss forecasts where only the depreciation may be shown).

Payments and receipts are shown in the projection for the period, e.g., month, during which that money is expected to change hands, not the date of an invoice (or even the date when a payment or receipt become due, unless settlement is expected to take place on time).

Your projections are shown in the 'budget' column, with the actuals for each period entered next to them when they become available. Any differences between the budgeted and actual figures will help you see how close performance and costs compare to target, and suggest ways in which your assumptions might be changed for the future.

When looking at the 'net cash flow' figure, remember that this is the difference between the total receipts and total payments for the whole of that period (e.g., in one month). Unless you have only limited business activity the net figure will change throughout the period (i.e., every time a payment is made or received), and the cash balance on any day is likely to differ from that as at the end of the period. In practice this means that the maximum amount of cash you have or you need intra-period can be very different from the figure shown for the end of that period. If, for example, you normally receive payments from debtors at a month end but have to make payments to creditors throughout the month, then your projections for the month overall may not show the worse cash position. This can be important if you are borrowing from a bank, and allowance must be made for mid-period 'peaks' if you do not want to go into 'excess' against the agreed level of facility. The alternative is to select periods that end at the worst time, e.g., mid-month.

Profit and loss forecasts

Forecasts of profit and loss differ from cash flow forecasts in the following ways.

- Cash flows are only concerned with the actual cash in and out of a business, whereas profit and loss accounts seek to show the difference between revenues and expenditure over a specified period of time, irrespective of whether or not there is any movement of cash. A profit and loss forecast usually includes, for example, invoices issued or received for which payment is outstanding and costs such as 'depreciation' of assets that do not directly involve any cash payment.

- Profit and loss accounts are prepared in accordance with the applicable 'accounting standards', which often allow room for some 'creative accounting' by the managers of the business. With cash you either have it or you don't.

As with cash flow projections it is important to state the assumptions upon which your profit and loss forecast is based, and usual to provide for comparison of the actual figures with the forecasts. Keep your working papers for reference.

A typical profit and loss forecast will show the following items.

- **Earnings,** for example, sales, excluding sales taxes collected from customers for subsequent payment to the government. It may be necessary to apportion a single sale over two or more periods, to reflect the dates on which the earnings are 'booked' for the purpose of being taken to profit.

- **Variable costs,** being those costs of a business that vary with the level of turnover (e.g., materials and labour directly incurred in the manufacture of a product or provision of a service). As with earnings it may be necessary to apportion costs over the period of time to which they relate.

- **Overhead (fixed) costs,** being those costs of a business that do not vary with the level of turnover (e.g., usually including salaries, rental/premises costs, depreciation, lease and hire purchase payments, insurance premiums, professional fees and communications costs). Depreciation is sometimes shown separately.

The profit or loss from each period (e.g., each month) is added to the total profit or loss carried forward from previous periods to show the cumulative profit or loss for the accounting period to date (see Figure 3.2).

	Month 1		Month 2		Month 3		Month 4		Month 5	
	Budget	Actual	Budget	Actual	Budget	Actual	Budget	Actual	Budget	Actual
Earnings (a)	150	150	150	200	150	210	200	250	etc.	etc.
Less Variable costs (b)	70	100	80	120	70	110	100	120		
Contribution (a - b) = (c)	80	50	70	80	80	100	100	130		
Less Overheads (d)	50	60	80	70	80	75	90	80		
Trading profit (c - d) = (e)	30	(10)	(10)	10	–	25	10	50		
Less Depreciation (f)	10	10	10	10	10	10	10	10		
Net profit before tax (e - f)	20	(20)	(20)	–	(10)	15	–	40		
Cumulative net profit	20	(20)	–	(20)	(10)	(5)	(10)	35		

Fig. 3.2 Profit and loss forecast

Types of funding

Equity

'Equity' is the capital provided by the owners of a business, who may or may not be the same people as the managers.

In return for their investment, shareholders in a company hope to receive dividends and to benefit from an increase in the value of their shares, but will only get all or part of their investment back if they sell their shares to someone else, or if the company is wound up and there is a surplus after paying creditors (in which event the individual equity investors would normally receive a share of the surplus *pro rata* to their percentage stake in the company).

Equity investors are also usually entitled to receive information about the company, and to vote on important matters (e.g., the constitution of the board of directors). These rights may differ between different classes of shares in the same company (e.g., Class A shares or Class B shares).

Even though there may be an entitlement to receive information there are often statutory or regulatory restrictions on using that knowledge for personal gain. This arises where, for example, the information is 'price sensitive' (i.e., knowledge of it could affect how much someone would be prepared to pay for shares in a publicly quoted company) and 'insider trading' is an offence in that jurisdiction (i.e., using knowledge that is not publicly known to trade at an advantage against other existing or potential investors).

There are many different types of equity holding, including the following.

Ordinary shares (common stock)

These are the basic equity investment in a company, giving rights to a share in any dividends and usually to vote on specified matters. There may be legal restrictions on the payment of dividends by a company, typically depending on the levels of profits and reserves. Subject to any such constraints, the amount of the dividend is decided by the board of directors and there may be one or more 'interim' dividends in addition to any 'final' dividend for an accounting period. Dividends are paid from after tax profits of a company whereas, in many jurisdictions, the interest on borrowings can be deducted from the profits before calculation of tax.

A potential problem, particularly for a publicly quoted company, is that meeting the expectations of shareholders for dividends may conflict with the need to retain sufficient monies in the business for its development. Look at the accounts of quoted companies to see how many have substantial and often costly borrowings but still pay dividends. This inherent conflict can, however, help to ensure the optimum balance of funding between debt and equity.

Existing ordinary shareholders may be invited to subscribe for new shares *pro rata* to their existing holdings, and usually at a discount to the current market price. This is known as a 'rights issue'.

Where existing shareholders are issued with free additional shares *pro rata* to their current holdings this is known as a 'capitalization (scrip/bonus) issue'. The resultant availability of more shares at a reduced price per share (as the issue by the company of the extra shares 'dilutes' the stake in the company represented by each share), often makes the shares more attractive in the market. The existing shareholders do not suffer. For example, if the company had net assets of £15m and 1m shares in issue, then each would represent £15 of assets. A capitalization issue of 1 new share for every 2 held would mean that each shareholder would have 3 shares for every 2 they originally held, each representing £10 of assets. Instead of 2 shares representing £30 of assets they would have 3 shares representing £30 of assets. Hopefully, as often happens, the capitalization issue is seen as a positive move by the company, and the market price of the shares (which may have little relationship to the net assets of the business) will rise.

Preference shares (prior-preferred stock)

Holders receive a dividend at a fixed rate irrespective of the profits of the business, unless these are insufficient for the payment of that dividend in whole or part. If this happens some preference shares are 'cumulative', i.e., the fixed dividend will be paid when the company is able to do so, whilst others are non-cumulative, i.e., the dividend for that period is forfeited. The fixed dividend is paid before any dividend payment to holders of ordinary shares, and if the company is wound up the preference shareholders rank before the ordinary shareholders for any repayment of their capital. Some preference shares are 'participating', which means they receive a share of the profits of a business in addition to the fixed dividend. Others are 'convertible' into ordinary shares on a specified basis, or 'redeemable' by the company on set terms.

Preference shareholders cannot normally vote at the meetings of the company.

Convertible shares

These 'hybrids' pay a fixed rate of interest unless, on the occurrence of specified events, they are converted into ordinary shares (common stock) in the company. They can be attractive to companies as the rate of interest is usually lower than that for bank borrowings or bonds, and may appeal to investors as there is usually a set 'conversion price' which may be lower than the market price at the conversion date.

Warrants (subscription or stock purchase warrants)

These may be issued as a 'sweetener' with preference shares or bonds, giving the holder the right to buy ordinary shares (common stock) in the future at a set price. The price is normally above the market price at the time the warrant is issued, and the warrants can be traded on exchanges separately from the shares or bonds with which they were issued.

Stock markets (securities exchanges)

Stock exchanges are the regulated markets in which the shares (stock) and, as appropriate, bonds and warrants of 'listed' companies (i.e., companies whose shares are available to the public and are traded on the exchange) may be bought and sold. The aim should be to provide liquidity for the shares in an orderly and fair marketplace.

When a company issues new shares they are sold in the 'primary market'. Once the issue has closed the shares are subsequently traded by shareholders in the 'secondary' market. There may be a 'grey market' if shares are bought or sold during the period between an offer closing and the date on which secondary trading starts.

A 'privately' owned company has some hard decisions to make before asking for its shares to be listed on an exchange. The advantages of a 'flotation' are that:

- additional cash can be raised by the issue of new shares (stock) which will strengthen the balance sheet and, unlike borrowings, does not incur liability to pay interest
- the 'liquidity' it offers (i.e., a market in which to buy and sell shares) may encourage investors who would not invest in a company where there was no 'exit route'. The 'owners' of the business may be able to realize some of their holding (thereby spreading their risks)
- it may be possible to acquire other businesses by giving their owners 'paper' (i.e., shares in the acquiring listed company instead of cash, which may also have tax advantages to the vendors)
- rightly or wrongly, some customers may consider a listed company to be an inherently better credit risk.

The disadvantages of a 'flotation' are that:

- it can take a lot of management time and incur considerable costs to complete the formalities necessary to obtain a listing
- there may be extensive regulatory requirements of the stock exchange on which the shares are listed
- it will be necessary to meet the regulatory requirements for disclosure of information, including details of directors' remuneration
- the affairs of the company are subject to public scrutiny, and fluctuations in share price can give rise to concern by customers and staff
- there will usually be pressure from shareholders to declare dividends, which may not have been important (or tax efficient) when the company was privately owned
- there is often a requirement for a minimum percentage of the company's shares to be in 'public hands' after the listing
- the holdings of existing shareholders will be 'diluted' by issues of new shares, and they may even lose control of the company
- there may be restrictions on directors and others buying or selling shares as an 'insider', i.e., whilst being in possession of information that is not generally available.

Borrowing from banks and elsewhere

In many countries banks are increasingly competing among themselves and with other groups, such as asset-based financiers, to provide a wide range of lending facilities.

The forms taken will vary depending on local law and practice, but a borrower needs to know:

- how much is available

- in what currency(s)

- the purpose(s) for which the facility can be used

- the term (duration) of the facility and the specified repayment date(s)

- whether the lender can call for repayment on demand

- any conditions precedent (see page 153) to be complied with before the facility can be utilized, including provision of security

- the conditions subsequent (covenants; see page 154) to be complied with after drawing down the facility, if the lender is not to have the right to demand early repayment of a term facility

- what it will cost by way of interest and fees, and when these are payable (including the costs if the facility is not fully utilized)

- if the interest rate is fixed or variable.

See also *Lending*, page 52 and *The documentation (loan agreements)*, page 138.

Mergers and acquisitions

When you agree to buy a business, or to merge your business with another, any payments in consideration can either be made on completion of the deal or over an agreed period of time (in which latter event the vendor will often require a suitable guarantee of payment, or retain some form of charge or other interest over the business or the shares in the business being sold until they have been paid in full).

The purchase price may include a deferred payment ('deferred consideration'), perhaps based on the future profits of the business, and you might be keen to retain the services of the previous owner(s) on an agreed basis ('golden handcuffs', as distinct from the 'golden parachutes' given to encourage executives to leave a business). Any deferred payment can be dangerous if, for example, it falls due after a period of high profits but at a time when the business is currently short of cash or experiencing other problems. Another practical difficulty can be in agreeing the actual profits on which any deferred payment is to be based, as profits are potentially subject to 'creative accounting' by the new owner of the business.

The prospective purchaser should try and obtain from the seller a 'lock-out' agreement, giving time to complete the due diligence process and negotiate a deal before other potential purchasers are approached. This is particularly important if substantial professional fees are likely to be incurred in advance of the completion of any purchase.

If you make an offer for the shares of a company listed on a stock exchange this is likely to demand compliance with extensive rules and regulations, and professional advice will almost certainly be needed. The normal requirement is that all shareholders must be treated equally, and an offer made to any single shareholder or group of shareholders must be made to all shareholders. Indeed, in many countries anyone acquiring more than a specified percentage of the shares of a publicly quoted company must offer to buy all the remaining shares, usually at the price they had paid for the shares that took their holding over the specified limit. You may also be required to notify the stock exchange on which they are listed or other regulatory body once you hold more than a small percentage of the total shares.

The opportunity for the purchase of an existing business by all or part of its management team (a 'management buy-out', or 'MBO') may typically arise because the current owners have reached retirement age or need funds for other activities, or when the business is in difficulties. Depending on the structuring of the purchase the management may end up owning all or part of the business.

The management often need to borrow from banks or venture capitalists to help pay the previous owners for the business, but will usually be expected to put some of their own money at risk. They need to ask themselves if they have the collective skills and ability to run their own business, accepting the inherent risks as well as the rewards. This may include giving personal guarantees to the providers of finance.

Subject to the jurisdiction there may be restrictions on using the assets of the business that is being acquired to help in financing the purchase of its shares.

The management team will probably need to declare their intentions at an early stage, to avoid accusations of conflicting interests or breaches of their employment contracts. They are also likely to require the services of professional advisers.

Management have the advantage over other prospective purchasers of the business in that they should know what they are buying, whereas third parties will need to undertake time-consuming and costly due diligence. A non-management buyer may ask the current owner and the executives for 'representations and warranties' as to the assets and liabilities being acquired, but in an MBO situation the management often find it difficult to obtain 'reps and warranties' from the owners.

The buyer may have to decide whether to purchase the existing business (with both its assets and liabilities) or only the assets, which can then be used in starting up a new business. This will depend on considerations such as the nature and extent of the actual and contingent liabilities and whether assets such as customer contracts and property leases can be assigned to a new business.

The finance for an MBO may typically involve:

- **equity** – ordinary shares
- **senior debt** – conventional bank lending

- **mezzanine debt** – often in the form of a medium-term loan, the servicing and repayment of which is subordinated to any senior debt, or as preference shares (the risks and rewards to a provider of mezzanine debt lie between those of equity and senior debt).

The provider of the mezzanine finance may receive options or warrants to convert all or part of its debt into equity or to acquire equity at a discount at a future date (these rights often being exercised by their holder if the shares of the business are subsequently listed on a stock exchange), or other incentives to compensate for the higher risk.

An added benefit to the MBO buyer of the business is that, because mezzanine finance is subordinated, banks may be prepared to regard it as 'quasi-capital' when considering the level of gearing, and agree to lend more than they would otherwise find acceptable.

A 'leveraged buy-out' is where the purchaser takes on a higher than usual level of debt to fund the acquisition.

The availability and form taken by venture capital varies from country to country, and may be provided by private individuals, financial institutions or large corporates. The funds made available by venture capitalists are typically invested into potentially 'high-risk' situations such as new business start-ups and management buy-outs. In addition to providing finance the venture capitalist can often offer good advice and valuable business introductions to the management of the businesses in which they are investing. They will usually want to have a representation on the board of directors, and may step in to help if things go wrong.

A venture capitalist will hope to make a profit if the business is subsequently sold, or if its shares are listed on a stock exchange, or if the business buys back the shares.

When a management team not already running a business are put in to run it after it has been acquired it is called a 'management buy-in', or 'MBI'. The selection and appointment of the team might be made by the venture capitalist providing the finance for the purchase. The management may be required to put in some of their own money, and be offered a 'ratchet' whereby they receive an increased equity stake in the business if specified performance criteria are met.

Whatever the nature of your proposed merger or acquisition it is a good discipline to occasionally stop and ask yourself if the deal is still one you want to do. Once into the heat of negotiations, with heavy professional fees already incurred and your advisers keen to score another success, it is very hard to say that you no longer wish to proceed. But the attractiveness of a deal changes as fresh facts come to light, and never forget that the day you complete the transaction is when the responsibility and hard work to make it successful starts.

Bond markets

These are the markets in which governments, supra-nationals (organizations outside the regulation and control of a single government, e.g., the World Bank), financial institutions and large corporates borrow and invest for the medium and long term. The amounts involved are large and the term to maturity is usually a minimum of one year from the date of issue, but more often two years or longer.

Although banks and brokers often act as intermediaries the markets are an example of 'disintermediation'. This means that the investors and the borrowers can deal directly with each other, rather than the investor depositing its money with a bank which then, as entirely separate transactions, lends money to borrowers.

Subject to applicable legislation the instruments traded may be 'bearer' (where ownership and the right to be paid interest or repaid principal is evidenced by possession of coupons or other documents) or 'registered' (where ownership and its associated rights are evidenced by some form of registration).

Until purchased from the issuer by the original investor the instruments are traded in the 'primary market' (where the proceeds go to the issuer), and thereafter in the 'secondary' market (where the proceeds go to the previous holder).

Bonds may be:

- fixed interest rate
- floating interest rate
- zero coupon – not paying interest but issued at a discount to their 'par' (face) value, so that a capital gain can be made at maturity (subject to any applicable taxation in the hands of the investor)
- callable – the issuer can redeem the bond prior to its specified maturity
- puttable – the investor can require the issuer to redeem the bond prior to its specified maturity.

Bonds typically have maturities in the five to ten year range, and can be secured or unsecured.

Assuming the credit risk on the issuers to be equal (and the bond not to have been issued at discount to its par value) the price of a bond in the market will vary depending on the comparison of the interest rate it pays (its 'coupon') against other bonds and investment opportunities.

The available debt instruments include Eurobonds, which are bearer bonds sold internationally to investors outside of the country of the currency of the issue. Any interest ('coupon') is paid without deduction of tax.

Eurobonds differ from 'domestic' bonds, that are issued to investors in the country and currency of the issuer (e.g., a sterling bond issued in London by a

UK corporate) and from 'foreign' bonds that are issued in a country (and in the currency of that country) other than that in which the issuer is domiciled (e.g., a sterling bond issued in the UK by a non-UK corporate, known as a 'Bulldog' bond, or a US dollar bond issued in the USA by a non-US corporate, known as a 'Yankee', etc).

By way of background, it is worth noting that the terms 'Eurocurrency' and 'Eurobond' do not relate only to Europe. Eurocurrency is any money which can be lent and borrowed in countries other than the country of issue of that currency (e.g., US dollars deposited with a UK bank, or French francs deposited with a Japanese bank). A Eurobond can be in any currency provided it is issued outside of the country in whose currency the issue has been denominated.

With floating rate notes (FRNs) the interest rate is periodically adjusted in line with a money market index, such as Treasury bill rate or LIBOR. As the coupon (interest rate) is floating, the price of an FRN should, at least in theory, be subject to less movement than that of a fixed rate bond. 'Perpetual' FRNs have no redemption date.

Euro commercial paper (ECP) is short-term, unsecured, bearer promissory notes issued in US dollars and other major currencies by governments, financial institutions and large corporates and mostly purchased by financial institutions and fund managers (another example of 'disintermediation'). They do not usually pay interest but are issued at a discount to par (face) value and redeemed at par, with the difference being the return to the holder. The amount of the discount reflects the interest that could have been earned if the funds had been invested at similar risk elsewhere. A typical issue might be for a total of US$100m in multiples of US$500,000 or its equivalent, with maturities of up to 1 year. Being short term most of the 'paper' is held to maturity by the original investors, although they can be traded in the secondary market.

Markets for domestic commercial paper also exist within individual countries, providing a convenient and relatively inexpensive method for high-rated issuers to obtain short-term unsecured funds, e.g., US commercial paper (USCP) and sterling commercial paper.

Similar to ECP are 'medium-term notes' (MTNs) with maturities of one to five years, issued mostly in US dollars; and 'Euronotes', which are short-term unsecured bearer promissory notes underwritten by banks (within agreed facility limits).

Rating agencies

Credit rating agencies, of which Standard & Poor's and Moody's are amongst the best known, are vital to efficient capital markets. Investors attach considerable importance to their published ratings, which greatly influence the pricing of individual issues. Combining qualitative and quantitative assessments, the ratings produced by these agencies have provided a consistently reliable indicator of risk, and facilitate cross-border comparisons between issuers.

An agency's ratings grade the likelihood of a default in the *timely* payment of interest and repayment of principal, providing investors with internationally recognized credit risk benchmarks. Agencies do *not* comment on trading movements in market prices.

Although some rating agencies issue 'unsolicited' ratings, the majority are 'rate-by-request', with the issuer of a bond or other financial instrument paying a fee to an agency for them to undertake the necessary analysis and publish a rating. Without a bond rating, it can be difficult for the issuer to attract investors, or decide upon the appropriate pricing or rate of interest, and in some countries, investment in lower-rated bonds is restricted by regulators.

Whether the issuer is a country or a corporate body, its representatives meet with the rating agency in advance to discuss the key financial and other factors underlying any evaluation. The credibility of an agency, however, depends upon maintaining its independence. To be unduly influenced by any issuer into setting an inappropriate rating would be to destroy the very foundation of their business.

With over 70 years' experience and more than 600 analysts, a great deal can be learned by looking at the way Standard & Poor's evaluate risk, and the following summary appears with their kind permission.

The details will, obviously, vary with the nature of the issuer and the instrument being analyzed. Is it a long-term government bond or corporate commercial paper. You can even obtain an 'issuer credit rating', giving an opinion of creditworthiness that is not linked to any specific debt instrument. But certain fundamentals remain, and are the key to consistent ratings.

Standard & Poor's evaluations for corporate debt instruments typify their approach. They start by looking at the country risk, then the business risk of the industry and finally the business position of the issuer itself. Once a business risk analysis is complete, a 'quantitative' assessment is made which involves analysis of published financial information, cash flow sources and uses, and the resultant ratios, taking into consideration the accounting principles and conventions that have been applied. 'Qualitative' factors such as economic and technological issues and evaluation of the management are also considered.

Significantly, the final decision on any rating is made by a team of experts combining knowledge of the industry, country and other risks being considered, and not by a mathematical weighting of the evaluation criteria.

For a corporate issuer, the analysis would normally be based on a minimum of five years' historic results and projections for at least the next two years. The historic accounts are accepted in the form, and subject to the accounting principles, normal in the country of the issuer. Where this provides an inadequate basis for evaluation, then Standard & Poor's may ask for supplemental information.

The future projections are especially important for the insight they give into the issuer's thinking and planning.

As already mentioned, Standard & Poor's start by looking at country risk.

Country risk

The creditworthiness of a country is indicated by its 'sovereign debt' rating, reflecting both *political* and *economic* risk.

One difference between sovereign and other (e.g., corporate) debt is that even when economic factors would allow a country to meet its liabilities, it may decide not to do so for political reasons.

With certain specific exceptions, the rating of an individual issuer is not typically higher than the sovereign rating of the country in which it is domiciled.

If the issuer is a State-owned business rather than the State itself then, unless there is a State guarantee for the issuer, the evaluation is made on the business itself, including the likelihood of government support if needed. This will reflect the strategic and economic importance of the business to the country, the extent to which aid has been forthcoming in the past and any international restrictions on support for such State-owned industries.

A State's decision on whether or not obligations are met when due may depend upon its social and political stability. Does a weak or unpopular government have the desire or ability to implement any domestic austerity measures needed to strengthen creditworthiness, or is it more likely to pursue popular policies? Will it recognize the importance of honouring its external obligations, and maintaining sound international trading and financial links? Are influential power groups looking after their sectoral interests at too high a cost to the country? Are there significant internal or external security risks?

Can a country meet its debts even if it wants to? This will depend upon the balance of payments, economic position and nature or extent of external obligations. Elements factored into Standard & Poor's sovereign evaluation include:

- the level and cost of public debt
- exchange control and currency convertibility
- monetary reserves
- natural resources
- overseas assets
- levels of taxation and public expenditure
- economic policies, strengths, diversity and volatility
- size of the economy, its strengths and weaknesses
- exports
- dependence on trade with other countries.

STANDARD & POOR'S COUNTRY RISK RATING METHODOLOGY PROFILE

Given the importance of country risk to so many business dealings, the rating methodology used by Standard and Poor's is summarized below. It should be studied carefully by anyone thinking of doing business with the government or any enterprise in another country. Remember, the rating of any individual business will not typically be higher than the sovereign risk of its country.

Political risk

Political system

- Form of government.
- Orderliness of leadership succession.
- Adaptability of political institutions.

Social environment

- Living standards and income distribution.
- Labour market conditions.
- Cultural and demographic characteristics of population.

International relations

- Integration within international economic system.
- Security risks.

Economic risk

External financial position

- Size and structure of gross and net external debt.
- Debt service burden.
- Adequacy of international reserves.

Balance of payments flexibility

- Structure, performance and responsiveness of the current account.
- Adequacy and composition of capital flows.
- Ability of policymakers to manage external payments.

Economic structure and growth

- Resource endowment, level of development and economic diversification.
- Size and composition of savings and investments.
- Rate and pattern of economic growth.

Economic management

● Willingness and ability to ensure economic balance.

● Effectiveness of fiscal, monetary and income policies.

● Structural economic reforms.

Economic prospects

● Long-term economic projections, including reasonable worst case scenario.

● Costs of policy trade-offs.

Fiscal policy and public debt

● Public-sector financial balances.

● Currency composition, structure and public debt.

● Public debt and interest burdens.

● Contingent liabilities, including banks.

● Debt service track record.

Monetary policy and inflation

● Trends in price inflation.

● Exchange rate policy.

● Rates of money and credit growth.

● Degree of central bank autonomy.

Industry or business risk

To quote Standard & Poor's on this vital component of the evaluation of corporate issuers:

'The key considerations in assessing industry or business risk are:

● understanding the sector(s) in which the company is active

● prospects for growth, stability or decline

● the pattern of business cycles

● vulnerability to technological change, labour unrest or regulatory interference

● levels of fixed or working capital intensity

● on-going needs for spending on capital equipment or research and development

- the nature and intensity of the competitive environment
- 'SWOT' analysis may be used to assess the company's strengths, weaknesses, opportunities and threats.

In addition, the analysis of corporate issuers of differing nationalities calls for an appreciation of the issuer's specific geographical and business mix. Consideration is given to both domestic and worldwide demand and supply factors. Industries where competition takes place on a local basis, such as retailing, are viewed differently from those that are exposed to international forces, such as semiconductors or energy. Other industries, for example, automobiles, face a combination of global and regional market considerations. As such, perceptions of industry risk can vary from region to region.'

Issuer business risk

Factors considered include the following.

Competitive position

Does a corporate issuer have or lack what it takes to succeed in its industry sector? Look at the:

- structure of industry
- product quality, pricing and differentiation
- management competence, depth, strategies, goals and motivation
- past performance of management
- organizational structure
- intangible and human resource assets
- diversity, with each business activity being considered separately
- market shares and geographic spreads
- order books, and the duration of contracts
- price sensitivity
- litigation
- quality of planning process
- structure of balance sheet – nature and size of assets and liabilities
- how much debt
- effect of inflation on earnings and debt
- number and size of competitors
- barriers to entry
- political influences on larger corporates
- government intervention, regulations and deregulation

- research and development
- distribution networks
- economies of scale
- SWOT analysis.

Financial risk analysis

For historic financial information, Standard & Poor's primarily relies on audited accounts.

It is essential to understand and allow for the various accounting policies and practices encountered in different countries. As with any financial evaluation, this includes consideration of the bases of revenue recognition, depreciation, write-offs, foreign currency translation, valuations, tax, consolidation and off-balance-sheet financing.

Particular attention is paid to core factors such as cash flow and the level and cost of debt, which remain crucial whatever the accounting practice.

What is the structure of the balance sheet, and the nature and size of assets and liabilities respectively?

The rating agencies are especially interested in the management's setting of financial targets, and the ways in which they assess their own performance. What is their attitude to debt and financial risks, and how are prospective acquisitions to be funded?

The profitability and, hopefully, resultant positive cash flows of a business are key factors in its ability to raise capital and service its financial obligations and meet its debts, including interest and preference stock dividends and ordinary shareholders' dividend expectations.

Benchmarking within business sectors and countries provides an essential balance when preparing evaluations on a cross-border basis, allowing due consideration to be given to different accounting practices and business cycles.

Is the issuer potentially helped or hindered by its relationship with other members of its 'group'. Would they come to its help, or expect financial assistance if themselves in trouble?

To what extent is the business dependent on debt to fund its activities and acquisitions? Is this debt:

- short- or long-term?
- fixed or floating rate?
- off-balance-sheet?
- in local or foreign currency?

How easily will a business withstand a period of financial stress? Is everything already stretched with little in reserve, or are there 'hidden' strengths and assets that would enable finance to be raised in times of difficulty? What is the effect of inflation on earnings, assets and debt? How good is the relationship of the business with its existing bankers and investors, and can it expect a favourable market response and pricing to its financing needs? What kind of financial flexibility does a company have (e.g., cash, non-core investments, access to equity market, committed bank lines, etc.)?

Rating definitions

Each rating agency has it own system of gradings, which vary according to the nature of the debt or other instrument being evaluated.

By way of example, the ratings applied by Standard & Poor's to *corporate debt* (a corporate bond is a debt instrument issued by a company) are summarized in the box.

A rating is *not* a recommendation to buy or sell, but is an assessment of the creditworthiness of the issuer, usually in respect of a specific instrument. It assesses the likelihood of a default in the timely payment of interest and repayment of capital. Ratings from AA to CCC may be modified by the addition of a plus or minus sign to show relative standing within the major rating categories.

RATINGS APPLIED BY STANDARD & POOR'S TO CORPORATE DEBT   Key points

Investment grade

AAA   Highest rating. Extremely strong capacity to pay interest and repay principal.

AA   Very strong capacity to pay interest and repay principal.

A   Strong capacity to pay interest and repay principal but somewhat more susceptible to the adverse effects of changes in circumstances and economic conditions than AAA- or AA-rated debt.

BBB   Adequate capacity to pay interest and repay principal, but adverse economic conditions or changing circumstances are more likely to lead to a weakened capacity than in higher-rated categories.

Speculative grade

(Debt with predominantly speculative characteristics as regards the capacity to pay interest and repay principal.)

BB   Less near-term vulnerability to default than other speculative issues. However, it faces major on-going uncertainties or exposures to adverse business, financial, or economic conditions which could lead

---

	to inadequate capacity to meet timely interest and principal payments.
B	Greater vulnerability to default than BB, but currently has the capacity to meet interest and principal payments
CCC	Currently indefinable vulnerability to default and is dependent upon favourable business, financial and economic conditions to meet timely payment of interest and repayment of principal.
CC	Rating typically applied to debt subordinated to senior debt with a CCC grade.
C	Rating typically applied to debt subordinated to senior debt with a CCC- (minus) grade. For example, a bankruptcy petition may have been filed, but debt service payments are continuing.
D	Payment is in default. Interest payments or repayments of principal have not been made on the due date.

Project finance

Definition | *The financing of a project where the servicing and repayment of the funding depends on the revenue stream or capital value of the completed project rather than on the covenant of the borrower or on a charge over other assets.*

Typically the projects involve substantial amounts and may be inherently high risk, with high financing costs to match.

Financiers will be concerned with the technical and economic feasibility of the proposal, and usually need to undertake in-depth viability analysis and on-going monitoring (using either 'in-house' or independent experts).

Typical projects would be the construction of airports, roads, bridges, tunnels, ports, telecommunications systems, railways, water treatment plant, power stations and oil refineries.

The principal parties to a project financing include the following.

- **Sponsor(s)** – the parties behind the project, which may be a single entity or a consortium of, for example, the principal contractors and the prospective buyers of the output of the project when it is completed.

- **Borrower(s)** – the choice of legal entity to act as borrower will be dependent upon, for example, the applicable laws, taxes and exchange controls. If the sponsor is a consortium then two or more members may separately raise finance, and there can then be more than one borrower for that project.

● **Financier(s)/lender(s)** – because the amounts involved are usually large and the risks high it is normal for any facility to be syndicated between two or more providers of finance. One bank is usually 'mandated' by the other to act as the 'arranger', putting together the funding package. That bank, or another as appropriate, then acts as 'agent' to coordinate the syndicate of financiers once the funds have been made available. Those banks providing the most are often named as 'managers' or 'lead managers'.

Some banks may not themselves lend, but will instead provide guarantees to other banks or organizations able to provide subsidized or lower-cost finance (but who themselves cannot or do not want to carry the credit risk).

Projects in developing countries may be financed in whole or in part by international agencies, such as the World Bank.

The finance may be provided in the form of a loan or, for example, bonds, guarantees, export credits, commercial paper or leases.

Interest on the facility is often 'rolled up' and added to capital during the construction phase of a project.

Charges on the project assets and revenue streams are sometimes taken by lenders solely to stop third parties obtaining prior charges.

Where there are restrictions or taxation disadvantages to an outright lending the finance is sometimes provided by means of a 'forward purchase' or by 'production payments', where the provider of finance receives all or some of the output from the project to service and repay the debt.

Depending on the skills that each of the consortium financiers has available they may divide between them the responsibility for the initial feasibility study and the subsequent monitoring of different aspects of the project.

Most projects have a lengthy development or construction period, with the risks having to be evaluated well into the future. These risks include:

● political ('political risk' insurance may be available)

● market for output (volumes and prices)

● costs

● technical feasibility, especially if the techniques upon which the project depends are untested, and including where appropriate the existence of projected reserves (e.g., oil)

● performance of contractors, suppliers and operators

● the income stream and its adequacy for servicing the debt after operating expenses, taxes, royalties, etc.

● taxation and tax allowances

- price regulation affecting the output
- time and cost overruns
- trade barriers/tariffs
- operating risks when complete
- counterparty risk on the borrower and/or sponsor (where the facility is 'with recourse'), and on any insurers and guarantors
- currency exchange rates
- exchange controls
- applicable laws and their effective application
- available security
- licences and permits
- legal risks of the project structuring, operations, any security and for the resolving of disputes
- inflation
- environmental risks
- availability of human and other resources
- insurance.

The availability of political and other risks insurance is often critical, with the insurers frequently undertaking their own detailed feasibility studies.

Whilst the financiers will be principally concerned with the inherent viability of the project, and the financing might be provided on a partial-recourse or non-recourse basis (relying for servicing and repayment on the revenue streams and asset value of the project), the sponsors or borrower may also be required to provide guarantees, equity or subordinated loans (ranking for repayment after the financiers).

Borrowing

The documentation (loan agreements)

For convenience in this subsection, the provider of financial facilities will be referred to as the 'lender' and the recipient as the 'borrower', even though no loan or other cash advance may be involved. A facility might, for example, cover currency exchange transactions or the issue of documentary credits.

The documentation setting out the terms and conditions of borrowing and of other financial facilities comes in many shapes and sizes. At its simplest, it may be a short letter from a lender addressed to a borrower, agreeing to provide a loan for a stated amount of money at a specified rate of interest and repayable on demand by the lender.

The other extreme might involve a number of participating lenders and lengthy documentation detailing the terms and conditions of a multi-option facility for group borrowers.

Facility agreements, in common with other contracts, are all too often entered into without considering the possibility that things may later go wrong, or that the parties could find themselves in dispute. Both the borrower and the lender need to ensure that the documentation accurately records the basis on which they have agreed to do business, and that they wish to be bound by its terms and conditions.

Banks and other lenders usually try to make the wording of agreements (which often take the form of an 'offer letter' to be accepted by the borrower) as clear as possible, but the need to produce legally binding documents may make it necessary to include terminology that sometimes appears less than straightforward.

There are, however, certain common fundamentals, and for other than the simplest agreements, the facility documentation will usually state:

- who is the lender
- who is the borrower
- the amount(s) of the facility(s), in which currency(s) and whether the lender or borrower are taking any exchange rate risk
- when the facility must be repaid or is otherwise to be terminated
- the purpose(s) for which the facility can be used
- the rate(s) of interest to be applied to the facility, including any 'margin', and when this is due and payable
- who is liable for any fees or costs, and the amount or limit of these where appropriate
- any security to be given to the lender by, or on behalf of, the borrower
- any conditions to be met by the borrower before the facility becomes available ('conditions precedent'), and the latest date by which a prospective borrower can formally accept the offer of the facility
- any conditions to be met by the borrower after the facility has been drawn down or otherwise utilized ('conditions subsequent', 'covenants' and 'undertakings'), and what happens if these are breached ('events of default' and 'remedies').

The lender

Borrowers need to be very careful from whom they take money or other facilities. If their lender finds itself under financial pressure or decides upon a change of strategy, that can be very bad news. The last thing most borrowers need is for their lender to unexpectedly withdraw the facilities upon which they depend, or to run for cover at the first sign of trouble. If a business is dependent on borrowing or other facilities, and its lenders have the right to cancel the facility or to immediately demand repayment (either because the facility is repayable on demand or its terms and conditions have been breached), then it no longer controls its own destiny. Before signing any agreement a borrower should consider whether it wants that particular lender to have the potential power of life or death over the business.

The facility documentation will show the name and usual contact address of the lender and, where appropriate, a separate address to which any formal notices should be delivered by the borrower. It should also state where any payments by the borrower to the lender are to be made.

When a facility is 'syndicated' amongst two or more lenders (syndicate or club 'members'), one is normally named as the 'agent' to whom all communications are addressed by the borrower. The agent then passes any relevant information it receives on to the other lenders. All syndicate lenders are usually named in the document, unless some have taken 'hidden (silent) subparticipations' when the borrower will be unaware of their involvement. If a facility agreement includes details of the respective duties and responsibilities of the agent and syndicate lenders to each other, then it can become a very lengthy document. Where there is a syndicate of lenders some decisions may be made by the 'majority lenders', being those whose participations when added together represent a specified minimum percentage of the facility which can protect against a minority lender being obstructive.

The borrower

As the detailed terms and conditions of any agreement will vary with the type of borrower, a lender needs to know whether a borrower is:

● a company with limited or unlimited liability

● a publicly listed or a privately held company

● a holding company or a subsidiary

● a partnership (or some other arrangement whereby two or more individuals are jointly and/or severally liable)

● a sole trader (i.e., an individual trading for their own account), and if there is legislation or regulation governing lending to an individual even though for business purposes

● a trustee

- a governmental, quasi-government or supra-government organization
- some other body
- incorporated, registered or otherwise based in the country of the lender for legal and/or taxation purposes, and if not, then where?

What legislation, regulation or other special factors apply to the provision of facilities to any class of borrower, e.g., local government authorities or insurance companies? Subject to the nature of the entity and its jurisdiction, legal advice may be needed as to the capacity and authority of the borrower and its representatives.

A lender needs to take particular care when the borrower is a holding company or a subsidiary, to ensure that the lender:

- knows which company it is contracting with
- can monitor and/or control the application of the facility(s) within the borrower's group
- has good security and/or recourse within that group
- includes in the agreement such financial and other covenants as are effective and meaningful to a group situation.

For a corporate borrower, the lender will want to see its charter/memorandum and articles of association/certificate of incorporation (etc., depending on its structure and country(s) of registration and/or operations).

The facility agreement is likely to contain what are known as 'representations' and 'warranties,' which usually include statements that the borrower:

- has the power and authority to enter into and perform its obligations under the agreement, to execute legally valid and binding documents to that effect and to provide any specified security – for a corporate borrower a certified board resolution or its equivalent is usually required, authorizing acceptance of the facility and execution of the documents and naming those individuals nominated to sign on behalf of the company (in some countries the local Chamber of Commerce maintains a list of authorized signatories)
- is not, by entering into the agreement, breaching any laws or regulations, nor any undertakings or agreements with third parties, and is not otherwise in default of any obligations (including payment of taxes) that might affect either the facility or any security to be provided in its support, including any requirement for the borrower to take actions that might be detrimental to the lender's interests
- is not subject to litigation or arbitration, and that none is pending or threatened
- is not in default of any of the terms and conditions of the facility or other facilities (this statement is often required to be repeated by the borrower at the

time of any subsequent variation or utilization of the facility – wording to that effect may be included in the notice a borrower has to give to the lender when it wishes to draw down or otherwise utilize the facility at any time – such 'repetition of representations' can become extensive and contentious, with the borrower being required to re-state all covenants, representations and warranties and events of default)

● has provided accurate information to the lender, including details of any charges over assets, and that its financial position is not materially different from that as at the date of its most recent audited (statutory) accounts.

Depending on the group structure, it may be important that the representations and warranties relate to all companies within a group, and not just the borrower and the holding company if different.

A bank lender will usually require the borrower to provide a 'mandate' specifying those individuals authorized to give instructions on its behalf to the bank, and setting out any conditions or limits to their powers.

The agreement should include the usual contact address of the borrower and, where appropriate, the separate address to which any formal notices are to be delivered by the lender. Care should be taken by the lender as to the persons to whom any documents are addressed, e.g., to 'the directors' of a corporate borrower.

If the borrower is registered or is otherwise based or operating outside the country of the lender, different rules (including exchange controls and withholding tax) may apply, and the lender might need to register any agreement or other documents in territories other than its own. Any necessary legal advice should be sought *before* lending or borrowing.

Businesses can change their names, and it is not uncommon for companies within a group to do so (sometimes with specific fraudulent intent). As a lender needs to know who they are contracting with, it is good practice to check a corporate borrower's or guarantor's name against their company registration number, and to include that number in any documentation for identification purposes. Lenders have lost money by failing to observe this simple precaution.

Amount

The agreement may relate to a short-term loan, an overdraft, a long-term loan, an acceptance credit, a guarantee or a bond, international trade instruments, currency dealing limits, derivative trading limits, etc. – or any combination of these and other facilities. It may commit the lender to provide the facilities, subject to the borrower meeting all specified terms and conditions, or be an 'uncommitted facility'. The latter is a type of facility, usually only available for larger amounts, where the agreement details the terms on which a lender would lend to a borrower, but the lender is not committed to lend nor the potential borrower to borrow. When the bank has funds surplus to its requirements which it is looking to lend (often only overnight), it can then contact the counterparties with whom it has entered into such uncommitted facility agreements, asking if they would like to borrow. If any of the counterparties can use the funds to balance their own 'treasury' operations, there is no delay while an agreement has to be prepared and signed.

The documentation must specify the maximum total facility amount, any 'sub-limits', whether the facilities are available in local and/or foreign currency, and if the borrower or the bank are liable for any exchange rate risk.

If interest, fees and other costs can be added to the principal debt, the agreement should mention this, together with any maximum limit.

Some facilities must be drawn down or otherwise utilized in full in a single 'tranche' (instalment), while other agreements permit 'stage' drawings.

Undrawn commitments may initially be nil-weighted for the lender's capital adequacy purposes, but even if they remain unused this cost usually starts to impact after a set period of time.

The agreement should specify the earliest and latest dates on which the facility(s) can be utilized, and the minimum amount permitted for any drawing (it may be necessary to incorporate a schedule giving the dates on which amounts become available). It is also normal practice for loan agreements to specify the period of notice of a drawdown of cash, or other usage of the facility, that must be given by the borrower to the lender, so that the latter can ensure funds or other resources are available. This is particularly relevant for foreign currency facilities, where time may be required for delivery of funds. Notices should be irrevocable, so that a lender does not find itself with excess funds that are not utilized on the due date.

A lender should satisfy itself that the amount of any facility is within the borrowing or other 'powers' of the borrower, and of those individuals signing the agreement on its behalf.

Repayment

An agreement may provide for a facility to be:

- repayable, or subject to immediate termination, on demand (depending on any legislation requiring a lender to give the borrower a minimum period of notice of termination or repayment), and even when a facility is repayable on demand, the agreement may specify those dates on which the total limit and/or any sub-limits are subject to reduction (it is also common practice for the lender to include in the agreement a reference to dates when they will 'review' the facility, but for an 'on demand' facility care may need to be exercised in case this provision might be legally interpreted as creating a term facility

    or,

- a 'term' arrangement, with repayment of any indebtedness, and termination of any non-cash options, at a specified future date or dates – repayment and/or termination of a term facility can only be accelerated by the lender if the borrower is in default of its obligations under the agreement (or if required by law or other binding regulation).

With a 'revolving' facility the amount drawn down can be repeatedly repaid, and non-cash options closed out by the borrower, and then re-drawn or re-utilized throughout the term of the facility. By contrast, amounts repaid, and non-cash options closed out by the borrower, under a non-revolving facility cannot be redrawn or re-utilized.

Repayment of a facility can either be in instalments ('tranches'), by way of a 'bullet' (i.e., repayment of the entire liability in a single tranche at, or no later than, a specified date) or by way of a 'balloon' (i.e., partial amortization by tranche repayments with a lump sum payment for the balance at expiry of the facility). When repayment is by instalments, these can either be for equal amounts at set intervals during the repayment period, or for uneven amounts and/or frequencies.

The agreement might specify a fixed equal amount for each repayment, covering both interest and capital. In this event the borrower's payments early in the repayment period will meet all interest that has accrued since the last such payment, with the balance of each payment reducing the debt (the 'capital' or 'principal'). As the debt reduces, the amount of interest payable declines in line with the debt upon which it is based, leaving a greater balance from each fixed payment amount to further reduce debt. In theory, the amount of each fixed repayment is set, so that by the end of the repayment period all interest has been paid and the capital debt is fully repaid. The problem comes if the rate of interest payable by the borrower increases with market changes, so that there is not enough left from each fixed payment after meeting the interest to achieve an adequate reduction in the capital debt (or even to pay the accruing interest in full). It will then be necessary for the amount of the fixed payments to be increased. Facilities of this type frequently provide for the interest rate to be fixed for a certain period, at the end of which the interest rate is re-fixed for the next period and the amount of the repayments re-calculated. For example, a 15-year loan may provide for the interest rate and repayment amounts to be re-fixed/re-calculated every three years. Despite this potential problem, a fixed repayment amount covering both interest and capital can be very helpful to borrowers who could not afford higher payments early in the repayment period.

The lender may agree to an initial 'holiday' period during which repayments of capital are not required to be made by the borrower. (The holiday period may also cover interest or fees due to be paid by the borrower, which is instead added to the principal amount of the debt. It will then be necessary to ensure that the agreement and/or local law permit the charging of compound interest.) A holiday period may be appropriate where the facility will be used to create a future revenue stream (e.g., to acquire plant and equipment that, once installed, will produce income for the borrower).

An 'evergreen' facility is agreed at the outset for a specified term. At a pre-set frequency, and provided that both the lender and borrower agree at that time, the facility can be renewed for its original term, For example, a three-year revolving loan might be reviewed by the lender and the borrower at the end of the first year. If both agree it will be renewed for a three-year term from the review date. In this example, a borrower would always have a minimum of two years' notice of the repayment date, but the commitment of the lender would never be longer than three years.

An agreement may also specify the following.

- The minimum period for which any facilities are to be utilized by the borrower, with an additional fee if this requirement is not met. This is to ensure adequate remuneration to the lender, in return for them holding the facilities available.

- Whether a borrower is entitled to cancel the agreement before its stated expiry date, either because it is no longer required and the borrower wishes to save on commitment or other fees or to 'free up' the limit for other purposes, or because the facilities can be obtained more cheaply elsewhere. The agreement should state what, if any, fees or costs must be paid to the lender if the facility is cancelled by the borrower, as the lender may itself have had to borrow or set aside the funds or limits needed for the facility.

- If, for other than a revolving facility, the borrower can repay a cash borrowing (or close out any non-cash utilization) before the scheduled repayment or termination dates, and, where this is permitted.

  - How much notice must be given to the lender.

  - What fees or costs ('breakage costs') must be paid to the lender, who may itself have had to borrow or set aside the funds or limits needed for the facility, or have entered into a swap or other arrangement to hedge the risk of adverse interest rate movements on a fixed rate loan, and is faced with termination costs.

  - Are partial repayments permitted (in addition to any regular repayments provided for in the agreement), or must repayment be for the entire outstanding amount of the facility? If partial repayment is allowed, then what is the minimum amount that can be repaid at any time and is the borrower entitled to ask for the release by the lender of any security? Other than for revolving facilities, amounts repaid cannot normally be re-drawn.

It is a good discipline to have pre-set dates (usually annually or semi-annually) when the lender reviews the borrower's obligations and performance, which would normally only affect the term of the facility if the borrower was found to be in default. For corporate lenders, such as banks, it is also the occasion on which an updated report may require to be submitted by the lending officer(s) to their head office or other 'control'.

Purpose

An agreement will normally specify the purpose(s) for which the facility is to be used by the borrower. This may be general, for example 'trading purposes', or specific, for example to fund the acquisition of a particular asset.

The lender will wish to be satisfied that the purpose is not an activity contrary to the permitted activities of the borrower, which might make the facility *ultra vires* and prevent the lender from being able to enforce repayment. Similarly, if a facility is provided for illegal purposes it may be unrecoverable, and the lender might even be liable to criminal proceedings.

Would the lender be happy for it to be widely known that they had provided a facility for the stated purpose?

Unless the borrower is well-known to the lender, and considered to be of good covenant, it can be important for the lender to ensure that the facility is actually used for its specified purpose. For example, loan monies might be released only to a firm of solicitors and against their written undertaking to apply those funds in paying for a specified asset, which is in turn to be charged to the lender by way of security. All too often lenders have released monies intended for one purpose, only to find later that the borrower has used them for another.

Interest

The rate(s) of interest payable by the borrower on any debt may be either:

- fixed for the entire term of the facility *or*

- fully floating, i.e., not fixed for any period but changing as the market or other rate on which it is based changes *or*

- fixed/floating, i.e., fixed for specified periods during the term of the facility, with the rate for each period being in line with a specified market or other rate for that period.

A lender will wish to be paid:

- the cost to it of the monies it lends to the borrower – this may be the actual cost of obtaining those funds in the market (or, in the case of banks, the interest it pays on deposits from its customers), or a notional figure to represent the rate of return the lender wants to see from lending its own capital *and*

- a 'margin', to provide against bad debts and, if all goes well, leave the lender with a profit – it may be argued that the costs of establishing, administering and controlling a facility should be separately covered by fees, but these expenses are often borne in whole or part by the interest margin, *and*

- any 'associated costs' and other costs imposed by, or resulting from the requirements of, central banks or other government bodies or regulators.

The facility agreement may either specify the above interest rate components separately, or quote an 'all up' figure.

Where the interest charge is broken down into its elements, the agreement should state the following.

- *The 'base' to be used in calculating the interest charge, e.g. 'three-month LIBOR'.* The base selected need not be the same as any against which the lender might actually be borrowing to obtain the funds it is on-lending, but it should be relevant to the type of facility being provided and be a generally accepted benchmark for such purposes. Ideally, the borrower will be able to check the base independently, without having to ask the lender. For example, most commonly used bases are quoted in newspapers or on electronic databases.

A bank lender often uses its own standard base rate for lending purposes, the interest rate on which may be internally decided by that bank from time to time (it is usually published in their branches and in the newspapers). In most countries, the standard lending rates of different banks are likely at any time to be the same or very similar, and banks do not normally abuse their right to vary the rate (which could be very damaging to their reputation). But that possibility still exists, and on large amounts, even small percentage differences in the base rate between banks can be significant (unless a borrower has the right to repay without penalty and could then arrange suitable alternative facilities elsewhere). It is also common practice to specify a substitute base that could be used if the normal base was not available for any reason. In such an event, the borrower may be given the option of repaying the facility without penalty if they consider the substitute rate to be unacceptable.

- *The formula for calculating any 'associated costs', which are normally 'rounded' up or down to a specified number of decimal points.* These usually represent only a small percentage of the total interest charge, but can be significant if the debt is large.

- *The 'margin', to be added to the base and any 'associated costs'.* The facility document may provide that the lender is entitled to an increased margin for utilizations it allows in excess of the limits specified in that document, or if the borrower is in default of its obligations. This is likely to depend upon the local legislation governing 'usary', consumer protection, post-insolvency or judgement debts and the general enforceability of penalty clauses. In some jurisdictions, default interest is liable to be set aside by the courts if it exceeds an amount equal to 'liquidated damages', i.e., the loss actually suffered by the lender. There may be provision for reduction in the margin if the credit risk on the borrower improves.

It is also normal for the agreement to detail the following.

- Whether the borrower can choose ('elect') the length of each or any interest rollover period(s), and the 'default' rollover period that will be applied if the borrower fails, or is not entitled, to make such an election. A rollover period can apply only where the rate is fixed for a specified period less than the term of the facility, and is the length of time between one fixing of the interest rate and the date when it is next due to be fixed. It is also normal practice for accrued interest to be paid by the borrower to the lender on the rollover date (although interim interest payments may also be due if the rollover period is particularly long, e.g., greater than 6 months).

EXAMPLE

The interest rate on a loan subject to rollovers would be fixed in line with the market rate for the amount drawn on the date of the first drawing under the facility. The rollover period might typically be one month, three months or six months, etc., depending on the type of base and any permitted election by the borrower. If the rollover period was for three months and the borrower made a second drawing under the agreement one month after the first, then the rate for the second drawing would normally be fixed in line with the market rate at that time for a rollover period of two months, so that it expired on the same day as that for the first drawing (but see below). On the date three months from the first draw down (and two months from the second draw down) the rollover periods for both tranches would expire, the accrued interest on each would be paid by the borrower to the lender (or, if permitted, added to the principal debt) and a new rollover period fixed for the combined amount.

Subject to the terms of the agreement, there is no reason not to have a number of different rollover expiry (maturity) dates for different amounts (tranches) within the available facility, which can have an attraction to the borrower as it provides an opportunity to spread their interest rate risk.

The length of rollover period selected by the borrower can be very important. If, for example, it was fixed for six months and after three months the market rate fell, then the borrower would pay more interest in total over the six months than if the rate had been fixed for only three months and then refixed for another three months (in practice, the market rates on any day for terms of, say, three and six months are likely to be different, but the principle holds good for general movements in the market).

The final rollover period must end no later than the date on which the facility expires.

- The dates on which interest is due to be paid by the borrower to the lender. For a fully floating rate facility, interest is typically payable every three, six or 12 months in arrears. For a facility with fixed rates, the interest would usually be payable on a rollover date, or at a specified frequency (e.g., six-monthly) if the rollover period was particularly long or where the rate had been fixed for the entire term.

The agreement may provide for the borrower to make an additional payment to the lender to recompense them for any tax or other deductions, subject to double taxation treaties, etc. It is important that before entering into an agreement, the lender and the borrower both understand the nature and impact of such statutory and contractual burdens or obligations.

Payments are normally specified as having to be made without any right of set-off by the borrower, e.g., for any amounts owed to them by the lender.

- Whether interest that is due and payable can be added to the principal amount of the debt ('capitalized/compounded'). This might, for example, be appropriate where the lender is funding a construction or other project that will not produce income until its completion. In some jurisdictions, as previously mentioned, interest cannot be charged on the amount of capitalized interest unless compound interest is specifically provided for in the agreement.

- The number of days in a year used for the purposes of calculating the interest charge. In some instances, or countries, it may by law or convention be 365, and in others 360, but the agreement should be specific where necessary.

- The right of the lender to charge an increased rate of interest if, as a result of any change of applicable law or other binding regulation, the cost to the lender of providing the facility is increased ('margin protection'). In such an event, it is common for the borrower to have the right to repay the debt without penalty.

Fees and costs

The fees charged by a lender for a facility can be many and varied, and their size and form often depends on the relative negotiating strengths of the lender and borrower. Amongst the categories of fee in a lender's armoury are:

- **arrangement** – for negotiating the facility; normally payable no later than the date when a prospective borrower signs the agreement and not refundable even if, for whatever reason, the facility is unused

- **commitment** – on the undrawn or otherwise unutilized portion of a facility, to reimburse the lender for any capital adequacy costs and for tying up its funds or limits in case they are needed by the borrower

- **annual ('management')** – similar to an arrangement fee, but payable on the anniversaries (or at other agreed frequencies) throughout the term of the facility

- **cancellation** – where the borrower, if permitted, asks for the facility to be cancelled before its specified expiry date (thereby saving the borrower further annual, commitment and other fees)

- **pre-payment** – if the borrower repays all or part of the facility in advance of the due dates
- **repayment** – due on the repayment of a facility, and sometimes calculated as a percentage of the profits made by a borrower from using the facility for a specific purpose (e.g., the purchase of an asset subsequently sold for a profit)
- **agency** – to the agent bank in a lending syndicate, for the work it undertakes in that capacity.

In territories where value added or similar taxes are charged there may be differentiation in their application to various classes of fees.

Normally all costs and expenses specifically related to the facility are borne by the borrower (excluding taxes the lender has to pay on its profits from the facility).

The lender may initially agree to pay the fees, costs and other expenses on behalf of the borrower, in which event these are then added to the loan amount ('capitalized').

Security

During their negotiations for a facility the lender and borrower may have agreed upon the security required in its support. The agreement should then record the following.

- The specific security to be provided before the facility can be utilized (i.e., as a 'condition precedent'), and that any documentation relative to that security must be in a form and have a wording acceptable to the lender. In many cases the lender will have its own forms for charging security, containing 'standard clauses'. Even if these are on pre-printed forms, a borrower should ask for changes if there is a good reason to do so. Indeed, most reputable lenders prefer to end up with a mutually acceptable agreement, rather than arbitrarily imposing wording or conditions that a borrower is unhappy with. Until the documentation is signed, everything is potentially negotiable.
- Any security to be provided subsequent to the facility first becoming available (i.e., as a 'condition subsequent'), and whether future utilizations are dependent on this. It may, for example, be appropriate to incorporate this requirement where the borrower will be using the facility to acquire assets.
- Whether the facility limits will vary with the value of the security from time to time, and the rights of the lender to resolve any security at the borrower's cost. The borrower may be required to 'top up' the security so that it always provides an adequate margin of cover for the facility. For example, the agreement may provide that the borrower must charge in favour of the lender shares which have a market value equivalent at all times to at least twice the outstanding amount of the facility. If the market value of the shares falls, then the borrower must either charge additional shares to the lender or reduce its utilization of the facility (alternatively, the lender can sell some of the shares

until the required margin is restored unless, of course, the shares are unsaleable or the market price has fallen dramatically and the shares cannot be sold for enough).

- When, and subject to what, if any, conditions or notice periods the lender can enforce or otherwise have recourse to the security. This is normally for any serious, unremedied default under the terms and conditions of the facility agreement. Depending on the applicable law, a specific 'power of sale' or right to take possession of the charged security may be essential. The rights and methods of enforcement by the lender may differ from one jurisdiction to another, and it might be necessary to obtain a court order before proceeding.

The range of potential security is almost endless, including cash, fixed and floating charges over the assets (real and intellectual) and undertakings of a borrower, guarantees (which may themselves be separately secured), other 'third party' security, 'key man' life insurance policies on individuals considered critical to the borrower's ability to service and repay the debt, and a 'letter of comfort' from the borrower's holding company or another company in its group (which may have moral but not legal force). What is available will differ from territory to territory. For example, in some jurisdictions, a lender can obtain a charge over book debts (debtors/receivables), whilst in others that is either not possible or only valid if notice is given to each individual debtor.

In some jurisdictions, the agreement can incorporate 'consolidation' and 'all monies' clauses, giving the lender the right to consolidate the security referred to therein with any other security charged in its favour by that borrower, so as to provide cover for all present and future facilities to the borrower (i.e., it provides 'continuing security').

If the agreement contains a 'set off' clause, this empowers the lender to offset any liability of the borrower against any assets of the borrower in the lender's possession, subject to the borrower being in default or as otherwise specified. Depending on the jurisdiction, such a provision may not, however, be valid in the event of the borrower's insolvency (when any uncharged assets may have to be available for all creditors). By contrast, the borrower may be prohibited from offsetting against its debts to the lender any indebtedness to the borrower by the lender.

Normally a borrower is prohibited from redeeming any individual item of security unless it repays the entire debt and clears any other liabilities to the lender. This is to prevent a borrower taking away the good security and leaving the lender with inferior security, although in some jurisdictions there are restrictions on 'over-collateralization'.

Guarantors are usually required to waive any right of recourse they might have against the borrower for amounts paid on their behalf to the lender. This is to prevent guarantors proving as a creditor for the debt if the borrower becomes insolvent, and thereby 'diluting' the amount which might be available to the lender. Once the lender has been repaid in full, this restriction would normally fall away.

Subject to the nature of the assets and to the jurisdiction, there may also be a requirement in the agreement that the borrower will charge in favour of the lender any 'after acquired assets', being those coming into ownership of the borrower subsequent to the date of the agreement. In some territories, this can only be achieved by the lender taking further steps to 'catch' such additional assets.

If any assets are already charged in favour of another lender who is continuing to rely on it, their consent may be required before a new lender can also take a charge on those assets. Even where that is not necessary, the lenders may enter into a 'deed of priority', or some other form of agreement, for the prioritizing or sharing of the security (often by way of fixing the maximum amount to which the original lender can continue to have recourse to the security, which usually means that they then restrict any facility to that amount) and, possibly, the new lender will require a written confirmation from the original lender that they are not currently intending to exercise the security.

The covenants section of the agreement normally requires the borrower to insure, protect and maintain any security in good order, failing which the lender can do so at the borrower's cost. This is very important as, if the charged asset is damaged or destroyed, the only security may be the insurance. It will also usually stipulate that the security cannot be sold, leased, rented or otherwise disposed of or transferred elsewhere or used as security to third parties or become subject to any liens or encumbrances, without the lender's consent. In the case of real property, the lender would normally need to approve in advance any new or amended leases, to prevent lettings on terms that reduced the value of the realty or otherwise made it less attractive as security.

If the subsidiaries of a corporate borrower have given guarantees to support their parent, then the agreement will normally stipulate that any future subsidiaries of the borrower must also provide guarantees (it might be necessary to define 'subsidiaries' for this purpose). This assumes that subsidiaries are even permitted to issue guarantees on behalf of their parent. Such 'upstream' guarantees are prohibited in some jurisdictions as 'an abuse of corporate assets'. Even where they are allowed, it may be necessary to ensure that there is valid 'consideration' for the subsidiaries to guarantee the debts or other liabilities of their parent, or of any other companies within their group. In the absence of such consideration, the guarantee may not be enforceable.

The actual charging of the security in favour of the lender is usually achieved by documentation linked to, but separate from, the facility agreement. A lender needs to ensure that the charge is valid and binding, is registered if necessary, and that any duties, taxes, registration, notarial and other costs and fees resulting from the provision of security are paid. Legal and taxation advice should be sought as appropriate. Legal and taxation advice may especially be required if the borrower or the asset(s) comprising the security are located in a jurisdiction other than that of the lender.

When a lending 'goes bad', one of the first things a lender does is to check the security, and all too often it is found to be 'imperfect'. This inevitably governs the approach a lender can take in seeking to recover any debt. A lender may have to attempt the delicate balancing act of pressuring a borrower to repay, whilst knowing that its own position is weak. In any restructuring of such a facility, a priority for the lender will be to have the borrower sign new (and valid) security documentation. When things go wrong, it can therefore be worth the borrower asking its solicitor to review the security documentation, for an opinion as to its validity.

Similarly, it can pay a lender to have a solicitor review as part of an audit process the security it holds for existing facilities. The cost of such an exercise may be more than covered by the subsequent reduction in bad debts, if mistakes can thereby be corrected before any problems arise.

Conditions precedent

Even though both the borrower and the lender may have signed the facility agreement, this will not become effective until the borrower has complied with any 'conditions precedent' it contains. There may also be further conditions to be met at a later date before additional facilities become available (e.g., specified financial criteria are to be achieved, or an asset purchased).

The 'conditions precedent' will vary, depending on the nature of the facility, purpose of the loan and the relationship between the borrower and lender, but typically might make the following requirements.

- The borrower to provide a mandate specifying those individuals authorized to give instructions on its behalf, and setting out conditions or limits to their powers.
- The borrower to pay any 'upfront' fees due to the lender.
- The lender to be provided with the security specified in the agreement.
- The lender to receive a valuation(s) of the asset(s) constituting all or some of its security, in a form and from a valuer acceptable to the lender. As the valuation figure may vary, depending on the basis on which it is prepared, the lender will usually wish to formulate the instructions to be given to the valuer (e.g., 'open market' or – where vendors are willing to provide it – 'forced sale' value, etc.). Lenders usually insist that the valuer is independent of the borrower (i.e., does not have an existing or intended future relationship with the borrower). The costs of valuations are normally paid by the borrower even if, in the event, the facility is unused or unavailable for any reason. Valuations are normally addressed by the valuer to the lender, so that the lender may be able to take legal action against the valuer if they are negligent, and often include statements to the effect that the valuer knows the lender is relying on the valuation for lending purposes. The valuer might also be asked to confirm that the asset will provide suitable security upon which the lender can rely, although that may involve legal or other issues outside of the valuer's competence.

- Any legal, regulatory, planning, or other requirements, consents or licences necessary for the borrower to fulfil the purpose of the facility, being met or obtained. The lender would normally require satisfactory evidence to that effect. This will include any relevant exchange control approvals.

- That if the security is real property the lender receives a satisfactory report on legal title, structural and/or mechanical or electrical survey, details of tenancies and satisfactory references on tenants. Any fees or costs in obtaining these would be for the borrower. Careful attention would be given to any environmental or pollution issues.

- The lender to be satisfied as to the power of the borrower, and of the individuals representing it, to enter into the agreement.

- The borrower to arrange any insurance specified in the agreement (for example on an asset charged as security, or 'key man' policies on directors or employees), and these being charged in favour of the lender as appropriate (or, at least, the insurer acknowledging that they are on notice of the interests of the lender in the policy, as they will then usually notify the lender if premiums are not paid or if the cover might be invalidated for any other reason).

- The lender to receive any legal or auditor's opinions necessary to satisfy itself that the appropriate terms of the agreement have been fulfilled.

The agreement will normally specify the latest date by which the conditions precedent are to be met, after which time either the offer expires or the lender has the right to cancel the facility (usually without refunding any 'upfront' fees).

Covenants (conditions subsequent/undertakings)

There are two types of covenants, being those that:

- require the borrower to do something (positive/affirmative)
- require the borrower not to do something (negative).

Covenants are important because:

- they are the 'ground rules' for the future relationship between the lender and borrower
- both the lender and the borrower know what constitutes a breach of the agreement.

Even if the facility is repayable on demand, covenants can constitute a valuable 'benchmark' – but care is needed as they can have the legal effect of negating the 'on demand' nature of the agreement.

In times of competition between lenders to provide facilities, it is common to see these covenants 'diluted' to win business. This can be a serious mistake for the lender, as their position may be greatly weakened if things subsequently go wrong.

Just as the borrower enters into covenants, the agreement may include undertakings by the lender. These would set out any lender's obligations to the borrower, and must be studied carefully by a prospective borrower.

It is important that any covenants are clearly defined, to avoid disputes over interpretation.

The exact nature of the covenants included in any agreement depends upon the purpose of the facility and the relationship between the lender and borrower, but might typically include the following undertakings by the borrower.

- *That at no time will they (and their subsidiaries, as appropriate) allow any charge, mortgage, lien or other encumbrance on all or part of their assets, including permitting any third party to have the right to such charges in the future.* This is known as a 'negative pledge', and may extend to prohibit charges that would have inferior ranking (as these might inhibit any power of sale of the 'senior lender'). Even when the borrower does not have subsidiaries, it is usual to include provision for this covenant to cover any it might acquire in the future.

  If the borrower subsequently acquires a new subsidiary which has already given such charges to a third party, these are normally allowed to continue, but any debts they secured would not usually be permitted to be increased. The purpose of negative pledges is to stop any future lender(s) obtaining a priority charge over the assets of the borrower (i.e., ranking before that of the existing lender). Where this is permitted there may be a 'pari passu' clause, that in the event of liquidation of the borrower, the lenders have the same priority against assets.

- *Not to borrow from third parties.*

- *To meet specified financial criteria.* It is important that these be realistic, and that the accounts on which they are based are prepared in accordance with recognized accounting principles and practices. All too often lenders have 'standard' covenants that they impose irrespective of individual circumstance. If, for example, a borrower has never previously achieved a level of outstanding good debtors twice the amount of the facility, and their business plan predicts a maximum of, say, $1^{1}/_{2}$ times cover, then why stipulate twice cover in the agreement? The borrower must feel comfortable that they can achieve and sustain the financial (and any other) covenants, otherwise they are giving a hostage to future fortune.

  Financial covenants may include:

  - maximum total liabilities
  - minimum ratio of current assets to current liabilities
  - minimum good debtors/receivables (normally 'aged', for example to be outstanding not more than 60 days from, say, the date of invoice or from

the due date of payment; also, usually to be 'well spread', i.e., not more than, say, 20% of debtors (receivables) to be from the same debtor or connected group of debtors; any debtors outside of these aging and spread limits would be ignored for the purposes of the covenant, although they will normally still be caught for the benefit of the lender under any security charge over receivables

- minimum stock/inventory levels, and the basis of valuation for that purpose
- maximum total borrowing
- minimum net worth (net tangible assets)
- maximum (and sometimes minimum) subordinated debt
- minimum pre-tax profit
- minimum coverage of interest and other finance charges by cashflow and profits (usually the profits before deducting interest and tax, known as PBIT)
- maximum preferential creditors
- maximum gearing/leverage and if including the liabilities and assets of subsidiaries (the agreement should define the meaning of gearing/leverage for the purpose of this covenant – consider, for example, definitions using 'borrowings' as against those using 'total liabilities including creditors': the latter may encourage a borrower to avoid a breach of covenant by not paying creditors, which could ultimately be harmful to its business, and does the definition of borrowing include bonds and the capitalized values of leases and hire purchase contracts, and are assets valued after deducting goodwill and intangible assets?)
- maximum directors' remuneration
- maximum payments or declarations of dividends (this can be difficult for a quoted company, particularly if they might need to raise capital in the market)

The frequency with which these financial covenants are to be tested should be specified, and it may sometimes be appropriate to require periodic verification by the borrower's auditors that specific covenants have not been breached.

● *To meet specific non-financial criteria that are important to the business.* These must be measurable and, depending on the industry, might typically set standards for customer response or delivery times.

● *To provide specified information, together with such other information as the lender may (sometimes 'reasonably') require from time to time, within set time limits.* This usually includes management and statutory accounts, and circulars to shareholders and holders of loan stock. Late submission of this information to a lender is often the first sign that the borrower is in trouble. If in any doubt as to its reliability, a lender should verify the information it receives.

- To *maintain in good condition, any security or other assets necessary for the business.* This might include restrictions on the borrower agreeing new or amended leases on real property.

- To *pay any due taxes.*

- That *all monies received by the business will be paid into specified accounts* (to avoid funds being diverted).

- To *advise the lender of any changes to the business* (these may require the lender's prior consent).

- To *advise the lender of actual, threatened or anticipated litigation or regulatory impositions.*

- To *arrange and pay for any insurances specified in the agreement.*

- Not *to sell, transfer or otherwise dispose of those assets not already charged to the lender by way of security other than in the normal course of business* (e.g., the business can sell its stock, but not its plant and machinery). Sometimes a maximum limit is set for such disposals, in either a single or a series of transactions during any set period, below which they are permitted.

- Not *to invest in shares or in third party assets or to acquire new businesses.* A financial limit may be set, below which the restriction does not apply.

- Not *to give financial support (including guarantees) to third parties* (including subsidiaries of the borrower unless otherwise agreed).

- Not *to purchase its own shares, or to accelerate the repayment of its bonds or stock.*

- Not *to permit a change in control of the business, or to merge with another business.*

- To *advise the lender of changes in the management of the business.*

- Not *to amend its charter/memorandum and articles of association, etc.*

- To *notify the lender of any events that might affect the facility or the security.*

Miscellaneous

An agreement is also likely to include some or all of the following.

- Definitions of the principal terms and expressions used in the agreement. It is important to study these, as they are critical to understanding and interpreting the document. Be especially alert for differences of definition between documents, e.g., between the agreement and any security documents.

- A definition of 'business day' for the purposes of the agreement, which is important for clarifying the dates when rollovers and payments are to be made. In some countries, it may typically be specified as 'a day other than a Saturday or Sunday when banks are open for normal business transactions'. It is also necessary to specify whether, when a rollover or payment date falls on a non-business day, it is adjusted to the previous business day or to the next business day. Even then there can be problems where, for example, a derivative instrument is being used to hedge a loan, as for a non-business day at the end of a month the derivative settlement date might be adjusted to either the last business day in the month or the first business day in the next month, whilst that for the loan rollover or payment is carried in the opposite direction. Such a mismatch could prevent an effective hedge, and prove costly if market rates changed adversely between the two dates.

- A statement that any waivers of breaches must be in writing. It may, additionally, be stipulated that any amendments to the agreement are to be in writing (e.g., by a 'letter of variation'), although some jurisdictions recognize oral amendments.

- A 'severability' clause, which states that if any individual terms or conditions of the facility become invalid for any reason the remaining terms and conditions remain valid.

- A statement that delay by the lender in exercising any of its rights is not to be taken as a waiver of those rights, in the absence of which there may be deemed to have been a constructive waiver. In some jurisdictions such a clause is insufficient to protect a lender, who needs to write to the borrower specifically reserving their rights in the event of a breach (otherwise they 'go stale'). It is very important for the borrower that, if a lender agrees not to exercise its rights when the borrower has defaulted, a 'letter of waiver' of that breach be obtained from the lender. This confirms that the lender will not use the default(s) specified therein as a basis for an action against the borrower. In the absence of such a document, the lender might at any later time be able to use an historic default by the borrower as grounds for terminating a facility.

- Whether the lender can sell, transfer or otherwise assign the facility in whole or part to another lender and, if so, whether the borrower has the right at that time to cancel or repay the facility without penalty.

- What happens if the agreement and security documents differ, i.e., which is the governing/binding document.

- The legal jurisdiction and/or governing law to which the contractual terms of the agreement and any disputes are subject, and what happens if there are changes in the applicable law. The forum for legal actions may be very important. For example, there might be no point in suing your contractual counterparty(s) in one country, if their assets are in another country which does not recognize the decisions of courts in the former jurisdiction. Are there any applicable treaties or conventions between the countries?

'Exclusive jurisdiction' means you can only take legal action in one specified country. 'Non-exclusive jurisdiction' means that whilst it would be the intention for legal actions to be taken in a specified country, each of the parties reserves the right to commence proceedings in another country.

- That the agreement supersedes any previous agreements relating to the facility, unless otherwise specified.

There are three phrases in common usage of which to beware.

- The first is that the lender will not 'unreasonably withhold' its consent to specified future requests by the borrower. If they disagree as to what is reasonable then, subject to any applicable legislation, the borrower may be in a very weak position.

- The second and third are 'best efforts' and 'reasonable efforts'. The former means that you will do everything you possibly can to make something happen, whilst the latter only requires you to make 'reasonable efforts,' albeit in good faith.

Events of default by the borrower

Typically, these include:

- breaches of the terms and conditions of the facility and defaults under the security: the agreement, or applicable laws, may require these to be 'material'
- not making payments of interest or capital when due
- making false representations and warranties
- breaching the terms of other financial facilities from the same or from other lenders (known as a 'cross-default' clause)
- being subject to liquidation, bankruptcy, administration, receivership or any winding-up petitions or judgements
- being unable to pay debts when due or entering into a 'composition' with creditors
- control of the borrower passing to other parties, or changes in its senior management
- guarantors giving notice to terminate their guarantees(s)
- failing to provide by the due dates the financial and other information specified in the agreement
- any 'material adverse change', as decided by the lender: whilst this clause is common, and often insisted on by the lender, it is less usual for it to be exercised in practice; failure to prove that it was validly exercised can render the lender liable for damages for breach of contract.

Remedies

The normal rights of a lender in the event of any breach of covenant or other default by the borrower are:

- to terminate any obligation on the part of the lender to continue to provide the facility(s)

- to renegotiate the terms of the facility, and/or to impose additional controls

- to demand immediate repayment of outstanding debts and settlement of any other liabilities

- to have recourse to any security if the borrower's obligations are not met in full after demand has been made: sometimes the borrower may have a specified period of time in which to remedy any failure to comply with the terms and conditions of an agreement, but this may only apply to specific defaults, for example, giving a borrower a short period of time to remedy a shortfall in the specified security cover by either reducing the outstanding liability or providing additional security acceptable to the lender

- subject to the jurisdiction to take over control of the borrower and realize its assets, or instigate a winding up.

It is when things go wrong that the borrower will find out whether their lender is prepared to give help in remedying the problems, or simply exercises its legal rights. This may depend in part on the past actions of the borrower. If they have failed to keep the lender fully and honestly informed, or to act in good faith, then a borrower cannot complain at the treatment it receives from the lender. The effort put into the relationship during the good times usually pays dividends when problems arise.

Asset-based financing

The time has long since passed when factoring and confidential invoice discounting against book debts (receivables) were regarded as last resort finance, and they are rightly recognized as legitimate components of business funding. Indeed, the market has polarized and some of the finance companies who offer these services can now provide a very much wider range of 'asset-based financing', and will consider as collateral not only receivables, stock, plant and equipment and property but such intangible assets as trademarks, licences, franchise rights and intellectual property.

To quote BNY Financial Limited:

Many companies find themselves with imbalanced, inefficient capital structures. Some finance long-term assets with short-term debt, or vice versa. Others fail to consolidate their debt during a growth phase. Too often, a company's receivables contain barriers to profitability and growth: uneven cash flow, bad debts, the high costs of administration and control.

By purchasing receivables, we provide immediate working capital to fund stock, sales and marketing efforts, or day-to-day business needs – we can even remove the risk of bad debts. We also can reduce a business's overhead by taking on certain administrative operations.

As an example, BNY Financial helped a major advertising agency to increase its reach by acquiring similar firms. The problems the agency had faced included negative tangible net worth (from previous acquisitions) and a bank with a restrictive lending limit. BNY used the agency's high-quality receivables to more than double their financing capability, then financed a dozen acquisitions, each time maximizing the receivables of the acquired company. The agency grew five-fold as the facility quadrupled.

Confidential invoice discounting

> *The 'undisclosed' sale by a business (discountee) of its book debts (receivables) to a finance company (discounter) in return for an immediate cash payment (advance) within pre-set limits.*

Definition

The maximum advance is normally set at between 70% and 100% of the value of invoices issued by the discountee (usually including VAT/sales tax where applicable), but the discountee is not required to draw down more than it needs.

Other limits are on the total of all advances outstanding at any time, and (usually) the maximum exposure to any single debtor.

A schedule is sent by post or fax from the discountee to the discounter listing the invoices issued and against which an advance is requested. The invoices themselves are sent direct by the discountee to the debtors, but, without any reference on them as to the sale of the debt to the finance company.

The discounter pays the discountee the amount it has requested, up to any set limits and usually within one business day.

The balance of the invoice amount, e.g., 30% where the initial advance was 70%, is received by the discountee when the debtor pays in settlement of the invoice. Although the debtor sends the payment direct to the discountee, the usual practice is for it to be paid into a bank account controlled by the discounter, who deducts the amount already advanced and then remits the balance to the discountee (see Figure 3.3).

The facility is 'confidential' (undisclosed) because the individual debtors need not be aware that the book debts have been sold to the discounter, and the discountee continues to be responsible for collecting payment of the debt.

Discountee   The business which sells its book debts (receivables) to an invoice discounting company (discounter) for an immediate cash payment (advance).

PARTIES

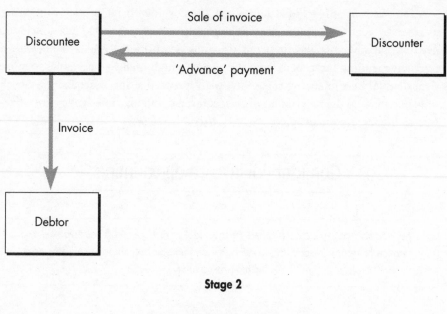

Stage 1

Discountee → Sale of invoice → Discounter

Discountee ← 'Advance' payment ← Discounter

Discountee → Invoice → Debtor

Stage 2

Discountee ← Balance (debtor's payment less advance) ← Discounter

Discountee → Debtor's payment sent to bank account controlled by discounter → Discounter

Debtor → Pays invoice → Discountee

Fig. 3.3 Example of confidential invoice discounting

Discounter (invoice discounting company) The finance company, many of which are subsidiaries of banks, which buys the book debts (receivables) from the discountee.

Debtor The party receiving an invoice from the discountee, for the supply on credit terms of goods or services, and who need not be aware that it has been sold to the discounter.

Factoring

> *The 'disclosed' sale by a business (factoree) of its book debts (receivables) to a finance company (factor) in return for an immediate cash payment (advance) within pre-set limits.*

Definition

The maximum advance is normally set at between 70% and 100% of the value of invoices issued by the factoree (usually including VAT/sales tax where applicable), but the factoree is not required to draw down more than it needs.

Other limits are on the total of all advances outstanding at any time, and (usually) the maximum exposure to any single debtor.

A schedule is sent by post or fax from the factoree to the factor listing the invoices issued and against which an advance is requested. The invoices themselves (see Figures 3.4 and 3.5) are usually sent direct by the factoree to the debtors, although occasionally they may be sent first to the factor who then posts them to the debtors.

The factor pays the factoree the amount it has requested, up to any set limits and usually within one business day.

Factoring is 'disclosed', because the individual debtors are aware from a statement on the invoice that the book debt has been sold, and are instructed that payment in settlement must be made direct to the factor.

The balance of the invoice amount, e.g., 30% where the initial advance was 70%, is paid by the factor to the factoree when the debtor pays in settlement of the invoice (see Figure 3.4).

Factoree The business which sells its book debts (receivables) to a factoring company (factor) for an immediate cash payment (advance).

PARTIES

Factor (factoring company) The finance company, many of which are subsidiaries of banks, which buys the book debts (receivables), manages the factorees sales ledger and collects the debts.

Debtor The party receiving an invoice from the factoree for the supply on credit terms of goods or services, the sale of which has been disclosed to the debtor, and who makes payment in settlement direct to the factor.

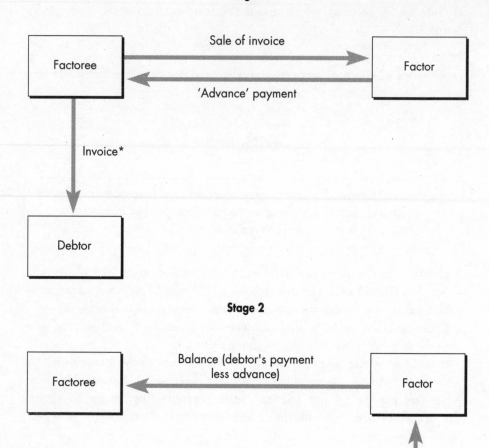

Stage 1

Factoree — Sale of invoice → Factor

Factor — 'Advance' payment → Factoree

Factoree — Invoice* → Debtor

Stage 2

Factor — Balance (debtor's payment less advance) → Factoree

Debtor — Pays invoice → Factor

*Invoice may, alternatively, be sent to the factor who forwards it to the debtor.

Fig. 3.4 Example of factoring

INVOICE

Name of Buyer

INVOICE No.:
INVOICE DATE:
ORDER No.:
ACCOUNT No.:

DETAILS (e.g.)	NET PRICE	VAT
8CM DEEP BORDERS FOR FIVE ADS	150.00	26.25

Items Net	150.00
Total VAT	26.25
Invoice Total	176.25

This account has been purchased by, and is to be paid direct to, **XYZ Factoring Ltd**, XYZ House, Straight Row, London. Payment to, and for credit of, XYZ Factoring Ltd alone will discharge your obligations in respect of this account.

Name and address of seller

Payments due within 30 days. Accounts strictly net. Errors and omissions are excepted.

Fig. 3.5 Specimen factored invoice

INVOICE DISCOUNTING AND FACTORING COMPARED

Points in common

- The book debts (receivables) are traditionally *sold* to the finance company. However, some finance companies are now prepared to consider advancing monies solely against a charge over book debts rather than against their purchase, increasingly competing head-on with the traditional overdraft and loan facilities provided by banks.

- The finance company buys the book debts for cash.

- The limit (maximum percentage) available by way of advances against book debts is agreed between the business and the finance company, and depends upon:
  - the industry sector
  - country risk for exports
  - historic experience
  - the spread of debtors
  - individual debtor limits (if any)
  - how long debts are allowed to remain unpaid before the discountee/factoree has to reimburse the finance company for the initial advance (unless without recourse, see below).

- Individual limits are usually set for each debtor (for small amounts this may be at the discretion of the discountee/factoree).

- There may be an agreed limit establishing the maximum amount that the finance company will advance *in total* at any time.

- The advances are made by the finance company on either a 'with recourse' or a 'without recourse' basis.

With recourse
If the debtors do not pay in settlement of their invoices, then the discountee/factoree has to repay the advance to the finance company. This is often achieved by setting off the amounts due by way of repayment against the sale to the discounter/factor of fresh book debts. A discountee/factoree may protect against having to repay all or part of advances, especially should a debtor become insolvent, by taking out credit insurance with the discountee/factoree or an independent insurer (see *Credit insurance*, page 62)

Without recourse
Where the discounter/factor agrees to carry the credit risk within agreed limits. This arrangement is more common with factoring than with invoice discounting.

- Within the limits agreed for percentage and total advances, the discountee/factoree decides how much to take from the finance company at any time.

- The contract between the business and the finance company is set out in a 'discounting/factoring agreement'.

- In addition to its recourse to book debts, a finance company may also require a charge over other assets of the business.

- Once negotiated, and subject to audit and annual (or other periodic) review, the agreement between the business and the finance house provides a 'continuing facility'. In the absence of default, any termination by the finance company is subject to an agreed period of notice (i.e., it is not 'on demand').

- By way of interest charge the discountee/factoree pays the finance company a 'discount rate' ('discounting charge') on the daily outstanding balance, often the base rate of a specified bank (usually the banker to the finance company) plus a margin, together with an 'administration fee' which is either a fixed amount or based on turnover. These charges are usually paid monthly in arrears, rather than being deducted from the advance.

- Amounts already drawn down can normally be repaid by the discountee/factoree at any time without penalty.

- It is important to know the number of days allowed for clearance of cheques.

- Where the debts relate to exports, it is usual for these to be on an open account basis (see page 65), although exceptions may be made by agreement.

- The help of the discounter's/factor's credit approval and control systems may be of especial value when dealing with buyers in another country, and a factoree can potentially forget about the problems of long-distance debt collection. Exporters have been known to factor their debtors for these reasons alone, even when they do not need to take advantage of the available cash advances. The discounter/factor can also give valuable advice on trading and resolving disputes in territories with which the exporter is unfamiliar.

Differences

- **Invoice discounting** – the debtors need not know the book debts have been sold.

    Factoring – the debtors know the book debts have been sold.

- **Invoice discounting** – the debtors pay the discountee direct in settlement of the invoices.

    Factoring – the debtors are instructed to pay the factor direct in settlement of the invoices.

- **Invoice discounting** – the business runs its own sales ledger and collects the debts.

- **Factoring** – the factor runs the factoree's sales ledger and collects the debts.

Discountee/factoree

- A higher percentage advance against the book debts can be obtained than would normally be the case for a bank overdraft or loan.

- In the absence of default, the finance company is required to give a specified period of notice before the facility can be terminated (i.e., repayment is not 'on demand').

- Amounts drawn down by way of advances can usually be repaid at any time without penalty.

- A factor maintains the factoree's sales ledger, will normally send out monthly statements and provides overdue debt collection services to an agreed level. This can represent a considerable saving on staff, equipment/systems, administration and credit control costs for the factoree.

- The discountee/factoree has the backing of the discounter's/factor's sophisticated credit control systems for setting and monitoring trading limits with individual customers.

- Substantial benefit can be derived from the regular audits undertaken by the discounter/factor. Their specialist skills provide not only a check on the integrity of financial systems, but also valuable input on business trends and developments.

- Invoice discounting and factoring facilities have proved particularly helpful for management buy-outs (MBOs), in meeting working capital funding needs.

- The finance company is primarily interested in the current and forecast levels of activity, not in historic accounts. This is especially useful to growing businesses needing a flexible facility.

- If entering fresh (e.g., export) markets, the experience of the finance company can be very helpful.

- When the debts (receivables) relate to exports, the discounter/factor may have a representative in the importer's country who can advise on credit risk and help with debt collection or other problems. They might even be able to assist the importer in arranging its local financing.

- The advance payment can usually be received within one business day of the invoices being issued to debtors – making it easier to predict and manage funding requirements.

Discounter/factor

- Earns interest (discount rate) and an administration fee.
- May earn commission on provision of credit insurance.
- Establishes relationships with businesses that might enable it to offer additional services in the future.

- If their parent is a bank, it keeps the business within the group, and reduces the risks of another financial institution becoming the principal financier.

Discountee/factoree

- That a debtor will not pay in settlement of invoice(s) and the advance(s) will have to be repaid to the finance company (unless credit insurance has been arranged or a non-recourse agreement provides for the finance company to bear such losses in return for an additional fee). If the debts are in foreign currency, there will be an exposure to adverse exchange rate movements on repayment unless the discounter/factor has agreed to accept this risk.

- A minimum level of turnover is usually required.

- When invoice discounting, your sales ledger systems must be reliable, and on an 'open item' basis (i.e., showing every outstanding invoice separately and not just the net balance of receipts and payments).

- To control your financing, you need to be able to forecast future invoicing levels with reasonable accuracy.

- Whereas a bank borrowing facility is generally available, albeit often subject to repayment on demand, up to its limit at all times, this is not true with invoice discounting or factoring. If you do not have outstanding acceptable book debts, then you cannot obtain finance. Even where your bank requires a facility to be covered by book debts (receivables) with a specified margin, the reality is that by the time you submit any required return to the bank (usually monthly) and they have looked at them and got back to you, the debtor position will probably have changed. For that reason, the available level of a bank facility linked to debtors is rarely, in practice, as closely related to the level of book debts as might in theory be supposed. With invoice discounting or factoring, immediate adjustment of the facility occurs every time an invoice is issued, is paid or is overdue.

- Once a discountee/factoree enters into invoice discounting or factoring, its bank will usually withdraw all or part of any facility that was dependent upon the bank having a charge on book debts (receivables). The discountee/factoree may, therefore, have nothing to fall back on if drawings are not available from the discounter/factor. In practice, most discounters/factors are prepared to be flexible, and will accommodate temporary excesses on an agreed basis.

Discounter/factor

- If a debtor does not pay by the due date for settlement of an invoice, then any 'with recourse' advance has to be recovered from the discountee/factoree.

- Where the facility is provided on a non-recourse basis (and without third party credit insurance), the discounter/factor will have to bear any bad debts within the pre-determined limits.

- When invoice discounting, the discountee may receive payment from a debtor but not pay the monies into the discounter's bank account, thereby retaining the original advance when it should be repaid (or have been offset against advances on fresh invoices). The discounter has to recover the advance from the discountee, which could be a problem if they are insolvent.

- Where the debtors (receivables) relate to exports, there may be additional exposure to adverse exchange rate movements if the advance is not recovered.

- If factoring, the debtor may make the payment to the factoree rather than to the factor. Will the factoree account for these monies to the factor? If not, then the factor is normally entitled to demand a second payment in its favour from the debtor, but can that be obtained?

- A fraudulent discountee/factoree could draw advances against non-existent debtors, or against the issue of invoices where the goods or services have not yet been provided.

- Invoices could be 'double discounted' by entering into agreements with two or more finance houses, and drawing advances from each.

- The costs to a factor of initially setting up the systems for any individual factoree can be considerable, and may not be recovered if the facility is terminated after only a short period. For that reason, a minimum term of, say, one year is usually specified in the agreement.

Forfaiting

Definition

> Forfaiting ('à forfait') is the purchase for an immediate discounted cash payment of tenor ('usance'/'term') bills of exchange ('drafts'), promissory notes, letters of credit or other instruments (for example, book receivables) evidencing a sale and deferred payment, without the purchaser having a right of recourse to the beneficiary or to any previous holders if payment is not received at maturity.

Historically, forfaiting was most commonly associated with the provision of medium-term finance for exported capital goods, but in recent years it has been extensively used to finance commodities and lower-value exports over shorter credit periods of 60–360 days.

PARTIES **Exporter** Who draws the tenor bills of exchange (drafts) which are accepted by the importer, or receives the other documents (instruments) evidencing a sale and deferred payment, and then sells them for cash to the forfaiter. For medium-term finance there is typically a series of drafts payable at, say, six-monthly intervals over a period of between one and five years or longer. For shorter-term finance, a single 'bullet' repayment is usual.

Importer   Who accepts the tenor drafts drawn up by the seller, or issues the other instruments evidencing a purchase and the undertaking to pay at maturity.

Guarantor (who might be an 'avalor' – see page 105)   The bank, financial institution or government department which provides a guarantee or adds their 'aval' to the draft or other instrument, guaranteeing that it will be paid ('honoured') at maturity (see Figure 3.6). In the case of an aval, the guarantor signs above their name on either the face or reverse side of the draft or instrument, guaranteeing payment 'pour aval' ('for value').

Alternatively, the guarantor may itself accept a draft or issue a promissory note in favour of the exporter, which can be endorsed by the exporter in favour of the forfaiter.

Without a guarantee or aval, there would be no-one against whom the forfaiter could claim if the drafts or instruments were not honoured on their due date, as the forfaiter has no right of recourse against previous holders (which includes the exporter who sold them to the forfaiter).

Forfaiter   The company, bank or financial institution that buys the tenor drafts or instruments for cash at a discount to face value, without recourse to any previous holder.

The 'discount rate' deducted by the forfaiter when buying the drafts or instruments covers the cost of financing their purchase until maturity plus a margin for their perceived risks. If the tenor until maturity is long, particularly where the transaction is in foreign currency, it can be very difficult to forecast future interest rate movements for the purposes of calculating the discount.

The forfaiter may 'rediscount' (i.e., sell) the drafts or instruments in the secondary market to refinance the transaction or to crystalize its profit.

Forfaiting can also be used to finance domestic trade provided the forfaiter is comfortable with the payment risk on the buyer or other obligor (i.e., a party obliged to pay, usually an acceptor) or an acceptable third party guarantee is available.

Forfaiting is best arranged well in advance, ideally at the same time as the importer and exporter are negotiating the underlying trade contract.

Figure 3.7 shows some specimen forfaiting calculations provided by London Forfaiting Company UK Limited. In this case, a three-year credit period is being provided to a buyer in Thailand, against six half-yearly bills of exchange drawn on and accepted by a first-class Thai bank under their irrevocable letter of credit.

For Acceptance

Pour Aval for account of the drawee:

31.1.97 (PLACE OF ISSUE)..................

US$101,861-11

At/On · 31.10.97 .... for value received, pay against this bill of exchange to

the order of .... (NAME OF EXPORTER) .... **the sum of**

ONE HUNDRED AND ONE THOUSAND, EIGHT HUNDRED AND SIXTY-ONE – 11

effective payment to be made in UNITED STATES DOLLARS , **without deduction for and**

free of any present or future taxes, impost, collection charges, levies or duties of any nature.

This bill of exchange is payable at (NAME AND ADDRESS OF AVALOR/GUARANTEEING BANK)

Drawn on:
(NAME AND ADDRESS OF IMPORTER)

For And On Behalf Of (EXPORTER)

Authorized Signatures

Fig. 3.6 Example of an aval (source: courtesy of London Forfaiting Company UK Limited)

The importer signs the 'Acceptance' box and the avalor signs the 'Aval' box. On the reverse, the exporter makes an endorsement in favour of the forfaiter, for example, 'Pay to the order of London Forfaiting Company UK Limited without recourse. For and on behalf of ... (Exporter). Authorized signature ...'

```
        EXPORT CALCULATION Our Reference: SAMPLE/1

    From:              UK EXPORTER.
    Your reference:    J. SMITH.
    Importer:          BUYER IN THAILAND.
    Guarantor:         FIRST-CLASS THAI BANK.
    Details 1:         EQUIPMENT


                    BASIS OF CALCULATION

    Currency                             US DOLLARS
    Required amount                      500,000.00
    Number of bills                               6
    Interest paid by importer % p.a.          7.1/4
    Method of interest calculation          365/360
    Commitment date                       31/ 1/97
    Interest/shipment date                30/ 4/97
    Discount date                         30/ 5/97
    Commitment fee % p.a.                    0. 3/4
    Days of grace                                 5
    Method of discounting         Semi-annual yield
    Discount rate % p.a.                     7. 3/8


                   SUMMARY OF CALCULATION

    Contract value                       500,000.00
    Principal                            500,000.00
    Interest                              64,410.89
    Total face value                     564,410.89
    Discounted value                     501,404.14
    Total proceeds to exporter           501,404.14
    Commitment fee (119 days)              1,399.27
    Final proceeds                       500,004.87


                      BILL DETAILS

No.  MATURITY   PRINCIPAL    INTEREST    FACE VALUE   NET VALUE
 1   31/10/97   83,333.33   18,527.78   101,861.11   98,647.86
 2   30/ 4/98   83,333.33   15,188.08    98,521.41   92,002.26
 3   31/10/98   83,333.33   12,351.85    95,685.18   86,073.59
 4   30/ 4/99   83,333.33    9,112.85    92,446.18   80,218.61
 5   31/10/99   83,333.33    6,175.93    89,509.26   74,833.77
 6   30/ 4/00   83,333.35    3,054.40    86,387.75   69,628.05
                500,000.00   64,410.89   564,410.89  501,404.14
```

Fig. 3.7 Specimen forfaiting calculations (source: courtesy of London Forfaiting Company UK Limited)

EXPORT CALCULATION Our Reference: SAMPLE/2

From:	UK EXPORTER.
Your reference:	J. SMITH.
Importer:	BUYER IN THAILAND.
Guarantor:	FIRST-CLASS THAI BANK.
Details 1:	EQUIPMENT

BASIS OF CALCULATION

Currency	US DOLLARS
Required amount	500,000.00
Number of bills	6
Interest paid by importer % p.a.	7
Method of interest calculation	365/360
Commitment date	31/ 1/97
Interest/shipment date	30/ 4/97
Discount date	30/ 5/97
Commitment fee % p.a.	0. 3/4
Days of grace	5
Method of discounting	Semi-annual yield
Discount rate % p.a.	7. 3/8

SUMMARY OF CALCULATION

Contract value	500,000.00
Principal	500,000.00
Interest	62,189.81
Total face value	562,189.81
Discounted value	499,377.59
Total proceeds to exporter	499,377.59
Commitment fee (119 days)	1,393.76
Final proceeds	497,983.83

BILL DETAILS

No.	MATURITY	PRINCIPAL	INTEREST	FACE VALUE	NET VALUE
1	31/10/97	83,333.33	17,888.89	101,222.22	98,029.13
2	30/ 4/98	83,333.33	14,664.35	97,997.68	91,513.19
3	31/10/98	83,333.33	11,925.93	95,259.26	85,690.46
4	30/ 4/99	83,333.33	8,798.61	92,131.94	79,945.93
5	31/10/99	83,333.33	5,962.96	89,296.29	74,655.72
6	30/ 4/00	83,333.35	2,949.07	86,282.42	69,543.16
		500,000.00	62,189.81	562,189.81	499,377.59

Fig. 3.7 (Continued)

EXPORT CALCULATION Our Reference: SAMPLE/3

From:	UK EXPORTER.
Your reference:	J. SMITH.
Importer:	BUYER IN THAILAND.
Guarantor:	FIRST-CLASS THAI BANK.
Details 1:	EQUIPMENT

BASIS OF CALCULATION

Currency	US DOLLARS
Required amount	500,000.00
Number of bills	6
Interest paid by importer % p.a.	7
Method of interest calculation	365/360
Commitment date	31/ 1/97
Interest/shipment date	30/ 4/97
Discount date	30/ 5/97
Commitment fee % p.a.	0. 3/4
Days of grace	5
Method of discounting	Semi-annual yield
Discount rate % p.a.	7. 3/8

SUMMARY OF CALCULATION

Contract value (multiplier = 1.0040)	502,024.34
Principal	502,024.34
Interest	62,441.59
Total face value	564,465.93
Discounted value	501,399.39
Total proceeds to exporter	501,399.39
Commitment fee (119 days)	1,399.41
Final proceeds	499,999.98

BILL DETAILS

No.	MATURITY	PRINCIPAL	INTEREST	FACE VALUE	NET VALUE
1	31/10/97	83,670.72	17,961.32	101,632.04	98,426.02
2	30/ 4/98	83,670.72	14,723.72	98,394.44	91,883.69
3	31/10/98	83,670.72	11,974.21	95,644.93	86,037.39
4	30/ 4/99	83,670.72	8,834.23	92,504.95	80,269.91
5	31/10/99	83,670.72	5,987.10	89,657.82	74,957.97
6	30/ 4/00	83,670.74	2,961.01	86,631.75	69,824.71
		502,024.34	62,441.59	564,465.93	501,399.39

Fig. 3.7 (Continued)

1st Bill

$$\frac{\text{No. of days} \times \text{Discount rate}}{360} = a$$

$$\frac{100}{100 + a} = \text{Factor 1}$$

Face value × Factor 1 = Net value

2nd Bill

1. $$\frac{183 \times \text{Discount rate}}{360} = b$$

$$\frac{100}{100 + b} = \text{Factor 2}$$

2. $$\frac{\text{Remaining days} \times \text{Discount rate}}{360} = c$$

$$\frac{100}{100 + c} = \text{Factor 3}$$

Face value × Factor 2 × Factor 3 = Net value

3rd Bill

1. (Factor 2 – above)

2. $$\frac{182 \times \text{Discount rate}}{360} = d$$

$$\frac{100}{100 + d} = \text{Factor 4}$$

3. $$\frac{\text{Remaining days} \times \text{Discount rate}}{360} = e$$

$$\frac{100}{100 + e} = \text{Factor 5}$$

Face value × Factor 2 × Factor 4 × Factor 5 = Net value

Fig. 3.7 (Continued)

Notes

1. 'Remaining days' is the number of days between the discount date and the maturity date, plus the days of grace, plus any business days adjustment, less the number of days used up in calculating preceding factors. For example, with Bill 3 the number of days between 30.5.97 and 31.10.98 is 519, but 31.10.98 falls on a Saturday so a further 2 days must be added to bring the calculation to the next business date. The 5 days of grace must also be added, bringing the total to 526. From this must be deducted the days used in calculating the preceding factors, i.e., 365. Hence, there are 161 remaining days.

2. The interest charge for Bill 6 allows for the fact that, as 2000 is a leap year, there are 182 days between 31.10.99 and 30.4.00, although the calculation remains based on a 'year' of 360 days.

For the purposes of the calculations it is assumed:

- contract/commitment date   –   31.1.97
- shipment date   –   30.4.97
- discount date   –   1 month after shipment.

Calculation SAMPLE/1: This shows that the exporter would need to charge interest to the buyer at 7.25% p.a. on reducing outstanding principal amounts in order to recover all discount and commitment costs.

However, an exporter may decide to subsidize the interest rate in order to put forward a more attractive package to the buyer.

Calculation SAMPLE/2: This shows that if the exporter subsidizes the interest rate to 7% p.a. their final proceeds would represent a shortfall equal to 0.40% flat of the original contract price. The principles and basis of calculation can be applied to whatever level of subsidy is chosen by the exporter.

Calculation SAMPLE/3: This shows how the contract value would need uplifting to recover this shortfall.

Exporter

BENEFITS
including risks
avoided

- Obtains an immediate cash payment for up to 100% of the contract price or for the face value of the drafts (which may include the cost of the discount rate) or other instruments, less the discount rate, on a non-recourse basis. The advance cannot be for less than 100% of the face value of a draft, but the draft might be for less than 100% of the contract price – with the balance having been paid, for example, by the importer to the exporter in cash.

- Does not tie up the normal trading finance facilities provided by the exporter's bank.

- The forfaiter usually provides a speedy response as to whether it will finance individual contracts.

- There is normally no restriction on the country of origin or type of goods being forfaited.

- Uncertainty as to future exchange rate movements until payment at maturity of the drafts or instruments is removed. The forfaiter pays the exporter in the currency of the draft or other instrument (usually a major currency if forfaited), which the exporter can then sell if necessary to obtain local currency.

- By offering the importer credit, the exporter may secure sales that would otherwise not have been possible. The exporter can also subsidize the interest cost normally borne by the importer if it helps to win the business and still leaves enough profit to be worthwhile.

- The documentation is straightforward.

- The exporter does not have to collect the payment at maturity.

Importer

- Does not have to pay until maturity. In practice, there are usually a series of drafts with different maturity dates, so that the importer is effectively 'paying by instalments'.

- Can obtain credit for up to 100% of the contract price, or the face value of the drafts or other instruments, at a fixed rate of interest. The forfaiter's discount rate, including provision for interest at a fixed rate, is normally borne by the importer and included in the amount of the drafts (unless otherwise agreed with the exporter).

Forfaiter

- The drafts can be sold in the secondary market, making it possible for the forfaiter to raise funds at attractive rates.

RISKS
REMAINING

Exporter

- Is still liable to the importer for satisfactory performance of the contract.

- If the exporter bears the discount rate, the fixed rate of interest it incorporates may, over the period of the finance, prove to be higher than the average of the short-term market rates.

Importer

- If the fixed rate of interest charged by the forfaiter is borne by the importer (i.e., included in the amount of the drafts), it may prove to be higher than the average of short-term market rates over the period of the finance.

- If the finance is in a currency other than its local currency, the importer will have an exchange rate risk until payment. Forfaiting is usually only available if the drafts or other instruments are in a major currency.

Forfaiter

- That the acceptor or avalor of the draft (or other party liable under any forfaited instrument) will not pay on maturity, or will be prevented from doing so. Country risk is an important factor – including exchange controls. Forfaiters, like banks, must mark 'country limits'.

- If the projections as to future interest rates are incorrect then the discount rate may be too low and a loss incurred.

- The drafts or instruments must provide for an unconditional payment at maturity, to avoid the risk that the importer will claim a failure by the exporter (against whom the forfaiter has no recourse) to fulfill its contractual obligations as grounds for non-payment.

Acceptance credits

> *An acceptance credit (banker's acceptance) is a source of short-term finance where a bank accepts a bill of exchange (draft) drawn on it by a customer, which is discounted after acceptance and the discounted value paid to the customer.*

A draft (bill of exchange) usually for a maximum tenor of six months and relating to a trading transaction, is drawn by a customer on its bank. The bank accepts the draft (it is then a 'bank bill'), and pays its face value to the customer less a discount (to cover interest at a fixed rate for the tenor of the draft) and an acceptance commission.

Because it is a bank bill, it can be sold in the discount market by the bank at an advantageous rate, to raise the funds used to pay the customer. Alternatively, it may simply be held by the bank until maturity. (Sometimes the draft is returned to the customer after acceptance by the bank, and the customer itself rediscounts it in the market.)

At the maturity date, the customer pays the bank the face value of the draft and, if it had been sold into the market, the holder at that time will present it to the bank for payment.

This facility is usually only provided to established customers for transactions of a reasonable size.

In practice, the bank normally holds a stock of drafts already signed by the customer, but otherwise blank. When the customer needs funds, it asks the bank to fill in a draft with the amount and maturity date, which the bank then accepts, making the payment to the customer.

In some countries, the drafts accepted by certain banks are eligible for 'rediscounting' at attractive rates in either the market or with the central bank ('as lender of last resort'). Depending again on the country, the draft may either need to be 'claused' (as in the UK), with details of the underlying trade transaction, e.g., to finance the sale of printing machinery from UK to France and/or (as in the US) be supported by documentation evidencing the trade transaction. It is not usually necessary for any underlying import/export to directly involve the country where the accepting bank is located.

Negotiating a bill of exchange/draft

Definition	*The sale of a bill of exchange (draft) for an immediate cash payment.*

The buyer of the draft usually has recourse against its seller if it is not honoured at maturity.

See also *Advances against collections (bill advances)*, page 182.

EXAMPLE **Collections**

At the same time as asking its bank (remitting bank) to undertake a collection, an exporter can also request it to 'negotiate' the draft. This means that the bank buys, with recourse to the exporter, the bill of exchange (draft) together with any other documents, paying upfront 100% of the draft's face value. The bank then proceeds with the collection as *principal*. The collecting/presenting bank is not usually aware of the negotiation.

Interest, calculated to the date when payment *should* be received, is charged by the bank to the exporter (at the applicable currency interest rate if the negotiation is of a currency draft), together with any bank's commission. As the date when payment will be received cannot be known with certainty, the usual practice is to allow a safety margin of time in the bank's favour when calculating the period for which interest is charged.

If the draft is dishonoured (notice of which may be delayed for a considerable period of time), the negotiating bank can claim reimbursement in full from the exporter, and/or proceed against the importer if they had accepted the draft. The bank normally has title to the goods to which the collection related, although these may already have been released to the importer (it is obviously safer if the collection is 'documents against payment' (D/P) than if 'documents against acceptance' (D/A), as with the latter the importer can obtain the goods and then subsequently dishonour the accepted draft).

EXAMPLE **Documentary letters of credit**

When issuing a letter of credit the issuing bank can nominate the advising, or any other, bank to negotiate drafts (which for a letter of credit must have been drawn on a bank) against presentation by the beneficiary of the specified documents in good order. Repayment to the negotiating bank comes from payment by the issuing bank under the letter of credit.

If the negotiating bank is also the confirming bank under a letter of credit, then it does not have recourse to the exporter. Similarly, even where the letter of credit is unconfirmed, the negotiating bank loses the right of recourse against the exporter if payment is refused by the issuing bank on the grounds of errors in the documents that the negotiating bank overlooked.

Seller of draft

- Receives cash upfront.
- Can immediately convert the proceeds of a foreign-currency negotiation into local currency at spot rate, eliminating exchange rate risk unless the negotiating bank claims recourse on non-payment.

Negotiating bank

- Earns interest and commission on the negotiation and any foreign exchange or other related transactions.
- The source, and approximate timing, of anticipated reimbursement of the amount negotiated is known.

Seller of draft

- Has to repay the negotiating bank if the draft is not paid.
- Exposed to any adverse exchange rate movements if it has to buy currency to reimburse the negotiating bank in the event of non-payment.

Negotiating bank

- Has to consider the credit risks of the seller of the draft (unless the negotiating bank is also the confirming bank under a letter of credit when it has no right of recourse), the drawee and any acceptor (including country risk and after taking into account any credit insurance), the likely saleability of the goods if that became the method of repayment, whether possession of the goods could be obtained and if collection is D/P or D/A.
- Potential exposure to adverse exchange rate movements on non-payment of a currency negotiation if recourse cannot be had from the seller of the draft.
- The right of recourse against the seller of the draft only arises when the draft is dishonoured.
- Overlooking errors in documents presented under a letter of credit.
- Ensuring a tenor draft is presented for payment on its maturity, and protested if dishonoured.
- The issue or any acceptance of the draft *ultra vires*, and do all previous parties have good title (e.g., if stolen, a subsequent holder does not acquire a good title)?

Noting and protesting

If, when presented for acceptance or payment, a draft is not paid or accepted by the drawee or intended acceptor, it is dishonoured. Then it is the usual practice (and often essential if legal rights are to be protected) for a lawyer, notary or other person, depending on the jurisdiction in the non-acceptor's country, to be requested to re-present the draft for payment or acceptance and to 'note' any dishonour (which is recorded on the draft itself or on an attached piece of paper). This may be followed by a formal document known as a 'protest'. In the protest the notary or other party gives details of the bill and its dishonour. These actions need to be taken within a short time of the original dishonour in a way that is acceptable to courts of law.

Advances against collections (bill advances)

Unlike negotiations, where the bank 'owns' the documents, with an advance against collection (bill advance), it only lends against them (although it may take a pledge of the documents as collateral). The loan is usually limited to a percentage of the face value of the draft, but for some customers, this may be a full 100%.

The bank undertakes the collection on behalf of a customer, against whom it has recourse if the draft is not paid. A key difference from negotiations is that an advancing bank can usually demand repayment of the loan at any time, whereas a negotiation only becomes repayable by a customer on non-payment of the draft.

Advances can be particularly useful where a customer needs to borrow only part of the face value of the draft.

Derivatives: the basics

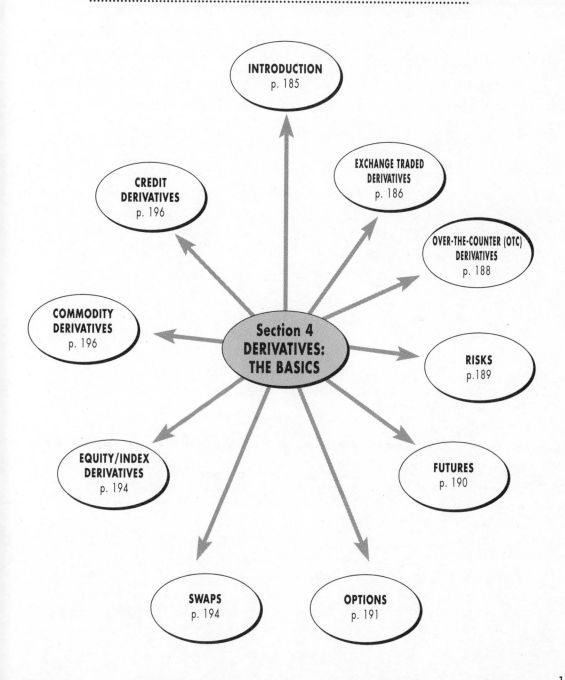

Introduction

....

Derivatives can be used:

- to protect ('hedge') against risks *or*
- to speculate in the hope of profit.

They fall into three principal categories:

- futures
- swaps
- options.

Derivatives are available to cover many types of exposure, including:

- interest rates
- foreign currency exchange rates
- commodities: energy (e.g., oil and gas), bullion (e.g., gold and silver), base metals (e.g., copper and nickel) and agricultural (e.g., sugar and pork bellies)
- equities.

The gain or loss under a financial derivative depends on (or 'derives from') movements in the market price of the asset or index to which the contract relates (known as the 'underlying').

Derivatives where one counterparty has to pay a premium (see *Options*, page 191) give that counterparty the choice of whether or not to exercise their rights under the contract. If it is in their interests not to exercise the contract, then they can simply let it lapse (e.g., because at the settlement date(s) they can get a better deal in the market than under the derivative contract). By contrast, the counterparty who is paid the premium has no choice but to meet its obligations under the contract if requested to do so by the payer of the premium.

Derivative contracts where no premium is paid at the outset (e.g., futures and swaps) commit *both* counterparties to complete the transaction at settlement date(s), which normally means that one of them will have to make a payment to the other.

Derivatives can be either 'exchange traded' or 'over the counter' ('OTC').

Exchange traded derivatives

Exchange traded derivatives are bought and sold on recognized exchanges throughout the world, amongst the best known being the Chicago Board of Trade (CBOT) and the London International Financial Futures and Options Exchange (LIFFE – pronounced 'life' not 'liffy').

If derivative contracts are readily tradeable in volume on an exchange, they are said to have 'liquidity'. This requires the contracts to be of standard unit sizes and specification (ie, to be fungible).

To deal in larger amounts than a standard contract unit, you simply buy or sell more contracts.

Trading may be conducted by 'open outcry' and/or by 'electronic' computer-based dealing, subject to the rules of the exchange.

Open outcry is where traders, who are either members of the exchange or the authorized representatives of a member, stand in areas known as 'pits' – there are different pits for different derivative contracts – on the 'trading floor', and shout out their buying or selling needs, using hand signals to complement the procedure. Depending on the arrangement of fingers, and whether the hand signals show the palm or back of the hand, the other traders know whether a trader is in the market to buy or sell, in what quantity of the standard contracts, the contract month and the price at which they wish to trade.

For example, a trader on LIFFE wishing to buy (bid) shows the back of their hand to a potential seller (keeping the palm towards their own body). A trader wishing to sell (offer) shows the palm of their hand to a potential buyer. The last digit(s) of the price at which they wish to trade is shown by the fingers of the hand (prices 1 to 5 by fingers held vertically, prices 6 to 9 by fingers held horizontally, 10 and 0 by a clenched fist and 00 by a clenched fist shown twice). The number of contracts they wish to trade is indicated using fingers as for prices (and showing the back of hand or palm for buying or selling respectively) but touching the chin for 1 to 9, touching the forehead for tens (e.g., three vertical fingers on the forehead show 30, two horizontal fingers on the forehead show 70), and a combination for intermediate numbers (e.g., five vertical fingers on the forehead, then two horizontal fingers on the chin for 57).

There are separate signals to show option puts and calls, prices in fractions, the trading month and acknowledgement that a trade has been accepted by another trader.

Each trader wears a jacket, the colours of which show the firm that they work for, or if they are trading on their own behalf. Members of the exchange trading for themselves are called 'Locals'.

At close of business in the pits, trading continues 'after hours' by means of computer links between the members of the exchange, and for some contracts between exchanges in different countries.

Once the deal has been agreed, a 'clearing house' associated with the exchange (and which may be owned by the exchange itself or by banks or other financial institutions) steps in. From that point onwards, the clearing house act as the counterparty to *both* the buyer and the seller of the contract. Each counterparty is, therefore, taking its credit risk on the clearing house and not on the other counterparty. As some derivative exposures can last for years, this is a valuable safeguard.

If you want to deal in exchange traded derivatives, but are not a member of an exchange, it will be necessary to act through a broker, who transacts the trade on your behalf. It is important to note that the clearing house is not a party to the contract between a broker and the client for whom the broker transacts trades on the exchange.

The price of an exchange traded derivative is whatever it fetches in the market, e.g., through 'open outcry'. There are, however, restrictions on the minimum amounts by which prices for each of the standard derivative contracts can move. These minimum movements are known as 'ticks', and differ from one type of derivative to another.

For example, the unit of trading on LIFFE for a three-month Euro-deutschmark ('Euromark') interest rate future is DM1,000,000 and the 'tick size' (i.e., the minimum permitted price movement when trading on the exchange) is 0.01%. The 'tick value' is, therefore, DM25; being:

$$ \text{DM1m} \times \frac{0.01}{100} \times \frac{3}{12} $$

(3/12, as the contract is for three-month Eurodeutschmark.)

At the time of committing to a contract, *each* trader has to pay an amount of money know as the 'initial margin' to the clearing house. Both traders pay the same initial margin, whether they are buying or selling. This initial margin is a set amount which differs for each standard derivative contract and is calculated to cover the likely maximum trading loss on that contract on any single day (the set amount is based on trading experience and projections, and will be changed by the clearing house as market circumstances alter using the standard portfolio analysis of risk system – 'SPAN'). Each business day, every outstanding contract (i.e., those recorded by the exchange as not having reached their settlement date) is 'settled to market'. The contracts are 'marked to market', being revalued at the current price in the market. If the value of the contract has changed since the previous business day, the amount of that change is credited by the clearing house to one of the counterparties (in whose favour the market has moved) and debited to the other (against whom the market has moved). This means that profits and losses are crystalized and paid every business day. The daily payment is known as the 'variation margin', and is in addition to the initial margin (active traders are required to top up their margin deposit when it falls below a set minimum 'maintenance' level). Whether it is the trader who bought or the trader who sold the contract who has to pay depends on the way the price has moved. Neither trader knows from day to day if they will be the one paying or receiving the variation margin, nor how much, as it depends on the movement in the market.

The initial margin should, at any time, be sufficient to protect the clearing house from loss if it has to 'close out' a contract because, for example, a counterparty fails to pay the variation margin on any day. Thus, the margin system enables the clearing house to act as counterparty to both the buyer and the seller of the contract without incurring undue financial risk.

Imagine the problems in trading, and lack of market liquidity, if counterparties had to assess the credit exposure and directly settle margins with all other traders with whom they were dealing.

Whether they have bought or sold a contract, a counterparty can at any time let it lapse by failing to pay that day's variation margin. The clearing house will then close out the contract.

Counterparties, therefore, know the extent of their profits or losses, and can choose to terminate the contract, on any day.

At the 'settlement' (or 'delivery') date on expiry of a contract (these are pre-set dates, usually quarterly, for each type of exchange traded contract), there is a final settlement between the parties, and the initial margins, together with the interest earned thereon, are refunded to the respective counterparties.

In practice, few exchange traded contracts run their full term until the settlement date, as most are closed out before then.

Over-the-counter (OTC) derivatives

Over-the-counter derivatives are contracts written to meet the specific needs of individual clients, such as businesses, banks or governments. They are usually provided by banks or other financial institutions, *and cannot be traded on any exchange*. The actual contract document is likely to be based on the standard terms and conditions of an organization such as the International Swaps and Derivatives Association (ISDA).

OTC derivatives can be very attractive products for banks to offer, as they may enable them to satisfy a client's financial needs without having to mark the higher 'limits' required for conventional facilities (as the risk on the derivative is usually only for market movements and not for the entire principal amount on which the contract is based). This leaves limits free for other services or customers, and may reduce the bank's capital adequacy requirements.

As there is no need for OTC derivatives to be in the standardized units necessary for trading on an exchange, they can be for whatever amounts and periods best suit an individual client.

The disadvantage of an OTC derivative is that it may not have the 'liquidity' that comes from exchange trading, although (whilst not obligated to do so) banks will usually agree to close out or repurchase their contracts at a price.

The most common OTC derivatives are 'swaps' and 'options'.

With an OTC contract, the pricing of the derivative is negotiated between the counterparties (i.e., normally between a bank and a client), although it is often possible for a client to obtain comparative prices from different banks.

As there is no clearing house to take the credit risk, it falls to each counterparty to accept any credit risk on the other counterparty, and for some derivative instruments this exposure can last for years. The credit risk is for that amount which would be required to close out or replace a transaction if a counterparty defaulted, being usually equivalent to only a percentage of the notional principal. As with any risk, the longer its term the greater the chance of something going wrong.

There may also be exposure to 'settlement risk'. This is usually for the entire amount due under the contract, and exists from the point of settlement of the contract until the cash payment or other 'delivery' is actually received from the counterparty. For some derivatives payment may not be due until several days after the settlement date, but often the settlement risk only exists during the day of settlement ('daylight' exposure) or until the next day ('overnight' exposure). However long it takes, the exposure remains until payment is received.

In a swap contract, a bank or other provider may be acting as an intermediary between two counterparties, who may not even know the other's identity. Each counterparty is then taking a credit risk on the bank, whilst the bank has an exposure to both counterparties.

A counterparty may be required to provide collateral security if their unsecured covenant would otherwise be regarded as an unacceptable credit risk, although this is unusual.

Risks

The risks that may be associated with exchange traded or OTC derivatives include:

- **credit risk** – on counterparties, including country exposure
- **settlement risk** – where one counterparty pays cash or delivers assets before the other counterparty is known to have honoured their obligations
- **aggregation risk** – where the derivative transaction involves more than one market in which problems could be experienced

- **operational risk** – e.g., are there defects in a trader's risk or pricing models, or in their 'back office' administrative systems?

- **market risk** – being the exposure to potential losses resulting from market rate movements

- **liquidity risk** – if the markets are not liquid enough to trade out of problems or may even 'dry up' (e.g., can you deal in the amounts needed without moving market prices?)

- **legal risk** – of contractual non-validity, e.g., with netting agreements and cross-border insolvency or the counterparties' powers (ultra vires)

- **reputational risk** – where the actions of a financial institution damage its reputation to the extent that they lose business or offer to bear or share losses suffered by their customers

- **concentration risk** – by being exposed to too high a level of risk in any product or sector, i.e., inadequate diversity or 'spread' of risks (an extension of concentration risk is the risk to a market if too high a level of business in one area, e.g., swaps or options, is being conducted by only a small number of firms).

It will be seen that some of these risks, for example 'settlement', could involve the full amount of principal whereas others are more likely to involve only partial loss.

On a grander scale is 'systemic risk', where problems in one financial institution or market may cross over to others and to other countries on a domino effect, potentially threatening chaos in the global financial markets. This is the stuff of central bankers' and other supervisors' nightmares.

Futures

Interest rate futures... *page 212*
Currency futures... *page 256*
Equity/index futures.. *page 194*

Futures are exchange traded derivative contracts, which *commit* the counterparties to respectively buy or sell a pre-set amount of a financial instrument at an agreed price at a specified future date.

Being exchange traded, the size of the unit of trading, delivery dates and tick values are pre-set, and it will be necessary to buy whatever number of contracts is needed to match your requirements.

Each counterparty pays an initial margin to the clearing house with variation margin payments or receipts being made every business day throughout the life of the contract.

There is no 'premium' to pay.

Futures can be 'closed out' (buying or selling a contract opposite to that already held with settlement of the difference in cash) on any business day before the expiry date of the contract, and only a small percentage run their full term.

Being exchange traded, the credit risk is on the clearing house.

Options

Interest rate options .... *page 219*
Currency options .... *page 249*
Equity/index options .... *page 194*

An option contract gives the buyer (the 'holder') the right but not the obligation to buy or sell something (the 'underlying') at an agreed price (the 'strike price') within a specified time limit.

Options differ from other types of derivative in that one of the counterparties, called the buyer, *has the right but not the obligation* to exercise the contract. The other counterparty, called the writer (or 'seller') must perform their side of the contract if called upon to do so by the buyer.

There is no payment, receipt or other transfer of the notional amount of principal on which the option is based. Settlement is for the difference between the 'strike price' chosen at the outset by the buyer and the market rate on the date the contract is exercised.

An option which is not exercised lapses on its expiry date.

Options are both exchange traded and available over the counter, the latter mostly from banks.

The buyer, in return for the advantage of being able to decide whether or not to exercise the contract (which they will only do if the rates at that time are in their favour), pays a non-returnable fee called a 'premium' to the writer of the contract. The writer does not pay a premium to the buyer.

The only cost of an option to the buyer is the premium, but the potential benefit to the buyer is unlimited (i.e., there is no limit to how much the writer may have to pay to the buyer).

By contrast, the only benefit to the writer is the premium it receives from the buyer, but the cost to the writer if the buyer exercises the option is potentially unlimited.

An option contract which, if exercised by the buyer, requires the writer to sell something (i.e., to sell the 'the underlying') to the buyer is called a 'call option' (e.g., the buyer has the right to buy a specified amount of foreign currency from the writer).

An option contract which, if exercised by the buyer, requires the writer to buy something (i.e., to buy the 'underlying') from the buyer is called a 'put option' (e.g., the buyer has the right to sell a specified amount of foreign currency to the writer).

You can, therefore, be the *buyer* (holder) or *writer* (seller) of either a *put* or a *call* option.

In the case of interest rate options the contract is a 'lender's option' if the benefit to the buyer is that it has the right but not the obligation to *receive* a fixed amount of interest. It is a 'borrower's option' if the right is to *pay* a fixed amount of interest.

The price at which the writer must buy or sell the underlying if the contract is exercised by the buyer is called the 'strike'(or 'exercise') price (or 'rate').

The strike price is chosen by the buyer at the time of entering into the contract, to suit their needs.

There are two styles of option:

- **European** – where the contract can only be exercised by the buyer on its specified expiry date
- **American** – where the contract can be exercised by the buyer on any business day up to and including the specified expiry date.

The difference between the strike price and the current market rate for the underlying is known as the 'intrinsic value'.

If the strike price is more advantageous to the buyer than the market rate for the underlying, the contract is 'in the money' (ITM) (e.g., a call option where the strike price is below the market price, or a put option where the strike price is above the market price). The option has intrinsic value.

If the strike price is less advantageous to the buyer than the market rate for the underlying, the contract is 'out of the money' (OTM).

If the strike price is the same as the market rate the contract is 'at the money' (ATM).

Where the strike price is ATM or OTM, the intrinsic value is zero, as it cannot be a negative figure.

The more ITM the strike price chosen by the buyer at the date of entering into the contract, the higher the premium to be paid to the writer.

The premium is a combination of:

- the present value of the difference between the strike price and the market price for the underlying (i.e., the intrinsic value), so a put increases in value as the price of the underlying falls (as the buyer of the option can require the writer to buy at more than market price), and a call increases in value as the price of the underlying increases (as the buyer of the option can require the writer to deliver at less than the market price), *and*

- the 'time value,' which has two components:

  - the time to expiry of the option contract, as the risk to the writer that the underlying might cost more is greater the longer the contract has to run, and even with an American-style contract the longer the time to expiry, the more times there are when it might potentially be in the buyer's interest to exercise the option
  - the 'volatility' of the underlying: if the market price of the underlying normally shows little variation, then the risk of it costing more on the expiry date is less than for an unstable underlying, where there are potentially more occasions when the option might favour the buyer.

The nearer a contract gets to its expiry date, the less the uncertainty and, hence, the smaller the time value. By the expiry date itself, there is no uncertainty, as the exercise rate is known, and time value will be zero. The value of an option is said to 'decay' over time.

It will be seen that the difference between the intrinsic value and the premium is the time value.

The price of the option premium also allows for the interest the writer can earn on the premium. Hence, the premium may be marginally smaller if interest rates are high.

The date on which the writer has to deliver the underlying or make payment to the buyer is the 'value date'. For interest rate options, the value date is the same as the expiry date. For currency options, the value date may be later than the expiry date (e.g., say two days may be allowed between the expiry and value date for the writer to deliver the currency).

For a currency option, the market rate with which the strike price is compared differs depending on whether it is a European-style or an American-style option. For an American-style option, the market rate used would be the higher of the spot and the forward US$ to sterling £ (as the buyer could exercise the option on any business day it wished), whereas for a European-style option, the market rate used would be the forward rate for the specified expiry date (as the contract could be exercised only on that date).

Instead of waiting until the specified expiry date the buyer of an option can sell it back to the writer at any time before the expiry date for its 'fair value'.

Swaps

···········

Interest rate swaps .... *page 229*
Currency swaps.. *page 257*
Equity/index swaps .... *page 195*

Swaps are 'over-the-counter' derivatives where the counterparties commit to make and to receive payments, e.g., to swap fixed for floating rate interest streams and/or to swap one currency for another currency at an agreed rate of exchange at a specified future date.

They are used mostly by banks, governments and larger corporates.

Equity/index derivatives

···

Equity and index futures and options are used to hedge or speculate against market price movements in either individual equities (shares/stocks) or in equity indices.

For example, FTSE 100 Index exchange traded contracts (as available from LIFFE) enable a buyer to hedge or speculate against a weighted index of 100 UK blue chip quoted companies with an aggregate capitalization approximately two thirds that of the total UK equity market.

The Standard & Poor's 500 Index uses 500 major New York Stock Exchange stocks.

Each derivative exchange will offer contracts on the indices or shares appropriate to their traders' needs.

(With OTC contracts, you may be able to select your own index or basket of individual shares/stocks.)

If, for example, a fund manager wished to protect against the value of their portfolio falling, they could buy an option to hedge against that risk, whilst being able to let the option lapse and retain the profit (less the cost of the premium) if the market value of their portfolio increased.

A buyer of FTSE 100 Index futures at a price of, say, 3000 could either 'close out' the contracts before the final trading day, or settle for cash on the final trading day in the delivery month at the 'exchange delivery settlement price' ('EDSP'). Let us suppose that the buyer settles at an EDSP of 3200. The buyer's profit would be the size of the movement in index points (i.e., 200, being 3200 less 3000) multiplied by the standard trading unit for FTSE 100 Index futures of £25 per 'index point'. Their profit would be £5,000.

Whereas contracts for individual shares/stocks may be settled by delivery of those shares/stocks, contracts based on indices are cash settled.

With exchange traded equity and index put and call options on individual equities (e.g., British Telecom) or on an index (e.g., FTSE 100 Index) the buyer pays the premium upfront. The available strike ('exercise') prices are set by the exchange at levels above and below the current market price for the equity or index. For example, if the market price of an individual share in company ABC was 500p, the available options might be set with strike prices at intervals between, say, 450p and 550p. You could, therefore, buy call options in January giving the right to buy 1,000 shares in ABC at, say, 450p per share with expiry dates in March, June and September. If, for our example, the premium was 35p and the 'intrinsic' value (i.e., the difference between the strike price and the market price) was 20p, then the 'time' value element of the premium would be 15p. As with other options, the time value would depend on the length of time to the expiry of the contract and the volatility of the price of the company's shares in the market.

It will be seen that 'gearing' or 'leverage' is an important factor in equity/index trading, as the cost of the derivative is less than the cost of buying the portfolio/spread of shares that it represents.

If using an index to hedge a portfolio, you may need to weight the number of contracts, as the index is unlikely to be a perfect match to the portfolio (i.e., will not exactly 'track', resulting in 'tracking error').

Equity index swaps are OTC contracts where the two counterparties swap the income streams on either two indices (e.g., that on the Japanese Nikkei 225 Index for that on the Dow Jones Industrial Average Index) or on one index and a floating interest rate base (e.g., LIBOR). The amount payable by way of 'income stream' on an index is based on the movement of the index, which could be positive or negative (dividend income may be included in the calculation). It is, therefore, possible for one counterparty to have to pay both the floating rate interest and for the movement in the index, whilst the other counterparty pays nothing.

Normally the payments between counterparties would be netted off at pre-set dates during the life of the swap.

Use of an OTC equity index swap enables a fund manager to hold (or avoid the costs of selling and later repurchasing) a portfolio of stocks and shares for the longer term, while earning money market rates in the short term. Alternatively, cash can be held whilst benefiting from increases in the index.

Equity index swaps are also used in the hope of benefiting from gains in overseas indices without incurring the costs and problems of actually investing overseas, and can be highly tax-efficient.

It will be seen that the risks of equity index swaps can be substantial, as a counterparty can be exposed for the term of the swap to large market movements, and they may have additionally to pay the interest on any money market element.

- Swaps are based on indices, not on single stocks or shares.

- Futures are based on indices and very rarely on single stocks and shares.

- Options are based on indices and also on many single stocks and shares.

Commodity derivatives

Trading in commodity derivatives covers gold and other precious metals ('bullion'), oil and gas ('energy'), copper and other base metals, and agricultural produce (grain, pork bellies, coffee, sugar, etc., sometimes known as 'softs').

Commodity derivative instruments are similar to their financial equivalents, and may be exchange or over-the-counter traded. They are used both to hedge and to speculate.

A business wishing to hedge its exposure may enter into a reverse matching derivative. For example, if it is 'long the physical' (i.e., already owns the physical commodity, e.g., grain), then it can 'short the future' (i.e., enter into a futures contract to hedge the risk of falls in the market price of the commodity). The opposite terms are 'short the physical' and 'long the future.'

'Delivery' usually means settling the derivative contract for cash, although some involve physical delivery of the commodity.

To take another example: an oil company wishes to protect against a fall in the value of oil. If it enters into futures contracts, there is no premium to pay and the downside could be protected, but profit would be forfeited if oil prices increased rather than fell. The company could buy put options at an appropriate strike price. If the price of oil increases, the option will be allowed to lapse and the profit taken from sale of the oil at the higher price (less the cost of the premium for the option). If the price of oil falls, the option can be exercised and the company will receive the strike price (less the cost of the premium for the option).

Credit derivatives

Credit derivatives transfer the credit risk on transactions such as loans, bonds or other derivative instruments. They are over-the-counter derivatives.

In its simplest form, the 'credit swap' provides for one of the counterparties to the credit derivative contract to receive a cash payment from the other counterparty if the value of the 'reference debt' falls as a result of specified 'credit events' (which require careful definition in the documentation).

One alternative is the total return swap, where the counterparty owning the reference debt exchanges the income from it with a counterparty who pays in return (say) money market rate plus or minus a margin.

The debtor need not be aware that the debt has become subject to a swap.

Derivative swaps can open fresh credit (and bond) markets to banks and investors, whilst removing or reducing the credit risks and capital adequacy requirements on the original holder of the debt and creating greater liquidity of loan portfolios.

Interest Rate Risk

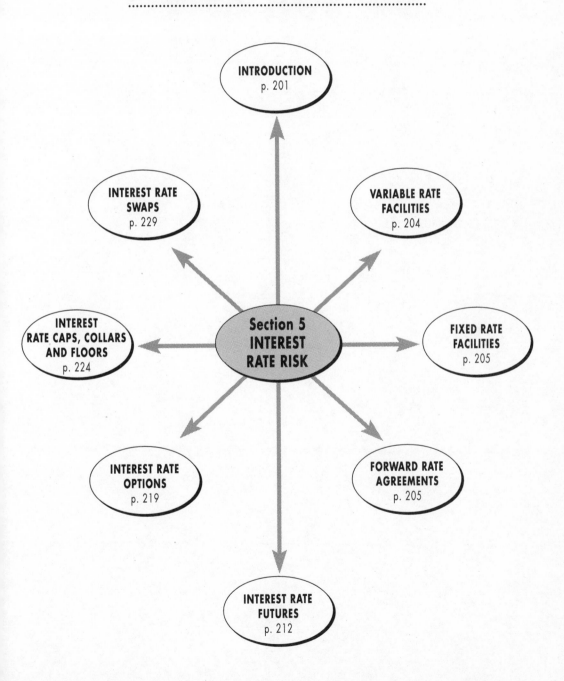

INTRODUCTION
p. 201

INTEREST RATE
SWAPS
p. 229

VARIABLE RATE
FACILITIES
p. 204

INTEREST
RATE CAPS, COLLARS
AND FLOORS
p. 224

Section 5
INTEREST
RATE RISK

FIXED RATE
FACILITIES
p. 205

INTEREST RATE
OPTIONS
p. 219

FORWARD RATE
AGREEMENTS
p. 205

INTEREST RATE
FUTURES
p. 212

Introduction

....

If lending or borrowing money, you will want to know the answers to these questions.

- On what basis is the interest rate determined?
- What is the rate of interest at the start?
- Is the interest rate fixed or variable, and for what periods of time ('terms')?
- What happens at the end of any rollover period for variable rate interest?
- When is the interest payable?

With a variable ('floating') rate the interest on your borrowing, lending or deposit changes, either immediately or on agreed 'rollover' dates, in line with any changes in the base upon which it is calculated. At a rollover date which ends a 'rollover period', a new rate must be set (unless the borrowing or deposit is repaid), by which time rates could have moved up or down.

The alternative is that the rate of interest is 'fixed' for the entire term of the facility. You are then insulated during that term from interest rate changes and know what you will pay or receive on your borrowing, lending or deposit for that period. To have fixed the rate is beneficial if the market rate subsequently moves in a way that would otherwise have been to your disadvantage, but you forfeit the opportunity of benefiting from movements that would have been in your favour.

It is to remove or limit the risk of adverse interest rate movements, or to profit from favourable changes, that the practices and instruments described in the following pages have been developed.

It is important to remember the following points.

- Interest is usually payable in arrears, often monthly, quarterly, half-yearly or annually. The longer the period of time before you pay or receive interest, the lower its present value.

- The rates of interest on borrowings or deposits in foreign currencies may, at any given time, be more attractive than you can obtain in your own domestic currency. If you need to borrow, but are expecting to receive income from trading or other activities in a foreign currency that could be used to service and repay a debt in that currency, then it can be worth while considering a matching currency borrowing in the interim (see page 244). Similarly, if you have surplus foreign currency, but will need it to make future payments in that currency, the funds can meanwhile be invested in a currency deposit. Otherwise, to borrow or deposit funds in foreign currency(s) simply because interest rates are better than in your domestic currency means that you are taking a risk on future exchange rate movements, which could potentially cost you far more than any interest rate benefits.

Whether you need to borrow or have surplus funds to deposit, the rate of interest to be paid or received will depend upon a combination of some or all of the following.

- **Risk** The greater the concern of the lender or depositor that they may be unable to recover all or some of their money, for whatever reasons, the higher the reward they will want for putting their funds at risk.

- **Term** (the length of time for which monies are to be borrowed or deposited) The longer the term, the greater the opportunity for something to happen that could prevent the borrower repaying the monies. The credit risk of this may be small if repayment is on demand or due within a short time, but who knows what the position may be in, say, two years, even less in five years.

- **Forecasts** If market interest rates are projected to either increase or decrease, then that will be factored into fixed rates for medium- and longer-term loans or deposits.

- **Amount** The rate of interest often varies according to the amount of money involved (the 'principal' or 'capital'). Other things being equal, larger amounts usually attract preferential rates, as the overhead and control costs may be proportionately lower.

- **Inflation** A provider of funds hopes (albeit often in vain) to earn a rate of interest at least equal to the rate of inflation over the term of the loan or deposit, as otherwise the amount they get back will in then-current terms be 'worth' less than their principal (capital) at the start.

- **Opportunity cost** What other opportunities does a provider of funds forgo by committing to any individual transaction. This may be especially important to a lending bank which is subject to capital adequacy constraints.

- **Market** The great efficiency of today's markets encourages international competition in a wide range of financial instruments and makes knowledge of prevailing rates readily available. However, laws or other controls on who can borrow or lend, on what basis or rates of interest and subject to which regulatory requirements or costs, may significantly affect a market.

The rate of interest charged by a lender such as a bank should be sufficient to cover the following.

- **The 'cost of funds'** (being the cost to the lender of obtaining the monies it then on-lends). This includes provision for the cost of any deposits or other impositions that may have to be made with, or as required by, the lender's government, Central Bank or other regulatory body (known as 'associated costs').

Although it is normal for the rate of interest to be linked to a single specified base (e.g., three-month LIBOR), the reality is that most lenders obtain their funds from many sources: for example, from their depositors, from issuing bonds and equity, and from inter-bank and other money markets. When a lender such as a bank lends at a rate linked to a standard market benchmark, such as three-month LIBOR, but is able to obtain funds from its own depositors at a lower cost (or even without cost where the bank's customers leave money in interest-free accounts) their profits can be greatly increased. In many countries, such benefits to banks have reduced as customers become more sophisticated and demand higher rates of interest on their deposits. Where, by contrast, there are legal restrictions on the rates of interest that can be paid by banks on deposits, this 'endowment' effect may be artificially maintained.

Care is required to ensure that the interest income a lender will receive matches its funding costs. An unmatched 'book' (e.g., lending long term at fixed rates whilst borrowing short term or at variable rates) might provide increased profits if the cost to the lender of obtaining its funds falls, but there is the risk of losses if the cost of funding increases.

(There is, of course, an additional risk when a lender borrows short term, or uses its customers' short-term deposits, and utilizes these monies in making longer-term loans. If, for whatever reason, it has to repay its short-term deposits and cannot replace this funding because perhaps there is anxiety in the market as to its creditworthiness, then the lender may itself become insolvent.)

- **The administrative and other costs of establishing, monitoring and controlling the lending** These are sometimes covered in whole or part by separate fees, which should be taken into consideration by a borrower when assessing the total cost of obtaining funds.

- **A bad debt contingency** It is a most fortunate lender who never experiences a bad debt, and a prudent lender builds into the interest rate a provision to cover such potential losses.

- **The lender's profit on the facility** Depending on the nature of the lending, and any applicable law or practice, this may be increased by additional fees and/or a share in profits. On religious grounds, it is the practice in some countries for lenders to require that any return on a lending be based on the profits derived from use of the borrowed monies, rather than by payment of interest.

If the market is very competitive, or if the borrower is a prime covenant in a strong negotiating position, the lender can find itself unable to charge a sufficiently high margin to leave any profit. However, they may still lend so as to maintain the client relationship or the lender's market share, whilst hoping to cover their costs and perhaps make a profit on other dealings with the borrower (for example, foreign exchange commissions and transaction charges).

Further, consider the interest margins charged to different business borrowers, where the cost to a first-class covenant may only vary by 2% or 3% from that to a secondary or high-risk borrower. This is unlikely to compensate for the additional costs of administering and monitoring lending to a weaker borrower, or of providing for the greater incidence of bad debts. If secondary borrowers were accustomed to paying rates of interest more accurately reflecting the costs and risks of lending to them (the 'risk vs reward' ratio), then lenders might be more willing to provide the funds they often desperately need.

See also *Borrowing*, page 138.

Variable rate facilities

Definition

> *Borrowings or deposits where the rate of interest paid or received changes, either immediately or on 'rollover dates', in line with movements in a specified base.*

For lending by banks the total interest charge will often comprise a variable ('floating') rate of interest plus a fixed 'margin'. Examples of commonly used bases are three-month LIBOR and the 'base rates' quoted by individual banks.

BENEFITS including risks avoided

- The gains from movements in your favour of the base on which the interest is calculated are passed on to you, either immediately or at the next rollover date, and over the term of the borrowing/deposit the aggregate of the floating rates may be more advantageous than the fixed rate which would have been offered at the outset for the entire term.

- If the borrowing/deposit is subject to the resetting of interest rates at intervals (rollover dates) you may have the right to vary the length of the rollover period (i.e., the period of time until the next rollover date). You can then select a longer or shorter rollover period depending on whether you think interest rates are likely to rise or fall. If, for example, a borrower considers it likely that rates will decline by the end of the next three months they could select a three-month rollover, to benefit from lower rates at the rollover date. By contrast they would elect for a longer rollover period (say, six months) if it was felt that rates were likely to be higher at the end of three months. It may, of course, be that the 'market' has already taken such anticipated increases or decreases into account, and factored them into the rates available for different terms. You should, therefore, obtain a range of quotes for different rollover periods before reaching any decision.

- The cost of a borrowing (or the income from a lending/deposit) cannot be known in advance for its entire term.

- You will suffer from any adverse movements in the base on which the interest is calculated, and over the term of the borrowing/deposit the aggregate of the floating rates may be less advantageous than the fixed rate which would have been available at the outset for the entire term.

- Any of the rollover dates (when the interest rate is re-set for a further period) may fall at a time when rates are disadvantageous. Unless you then have the option to select either a rate that changes immediately with movements in the base, or a shorter rollover period, you may be locked in to a disadvantageous rate for longer than you wish.

Fixed rate facilities

Definition

> Borrowings or deposits where the rate of interest paid or received is fixed for the entire term of the facility.

BENEFITS including risks avoided

- The cost of a borrowing (or the income from a lending/deposit) is known in advance for its entire term.

- You will not suffer from any adverse movements in the interest rate over the term of the borrowing/deposit, and the fixed rate available at the outset may be more advantageous than the aggregate of the floating rates over the same period.

RISKS REMAINING

- You do not benefit from any advantageous changes in the interest rate over the term of the borrowing/deposit, and the fixed rate offered at the outset may be less advantageous than the aggregate of the floating rates that might have been available over the entire term.

Forward rate agreements (FRAs)

Before reading this section, please see *Derivatives: the basics*, pages 183–97.

FRAs are over-the-counter derivatives that developed from exchange traded futures, and are mostly provided by banks. They are not traded on exchanges.

Definition

> A contract where two counterparties commit to respectively pay or receive an amount equivalent to the difference between:
>
> - an agreed rate of interest (the 'FRA rate') and,
> - the interest rate available in the market on a specified future date (the 'settlement' date)
>
> based on a notional loan or deposit for a specified term (the 'contract period').

FRAs can be used to hedge the cost of a future borrowing or the income from a future lending or deposit, or to speculate in the hope of profit.

They are usually regarded as instruments for short-term interest rate management.

The contract *commits* the counterparties to settle in cash the difference between the amount calculated at the FRA rate and the amount calculated at the market interest rate on 'settlement date', but there is no payment, receipt or transfer of the notional amount (principal) on which the interest is calculated.

Because FRAs are over-the-counter derivatives it is for the counterparties to agree between themselves the:

- notional amount on which the calculations of interest will be made (some banks will only deal for US$0.5m or its equivalent upwards)
- currency of the notional amount, FRAs being obtainable in most major currencies (this will also determine the market rate to be used for calculating the difference from the FRA rate at settlement date, e.g., if the FRA is in sterling with a six-month contract period, then the applicable market rate will be that for sterling six-month LIBOR)
- FRA rate
- settlement date
- contract period (usually up to three years, and being the period of time between the settlement and maturity dates of the contract).

By means of a FRA, the *interest rate is fixed for a specified term* (the 'contract period') *that starts at a known future date* (the 'settlement date') *and ends on a known future date* (the 'maturity date').

If the borrowing or deposit was being entered into today, then (provided there was a market) it would be a simple matter to obtain a quote for a fixed rate of interest for its term (i.e., the period until maturity). But where the loan or deposit is to start *at a future date* you cannot know the rate that will be available in the market until that day, which is where the FRA comes in.

To finance the purchase of equipment, a business arranges to borrow £1m from a bank, with the loan to be drawn down in three months' time (to coincide with the date when payment must be made for the equipment). The loan is due for repayment six months after drawing (i.e., it has a six months' term).

It has been agreed that the interest rate to be charged by the lending bank on the borrowing will be that for six-month LIBOR in the market at the date of drawdown, plus a margin to the bank of 1%. This means that the interest cost of the loan cannot be known until the date it is drawn down (i.e., in three months' time). If the six-month LIBOR rate today is 6% p.a., how can the business protect itself against the rate being higher on the date of drawdown (it could, of course, be the same or lower)?

The business could have arranged with its bank to immediately draw down a fixed rate loan of £1m with a term of nine months, and then put the money in an interest-earning deposit until it was needed to fund the purchase in three months' time. But the interest earned for those three months would normally be less than the cost of the interest payable on the loan. The bank might also be unhappy to release the monies before they are needed (particularly if it wanted to take a charge on the asset(s) being acquired as security for the loan), or to incur any reserve asset or capital adequacy costs for longer than necessary.

Where arrangements such as the above are made between a bank and a borrower, it would, in practice, be more usual for the bank to offset the loan (in our example, for nine months) and the deposit (in our example, for three months) on its own books and to simply quote a net rate to the borrower for a loan with a term of six months to be drawn down in three months. This is known as a 'forward–forward', as the loan is for a future (forward) period starting on a future (forward) date.

Instead, the business could *buy* an FRA contract from the bank providing the loan (or from any other bank or counterparty willing to enter into the FRA, even though they are not providing the loan).

As already mentioned, the FRA is not itself a commitment by the seller to lend money or by the buyer to borrow.

In our example, it is assumed that the FRA contract was taken out for a notional £1m on the day the business agreed the loan with its bank, with a settlement date three months later to match the drawdown date of the loan, and with a contract period of six months (i.e., so that the contract period expires on the date the loan is due to be repaid).

Because the settlement date is in three months' time, and the FRA contract matures six months after that, this FRA would be known as a '3s-9s' (or 'three on nine' or 'threes nines'). If, instead, the settlement date was, say, in six months and the FRA contract matured six months after that, then the FRA would be known as a '6s-12s.'

Assuming, for our example, that the FRA rate had been set at 6.25%, and that at settlement date in three months (which is also the date of loan drawdown), the market rate for six month LIBOR is 6.55% p.a., then the seller would pay the business in cash an amount equivalent to the 0.30% difference between the actual rate (6.55%) and the FRA rate (6.25%) calculated on the notional amount (in this example, £1m) for the contract period (in this example, six months).

The amount paid to the business by the seller of the FRA will be 'discounted back' for a term equal to the contract period, as the FRA payment is made upfront on settlement date (but interest on the borrowing will usually be paid in arrears by the borrower).

Thus, the payment by the FRA seller to the business would be:

$$\frac{6.55 - 6.25 \times £1m}{100} \times \frac{180 \text{ days}}{365 \text{ days}} = £1,479.45$$

to discount this back:

$$£1,479.45 \times \frac{1}{1 + \dfrac{6.55 \times 180}{100 \times 365}} = £1,433.16$$

See Figure 5.1 for an illustration of our example.

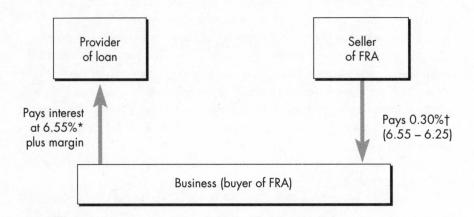

* Based on £1m loan, for the 6 months' term of loan. Payable at end of term.
† Based on a £1m notional amount for 6 months' contract period of the FRA. Payable at settlement date (i.e., on the same day as the loan is drawn down), and discounted back for the contract period.

Fig. 5.1 Example of FRA contract (1)

Net interest cost to business is the FRA rate of 6.25% p.a. (ignoring discounting back) plus the 1% margin on the loan.

If, however, in our example the rate for six-month LIBOR had fallen at settlement date to 5.75% p.a., then the business would pay the FRA seller (again discounted back to settlement date):

$$\frac{6.25 - 5.75 \times £1m}{100} \times \frac{180}{365} = £2,465.75$$

$$£2,465.75 \times \frac{1}{1 + \dfrac{5.75 \times 180}{100 \times 365}} = £2,397.76$$

Figure 5.2 shows what would have happened.

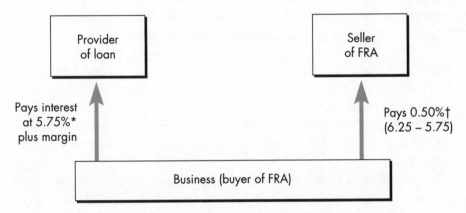

* Based on £1m loan, for the 6 months' term of loan. Payable at end of term.
† Based on a £1m notional amount, for the 6 months' contract period of the FRA.
   Payable at settlement date (i.e., on same day as the loan is drawn down), and
   discounted back for the contract period.

Fig. 5.2 Example of FRA contract (2)

Net interest cost to business is the FRA rate of 6.25% p.a. (ignoring discounting back)
plus the 1% margin on the loan.

*Notes: The number of days between the FRA settlement and maturity dates (i.e., the
contract period) has been assumed for the purposes of these examples to be 180. (It
would in practice be the actual number of calendar days between these dates.)*

*For sterling FRAs the year is assumed for the purposes of such calculations to have
365 days, but for many other currencies it is taken as having 360 days.*

*Money changes hands only on settlement date (i.e., there are no payments at the
date of entering into the FRA, nor at its maturity date).*

*FRAs are 'single settlement' contracts, as only one payment is made (i.e., at settle-
ment date).*

For our 3s-9s contract, the price quoted by a broker might be 6.20 to 6.25. The 6.25% would be the rate to a buyer of an FRA, and the 6.20% would be the rate to a seller of an FRA.

The rate is always higher to a buyer. (The FRA rate will be equivalent to the forward–forward rate described on page 207, plus any profit margin).

Whether the market rate for LIBOR rises or falls over the three months (between the date the business in our example agrees the borrowing with its bank and contracts for the FRA, and the fixing of the rate of interest on the loan as at the date of drawdown) the net cost to the business will be the FRA rate. If between the date of entering into the FRA contract and the settlement date the market rate rises, then the business receives a payment based on the difference between market rate and the FRA rate, and if the market rate falls, the business makes a payment based on its difference from the FRA rate.

Where a business was expecting to receive, say, £1m in three months, but would not need that money for a further six months, and meanwhile intended putting the money in a fixed interest rate deposit, then it could *sell* an FRA contract to a bank to hedge the income from its future deposit (see Figure 5.3). In this way, the rate of interest that will be earned on the deposit to be made in three months' time is known.

The 'seller' of an FRA is the counterparty who benefits under the contract if the market rate on settlement date is lower than the FRA rate. The 'buyer' of an FRA contract is the counterparty who benefits under the contract if the market rate on settlement date is higher than the FRA rate.

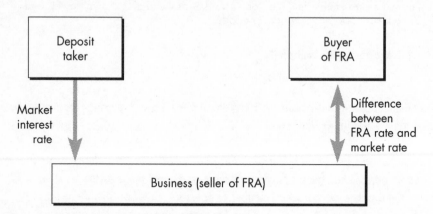

Fig. 5.3 Example of selling FRA contract as hedge

Net interest received by business is the FRA rate (ignoring discounting back).

Unless you are a sizeable user of FRAs it may be necessary to obtain the services of a broker, who will put you in touch with a bank or other counterparty willing to enter into the FRA. The broker provides this service for a fee and, as they are acting as agents not principals, you will still need to be considered a satisfactory credit risk by the bank or other counterparty.

The actual FRA contract should conform to an industry standard document.

- A borrower, lender or depositor can know the net interest payment or receipt for a specified term (the 'contract period'), starting on a specified future ('settlement') date and based on a specified ('notional') amount. They will not suffer if market rates move adversely in the interim.

BENEFITS
including risks
avoided

- Available separately from any borrowing or deposit they are being used to hedge.

- Neither counterparty has to pay anything until settlement date, as there is no upfront cost or premium with an FRA (unless dealing through a broker, to whom commission may be paid).

- The FRA contract is flexible in that it can normally be 'closed out' at any time by the counterparties entering into a 'reverse' contract and settling any difference in cash.

- A bank does not need to mark credit limits against the counterparty for the notional amount, only for the amount that might become due on settlement date (i.e., the difference between the FRA and market rates). This frees up limits for other facilities or customers, and normally reduces the bank's capital adequacy requirements.

- Although the borrower, lender or depositor know the net interest cost or income (i.e., the FRA rate) they do not know whether they will be the counterparty making or receiving the payment on the settlement date (being the difference between the market interest rate that day and the FRA rate).

**RISKS
REMAINING**

- If market interest rates move in favour of a borrower, lender or depositor they will not benefit, as they are committed to the FRA contract and will always pay or receive at a net rate equal to the FRA rate. The position is different for a speculator/trader entering into the FRA in the hope of profit rather than to protect (hedge) the rate on a borrowing or a deposit. A speculator will make a profit or a loss, depending on the difference between the market rate on settlement day and the FRA rate, but will not know the outcome until that date.

- Often only available for amounts of US$0.5m upwards.

- Each counterparty is taking a credit risk on the other for the amount to be paid on settlement date. Unlike exchange traded derivatives there is no clearing house acting as middleman, nor any initial or variation margin payments. If the FRA is in a foreign currency, the cash payment may not be due for two or more days after the settlement date of the contract.

- If the FRA contract is in a foreign currency there may be an additional exchange rate exposure if the counterparty defaults.

Interest rate futures

Before reading this section please see *Derivatives: the basics*, pages 183–97.

Interest rate futures are exchange traded. They are not available over the counter.

> *A future is a contract where the counterparties commit to buy or to sell a standard quantity of a specified financial instrument at an agreed price on a specified future date.*

A future does not require either counterparty to borrow or lend the notional amount. If they were to do so, that would be under a separate agreement, such as a loan document, and need not be with the same counterparty.

Interest rate futures can be obtained in most major currencies.

They are 'single settlement' derivatives, with settlement made at either the delivery date or on an earlier close-out date.

The notional amount of each contract is pre-set by the exchange, as are the 'delivery dates' on which they are settled and the 'tick values'. Most interest rate futures have quarterly delivery dates falling on a specific day in the 'delivery month' (e.g., third Thursday, although some long-term futures contracts can be delivered on any business day in the specified delivery month). This standardization is essential if the contracts are to be easily traded in volume on an exchange (i.e., are to have 'liquidity').

By way of example, LIFFE offer the following interest rate futures contracts (other exchanges around the world would have their own range of contracts):

- Three-month Eurodeutschmark (Euromark) – unit of trading DM1,000,000 – delivery months March, June, September, December – tick size 0.01 – tick value DM25. Cash settlement against the exchange delivery settlement price for three-month Eurodeutschmark deposits on the last trading day.

- Three-month sterling (short sterling) – unit of trading £500,000 – delivery months March, June, September, December – tick size 0.01 – tick value £12.50. Cash settlement against the exchange delivery settlement price for three-month sterling deposits on the last trading day.

- Three-month Eurodollar – unit of trading US$1,000,000 – delivery months – March, June, September, December – tick size 0.01 – tick value US$25.00. Cash settlement against the exchange delivery settlement price for three-month Eurodollar deposits on the last trading day.

- Other short-term interest rate futures including three-month Euroswiss, three-month Eurolira and three-month ECU, together with long-term bond futures based on long gilts, Japanese government bonds, German government bonds, Italian government bonds and medium-term German government bonds.

If you want to trade for larger amounts than the standard notional contract value (e.g., more than £500,000 for sterling), then it is necessary to buy two or more of the standard contracts.

Each future (e.g., sterling, Eurodeutschmark, Eurodollar, etc.) is based on the interest rate for a standard term (e.g., three-month LIBOR for sterling). It may, therefore, not be possible to obtain a future for a term that matches your needs. You cannot, for example, obtain a sterling LIBOR future for a four-month term (only for three months).

The percentage of futures contracts that continue until their specified delivery date is small, as most are closed out by a reverse contract ('offsetting trade') with cash settlement before that time.

Prices for short-term contracts are quoted by deducting the 'implied forward interest rate' from 100. For example, if the implied rate is 7%, the price will be 93.

The implied forward rate is the rate of interest the market expects to see on the delivery date (e.g., if the rate today for three-month sterling LIBOR is 6%, but the market expects the rate for three-month sterling LIBOR to be 7% in two months' time, then the implied forward interest rate (IFIR) for three-month sterling LIBOR as at a date two months ahead is 7%). As the delivery date gets nearer, the market should, at least in theory, have a better idea of what the rate is likely to be at that time, and the implied forward rate would change accordingly (on delivery date itself you know the market rate exactly, so the implied forward rate would then be the same as market rate).

To make a profit you need to:

- buy a contract low and close out/deliver high *or*
- sell a contract high and close out/deliver low.

The profit or loss is the number of contracts multiplied by the tick value multiplied by the number of ticks by which the price has moved.

If you are not a member of an exchange, then it will be necessary to trade through a broker, who acts for a fee and will arrange the documentation needed by the exchange and the clearing house before you can enter into any contracts. The broker will also be able to keep you informed of the continually changing prices in the market, and any margin payments due to the clearing house are made via the broker.

The only upfront payment is that for the initial margin, although variation margin payments may subsequently become due.

Interest rate futures can be used by banks and businesses to hedge their exposure on *future* loans or deposits (i.e., those starting at a future date), and by speculators (including banks) who think they know whether rates are going to rise or fall and can make a profit if they get it right and a loss if wrong.

EXAMPLE
....

It is 2 August, and to finance the purchase of an asset, a business has arranged to borrow £5m from its bank. The loan is to be drawn down on 8 November, with repayment due six months later. Under the loan agreement, interest will be charged at a fixed rate equal to that for six-month LIBOR on loan drawdown date plus a margin of 1%. On 2 August the rate in the money market for £5m at six-months LIBOR drawn that day is 6.4% p.a. The business is worried that interest rates may rise between 2 August and 8 November, and wishes to hedge its exposure.

On 2 August, the December sterling futures contract is priced in the market at 93.5 (such futures are known as 'short sterling' contracts, and are always based on three-month LIBOR. At any time, short sterling futures can be obtained with delivery dates at set quarterly intervals for the next three years). The price of 93.5 is calculated by deducting from 100 the 6.5% implied forward interest rate at which, in our example, traders expect sterling three-month LIBOR to be available in the market on the December futures delivery date.

The business decides to *sell* 10 'December contracts' at 93.5 ('December' as that is the delivery month for the contract). As mentioned on page 212, each sterling futures contract has a standard unit size of £500,000. The business pays the initial margin to the clearing house, together with the fee to a broker (unless the business is entitled to trade as a member of the exchange), and meets in cash any variation margin payments for which it subsequently becomes liable (or receives in cash any variation margin payments to which it subsequently becomes entitled).

On 8 November, when the business draws down the loan from its bank, the rate in the money market for six months' sterling is 7% p.a. (which, in our example, the business will have to pay on its borrowing together with 1% 'margin' to the bank).

The price of December sterling futures on the exchange on 8 November is 92.8, based on an implied rate of 7.2% (i.e., the implied rate has moved from 6.5% on 2 August to 7.2% on 8 November).

The business closes out its 10 contracts on 8 November by buying them back at the market rate of 92.8 and paying or receiving any difference between that price and the price the day before in cash (the difference on close-out is against the price on the preceding business day, as every business day since the contract was purchased on 2 August the counterparties have been making variation margin payments). The net total of the variation margin payments or receipts since 2 August including any final payment on close-out day will, therefore, equal the difference of implied rates between 2 August and 8 November.

If the interest rate has increased, the seller of the future will have received a net payment from the buyer, and vice versa if the rates have fallen.

Ignoring any interest earned on the initial margin (this being returned to the business at the close-out date) the business will have made the following gain on the future:

$$10 \text{ contracts} \times 70 \text{ ticks} \times £12.50 = £8,750.00$$

There has been a movement of 70 'ticks' as each tick is for a standard 0.01% p.a. (see page 212) and the price has fallen from 93.5 to 92.8, i.e., 0.70% or 70 ticks at 0.01%. Each tick is worth £12.50, as that represents 0.01% p.a. of the standard £500,000 sterling futures contract unit of trading for three months, i.e.:

$$£500,000 \times \frac{0.01}{100} \times \frac{3}{12} = £12.50$$

(3/12 as the sterling futures contract is based on three-month LIBOR)

Unlike FRAs, the amount received (or paid if the interest rate moves against you) is not 'discounted back'.

Offset against the gain on the future is any increased rate of interest the business in our example will have to pay the bank on its loan. We do not know at what interest rate the business could have arranged a forward–forward on 2 August for a £5m loan with drawdown on 8 November and a term of six months. However, we do know that on 2 August, the implied rate for three-month LIBOR with a December delivery date was 6.5% p.a. (as the price at which the future was purchased was 93.5, being 100 less 6.5%). Using this as a rough guide, the cost of borrowing has increased by around 0.5% p.a., being the difference between the above implied rate of 6.5% p.a. for three-month LIBOR with December delivery and the 7% the borrower actually had to pay based on the money market rate for six-month LIBOR on 8 November. In cash terms, such an increase in rates on the loan would cost the borrower:

$$£5m \times \frac{0.5}{100} \times \frac{6 \text{ months}}{12 \text{ months}} = £12,500$$

The £8,750 the business made on the future is not enough to cover the increased cost of borrowing. This is because the future is based on the implied rate for three-month LIBOR (as are all short sterling futures contracts), whereas the business has had to fix its loan in the money market at the actual six-month LIBOR rate. In our example, the implied rate for three-month LIBOR with December delivery has moved from 6.5% p.a. on 2 August to 7.2% p.a. on 8 November (i.e., by 0.70%), whereas the actual money market rate for six-month LIBOR on 8 November was 7% p.a. (i.e., only 0.5% more than the implied rate of 6.5% for three-month LIBOR on 2 August).

To illustrate, if we adjust the above gain of £8,750.00 for these differences, it equals the additional cost of borrowing:

$$£8,750.00 \times \frac{6}{3} \times \frac{0.5}{0.7} = £12,500$$

(6/3 as the loan is for six months, whereas a sterling futures contract is always based on a term of three months.)

The only way the business can adjust for these differences is to buy a greater or lesser number of contracts. The ability to do so may be dependent upon the mandate given to the business's treasury department as, ironically, it is often regarded as 'overhedging'. It could do this by, for example, buying twice as many (i.e., 20) futures contracts to compensate for the fact that sterling futures are based on three-month LIBOR, whereas the loan in our example was for a six-month term. The gain on the 20 futures contracts would then have been:

$$20 \times 70 \text{ ticks} \times £12.50 = £17,500$$

(70 ticks being the price movement from 93.5 to 92.8 at 0.01% per tick, and £12.50 the value of each tick).

The gain is greater than the £12,500 increased cost of the loan, as the loan was fixed at a six-month LIBOR rate of 7% whereas the implied rate on 8 November for a December delivery of three-month LIBOR was 7.2% (i.e., 0.5% and 0.7% more respectively than the implied rate of 6.5% on 2 August). This is shown by making appropriate adjustment:

$$\frac{0.5}{0.7} \times £17,500 = 12,500$$

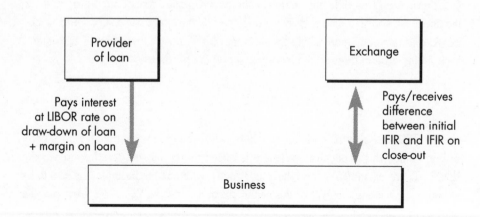

The business initially sells futures at a price of 100 less the implied forward interest rate (IFIR) at the time of selling.

The business subsequently buys back the futures at a price of 100 less the implied forward interest rate at the time of buying back.

The business borrows from the provider of the loan at the LIBOR rate applicable at the date when the loan is drawn down (and which is also the date futures are bought back) plus a margin (in our example, 1%).

The net cost to the business is LIBOR + the margin on the loan +/− the difference between the initial and close-out IFIR (plus any dealing costs and interest on the initial margin).

Fig. 5.4 Example of hedging exposure to an interest rate rise by selling futures

If, instead of being a borrower, a business had known on 20 May that it would be receiving £5m in cash on 16 August, which would not be needed for six months, then it might wish to protect against a fall in interest rates (see Figure 5.5). This hedge could be achieved by buying futures with a September delivery date.

The business could *buy* 10 contracts (each of the standard trading unit of £500,000) at a price of, say, 94.5 (i.e., 100 less an implied forward rate of 5.5% for September delivery).

The business would have to pay in cash the initial margin, any broker's fee and any variation margins.

If on 16 August, when the business received the £5m cash, the rate in the money market for six-month fixed deposits was 4.5% p.a. and each future was closed out by selling it back at 95.0 (i.e., 100 less the implied rate for September delivery on 16 August of, say, 5% p.a. for 3-month LIBOR, as sterling futures are always worked on LIBOR and not on LIBID, even when used to hedge a deposit), then the business would receive back the initial margin plus interest thereon, and make a gain on the futures of:

10 contracts × 50 ticks × £12.50 = £6,250
(50 ticks being 95.0 less 94.5 at 0.01% per tick).

To offset against this, the business is going to earn only 4.5% p.a. for its six-month fixed deposit against the implied forward rate in May of 5.5% p.a. for three-month LIBOR, i.e., a cost of:

$$£5m \times \frac{1.0}{100} \times \frac{6 \text{ months}}{12 \text{ months}} = £25,000$$

This difference between £6,250 and £25,000 results because a sterling futures contract is based on three-month LIBOR whereas the actual deposit was for six months, and the actual rate in the money market on 16 August was 4.5%, whereas the implied forward rate for September delivery was 5%.

To illustrate by adjusting for these differences:

$$£6,250 \times \frac{5.5 - 4.5}{5.5 - 5.0} \times \frac{6}{3} = £25,000$$

To cover its exposure for the full six months of the deposit the business would have needed to buy more contracts.

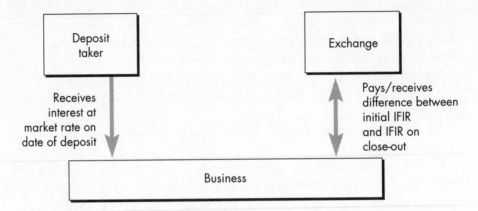

The business initially buys futures at a price of 100 less the implied forward interest rate (IFIR) at the time of buying.

The business subsequently sells back the futures at a price of 100 less the implied forward interest rate at the time of selling back.

The business makes the deposit at the market rate on the same day as it sells back the futures.

The net receipt to the business is the market rate for the deposit +/– the difference between the initial and close-out IFIR (plus interest on the initial margin, less any dealing costs).

Fig. 5.5 Example of a hedging exposure to an interest rate fall by buying futures

BENEFITS
including risks
avoided

- Can be used to hedge interest rate positions on future loans or deposits, foregoing the benefit of favourable movements, or to speculate in the hope of profit.

- Available in most major currencies.

- Futures can be closed out with cash settlement on any business day before the contract expiry (delivery) date (for the difference between the price that day and the previous day, up to which time the net cumulative variation margin will already have been settled).

- The amount of the initial margin, and the fee to a broker if you are not a member of the exchange, will be known when entering into the future.

- There is market liquidity to match changing needs.

- The credit risk is on the clearing house.

RISKS
REMAINING

- The amounts of each contract ('unit of trading') are fixed and large (e.g., £500,000 for three months' sterling).

- Even if you buy or sell two or more units of trading, they may not total the amount you want to hedge (e.g., if you want to hedge £700,000, the choice is one unit at £500,000 or two at £1,000,000).

- The delivery dates are fixed and, unless they fall on the date you need, it will

with settlement of any amounts due in cash (in practice, closing out happens in nearly all cases and is not a problem – although if you act through a broker it will normally incur an extra fee).

- Each future is based on a standard term (e.g., three-month LIBOR, three-month Eurodollar or three-month Eurodeutschmark). If your need is to hedge a borrowing or deposit for a different term (e.g., six months) then you can buy two or more contracts (e.g., two sterling three-month LIBOR-based contracts to cover a six-month deposit or loan). But this will not protect you from any inherent differences between the rates for three- and six-month LIBOR. Sterling futures are always worked on LIBOR, not LIBID, even when used to hedge a deposit.

- The documentation to be entered into with the exchange and clearing house is complex, and if you are not already a member of the exchange this needs to be completed before you can trade.

- Unless you are a member of the exchange, it will be necessary to trade through a broker for a fee.

- Unless you are a trader, it is hard to keep in touch with prices, although a broker can help.

- It is necessary for both the buyer and seller of a future to pay an initial and any variation margins.

These disadvantages are such that many businesses prefer to use over-the-counter FRAs, leaving the futures market to banks and larger corporates.

Interest rate options

Before reading this section, please see *Derivatives: the basics*, page 183–97.

Buying an option 'insures' against adverse interest rate movements, whilst enabling the buyer to take advantage of favourable movements.

Definition

In consideration of the payment of a non-returnable 'premium' an interest rate option contract gives the buyer the right, but not the obligation, to pay or receive interest calculated at an agreed rate (the 'strike' or 'exercise' rate) on a notional loan or deposit for a specified term starting from a specified future date.

It is called an 'option' because the buyer exercises the contract only when the difference between the market price and the strike price is in its favour. If the difference is not in its favour, the buyer allows the contract to lapse unexercised.

Unlike FRAs and futures the buyer is not, therefore, committed to having to settle at a rate determined by the market. The buyer has the freedom ('option') to instead let the contract lapse and deal at market rates if these are better.

If interest rates move against the buyer, they can exercise the option and receive a payment from the writer ('seller').

If interest rates move in favour of the buyer, they can let the option lapse and deal at the market rate.

The option does not commit either party to borrow or to lend the notional amount on which the contract is based, only to settle the present value of the difference between the market price and the strike price in cash.

Interest rate option contracts are both exchange traded and available over the counter from banks and other financial institutions.

Exchange traded interest rate options use futures contracts as the 'underlyings'. For example (for the relevant interest rate futures, see page 212), on LIFFE you can obtain options based on interest rate futures for three-month sterling, three-month Eurodeutschmark, three-month Eurodollar, three-month Euro Swiss franc ('Euroswiss') and three-month ECU.

The option based on the three-month Eurodeutschmark ('Euromark') interest rate future has the following characteristics:

- unit of trading – one three-month Eurodeutschmark futures contract
- delivery – March, June, September, December
- tick size – 0.01
- tick value DM25
- can be exercised any business day up to expiry on last trading day, with delivery the next business day
- nine exercise prices will be listed for each new option, with additional exercise prices introduced when the futures contract settlement price is within 0.12 of the fourth highest or lowest existing price
- the buyer does not make any payment to the writer at the time of purchasing the option.

Options on LIFFE are also available based on long-term bonds including long gilts and on German and Italian government bond futures.

The remainder of this section deals with over-the-counter interest rate options.

Unlike currency options, interest rate options are only written as European-style (i.e., a single specified exercise date), not as American-style contracts.

The period of time between the date when an option can be exercised ('expiry date') and the maturity date of any loan or deposit it is being used to hedge is called the 'reference period'.

The period of time from the date the option contract is written until the maturity date is called the 'option period'.

An over-the-counter interest rate option enables the buyer ('holder'), on payment of a fee (the 'premium') to the writer ('seller') of an option, to choose:

- the interest rate (the 'strike price', 'exercise price', 'exercise rate') *and*
- the expiry date to suit its needs.

On the expiry date the buyer can decide whether or not to exercise the option. If it is to the buyer's benefit to exercise the option, the writer pays an amount equal to the difference between the money market rate on that date and the strike price calculated on the specified notional amount. If the buyer does not exercise the option on expiry date, the contract lapses.

An option can be 'closed out' before its specified expiry date by a 'reverse contract' (or sold back to writer at 'fair value').

Interest rate options can be used by a borrower or by a lender to hedge against the risk of adverse interest rate movements on a loan or on a deposit.

- A call option is known as a borrower's option, as it protects a borrower against a rise in interest rates, as well as being used by speculators who think that rates will rise, and they can thereby make a profit. If the market rate at the expiry date is higher than the strike price, then the buyer is paid the present value of the difference in cash by the writer. Where the buyer of the option is having to borrow from its bank at the market rate, the amount received from the writer of the option compensates for the extra cost above the strike price.

  By contrast a speculator, who does not have to borrow in the market at expiry, can simply keep any amount paid by the writer as a profit.

- A put option is known as a lender's option, as it protects a lender from a fall in interest rates and gives a profit to a speculator who was correct in anticipating that rates would fall.

The option contract can be 'in the money', 'at the money' or 'out of the money', when compared with a comparative FRA.

EXAMPLE

On 2 April, a business arranges to borrow £10m from its bank for a three-month term, to be drawn down on 1 May. Under the loan agreement, interest will be fixed on 1 May for three-months at the rate for three-month LIBOR (plus a margin).

On 2 April, the rate for three-month LIBOR is 5.5% p.a. and the FRA rate for 1s-4s (i.e., for a term of three-months starting in one month) is 5.8% p.a. The money markets are very unsettled, and the business is uncertain whether interest rates are likely to rise or fall between 2 April and 1 May. It decides to protect itself by buying an over-the-counter 1s-4s call option contract, and chooses a strike price of 5.9%. At the outset, the contract is, therefore, 'out of the money' by 0.1% (as the chosen strike price of 5.9% is 0.1% higher than the current FRA rate of 5.8%). It is more common to choose an 'out of the money' contract as the premium is cheaper.

The writer of the option (which may or may not be the bank providing the loan) charges a premium of 20 basis points (calculated on a per annum basis), of which the intrinsic value is 10 basis points (being the difference between the strike price and the current FRA rate). The difference is the time value.

As there are 29 days between 2 April and 1 May expiry date, the upfront premium calculation is:

$$£10m \times \frac{29}{365} \times \frac{0.20}{100} = £1,589.04$$

Note: Most major currencies and Eurocurrencies are calculated on a basis of a 360-day year, not 365, as for sterling. In addition, Eurocurrencies are calculated assuming that every month is of 30 days.

If on 1 May, when the borrower draws down the loan from its bank, the interest rate in the money market for three-month LIBOR is 6.4%, then the borrower would exercise the option, as the market price is higher than the strike price and will receive in cash from the seller the difference between the 6.4% and the strike price of 5.9% (i.e., 0.5% on £10m for three months). Thus:

$$£10m \times \frac{6.4 - 5.9}{100} \times \frac{3}{12} = £12,500$$

The business will, therefore, be better off by the difference between the strike price and the market price less the cost of the premium (the receipt being discounted as it is paid 'upfront').

If the market rate for LIBOR on expiry date is lower than the strike price, then the business would let the option lapse unexercised as it has no value to the buyer. The business would, however, be borrowing from its bank at a current market rate less than the strike price. Thus, the strike price is the guaranteed maximum rate the buyer will pay, plus the cost of the premium.

A call option could be similarly used to hedge the rollover of a loan, and a put option to hedge the interest to be earned on a future deposit or lending.

This example is illustrated in Figure 5.6.

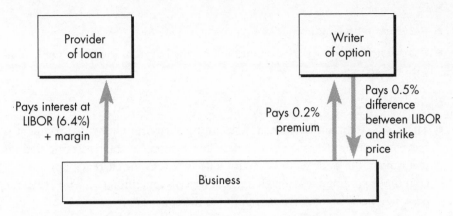

Fig. 5.6 Example of a business using a call option contract as a hedge against interest rate increases

Net cost to business is:

6.4% LIBOR + margin on loan + premium of 0.2% – 0.5% difference between LIBOR and strike price

i.e.:   6.4% LIBOR – 0.3% + margin on loan

i.e.:   6.1% + margin on loan.

The cost before the margin on the loan is, therefore, the strike price (5.9%) plus the cost of the premium (0.2%).

Buyer

- Knows the worst rate it will experience, whilst being able to benefit if rates move in its favour, as can choose whether or not to exercise the option (unlike an FRA or a future where they are committed).

- Selects the strike price, dates and notional amount to meet its needs, provided it can find a writer at an acceptable premium. Therefore, 'basis risk' can be avoided (i.e., where the available hedging instrument closely matches but does not exactly mirror or track the risk being hedged), as a nine-month loan or deposit can be covered by an option with a nine-month reference period.

- Options can be obtained for terms of up to two years or longer.

- Can normally be sold back to the writer at 'fair value' at any time.

- Can be written for substantial amounts.

- The cost (premium) is known at the outset.

BENEFITS
including risks
avoided

Writer

- Receives an upfront premium.
- It is not necessary to mark a credit limit for the buyer, as the buyer's only obligation is to pay the upfront premium.

RISKS REMAINING

Buyer

- There are credit and settlement risks on the writer until any due payment is received by the buyer. The 'value date' for settlement of interest rate options is normally the same as the exercise date, whereas for currency options it is commonly several days later. If a customer sells an option to a bank, then the bank will need to mark a credit limit for the contract.

Writer

- There is no limit to the potential amount that may have to be paid if the buyer exercises the option.

Interest rate caps, collars and floors

Unlike FRAs and options, which have a single expiry date, caps, collars and floors offer multiple settlement dates. They are, therefore, of value when used to hedge a loan or deposit with more than one date on which the interest rate is set.

For example, the benefit of a 1s–4s FRA is limited if a borrower needs to cover a one-year term loan that is to be drawn down in one month's time, but has quarterly 'rollover' dates for the setting of the rate of interest. The borrower could arrange a series ('strip') of FRAs to cover the loan but it would need four, being respectively 1s–4s, 4s–7s, 7s–10, 10s–13s, and each of the separate FRA contracts will provide cover at a different interest rate.

If a borrower or depositor wants to arrange cover for an entire period at a single interest rate, but with multiple settlement dates, this can be obtained using an over-the-counter interest rate cap.

Interest rate caps

Definition

A contract giving the buyer the right, but not the obligation, to fix the rate of interest (the 'strike' rate) for the entire term of a notional loan. The buyer pays a premium to the writer and, if the option is exercised on any of the specified settlement dates, is paid in cash an amount equal to the difference between the strike rate and the market rate on that settlement date (calculated on the notional loan).

A cap is effectively a strip of options.

As with all options, the buyer only exercises a cap if it is in its interest to do so.

Most caps are arranged to cover medium-term loans of two to five years, with the settlement dates matching the rollover dates on the cap buyer's loan. The writer of the cap may or may not be the same bank or other financial institution as is providing the loan. Caps can, of course, be used by speculators hoping to profit from a rise in market rates, rather than by borrowers seeking to hedge the interest on a loan.

Caps can be especially valuable if used together with a floating rate loan as an alternative to a fixed rate loan. With a fixed rate loan there are usually penalties for early redemption, which may be avoided by taking out a floating rate loan and protecting against increased interest rates with a cap. The borrower also retains the ability to benefit if interest rates fall. For an example, see below.

Interest rate floors

Definition

A contract giving the buyer the right, but not the obligation, to fix the rate of interest (the 'strike' rate) for the entire term of a notional deposit. The buyer pays a premium to the writer and, if the option is exercised on any of the specified settlement dates, is paid in cash an amount equal to the difference between the strike and the market rate that day (calculated on the notional deposit).

A floor is effectively a strip of options.

As with all options, the buyer only exercises a floor if it is in its interest to do so.

Most floors are arranged to cover medium-term deposits of two to five years, with the settlement dates matching the rollover dates on the floor buyer's deposit. The writer of the floor may or may not be the same bank or other financial institution as is accepting the deposit. Floors can, of course, be used by speculators hoping to profit from a fall in market interest rates, rather than depositors seeking to hedge the interest on a deposit.

From the above definitions, it will be seen that the difference between a cap and a floor is that the cap is purchased to hedge a loan (or to speculate in the hope of profit if market interest rates increase) and a floor is purchased to hedge a deposit (or to speculate in the hope of profit if market interest rates fall).

Caps and floors can be purchased in all major currencies, usually for US$0.5m or its equivalent upwards (although larger amounts are more common).

If on an exercise date the difference between the strike and money market rate, which is LIBOR not LIBID even if a deposit, would result in the writer having to pay the buyer the difference in cash (based on the 'notional amount', which for a borrower or depositor would normally be the amount of their loan or deposit, but for a speculator would be whatever notional amount they choose) then the contract will be exercised. If, on the other hand, the buyer would not receive cash if the cap or floor option was exercised, then the option would be allowed to lapse for that exercise date. Because caps and floors are 'multiple settlement' options, this happens on every exercise date during the term of the cap or floor contract.

As with any option, a cap or floor could be ATM (at the money), OTM (out of the money) or ITM (in the money), when compared to the rate at any time for a matching interest rate swap. (This differs from ordinary single settlement interest rate options, where the comparison is with the FRA rate rather than with the swap rate).

The essential difference with caps and floors, as distinguished from a 'string' of ordinary options, is that the same strike rate applies on every fixing date throughout the term of the contract.

As with all options, the size of the premium to be paid upfront by the buyer depends, in part, on the term of the contract (the longer the term the greater the risk of it being to the buyer's advantage to exercise the option on exercise dates) and the volatility of the market (as, again, the potential for the buyer finding it attractive to exercise the option increases with the volatility of the market).

EXAMPLE A UK business has entered into a loan agreement with its bank, to borrow £20m with a 'bullet' (i.e., single tranche) repayment of the entire debt at the end of 18 months. The loan has quarterly interest rate rollovers, on which dates the interest for the preceding three months is paid to the bank and the interest rate for the next three months is set, based on the market rate for LIBOR on each rollover date (plus a margin to be paid to the bank).

To protect against increases in market interest rates over the 18 months of the loan, the business enters into a cap with a bank (which may or may not be the same bank as is providing the loan) based on £20m (being a 'notional' amount, as the cap itself does not require the writer to provide the £20m loan to the buyer – if the writer does so, it would be because it was also the bank that, quite separately, had agreed to provide the loan to the buyer). On the date the cap contract is signed the market rate for an 18-month interest rate swap with quarterly interest rollover dates is 7%. The business chooses a strike rate of 9%, i.e., 2% 'out of money', and the seller asks for a premium of 1.1% of the notional amount (i.e., £220,000, which is payable by the buyer to the writer on the date of entering into the cap).

On every quarterly cap exercise date (each of which is chosen to match the rollover dates for the loan), the business decides whether or not to exercise the cap. It will do so if the market rate for three-month LIBOR on any exercise date is higher than the strike rate of the cap. The writer of the cap pays the buyer that percentage difference calculated on £20m for three months.

For example, if the LIBOR rate on a rollover date was 11%, the seller would pay the buyer:

$$\frac{11 - 9 \text{ (the strike rate)}}{100} \times \frac{3 \text{ months}}{12} \times £20m = £100,000$$

The cash payment of £100,000 received by the buyer would compensate for the fact that, under its separate loan agreement, it would be paying 11% interest to its bank for the next three months (ignoring the margin being paid to the bank in addition to LIBOR). Thus, the net cost to the buyer/borrower is 9% p.a. (being the strike rate) plus the premium. If the market rate for three months' LIBOR on a rollover date was lower than the strike rate, there would be no point in the buyer exercising the cap on that occasion, as the seller would not have to make a cash payment. However, the buyer would be able to fix the interest rate on its loan with the bank for the next three months at less than the strike price.

A cap, therefore, enables a borrower to fix the maximum interest rate it will pay on a loan.

A floor cannot be made to match so perfectly, as the underlying deposit may be earning LIBID, but the derivative contract is always based on LIBOR.

Interest rate collars

Options, including caps and floors, can guarantee either a minimum interest rate for a depositor or a maximum interest rate for a borrower, but allow the buyer to let the option lapse and simply deal in the market if that is cheaper. The buyer must, however, pay to the writer a cash 'premium' for the option contract.

With an interest rate collar, the party wishing to hedge its exposure *buys an option* from a bank or other financial institution, and at the same time *sells an option* to that bank or another counterparty, offsetting the respective premiums.

Definition

> *The simultaneous sale and purchase by one party of options for the same notional amount, term and rollover dates, but at different strike rates.*

A collar is a combination of a cap and a floor.

The party wishing, for example, to protect its interest rate exposure chooses for the option it is buying a strike rate that is the highest rate of interest it wishes to pay, and for the option it is writing (selling) a strike rate below which it accepts that it will not benefit. The premium earned on the option being written (sold) is offset against the premium to be paid on the option being purchased, so that the net cost of the option being purchased is either reduced or eliminated (or can even leave a positive premium if that for the sale is higher than that for the purchase). The two options can be with the same or different banks or other financial institutions.

There are credit and settlement risks on the writer of each option.

As with any option, the collar is not a commitment by either party to lend or to borrow the notional amount, and the only payments are for any net premium and the cash payments for differences at rollover dates.

EXAMPLE A UK business has arranged with its bank to borrow £20m with a 'bullet' (i.e., single tranche) repayment at 18 months and quarterly rollover dates on which interest for the preceding three months is paid to the bank and the interest rate is fixed for the next three months. The interest rate is based on the market rate for LIBOR, and the business is concerned that interest rates are expected to be volatile over the term of the loan.

The business has been quoted by a bank a premium of 1.1% of the notional amount for a cap at a strike rate of 9%, which was 2% 'out of the money'.

Keen as it is to hedge against increases in market interest rates, the business cannot afford to spend £220,000 (being 1.1% of £20m) on the cap premium. It, therefore, asks what premium the bank would pay if the business sold the bank a floor at 6%, and is quoted 0.6%.

The business decides to enter into the collar, and pays the bank a net 0.5% (i.e., 1.1% less 0.6%, being £100,000 on a notional £20m).

If the market rate for three-month LIBOR on any rollover date is higher than the 9% strike rate on the cap, the business will be paid the difference in cash. It has, thereby, fixed its maximum interest cost (as it will offset this receipt against the interest rate in excess of 9% it is paying on its loan).

If, on the other hand, the market rate for three-month LIBOR on any rollover date is lower than the 6% strike rate on the floor, then the business will pay the difference in cash to the bank. It has, thereby, fixed its minimum interest cost, and cannot profit if the market rate on a rollover date is less than 6% (as the difference will have to be paid to the bank, in addition to the interest rate it is paying on its loan).

If the market rate on a rollover date was between 6% and 9% neither option would be exercised.

The position would change on every rollover date with changes in market interest rates.

If the business had wished, it could have obtained a quotation for sale of a floor at a strike rate where the premium it would receive was £220,000. The two premiums would then offset each other to create a 'zero premium option'.

If the business had money to deposit (rather than a loan to hedge), it could buy a floor and sell a cap.

Interest rate swaps

A contract between two counterparties to exchange interest streams with different characteristics (e.g., fixed rate for floating rate) on the same principal amount.

Definition

Before reading this section, please see *Derivatives: the basics*, pages 183–97.

Swaps are typically arranged between:

- fixed and floating interest rates (if these are in the same currency it is called a 'vanilla' or 'coupon' swap)

- one floating interest rate to another floating rate (if these are in the same currency this is called a 'basis' or 'index' swap), e.g., six-month LIBOR to three-month LIBOR (or, say, to a rate linked to the US prime rate) or three-month LIBOR to three-month LIBOR plus a margin

- interest rates in the same currency ('single currency swap')

- interest rates in different currencies (see *Currency swaps*, page 257).

Unlike caps, collars and floors which are options where in return for paying a premium the buyer has the right but not the obligation to exercise the contract, a swap involves no premiums but commits both counterparties to swap the interest streams on the specified 'rollover' dates (which may be different dates for each side of the swap, e.g., the floating rate may be paid monthly and the fixed rate quarterly, in which case the pricing of the swap can allow for the discounted timing cost). The interest stream payments and receipts between the counterparties may be 'netted off'.

Swaps are principally used to manage medium- and long-term interest rate exposures, for example by banks needing to match fixed-rate lending with funds raised at floating rates and vice versa.

Where interest receipts are exchanged they are called 'asset swaps'.

Where interest payments are exchanged they are called 'liability swaps' (there are asset and liability swaps for other than interest rates).

As with most derivatives, the swap does not involve payment, receipt or transfer of the principal amount on which the interest rates are calculated, only that of the interest itself.

If the term of the swap is up to one year, it is a 'money market swap'.

If the term of the swap is over one year, it is a 'term swap'.

If quoted an 'all in' price for a coupon swap the 'swap rate' is that for the fixed rate, e.g., 3.6%:3.4% means a trader would pay fixed interest at 3.4% to a counterparty who paid floating rate, but would want to receive 3.6% fixed interest from a counterparty who wished to be paid floating rate (i.e., the trader is quoting a two-way price with a 'spread' or 'turn' of 0.2%).

For swaps in major currencies such as the US dollar, the quote will be for a swap spread against a benchmark interest rate. The benchmark will be the rate of interest on whichever government bond with maturity nearest to that of the swap has the greatest liquidity, e.g., a swap spread of 40/45 means the trader wants to receive interest at a fixed rate of 45 basis points over the benchmark interest rate, but would only pay 40 basis points.

In a coupon swap, the 'payer' or 'buyer' is the payer of the fixed interest stream and the 'receiver' or 'seller' is the receiver of the fixed interest stream. For basis swaps, it must be clearly defined as to who is paying or receiving each interest stream.

Each counterparty is taking a credit risk on the other counterparty for payment of the difference in interest streams, and swaps can involve terms of anything up to 25 years. Often a bank acts as intermediary between the two counterparties, taking the credit risk on each in return for a fee or profit turn.

If a party deals through a bank, they may never know the name of their counterparty. Indeed, as far as either counterparty is concerned, they have simply asked a bank to quote for the swap.

The 'vanilla' or 'coupon' swap (i.e., fixed rate to floating rate swap) is commonly used where one of the parties is able to raise finance on attractive terms by issuing bonds (hence 'coupon', which refers to the interest payable on a bond).

Swaps can be ended by:

- reversing out, using a matching swap
- termination by agreement of *both* counterparties, with settlement in cash equivalent to the discounted future benefit to either party
- assignment by either counterparty of their interest in the swap to a new counterparty, with the agreement of the remaining counterparty to the original contract to accepting the credit risk on the substitute counterparty. The transfer to a new counterparty is effected by cancelling the original swap contract and its substitution by an otherwise identical new swap contract with the new counterparty(s) – known as 'novation'.

Vanilla/coupon swap

Company A can issue bonds to raise £250m for 10 years at a fixed interest rate of 7% p.a. This is an attractive rate as they are a highly rated corporate. They would prefer to borrow at a floating rate, but their bankers are quoting what they regard as a high margin of 0.4% over the cost of funds for floating rate money.

Company B would like to borrow £250m for 10 years with the certainty of a fixed interest rate. As they are not highly rated in the bond market, a bond issue would have to be priced at 7.5% to sell. However, they could borrow from their bankers at a margin of 0.6% over the cost of funds, which is an attractive rate for a company with their rating.

Each of the parties, therefore, has a 'comparative advantage' in either the floating or fixed rate funding (Company A can obtain a better price for both fixed and for floating rate money, but its 'comparative advantage' is in the fixed rate market, whereas the 'comparative advantage' of Company B is in the floating rate market).

Company A has an advantage of 0.5% (7.5% less 7%) over Company B in raising fixed rate money by the issue of bonds and of 0.2% (0.6% less 0.4%) over Company B in raising floating rate money.

The companies agree to a swap, and each raises £250m – Company A by issuing 10-year bonds at 7% fixed with six-monthly 'coupon' payments of interest and Company B by borrowing from its bankers for a 10-year term at a margin of 0.6% over LIBOR with six-monthly rollover dates (at which times payment is made of interest for the preceding six months, and the interest rate is set for the next six months, based on the money market rate for six-month LIBOR on rollover date).

By entering into a swap, the companies agree to exchange the interest streams ('flows'). This exchange could be made direct between Company A and Company B, but is more likely to be via a bank acting as an intermediary and taking the credit risk on each counterparty.

Company A is called the 'fixed receiver' (as it pays at floating rate and is paid the fixed rate).

Company B is called the 'fixed payer' (as it pays at fixed rate and is paid the floating rate).

For our example, the companies are quoted by the bank a rate of 6.75/6.70 for the swap, being the fixed rate the bank will receive from company B (6.75%) and the fixed rate it will pay to Company A (6.70%) (i.e., the pricing for a swap is against the fixed interest rate). The difference is the bank's profit after capital and administrative costs and before any losses from defaulting counterparties.

On the rollover dates:

- the bank acting as intermediary will be paid by Company B an amount equivalent to 6.75% of £250m for six months, i.e., £8,437,500.

- the bank will pay to Company B an amount equivalent to the floating rate in the money market for six-month LIBOR; let us suppose that on the relevant rollover date

LIBOR was 7.1%, then Company B would be paid by the bank:

$$£250m \times \frac{7.1}{100} \times \frac{6}{12} = £8,875,000$$

(the £8,437,500 and the £8,875,000 could be netted off and the bank would pay Company B £437,500)

- the bank acting as intermediary will be paid by Company A an amount equivalent to the floating rate on £25m for six months, i.e., £8,875,000

- the bank will pay company A an amount equivalent to 6.70% on £250m (the swap quote having been 6.75/6.70, which relates to the fixed interest rates respectively received and paid by the bank) for six months, being £8,375,000 (the £8,875,000 and the £8,375,000 could be netted off and the bank would receive £500,000 from Company A).

Company A will pay an interest coupon of 7% to the bondholders from whom it raised its £250m, being £8,750,000, and Company B will pay to its bank interest for six months at the floating rate of 7.1% (£8,875,000), plus the margin of 0.6%.

In our example, the net cost to Company A is the floating rate it wanted to pay (which it pays to the swap bank) plus the 7% rate it pays to bondholders, less 6.70% (the rate paid to Company A by the swap bank). This is equivalent to the floating rate plus 0.30% – which is 0.10% less than the margin of 0.40% it was quoted for floating rate money by its lending bankers.

The net cost to Company B is the fixed rate of 6.75% it pays to swap bank, plus the margin of 0.60% it has to pay to the lending bank from whom it borrowed £250m (as the floating rate it received from the swap bank and the floating rate it paid to the lending bank cancel out). This totals 6.75% + 0.60% = 7.35%, which is 0.15% less than the 7.5% it would have had to pay to raise £250m from the bond market.

The bank has earned itself 0.05% (i.e., 5 'basis points', being the swap rate spread of 6.75% to 6.70%) for acting as intermediary and accepting the credit risk on both companies.

Figure 5.7 shows how the swap works.

Cost to Company A:

$$7\% - 6.70\% + LIBOR = LIBOR + 0.30\%$$

Cost to Company B:

$$LIBOR + 0.60\% + 6.75\% - LIBOR = 7.35\%.$$

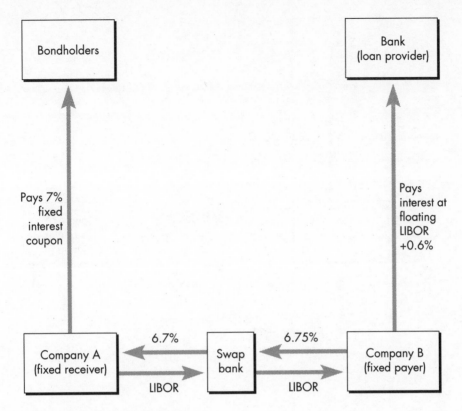

Fig. 5.7 Example of a vanilla (coupon) swap

The floating rate to floating rate (basis) swap is principally used by banks and other financial institutions who are borrowing and lending at floating rates, but for different terms. By entering into basis swaps they can 'match' their books, although still paying interest at a floating rate. A UK bank could, for example, enter into a 3s–6s basis swap (with a swap bank) if it wished to protect itself where it has borrowed at a floating rate of interest based on six-month LIBOR to fund a lending to a customer at a floating rate of interest based on three-month LIBOR.

An illustration of interest flows is shown in Figure 5.8.

Swaps can also be obtained based on different interest rate indices or with a margin added to one of the income streams.

The documentation for swaps is usually in a standard form using, for example, that of the International Swaps and Derivatives Association (ISDA).

Swaps can be obtained 'over the counter' in all major currencies for amounts normally of US$1m upwards and for terms of one to 25 years.

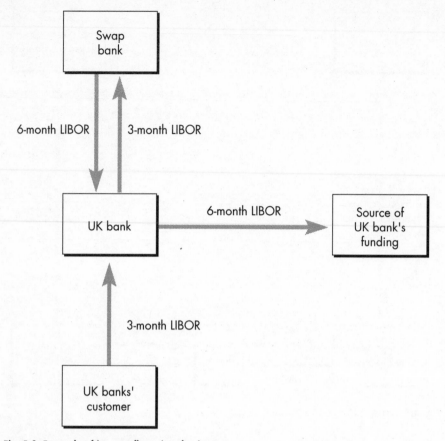

Fig. 5.8 Example of interest flows in a basis swap

BENEFITS
including risks
avoided

- No upfront premiums.

- Each counterparty can exploit any comparative advantage they may have to raise fixed or floating rate finance.

- Can provide access to finance in forms that might not otherwise be available, and non-fixed rates may move in your favour.

- Tailored to the needs of counterparties.

- The credit risk (including country risk) is only for the amount of the difference between the interest streams, not for the principal amount on which the interest is calculated (it is common for a bank to act as intermediary between the counterparties, taking the credit risk on each).

- Interest rate exposures can normally be hedged without affecting a counterparty's balance sheet.

- The documentation is usually in a standard form, e.g., that of the International Swaps and Derivatives Association (ISDA).

- Can be obtained in most major currencies, normally for US$1m upwards, for periods of up to 25 years (although up to 10 years is more common).

- As swaps can have a term of many years (up to, say, 25 years, although up to 10 years is more common) the credit risk (including country risk) on the counterparty can be considerable. It will be necessary to agree credit limits before entering into any swap.

- There may be settlement risk until you receive the interest stream due to you.

- If the rollover frequencies for the interest streams do not match, this can have cash flow implications.

- Non-fixed rates may move against you, or you may be unable to benefit from advantageous movements.

- There may be little liquidity in the swap.

- If a counterparty defaults, you may be unable to otherwise hedge the transaction ('replacement' risk).

Currency Risk

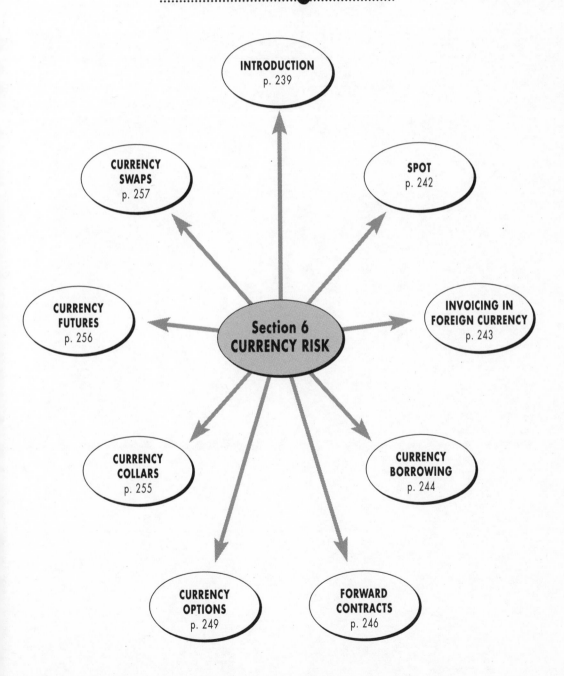

Introduction

Unless 'fixed' by their government at a set rate of exchange or within 'bands', the rate at which a country's currency can be converted into the currencies of other countries changes all the time, i.e., it 'floats'.

Even between major currencies, substantial movements may be experienced over relatively short periods of time. Whilst, if the movement is in your favour, this can result in an unexpected windfall, few businesses operate on margins that can comfortably absorb large negative swings.

Currency risk can affect:

- the value of your assets
- the amount of your liabilities
- your sales revenues
- your costs.

There is a 'balance sheet' ('translation') risk if you have assets (e.g., overseas property) or liabilities (e.g. borrowings) in a currency other than that in which the statutory accounts of your business are prepared. Even if the value of such assets or liabilities remains constant in that overseas currency, there is an impact on your balance sheet every time the exchange rate between that currency and your domestic currency changes.

EXAMPLE

You are running a company incorporated in the USA and, therefore, the 'domestic currency' in which your statutory accounts are prepared is the US dollar.

You buy a factory in the UK for £1m at a time when the exchange rate is £1.00:US$1.60, remitting US dollars from the USA for the purchase.

The balance sheet for your business as at the date of acquisition would show the factory as an asset at US$1.6m.

But the figure that has to be incorporated in your next set of statutory accounts will depend upon:

- the exchange rate used for the purposes of the accounts
- the value of the factory as at the date of the accounts.

(See Table 6.1.)

Table 6.1 The 'value' of an asset affected by currency movements

Value of factory £	At US$1.6:1 US$	At US$1.7: £1 US$	At US$1.5: £1 US$
1m (purchase cost)	1.6m	1.7m	1.5m
Gain (loss)	Nil	0.1m	(0.1m)
1.5m (£0.5m increase on purchase cost)	2.4m	2.55m	2.25m
Gain (loss)	0.8m	0.95m	0.65m
0.5m (£0.5m loss on purchase cost)	0.8m	0.85m	0.75m
Gain (loss)	(0.8m)	(0.75m)	(0.85m)

Table 6.1 illustrates two important points.

- Overseas assets or liabilities can result in balance sheet movements, irrespective of the trading activities they support (even when the factory remained worth £1m there was a gain of US$0.1m at US$1.7:£1 and a fall of US$0.1m at US$1.5:£1). Indeed, it is not uncommon for the trading profit or loss of a business to be exceeded by such balance sheet movements.

- If your domestic currency weakens against an overseas currency in which you have assets, then any gains in asset values as calculated in that currency are increased when converted to your domestic currency, and any falls decreased (when the factory was worth £1.5m, there was a gain of US$0.95m at US$1.7:£1 as against a gain of US$0.8m at US$1.6:£1, and when the factory was worth £0.5m, there was a fall of US$0.75m at 1.7:1 as against a fall of US$0.8m at US$1.6: £1). Similarly, if your domestic currency strengthens against an overseas currency in which you have assets, then any gains as calculated in that currency are decreased when converted to your domestic currency, and any falls increased (hence when the factory was worth £1.5m, there was a gain of US$0.65m at US$1.5:£1 as against a gain of US$0.8m at US$1.6: £1, and when the factory was worth £0.5m there was a fall of US$0.85m at US$1.5:£1 as against a fall of US$0.8m at US$1.6:£1).

The same principles apply if you have foreign currency liabilities instead of assets.

Notes: At an exchange rate of £1.00:US$1.50, the US$ is 'stronger' than at £1.00:US$1.60, as you will receive more £ sterling for every US dollar (e.g., £666,666 for US$1m).

At an exchange rate of £1.00:US$1.70 the US$ is 'weaker' than at £1.00:US$1.60, as you will receive fewer £ sterling for every US dollar (e.g., £588,235 for US$1m).

Rates can be quoted in either direction, i.e., £1.00:US$1.25 or US$1.00:£0.80 (these are commonly abbreviated to £/US$1.25 and US$/£0.80).

Whereas balance sheet risk was concerned with assets and liabilities, 'trading' ('transaction') risk is the impact of currency exchange rate movements on the costs and receipts of trading transactions.

Typically, these might involve purchasing raw materials from, or the sale of finished goods to, overseas countries.

It is not uncommon to see significant exchange rate movements over a short period of time, the impact of which can exceed any likely profit margins on your underlying trading and leave you with a loss (or increased profit).

All the effort of producing and selling goods or services can be wasted if currency rate changes wipe out your profit margin.

At a time when the exchange rates are £1.00:US$1.50 and £1.00:DM2.30, a UK **EXAMPLE** manufacturer wins an order to supply goods to the USA at a price of US$2m, with delivery and payment in three months. To fulfill the order it is necessary to obtain raw materials from Germany at a cost of DM1.5m, with payment on delivery in one month.

The calculations as at the date of winning the order are shown in Table 6.2.

Table 6.2 Calculations at date of winning order

	£m
Cost of raw materials	
(DM1.5m @ 2.30)	0.65
Other UK costs, say	0.55
Total costs	1.20
Sale proceeds	
(US$2m @ 1.50)	1.33
Profit	0.13

However, when the raw materials from Germany arrive at the end of a month the exchange rate has changed to £1.00:DM2.15, and when the finished goods are delivered in the USA the exchange rate is £1.00:US$1.70.

The result is as shown in Table 6.3.

Table 6.3 Calculations taking into account changes in exchange rates

	£m
Cost of raw materials	
(DM1.5m @ 2.15)	0.70
Other UK costs, say	0.55
Total costs	1.25
Sale proceeds	
(US$2m @ 1.70)	1.18
Loss	(0.07)

It will be appreciated that the position could change further if the payment dates for the goods purchased or sold were different from their delivery dates and currency exchange rates altered in the interim.

If you have the cash available, and forfeit the benefit of future favourable rate changes, the exchange rate risk on payments can be eliminated by settling debts early if the current conversion rate seems attractive.

'Strategic' exposure ('economic' exposure) is the effect of exchange rate movements on the value of a business (as distinct from on its immediate profit and loss account or balance sheet positions). It reflects the future rather than the present impact of currency movements. For example, will the medium-/long-term strengthening of your local currency make you uncompetitive in international markets ('indirect economic exposure')?

Key points

> **The questions to ask when considering currency risk**
>
> - Can your exposures be identified?
> - In what currencies are you exposed?
> - Over what time periods do the exposures exist?
> - Is any exposure a one-off, or is it recurring?
> - Is the exposure large in relation to the turnover of your business, and what impact could currency exchange rate movements have on your profit and loss account? Currency risk may need to be taken into consideration at the pricing stage.
> - What impact could currency exchange rate movements have on your balance sheet?
> - Who decides whether to hedge exposures, and is there any set policy? Clearly differentiate between actions taken to protect (hedge) a position and those taken for profit (speculating).
> - On the basis of what information are decisions being reached?
> - Will any exposures 'net off'?

Spot

When you buy or sell currency, it is normally, but not always, at 'spot value' with settlement (i.e., delivery of the currencies that are being exchanged) becoming due two business days later.

It is, therefore, very important to remember that when dealing at spot, the earliest time at which you will receive the proceeds from a sale of foreign currency, or be in possession of the foreign currency you buy, is normally at least two working days from when you enter into the contract.

If you need delivery to take place in less than two days that can usually be arranged at a price.

This is a different consideration from that of:

- the time to be allowed before funds remitted to an overseas party actually reach their destination, which will be subject to the practices and efficiency of the banks handling the transaction

- the 'settlement' risk, where an irrevocable payment is made before the currency due in return is known to have been received.

An exchange rate (whether at 'spot' or a forward contract) may be quoted as both a buy and a sell, e.g., 1.4953/62. The price at which the party providing the quote will sell the currency (the 'offer price') is the first and lesser figure (i.e., for every £1 sterling you give you will receive US$1.4953). The price at which the party providing the quote will buy the currency (the 'bid price') is the second and larger figure (i.e., for every US$1.4962 you give you will receive £1). When the giver of the quote does not know whether you wish to buy or to sell a currency they are more likely to offer a good price than if they know that your need is only to buy or only to sell. The difference between the two prices is the 'spread'.

Invoicing in foreign currency

Whilst it may be desirable to invoice customers in your own domestic currency, thereby eliminating exchange rate exposure and the costs of currency conversion, this may not be the most appropriate course of action, as the following examples show.

- You may know that at a future date it will be necessary to pay amounts away in the same foreign currency as that in which you are invoicing. Unless there is an urgent need for funds in your domestic currency, to pay creditors or to reduce borrowings, you can invoice in the foreign currency and place the payment when received in an interest-bearing currency deposit account until the monies are required. This eliminates any exchange rate risk on the currency you would otherwise need to acquire at a future date, and saves the costs of two conversions (although you would not then gain from any subsequent beneficial exchange rate movements, and interest receipts on the deposit account would be at the rate appropriate to that currency). Businesses that have frequent currency payments and receipts may operate 'current' bank accounts in a relevant currency, on which the interest rate for any borrowings or credit balances would be at the rate appropriate to the currency. Such accounts may be subject to exchange control and other regulatory requirements.

● Pricing sales in your domestic currency, rather than that of potential purchasers, can put you at a disadvantage against competitors. Unless themselves in receipt of funds in your currency, most customers usually prefer to buy goods and services priced in their own local currency, being as keen as yourself to avoid exchange rate exposure and costs. It is also easier for the buyer to compare the costs you quote with those of any local suppliers. If your competitors quote in local currency, then you may have no choice but to do the same. There are exceptions where industry custom is to price in a particular currency, for example, crude oil in US dollars.

● There might be difficulties, such as exchange control, for the prospective purchaser in obtaining the necessary foreign currency.

It is common practice to invoice in foreign currency, but build into the pricing a margin to cover the risk of adverse currency rate movements and the conversion costs. This can make you uncompetitive if your business rivals do not do so, and you have no way of knowing if the additional amount is enough to cover your actual risk. It may be preferable to cover the exchange rate risk by using a forward contract (once you have a firm order) or an option (particularly at the tendering stage where you do not know if your bid will be successful, but wish to protect against currency exposure). An alternative, where acceptable, is to quote in the domestic currency of the buyer, but with the right to vary the price if their exchange rate moves against you.

Currency borrowing

If a business is reasonably confident of receiving overseas currency amounts at future dates, and particularly where the exact timing of these is uncertain, it may (subject to exchange control and other regulations) be advantageous to consider borrowing in that currency. Reference has already been made on page 201 to the risks of borrowing or depositing in currency solely because the interest rates are more attractive than for your own currency.

In its simplest form, the business arranges a currency borrowing facility for an amount equal to or less than the total anticipated future receivables in that same currency. The currency obtained from the facility can then be either converted at spot rate into the domestic currency of the business (or some other currency if appropriate) and the proceeds used as needed, or kept in that currency and used to pay costs incurred in that currency.

As the foreign currency receipts arrive, they are used to reduce the currency borrowing.

Ideally, the outstanding borrowing is always matched by anticipated future currency receivables, eliminating exchange rate exposure on the borrowing.

This arrangement can be particularly useful if the business would otherwise have needed to borrow in its domestic currency to meet commitments, whilst having an exposure to exchange rate changes on its anticipated currency receivables.

Where the future receivables are in more than one currency, consideration can be given to borrowing in a principal currency with which the others have an exchange rate correlation.

For many businesses, currency borrowing will be an on-going requirement, with a steady flow of projected future receivables. This can be dealt with in two ways.

● If the bank is happy with a customer's covenant, the facility limit can be left at an agreed figure, with reductions to the balance from receivables and increases in the borrowing from payments. It may be important for the bank to have in place adequate systems to monitor the level of debt against outstanding receivables.

● Alternatively, the borrowing can be by way of a loan that is reduced by receivables. When the borrowing has fallen to an agreed minimum percentage of outstanding receivables, the loan is increased back to an agreed maximum percentage level, subject to any upper limit on the total debt.

There may be an added benefit if the interest rate on the foreign currency borrowing is lower than that for an equivalent borrowing in local currency, but the risk is that the currency interest cost will increase.

The risk with currency borrowing of this type is that anticipated receivables may not arrive, resulting in not only a bad debt but also an exchange rate exposure on that amount. The borrower may need to buy currency at spot to clear the debt, and there could have been an adverse movement in exchange rates since the currency borrowing was taken out.

Forward contracts

Definition

> *A commitment to exchange (buy or sell) one foreign currency for another at a specified exchange rate, with the exchange taking place on either a specified future date or during a specified future period.*

(The future date will be longer than the two days for spot: see page 242.)

The pricing of a forward contract is a wholly arithmetical process, involving no assumptions or guesswork as to likely future exchange rate movements. The seller of the contract, usually a market-making bank, simply adjusts the current spot rate of exchange to allow for the difference in interest rates between the two currencies covered by the contract.

A forward contract can be closed out by the bank's client before its maturity date by entering into a matching but reverse forward contract, and bearing any resulting costs.

'Broken dates' are contracts where the expiry is fixed for other than a round number of months.

The difference between the forward and the spot exchange rates is called the 'differential'.

EXAMPLE

A bank enters into a forward contract to buy US$50,000 from a client in two months' time, and to pay the client in sterling. For the purposes of our illustration the bank borrows US$50,000 which it immediately sells at spot rate in the market for sterling, placing the proceeds on deposit to earn interest in sterling for the next two months. At expiry of the forward contract in two months the bank receives from its client the US$50,000 it has agreed to buy under the contract, and uses that money to repay the US$50,000 it had borrowed. The bank pays the client the sterling it had received from selling the US$50,000 at spot two months earlier, which has been held in the interest-earning deposit account.

If the bank knows that it will earn a higher rate of interest on the sterling deposit than it will have to pay on the US dollar borrowing then the bank would give the client the benefit of the difference by buying the US$50,000 at a forward contract rate which is better for the client than the spot rate in the market on the day the forward contract is agreed. If the rate of interest the bank will earn on the sterling deposit is less than the rate of interest it will pay on the US dollar borrowing then the forward rate the bank quotes will be worse for the client than the spot rate in the market on the day the forward contract is agreed.

Where, instead, the forward contract was for the bank to sell its client US dollars and receive sterling (i.e., for the purposes of our illustration, the bank would borrow sufficient sterling to buy US$50,000 in the market at spot rate, placing the US dollars on deposit to earn interest in US dollars) then the forward rate at which the bank would sell US dollars will be better for the client than the current spot rate if the US dollar interest rate is higher than the sterling interest rate, and worse than spot rate if the sterling interest rate is higher than the US dollar interest rate.

In practice the bank is unlikely to actually borrow and sell the currencies, but the above illustrates the principles on which the calculations for a forward contract are based.

Whereas a standard forward contract can only be utilized on a single fixed date, an 'option dated forward contract' allows the client to complete the exchange of currencies at any time between two agreed dates (the 'option period'), usually subject to two business days' notice. The client may be permitted to utilize the contract in tranches (each of a specified minimum amount), provided the entire option date forward contract amount is taken up within the option period. The rate quoted by the bank remains constant throughout the option date forward contract period. As the client can choose the dates to suit its needs, the bank has to price the contract assuming utilization on the least attractive date to the bank. Normally, therefore, the shorter the option period, the better the pricing to a client.

If you are reasonably confident that it will be necessary to either purchase or sell foreign currency at a future date, the exact or approximate timing of which is known, you can do one or other of the following.

- Do nothing until the date when you actually receive or need to pay away the foreign currency, and then sell or buy at spot rate. If the spot exchange rate at that future time is the same as the spot rate today then you are neither better nor worse off. If the rate moves in your favour, you gain. If the rate moves against you, then you lose.

- Enter into a forward contract, usually with your bank, whereby they commit to exchange the foreign currency at an agreed rate of exchange on an agreed future date (or, for an option dated forward contract, between two agreed dates).You thereby remove both the risk of loss and the potential for gain that would result from exchange rate movements up to the date of settlement. The downside is that you are committed under the forward contract to deliver or receive the foreign currency at a future date. As with most hedging techniques, you can decide to cover all or only part of the exposure. (You could alternatively enter into a currency derivative contract: see pages 249 and 257.)

A forward contract can also be used to convert a cash flow stream from one currency to another. For example, a UK business needing to raise French francs for 9 months might be able to issue sterling commercial paper at a lower comparative interest cost than borrowing in French francs. It could then sell the sterling raised from issuing the commercial paper into French francs at spot rate and at the same time enter into a forward contract to sell French francs back into sterling in 9 months to repay the commercial paper.

BENEFITS
including risks
avoided

Client (buying the forward contract from the bank)

- Eliminates exchange rate risk for a specified amount and period (up to several years), both of which can be chosen by the client.

- The forward rate for the contract is known at the outset.

- Available in most currencies, depending on exchange control and other regulations, and for small amounts.

Bank

- Can make a profit on the currency exchange.

- Facilitates the relationship with the buyer from which other business may flow.

RISKS
REMAINING

Client (buying the forward contract from the bank)

- The client might lose the opportunity of making a currency exchange gain if rates move in their favour.

- The expected funds may not be received by the client by the date on which delivery of the foreign currency has to be made to the bank to which it has been sold under the forward contract. The client may then need to buy the currency in the spot market to meet its obligations, incurring any losses resulting from adverse exchange rate movements. This is a potentially open-ended risk. If the currency receipt has only been delayed, the client may be able to extend the forward contract at a cost (closing out and paying any losses on the old contract and entering into a new forward contract with the same spot rate as that used to close out the old).

- Similar considerations apply if the client enters into a forward contract to buy foreign currency and then finds that it is not needed, or the anticipated date of payment has changed.

- There is a settlement risk if funds are paid away before the currency is received from the bank.
- Care must be taken to monitor the dates on which forward contracts are due for settlement, to avoid overlooking liabilities that can be costly to cover at the last minute.

Bank

- At settlement date, the client may not have the funds it has committed to exchange (this might be because foreign currency failed to arrive when expected or because the client is short of the money and has already diverted the funds). When the client is unable or unwilling to meet the commitment, it may be necessary for the bank to close out the contract, taking a loss if there has been an adverse movement in exchange rates. The bank needs to record a credit exposure on the client for the potential cost of closing out the contract if it is not honoured. This is unlikely to be for the full amount of the funds to be exchanged, unless there are unusual reasons why the bank would suffer a total loss on closing out the contract. Any loss will normally be the difference between the forward contract and current spot rates.
- There may be settlement risk if currency or funds are paid away before the funds or currency in payment are received from the client.
- The allocation of part of a client's credit line for a forward exchange contract may prevent the bank providing other, possibly more profitable, services.
- Similarly, unless the bank is matching off transactions in its own books, it may use up part of the credit line marked for it by any financial institution providing the currency to the bank for the transaction.

Currency options

Before reading this section, please see *Derivatives: the basics*, pages 183–97.

A contract giving the buyer the right but not the obligation to exchange a specified amount of one currency into another specified currency on or before a specified date at a specified rate of exchange. The buyer of the option pays a 'premium' to its writer ('seller').	**Definition**

Currency options are both exchange traded and available over the counter from banks and other financial institutions.

Options can give the right to buy *or* to sell a currency, i.e., 'to call' or 'to put'. Each contract must, therefore, make it clear which currency is being bought and which sold.

This section concentrates on OTC currency options, where the exercise price and contract period can be tailormade to suit the needs of a buyer, instead of being pre-set or determined at regular intervals as for exchange traded options.

The buyer of an over-the-counter option chooses the exchange rate for the contract, known as the 'strike price', 'strike rate' or 'exercise price', and pays a premium upfront to the writer.

Whether the strike price is 'in the money', 'out of the money' or 'at the money' at any time depends upon comparison with the appropriate market rate. For an American-style option, this is the higher of the forward rate and the spot rate, and for a European-style, the forward rate.

The premium is paid in whatever currency is agreed between the parties.

Options can be:

- allowed to lapse by the buyer
- sold back in whole or part by the buyer to the writer in cash for 'fair value', reflecting both time value and intrinsic value (the intrinsic value is the difference between the market rate of exchange and the strike price, whereas the time value is the difference between the intrinsic value and the premium – see page 193)
- settled for cash at the expiry date: this can produce a profit even though the transaction being hedged has aborted, or taken place earlier than expected, or the amount of currency involved in the hedged transaction turned out to be different than expected
- 'exercised' with the buyer delivering one currency to the writer of the option and receiving in return another currency, with conversion taking place at the option strike price (if the amount of the option is greater than the currency actually needed it may be possible to sell the surplus amount of the option back to the writer).

The date on which a currency option is exercised must be a business day in the country of domicile of both the option currencies.

Actual delivery of currencies (on the 'value date') under the option would normally be two days after the exercise date, although it could be longer.

As with any option the premium depends on the strike price (whether 'in the money', 'at the money' or 'out of the money'), time to expiry ('maturity') and the market volatility of the underlying.

Writers of currency options have to take into consideration the difference in interest rates for the currencies involved in the transaction, as this affects present values and forward prices.

Although a business would normally *buy* an option from a bank or other financial institution, it could instead *sell* an option, provided a bank or other counterparty would accept the credit risk.

EXAMPLE

A UK business has a contract to sell electrical equipment to Germany for DM2m and needs to buy items from the USA for US$1m to meet the order. The current spot rates are £1.00:US$1.50 and £1.00:DM2.00.

The business has a number of alternatives, including the following:

- To sell in DM and buy in US dollars without taking any steps to hedge the transaction. The business will then be worse off if the £ sterling weakens against the US dollar before it has to pay for the items it is buying (e.g., from £1:$1.50 to £1:$1.40) or if sterling strengthens against the German Deutschmark before it receives payment for the electrical equipment it has sold (e.g., from £1.00:DM2.00 to £1.00:DM2.20).

To illustrate:

	at £1:US$1.50	at £1:US$1.40
Paying US$1m:	£666,666	£714.286

	at £1.00:DM2.00	at £1.00:DM2.20
Receiving DM2m:	£1,000,000	£909,091

- To enter into forward contract(s) to buy US$1m and/or to sell DM 2m. The business could choose to enter into only one of these forward contracts if it was prepared to accept the exchange rate risk on the other currency, or to only cover part of either exposure. This will fix the rate(s), but prevents the business benefiting from any subsequent advantageous movements in the exchange rates. There is also the risk that the actual dates of payment and/or receipt may differ from those the business anticipates. If, for example, the forward exchange contracts are for purchase of US$1m on 1 April and sale of DM2m on 1 May, the business has a problem if the US$ payment has to be made on 28 March and the DM sale proceeds are not received until 10 May. The business will have committed under the forward contracts to deal on the contractual dates at the agreed exchange rates for the specified amounts, and there may be a cost in closing out or extending the forward contracts.

- To try and renegotiate the sale and purchase contracts so that both the receipt and payment are in £ sterling. Alternatively, the business might, for example, ask the German buyer to pay in US$. On 1 April, the business could then borrow US$1m to pay its supplier. On 1 May, the business receives the sale proceeds in US$ from the German buyer, pays off the US$1m debt and either converts the balance into £ sterling or, if the money was not immediately needed, retains it as a US$ deposit to cover future purchases in that currency. Or, the business could borrow in DM, converting into $ at spot to pay the supplier, and repaying the loan when the sale proceeds are received.

- To buy a US$1m call option against sterling (the right but not the obligation to buy US dollars) and/or buy a DM2m put option (the right but not the obligation to sell deutschemarks). The business could choose to enter into only one or other option contract or hedge only part of its exposure in either currency.

The business chooses an American-style option for the US$ call at a strike price of $1.40 and a European-style option for the DM put at a strike price of 2.20. It could have chosen either style option for both the put or the call.

The bank arranging the options agrees to accept payment of the two separate premiums (say, 1% for the call and 0.6% for the put) in £ sterling (calculated at current spot exchange rates).

The chosen US$ and DM option expiry dates are 1 April and 1 May respectively.

If the US$ have to be paid value 22 March, the American-style call option could be exercised on 20 March (allowing two days after exercise for delivery of the currency and assuming both to be business days). The business would exercise the option provided the spot rate in the market that day was not better than the 1.40 strike price. If, for example, the spot rate was £1:US$1.45, then the business could let the option lapse and deal in the market (at 1.45, the US$1m would cost £689.655 plus commission, whereas at 1.40, the cost would be £714,285). If the DM2m were received on 1 May then the business would exercise the option unless the spot rate in the market that day was better than the strike price of 2.20, e.g., if the spot rate was £1:DM2.10 (at 2.20, the DM2m would convert to £909,091, whereas at 2.10 it would convert to £952,381). A mismatch would arise if the DM were not received on 1 May, as the option contract was European style and, therefore, only exercisable on the expiry date of 1 May. If there was benefit in exercising the option on the expiry date (or closing it out for cash) the business could still do so, but the rates in the market that day might be better or worse than those when the DM were actually received (whether this occurred before or after 1 May).

See Figure 6.1.

BENEFITS
including risks
avoided

Buyer

- Knows their worst position (i.e., the downside risk is limited, although there is no limit to the potential benefit).

- Knows the maximum cost at the outset (the premium plus the funding cost on making this upfront payment).

- Can choose the amount, the strike price and the expiry date (usually for up to one year, but may be longer).

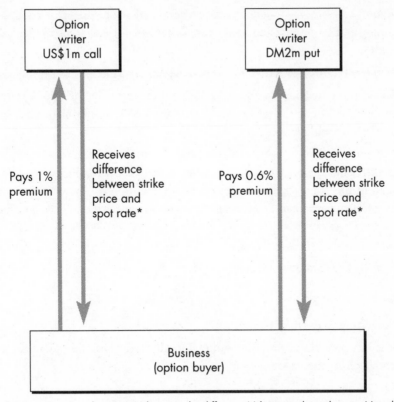

* If the business exercises the option(s) because the difference(s) between the strike price(s) and spot are in its favour.

Note: The call and the put may be provided by the same or by two separate writers.

Fig. 6.1 Example of how currency options are used by a business

- Is not committed to exchange currency at the strike price and can instead allow the option to lapse and trade in the market if the spot rate is better (i.e., has the right but not the obligation to buy or sell currency at the strike rate).

- Can adopt a strategy to suit their 'appetite for risk', e.g., if the strike price is chosen near to market rate then the risk is minimized. Alternatively, a strike price further out of the money could be chosen to reduce the premium but the buyer thereby accepts a higher potential loss or a reduced profit.

- Can purchase an option for all or only part of their exposure.

- Can be taken out at any time.

- If agreed at the outset there may be more than one delivery date, for specified amounts, to hedge a series of currency exposures with one option contract.

- Available for relatively small principal amounts, e.g., US$100,000 or its equivalent upwards.

- Available in most major currencies.

- Can use an option to hedge an uncertain currency payment or receipt (as to timing and/or amount), making them suitable for use in some tender bid situations.

- Can be sold back to writer for 'fair value' at any time.

- Does not tie up the buyer's credit lines with its bank, as the buyers only commitment is to pay the premium. (If you want to sell options to your bank, a credit limit will be needed).

- Currency options are available as both American- and European-style contracts. A European-style option can be exercised only on the expiry date specified in the contract, but an American-style option can be exercised on any business day up to and including the expiry date specified in the contract.

Writer

- Is paid the premium.

RISKS
REMAINING

Buyer

- Forgetting to exercise the option.

- It is not possible to purchase options in all currencies, although they can be obtained for the major currencies.

Writer

- No limit to potential cost to the writer, who in return only receives the premium.

As with all options, currency options can be used by speculators in the hope of profit, rather than by businesses wishing to hedge their trading exposures. The option is then likely to be sold back by a speculative buyer to the writer at fair value rather than exercised, as the buyer will not actually have an amount of currency that it wishes to convert (or to incur the costs of buying currency to do so). It is also better to sell back at fair value as that incorporates both the intrinsic and the time values, whereas the exercise price is at only the intrinsic value.

As both European- and American-style options can be sold back at any time prior to the expiry date, a speculator will not normally buy the potentially more expensive American-style option.

If the market for a currency is expected to be very volatile a 'straddle' can be purchased, i.e., both a call option and a put option each with the same strike price, underlying and exercise date, paying the premium for each. It is a gamble that the market volatility will be sufficient for one of the options to be sold back for sufficient gain to leave a profit after allowing for the upfront cost of both premiums.

A 'strangle' is a straddle with different put and call exercise prices.

'Cylinder options' (see *Currency collars* below) combine two European-style currency options at different strike prices – one bought and one sold (usually from/to a bank).

The cylinder limits the exchange rate risk whilst limiting the gain if market exchange rate movements are favourable. Cylinders cost less than ordinary foreign currency options as the premium received for the sale of one option is offset against the cost of buying the other. If the premiums are equal, it is a 'zero premium' option (the premium received might even exceed that paid, to produce a negative premium). Cylinder options should normally be considered only where there is certainty of the need to exchange currencies at a future date (unlike ordinary options where, if allowed to lapse, the only cost is the premium).

'Forward reversing options' ('Boston' options after their pioneer the Bank of Boston, or 'FROs') combine a forward contract with a European-style currency option. This gives the right to buy or sell one currency against another at an agreed forward contract rate with the ability to reverse out the transaction by means of the option if it is more advantageous to exchange the currency at spot rate in the market. The buyer chooses the strike price, the contract period (usually up to 12 months), the currencies and the amount. The cost of the forward reversing option is included in the rate for the forward contract and is settled at maturity rather than upfront (i.e., there is no upfront premium). A bank providing a forward reversing option to a customer will need to mark limits that incorporate the exposure on the forward exchange contract element of the contract.

Currency collars

To reduce or eliminate the premium for a currency option, the buyer could enter into a 'collar'. This involves buying a call or put option, and at the same time selling an offsetting option (either with the same or another bank, which will need to mark a credit limit on the counterparty for the option it is buying).

The strike price chosen for the first call or put is the worst rate at which the buyer wishes to buy or sell the currency. The strike price for the offsetting contract will be that at which the buyer of the first option (who is the writer of the offsetting option) is prepared to forfeit any further gain if exchange rates move in its favour.

It is advisable to use European-style options for collars, to avoid the situation where the bank to which you have sold the option exercises theirs on a different day to your exercise of your option, with the possibility of market rates moving adversely in the interim. The premiums on the two options are netted off and, depending on the amount of each premium, one or other party will pay the net figure. Alternatively, the strike price of the offsetting option can be set such that the premium exactly equals the premium on the first option, resulting in a nil or 'zero' premium position.

EXAMPLE

If a US business expects to receive sterling £10m in a month's time it could buy a put option from its bank, to sell the sterling £ for US$ (i.e., a 'sterling put dollar call' option). The business might wish to protect itself against the US dollar strengthening/sterling weakening beyond £1.00:US$1.45 (at £1:US$1.50, the US business could convert £10m into US$15m, whereas at £1.00:US$1.45 it would only get US$14.5m). However, the business's bank want a premium of 0.5% of £10m at a strike price of 1.45, which is considered too expensive.

To protect its downside without paying the 0.5% premium, the business could sell an offsetting option for £10m at one month to its bank at a strike price of 1.55, and thereby forgo any gain if the US dollar weakens/sterling strengthens beyond £1.00:US$1.55. The premium it receives for selling an option at US$1.55 to the bank is, let us suppose, 0.3%. The business enters into the two option contracts to create the collar, and pays the net premium of 0.2% on £10m. (It could, instead have asked the bank at what strike price for the offsetting option the premium would have exactly matched the premium for the first option so that none was payable, or even chosen a strike price for the option it was selling to the bank that would result in a net profit in favour of the business).

The business is now protected if the US dollar strengthens beyond £1:US$1.45 (it would exercise its option) but will not gain if the US dollar weakens below £1.00: US$1.55 (the bank would exercise its option).

Another way of potentially reducing the premium is to buy one option and sell another for the same currencies and strike prices but for different amounts. This is called a 'participating forward'.

Currency futures

Before reading this section, please see *Derivatives: the basics*, pages 183–97.

Currency futures are exchange traded only, and contractually commit the counterparties to buy or sell a pre-set standard amount of a specified currency at an agreed price on a specified future date.

As with other traded derivatives, the price of a contract is determined between traders on an exchange (e.g., by 'open outcry' in a 'pit'). Delivery dates are usually quarterly (e.g., March, June, September and December), but most contracts are closed out by buying/selling equal and opposite contracts before the delivery date (i.e., the market has 'liquidity'). The only upfront payment is for the initial margin, with variation margin adjustments being met if the market moves against a counterparty.

The clearing house takes the credit risk on each counterparty and there is, therefore, no need for a business buying a currency future to use up part of any credit limit marked for it by a bank (as would be the case with a forward contract).

For example, a US exporter is selling goods to the UK with payment due in three months. To hedge against an increase in the value of the US dollar against sterling (which would mean the sterling sale proceeds produced fewer US dollars on conversion), the business could buy an appropriate number of futures contracts (each contract being for the pre-set amount specified for such contracts by the exchange). If the US dollar strengthens, the value of each dollar futures contract increases and, when sold, the profit on the futures will offset the loss on conversion of the sterling proceeds from sale of goods by the business. If the US dollar weakens, the business will lose money on the futures but have gained on the conversion of the sterling sale proceeds. The business has, therefore, guaranteed its future exchange rate but, unlike a currency option, cannot benefit from advantageous movements in the exchange rate.

It is also possible to buy exchange traded options on currency futures, giving the right but not the obligation to buy or sell a currency futures contract at an agreed price.

Currency swaps

Before reading this section, please see *Derivatives: the basics*, pages 183–97.

Currency swaps differ from other derivatives in that the counterparties actually exchange the full principal amount. For example, if £10m and US$15m were swapped at £1.00:US$1.50, then the two counterparties to the contract would exchange the £10m and US$15m. For that reason, the credit risks involved are potentially greater than when, as for other derivatives, the only payments are for interest or currency rate differentials.

> *A contract to exchange at an agreed future date principal amounts in two different currencies at a conversion rate agreed at the outset. During the term of the contract the parties exchange interest, on an agreed basis, calculated on the principal amounts.*

The principal amounts can either be swapped at the outset and then re-swapped at maturity of the swap, or only swapped at maturity. In either case they *must* be swapped at maturity. Where there is an initial exchange of currency at the swap rate with the swap bank, with a re-exchange at maturity of the contract, the swap rate need not exactly match the spot rate in the market at the time of the original exchange.

They are only available 'over the counter', from banks and other financial institutions.

Currency swaps are used to hedge exposure to currency risk on future receipts (asset swaps) and payments (liability swaps), and to raise funds at a lower cost than would be obtainable in the currency sourced via the swap.

EXAMPLE **Straightforward cross-currency swap**

A major UK company needs to finance a US$60m project, and would prefer to raise floating rate US dollars. But it can obtain funds at a lower cost by issuing fixed rate Eurosterling bonds than by borrowing in US dollars, and decides to use a swap.

The company issues £40m of five year maturity bonds at, say, 10% and converts the sterling into US dollars at the spot rate of £1:US$1.5 to raise $60m.

Under the swap contract, the business agrees to pay interest to the swap bank throughout the 5-year term of the swap at, say, the floating rate for six-month US LIBOR on US$60m and to receive fixed rate sterling at 10.25% on £40m.

The swap bank providing the contract will match the swap by entering into an opposite swap with another counterparty (to whom, say, it charges fixed rate sterling at 10.5% and pays interest at six-month US LIBOR).

At the maturity of the swap contract, there is an exchange of currencies. The UK company pays $60m to the swap bank and receives £40m, which it needs to repay its bondholders.

The UK company has obtained floating rate US dollars and receives 0.25% in sterling (being the difference between the 10.25% fixed rate in sterling it receives from the swap bank and the 10% fixed sterling coupon it pays to the bondholders). The 0.25% could be sold into US dollars by way of a forward contract, thereby reducing the cost of the floating rate US dollars.

If the UK company has instead borrowed US dollars which will have to be repaid by converting sterling, then it could protect against a strengthening of the dollar (affecting both the principal and interest payments) by entering into a swap. It would then know the exchange rate at maturity and could swap the US dollar interest payments on its borrowing for fixed or floating rate sterling interest payments.

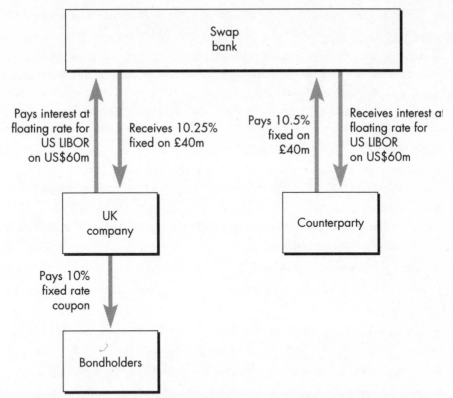

Fig. 6.2 Interest flows on a straightforward cross-currency swap (not of principal amounts)

The swap contract will specify the dates on which interest is to be paid (which need not be the same for each counterparty), and the rates of interest to be paid by each counterparty. Swaps can be at fixed rates in both currencies, or a fixed rate in one currency and a floating rate in the other ('cross-currency swap'), or floating rate in both currencies ('cross-currency basis swap').

Currency swaps can be obtained for terms of 15 years, or longer.

Each counterparty is a 'receiver' of interest in one currency and a 'payer' of interest in the other, e.g., if counterparty A is receiver of floating rate dollars and payer of fixed rate sterling, then counterparty B will be receiver of fixed rate sterling and payer of floating rate dollars.

The documentation for swaps is usually based on the standard formats of bodies such as the International Swaps and Derivatives Association (ISDA).

- Advantage can be taken of any comparative funding advantage (it may be that a borrower could issue favourably priced bonds in its own country, but be prohibited from issuing bonds in the country of the currency it requires, or can only do so on unattractive terms).

- The exchange rate at maturity is known at the outset.

BENEFITS
including risks
avoided

- The principal amount (usually US$5m or equivalent upwards) and term (typically 2–10 years) can be tailored to the needs of the swap parties

- Early 'termination' may be possible by agreement of the counterparties, e.g., by reversal (a matching opposite swap), or by a swap sale (buyout, where, with the agreement of the swap bank, a counterparty sells its participation to a substitute counterparty). In each case there may have to be cash settlement, either immediately or over the term of the contract, for gains and losses from rate movements to the date of restructuring.

- The basis on which interest is paid and received is known, and may be at variable or fixed rates. The cost of the swap is usually built into the interest rate.

- Available in most major currencies, often using the US dollar as an intermediary as that market has greater liquidity (i.e., swap first into US dollars, then into the required currency).

- There is no upfront premium.

- The principal amount can be a constant or increase or decrease during the term of the swap.

- The names of the swap counterparties need not be made public, as a result of which they have been used to 'circumvent' exchange control regulations.

- There is usually a right of set-off in the event of default by a counterparty.

- Where there are a number of swaps between the same counterparties, there can be a cross-default clause (so that a default on one swap triggers default on the others and gives a right of offset) or 'novation' (where all swaps are incorporated into a new swap contract that replaces the existing contract).

- Currency swaps can be entered into at any time during the life of the transaction they are being used to hedge.

RISKS REMAINING

- Advantage cannot be taken of advantageous exchange rate movements over the term of the swap, as the swap rate is agreed at the outset and the parties are committed to exchange the currencies at that rate at maturity irrespective of the spot rate in the market.

- As the principal amounts are exchanged, currency swaps are 'on balance sheet' instruments.

- Swaps are not available in all currencies, although they can be obtained in the major currencies. It may be possible to swap via an intervening swap in a common currency (known as a 'cocktail swap' and usually with the US dollar).

- The counterparties have to pay interest at the agreed fixed or floating rate, and to have the funds available for exchange or re-exchange of principal amounts at maturity of the swap. The amount at risk if a counterparty defaults is the cost of replacing the interest stream and any adverse movement in the exchange rate on the principal amount. It is the exchange of principal amounts that makes currency swaps fundamentally different from interest rate swaps, where no exchange of principal takes place. This imposes increased credit risk and if a counterparty defaults it may be too late to arrange alternative hedging.

Glossary

Abandon (options) When a **buyer** (holder) does not exercise an **option**.

Acceptance Credit See *Bankers' Acceptance*.

Acceptance (draft/bill of exchange) The signing of a **draft/bill of exchange** by the drawee, who thereby accepts responsibility for its payment at **maturity**. See also *Bank Bill, Bankers' Acceptance*.

Acceptance Pour Aval See *Avalising*.

Accepting Bank (documentary letter of credit) See *Nominated Bank*.

Acceptor A drawee who signs a **draft/bill of exchange**, thereby committing to honour payment in full at its **maturity date**.

Accommodation Party A party who signs a **draft/bill of exchange** as an **acceptor**, **endorser** or **drawer** and thereby becomes liable for its payment, but without receiving value, i.e. they 'lend their name'.

Accounting Period The period of time covered by a set of financial reports. Although the accounts of most businesses are drawn up to cover a 12-month period this may not always be the case. See also *Balance Sheet, Balance Sheet Date* and *Profit and Loss Account*.

Accounting Standards International and national accountancy bodies issue statements/directives as to acceptable accountancy standards and practices, with the detailed treatment sometimes varying from country to country.

Accounts Payable (Payables) The amounts owed to third parties (**creditors**) for goods or services.

Accounts Receivable (Receivables) The amounts due from third parties (**debtors**) for goods or services. See also *Asset-based Financing, Factoring* and *Invoice Discounting*.

Accrual Basis Adjusting accounts and other financial records or reports to allow for expenditure incurred but not yet paid, or payable, and income earned but not yet received or receivable. Alternative treatments include 'cash basis' where only amounts actually paid or received are recorded.

Accrued Expenditure/Expenses Expenditure incurred but not yet paid or payable.

Accrued Income Income earned but not yet received or receivable.

Accrued Interest Interest that has been earned but not yet become due for payment.

Acid Test See *Liquid Ratio*.

ADRs See *American Depository Receipts*.

Advance (Lending) When a banker or other lender makes funds available, also the amount lent (e.g., an advance of US$1000).

Advances Against Collections (Bill Advances) Where a lender advances monies to the seller of goods or services with repayment to come from the proceeds of a collection, whilst retaining full right of recourse against the borrower. See also *Negotiation*.

Advance Payment Bond A bond/contract **guarantee** undertaking that advance and progress payments made by the beneficiary (being the buyer in favour of whom the bond has been issued) to the principal (being the seller who asks the bank or insurance company to issue the bond) will be refunded if the principal fails to comply with its contractual obligations to the beneficiary.

Advising Bank (Documentary Letter of Credit) The bank asked by the **issuing bank** to advise the **beneficiary** of the issue and terms of the credit. See also *Confirming Bank* and *Documentary Letter of Credit*.

After Acquired A clause often incorporated into lending and security charge documents, whereby assets such as **real property** that are subsequently acquired by the borrower are taken by the lender as additional security.

After Market See *Securities Exchanges*.

AGM See *Annual General Meeting*.

Agent (Syndicated Lending) The bank coordinating a lending syndicate and liaising with the borrower. See also *Lead Bank/Manager* and *Syndicated Loan*.

Aggregation Risk Where a transaction involves more than one market in which problems could be experienced.

Air Waybill A contract of air transport carriage and receipt issued by a carrier to an exporter. They are non-negotiable and do not give title to the goods.

ALCO Stands for 'asset and liability committee', typically the body to whom the **board of directors** delegate responsibility for overseeing **asset** and liability management within a business.

American Depository Receipts (ADRs) Tradable receipts given to investors in respect of **securities** (e.g., **shares**) in non-US companies where the securities are being held on behalf of the investors by US banks. The investors receive the income (e.g., **dividends**) on the securities.

American-style Option (Derivative Contract) An **option** that the **buyer** can **exercise** on any **business day** up to and including its specified **expiry date**. See also *European-style Option*.

Amortisation (Amortization) A phased reduction in the **book value** of an **asset** or in the amount of a **debt** (for example, repayment of a **mortgage** over a **term** of years). See also *Depreciation (Amortization of Fixed Assets)*.

Annual General Meeting (AGM) Annual meeting of the **shareholders/stockholders** of a **company/corporation** at which the **board of directors** seek approval for the most recent **annual report,** report on performance, propose resolutions such as the election of directors and re-appointment of **auditors** and answer questions from the 'floor' by shareholders/stockholders.

Annual Rate of Return The 'average annual profit' = (inward **cash flow** [actual or estimated] from an investment less the amount of the initial investment) ÷ the number of years over which the inward cash flow has been calculated. Dividing the average annual profit by the amount of the initial investment and multiplying by 100 gives the average annual rate of return (as a percentage). See also *Yield*.

Annual Report The report of a company's activities and financial affairs (usually including at minimum a **balance sheet** and a **profit and loss account**) sent annually by the directors of a **company/corporation** to its **shareholders/stockholders**. See also *Annual General Meeting*.

Appetite for Risk The degree of willingness to accept known risks.

Applicant (Documentary Letters of Credit) The buyer/importer of the goods or services who asks the **issuing bank** to set up the credit, and is liable for payments made under it to the seller (**beneficiary**). See also *Documentary Letter of Credit*.

Arbitrage Because financial markets do not always move in perfect step with each other it is possible to take advantage of usually short-term anomalies to trade between them at a profit. An 'arbitrageur' is the party seeking to profit from arbitrage.

Arm's Length Transactions where the terms and conditions are not influenced by any close relationships between the contracting parties. For example, a contract between two unconnected companies, but not a contract between a **parent** company and its **subsidiary**.

Arranger (Syndicated Lending) The bank mandated by the prospective borrower or by other prospective providers of finance to put together a syndicated financing package. Also known as **lead bank/manager**. See also *Syndicated Loan*.

Articles of Association See *By-laws*.

Articles of Incorporation/Memorandum of Association The document, usually needing to be filed with a government agency, that covers its external dealings and sets out details of a company such as its name, activities and share structure. See also *By-laws/Articles of Association* and *Charter*.

Asking Price See *Offer Price*.

Asset Something that is owned, whether tangible (i.e., having a physical form, e.g., **real property** or, usually, being convertible into cash, e.g., **debtors**) or intangible (e.g., **goodwill** and patents). See also *Current Assets*, *Fixed Assets*, *Liabilities*, *Net Asset Value* and *Quick Assets*.

Asset-based Financing Lending that is principally reliant on assets of the borrower, typically **accounts receivable** and **inventory**. See also *Factoring* and *Invoice Discounting*.

Asset Stripping Acquiring a **company/corporation** and selling off some or all of its **assets** to potentially realize more than it cost to buy the entire business.

Asset Swaps (Interest Rate) **Swaps** involving an exchange of **interest** receipts (there are other asset swaps not involving **interest**). See also *Liability Swaps*.

Associate Company A **company/corporation** which is not a **subsidiary** or controlled by another company/corporation, but over which that company/corporation has significant influence. See also *Holding Company* and *Parent Company*.

Associated Costs The costs to a bank of providing or maintaining **loans** or other facilities, and which result from **reserve requirement/asset costs** or other government, central bank or regulatory requirements. See also *Capital Adequacy Requirement*.

At Call Repayable on demand or short notice, as distinct from being available for a specified **term**. See also *Call*.

ATM (Option Derivative Contract) See *At the Money*.

At Market To buy or to sell at the current **market price/rate/value**.

At The Money (Option Derivative Contract) An **option** where the **market rate** of the **underlying** is the same as the **strike price**. See also *In the Money* and *Out of the Money*.

Audit An independent professional check on the financial accounts of a business.

Audit Trail The verification of financial accounts or information by following a transaction step by step backwards until its starting point is reached.

Auditor The professional individual or firm (usually accountants) who undertake the **audit** of the financial accounts of a business. The auditor normally issues a signed report to the business or its shareholders (auditor's/accountant's opinion/certificate). This report may be 'qualified' if the auditor has doubts as to whether the accounts conform to required or accepted principles and practices, or if they have other reservations. See also *Annual General Meeting*.

Authorized Capital/Shares/Stock The amount of **equity** that a **company/corporation** can issue to **shareholders/stockholders**. See also *Articles of Incorporation/ Memorandum of Association*, *Issued Capital/Shares/Stock* and *Ordinary Shares/Common Stock*.

Aval See *Avalising*.

Avalising Avalising (an aval) is the guarantee by a bank, or other financial institution or government department (the avalor), that a **draft/bill of exchange, promissory note** or other **instrument** will be paid at **maturity**. Avalising is also known as acceptance pour aval. See also *Forfaiting*.

Average (Insurance) Where an insurance policy pays out on claims in the proportion of the value of the asset to any lesser amount for which it is insured.

Average Credit Given (Collection Period) A ratio showing the average number of days it has taken a business to collect payment from its trade **debtors**.

Average Credit Taken A ratio showing the average number of days it has taken a business to pay its trade **creditors**.

Back-to-back The matching of two opposing transactions. See also *Back-to-back Documentary Letter of Credit*.

Back-to-back Documentary Letter of Credit Where the **beneficiary** (seller) uses the letter of credit issued in its favour to obtain the goods or services needed to complete its contract with the buyer (**applicant**). The beneficiary asks its bank to issue a separate letter of credit in favour of the beneficiary's suppliers or subcontractors, relying on the original credit to produce the monies necessary to cover the payments to them when due. See also *Documentary Letter of Credit*.

Back Office The departments that deal with the administrative and compliance aspects of a business, but do not directly participate in its trading.

Backwardation Where prices are in inverse relationship to the length of time. For example, where the price for delivery of a future is higher at three months than at six months. It is the opposite of **contango**.

Bad Debt A debt that could not be collected and is written off.

Balance Sheet Risk (Currency) See *Currency Exchange Rate Risk*.

Balance Sheet (Statement of Financial Position) A summary as at a given date (**balance sheet date**) of the **assets** and **liabilities** of a business. It does not record trading performance over any period, other than the resultant increase or decrease in, for example, **debtors, creditors** and retained profits/losses. See also *Profit and Loss Account*.

Balance Sheet Date The date as at which a **balance sheet** is prepared, being the end of an **accounting period**. A business may, subject to local regulations, be able to change its balance sheet date.

Balloon Repayment The lump sum repayment that clears a **loan** or other **debt** at the end of an agreed term for the facility and is either the only repayment or is substantially greater than the amounts of any earlier stage payments. See also *Bullet*.

Bank Bill A **draft/bill of exchange** accepted by a bank. See also *Acceptance*.

Bankers' Acceptance (Acceptance Credit) A tenor draft/bill of exchange drawn on and accepted by a bank, which is then usually discounted to finance the **drawer's** short-term trading transactions. The accepted draft can be sold into the **money market**. See also *Acceptance, Bank Bill* and *Discounting (Drafts/Bills of Exchange)*.

Bankers' Payment A payment issued by a bank on behalf of a customer. The recipient's credit risk is on the bank.

Bankruptcy The legal **insolvency** of a business when it cannot pay its **debts**. It may result from a court action by an unpaid **creditor**, or be 'voluntary' if the insolvent business (i.e., its directors) takes action to be declared bankrupt. What happens next depends upon the applicable jurisdiction. In some countries a bankrupt business is simply wound up and any net proceeds distributed amongst creditors. In others there are options for continued trading and debt restructuring in the hope of reducing losses or saving the business. See also *Chapter 11, Insolvency* and *Liquidation*.

Barter The direct exchange of goods or services for other goods or services. See also *Countertrade*.

Basis Point One hundredth of one per cent, i.e., 0.01%.

Basis Risk Where the available **hedging instrument** closely matches but does not exactly mirror or track the risk being hedged. See also *Tracking Error*.

Basis Swap Also known as an 'index swap'. An **interest rate swap** between one floating **interest** rate and another floating interest rate in the same currency (e.g., six-month **LIBOR** to three-month LIBOR or three-month LIBOR to three-month LIBOR plus a margin). See also *Variable/Floating Rate Interest*.

Basket A combination of, for example, currencies, **commodities** or financial **instruments**, often providing an accepted **index** or point of reference.

Bear Someone taking the view that **market prices** will decline. To benefit from such a situation they may sell for delivery at a future date, say, **securities** they do not yet own, in the expectation of being able to buy them at a lower price before they have to be delivered. If they are wrong and prices rise the loss can be substantial. Bear is the opposite of **Bull**.

Bear Market A market where prices are falling. See also *Bull Market*.

Bearer (Securities) Where ownership and the right to be paid **interest** or repaid **principal** on **securities** is evidenced by possession of **coupons** or other documents. Can be attractive to those investors reluctant to let their financial interests be known by registration. See also *Registered*.

Bed and Breakfast The sale and re-purchase of **securities** to establish a new acquisition price, usually for tax reasons.

Benchmark A figure that can be used for comparison purposes e.g., the average

gross profit margin for an industry, or the ratio of staff costs to sales in (say) the 'top ten' companies within a sector.

Beneficiary (Documentary Letter of Credit) The seller/exporter of the goods or services who is the named beneficiary under the letter of credit and entitled to payment, or **acceptance** of a **tenor draft,** on presentation to a **nominated bank** of the documents specified in the credit in good order. See also *Documentary Letter of Credit.*

Beta A measure of price **volatility** against an **index** or other average. See also *Capital Asset Pricing Model.*

Bid-offer Spread The difference ('turn') between the prices at which, for example, a **market maker** offers to respectively buy and sell. The price at which the **trader** will buy (bid) is the lower figure and the price at which they will sell is the higher (offer). See also *Bid Price* and *Offer Price.*

Bid Price The price at which someone offers to buy. See also *Bid-offer Spread* and *Offer Price (Asking Price).*

Bid/Tender Bond A **bond/contract guarantee** given on behalf of a tenderer by a bank or insurance company in favour of the party to whom a tender is being submitted (the beneficiary), that pays if the tenderer is awarded the contract but then refuses to enter into a formal contract.

Big Figure Usually taken to be the second number, but sometimes the first two numbers, to the right of the decimal point in a foreign exchange quotation.

Big Ticket Refers to highly priced capital items, such as aircraft.

Bill of Exchange/Draft See *Draft/Bill of Exchange.*

Bill Advances See *Advances Against Collections.*

Bills of Lading Documents evidencing the contract of carriage and receipt for goods between an exporter and the carrier (a ship, shipping line or its agents). A 'clean bill of lading' is where the goods have been received for shipment in apparent good order, i.e., without obvious signs of damage.

Black-Scholes Pricing Model Fischer Black and Myron Scholes developed, with Robert Merton, an **option** pricing **model** critical to progression of that market.

Blue Chip Well-established **companies/corporations** that are considered to be sound investments.

Board of Directors The body of individuals (directors) with responsibility for running a **company/corporation,** usually elected by the **shareholders/stockholders.** Those involved in the day-to-day management are known as 'executive' (inside) directors whilst those who advise on policy but are not involved in day-to-day management are known as 'non-executive directors' (outside or board directors). See also *Shadow Director.*

Bond (Securities) A transferable **debt instrument** with **maturity** longer than one year, usually issued by substantial **companies/corporations**, local authorities, supra-nationals and governments. Bonds can have very long maturity dates, e.g., 30 years, whilst 'perpetuals' have no set repayment date. They may be issued at a **discount** to their **par** value and/or pay **interest** at **fixed** or **variable/floating** rates, be secured or unsecured, be in **bearer** or **registered** form, and may be convertible into **ordinary shares/common stock** of an issuing company/corporation. Government bonds are usually highly liquid, and in most countries are considered the lowest-risk investment. See also *Bond Markets, Callable, Domestic Bonds, Eurobonds, Foreign Bonds, Notes, Puttable* and *Zero Coupon*.

Bond/Contract Guarantee A written undertaking normally given on behalf of a seller (principal) in favour of a buyer (beneficiary), usually by a bank or insurance company, to make a payment under specified circumstances. There are two principal types of bond/contract guarantee: 'on demand' – where the beneficiary only has to make demand (accompanied by any specified documents) on the '**guarantor**' to be entitled to payment – and 'conditional' – where the beneficiary is required to claim a default by the principal, and may have to support this with specified documents. See also *Advance Payment Bond, Bid/Tender Bond, Counter Indemnity, Payment Bond, Performance Bond, Retention Bond, Standby Credits* and *Warranty/Maintenance Bond*.

Bond Markets The markets in which governments, supra-nationals (e.g., the World Bank), financial institutions and large **companies/corporations** borrow and invest for the **medium** and **long term**. The amounts involved are large and the **term** to **maturity** is usually a minimum of one year from the date of issue, but more often two years or longer. They include **domestic bonds** (under the jurisdiction of a single country) and **foreign** bonds (issued in a country, and in the currency of that country, other than of the issuer). Until purchased from the issuer by the original investor the instruments are traded in the primary market, where the proceeds go to the issuer, and thereafter in the secondary market, where the proceeds go to the previous holder. See also *Securities Exchanges* (for 'primary' and 'secondary' markets) and *Capital Markets*.

Bonus Issue See *Capitalization Issue*.

Book A trading record, showing what has been bought or sold and the net position.

Book Value The value of an **asset** as shown in the accounts of a business. It is normally the purchase price less any **depreciation**. Not to be confused with **market value**, which is what an asset might realize if sold at **arm's length**.

Borrower's Option (Derivative Contract) An interest rate **call option** contract where the benefit to the **buyer** is that it has the right to pay a fixed amount of **interest**. See also *Lender's Option*.

Borrowing Powers The extent to which an organization and its officers are respectively permitted to enter into financial commitments. See also *Articles of Incorporation/Memorandum of Association*, *By-laws/Articles of Association* and *Ultra Vires*.

Boston Option See *Forward Reversing Option*.

Breakeven When the sales revenues of a business equal its costs.

Bridging Loan A **loan** with repayment to come from the sale of a specific **asset** or the proceeds of a specific transaction. The risk is that the sale or transaction never happens, or is delayed or only achieved at a lower figure than expected, and there may then be no way of repaying the bridge in full or at all and on or after its **maturity** date.

There are two types of bridging loan, which are the following:

- 'Closed' – where the borrower has already entered into a contract for the transaction or asset sale from which repayment is to be made. In theory only time is needed for the monies to be received by the borrower and the loan repaid but things do not always work out smoothly in practice. What if the borrower's **counterparty** defaults, or the contract is conditional upon an act or event outside the control of the borrower?

- 'Open' – where the borrower has yet to enter into any contract with a third party for the transaction or sale. A typical example would be a borrower wishing to buy a new house but not yet having found a buyer for their present property. What if they cannot sell it, or house prices fall, or it simply takes much longer than expected to find a buyer. Given the added uncertainty and risk involved with open bridges a lender normally requires either a higher margin of security or some other comfort factor.

Broken Dates Contracts, e.g., currency **forward contracts**, where the **maturity** is fixed for other than a round number of months.

Broker Someone who acts between a buyer and a seller, for either a commission or a fee. See also *Broker-dealer*, *Dealer* and *Market Makers*.

Broker–Dealer Someone who trades for both their own account and for clients, i.e., as both a principal and a **broker**. See also *Dealer* and *Market Makers*.

Brokerage The commission charged by a **broker** for buying or selling on behalf of their client.

Budget A forecast of revenue and expenditure. See also *Cash Flow*.

Bull Someone taking the view that a market will improve. To benefit from such a situation they may buy, say, **securities** in the expectation of re-selling them at a higher price. If they are wrong and prices fall the loss can be substantial. Bull is the opposite of **bear**.

Bull Market A market where prices are steadily rising. See also *Bear Market*.

Bulldog Bonds **Bonds** denominated in sterling that are issued in the United Kingdom by non-UK issuers.

Bullet Where something is paid in a single lump sum rather than in installments (**tranches**), e.g., a **loan** repaid in a single payment at its expiry. See also *Balloon Repayment*.

Business Day The days and hours when a business or a market is officially open for trading.

Buy-back (Countertrade) Where the supplier of equipment, typically capital items such as mining equipment, receives some of the output of its use as payment. See also *Countertrade*.

Buy-back Agreement An arrangement whereby the seller of an **asset** or financial **instrument** agrees to buy it back at or before an agreed date at a specified price. See also *Repurchase Agreement (Repo)* and *Sale and Leaseback*.

Buyer (Vanilla Swap) See *Payer (Vanilla Swap)*.

Buyer (Option Derivative Contract) The party with the right but not the obligation to exercise the contract. Also known as the 'holder'.

Buyer Credit Where a bank in the country of an exporter lends (or otherwise commits) to a bank in the country of an importer, which in turn lends to the importer so that they can buy from the exporter. The bank in the country of the exporter is often, in turn, guaranteed by their government's export agency (to encourage trade).

Buyer's Market When sellers are keen, or even desperate, to sell and buyers can take a hard line in negotiations. See also *Seller's Market*.

By-laws/Articles of Association The rules set by an organization (e.g., **company/ corporation**) for the way it is to be managed. In some countries the articles of association and the **memorandum of association** form the 'constitution' of a company. See also *Charter*.

Call
- A 'margin call' is made by one **counterparty** on another, e.g., a lender on a borrower, requiring them to top-up the level of a deposit or other security to a pre-set limit.
- The demand by a **company/corporation** for holders of **partly paid capital/ shares/stock** to pay a further installment.
- When monies are deposited or lent without a fixed term they are said to be **at call**, and are repayable on demand.

Call Option (Derivative Contract) An **option** where the **buyer** has the right, but not the obligation, to buy a specified quantity of the **underlying** from the **writer** at an agreed price on or before a specified **maturity/expiry date**. The buyer can benefit from an increase in the **market price** of the underlying. See also *Put Option*.

Callable (Bonds) Where the issuer can redeem the **debt** before its specified **maturity date**.

Canons of Lending The fundamentals of good lending.

Cap (Interest Rate) A form of **option** derivative giving the buyer the right, but not the obligation, to fix the rate of **interest** (the **strike rate**) for the entire **term** of a notional **loan**. The buyer pays a **premium** to the **writer** and, if the option is exercised on any of the specified dates, is paid in cash an amount equal to the difference between the strike rate and the **market rate** (calculated on the notional amount of the loan). See also *Collar* and *Floor*.

Capital The assets invested or being used for business purposes. May be a **principal** amount.

Capital (Securities) See *Authorized/Issued Capital/Shares/Stock* and *Capital Market*.

Capital Adequacy Requirement Banks are required to show that they have sufficient **capital** to support their activities. They must have a minimum ratio of capital to assets, with the assets (e.g., **loans** to customers) on a bank's **balance sheet** 'weighted' according to their perceived degree of risk. If, as typically, the ratio is set at 8% then for every US$100 lent to a company (which would be accorded 100% weighting whereas lending to another bank may only be weighted at 20% of the **principal** amount) the bank must have US$8 of capital. As capital costs money to raise, and every unit of capital can only be allocated once, banks have to ensure that they put their capital to the best use. The bank's capital is, itself, 'tiered', i.e., classified by source. Part of the attractiveness of **derivatives** to banks is that, because these **instruments** have zero or low capital support requirements (as they may be off balance sheet or the amount of principal at risk is considered to be small) a bank can write greater volumes of such business on its capital base than it can write conventional 'on-balance-sheet' facilities such as loans. See also *Reserve Requirement/Reserve Asset Costs*.

Capital Asset Pricing Model (CAPM) A **modeling** technique based on the principle that the greater the **volatility** risk the greater the return required by investors. Where the risk on a specific investment (e.g., **shares/stock** in a single **company/corporation**) is the same as that of the market it has what is known as a 'beta' of one. An investment with a beta lower than one is less risky and its return should be lower, whilst a beta greater than one should provide a greater return. Once the beta is known it can be used to calculate the individual cost of capital as against that for the market (the return should equal that on a risk free investment plus a premium commensurate with the risk). See also *Internal Rate of Return* and *Hurdle Rate*.

Capital Employed Usually taken to be **net tangible assets** plus **term debts**.

Capital Gain/Loss The difference between the sale price and purchase price of an asset.

Capital Markets The equity, **bond** and **money markets**. See also *Securities Exchanges*.

Capital Reserve See *Reserve (Capital)*.

Capitalization/Scrip/Bonus Issue The issue of free additional **shares/stock** by a **corporation/company** to existing **shareholders/stockholders** *pro rata* the number they already hold, usually with any 'fractions' in cash. For example, one new free share for every four shares already held. The resultant availability of more shares at a reduced price per share (as the issue by the company of the extra shares 'dilutes' the holding in the company represented by each share) often makes the shares more attractive in the market.

CAPM See *Capital Asset Pricing Model*.

Carriage and Insurance Paid (CIP) An **Incoterm**. The supplier is responsible for carriage to a named place of destination, delivery into the custody of a carrier, export licence, duties and taxes and insurance during the carriage.

Carriage Paid To (CPT) An **Incoterm**. The supplier is responsible for carriage to a named place of destination into the custody of a carrier, export licence, duties and taxes and insurance until delivered to the carrier.

Cash Basis See *Accrual Basis*.

Cash Conversion Cycle The length of time between a business first expending cash in producing something and it receiving payment from the sale of that product or service. The longer the period of the cycle the more **working capital** a business needs.

Cash Cow An established business that produces a steady flow of net cash without the need for further substantial **capital** investment.

Cash Flow The net cash movements of a business, being actual receipts less actual payments, which may be positive or negative. It is the lifeblood of any business, hence the expression 'Cash is King'. Even the most profitable **company/corporation** can find itself in financial difficulties if, through poor 'housekeeping', it has insufficient funds to pay **debts** as they fall due. A cash flow forecast shows projected future cash revenue and expenditure. See also *Budget*.

Cash Ratio See *Liquid Ratio*.

CBOT See *Chicago Board of Trade*.

Cedel A **Eurobond** settlement organization, based in Luxembourg. See also *Euroclear*.

Ceiling Price The highest price a buyer will pay. See also *Floor Price*.

Central Banks The banking organization of a country that is typically responsible, *inter alia*, for issuing its currency, acting as bankers to the government, overseeing the monetary system and representing its government's interests in the financial markets.

Certificate (Securities) The document evidencing an investor's ownership of securities, e.g., **stocks/shares** and **bonds**. See also *Bearer* and *Registered*.

Certificate of Deposit (CD) A **negotiable debt certificate** issued by a bank or other corporate and repayable at a fixed date.

Certificate of Incorporation Document issued by or on behalf of a government evidencing a **company/corporation** as a legal entity. See also *Articles of Incorporation/Memorandum of Association* and *Charter*.

Certificate of Origin A statement evidencing the place of origin of goods, usually issued by an exporter or a local Chamber of Commerce.

CFR See *Cost and Freight*.

CHAPS The UK Clearing House Automated Payments System for same-day settlements between banks.

Chapter 11 of the 1978 Bankruptcy Reform Act in the USA allows an insolvent debtor to continue to control the operations of the business, whilst trying to resolve its financial problems.

Charter (Depending on the Country) The combined **Articles of Incorporation** and Certificate of Incorporation of a **company/corporation**.

Check/Cheque A **draft/bill of exchange** drawn on a bank and payable on demand. A certified check has its payment guaranteed by a bank.

Cheque See *Check/Cheque*.

Chicago Board of Trade (CBOT) The **derivatives** exchange in Chicago.

Chinese Wall Where different activities within an organization are separated (and kept confidential from each other) to avoid conflicts of interest.

CHIPS The US Clearing House Interbanks Payment System for same-day settlements between banks.

CIF See *Cost Insurance and Freight*.

CIP See *Carriage and Insurance Paid*.

Classes (Stocks/Shares) Where a **company/corporation** issues more than one type of **ordinary shares/common stock**, each having different voting or other rights.

Clean (Auditors' Report) A report that has not been **qualified** by reference to divergence from accounting practices, or to other reservations of the **auditors**.

Clean (Bills of Lading) See *Bills of Lading*.

275

Clean Collection See *Collection*.

Clearing House (Derivative Contracts) The counterparty to both participants of exchange traded derivatives, with whom the initial and variation margins are deposited. Usually owned by either the exchange or by banks or other financial institutions. See also *Netting Agreements*.

Close To conclude a transaction.

Close Out The elimination of an exposure by entering into an equal and opposite transaction. See also *Offsetting Trade*.

Closed/Private Company/Corporation A company/corporation privately owned by a small number of investors. See also *Public/Open Company/Corporation*.

Closing Creditors The creditors shown in the balance sheet at the end of an accounting period, which become the opening creditors for the next accounting period.

Closing Debtors The debtors shown in the balance sheet at the end of an accounting period, which become the opening debtors for the next accounting period.

Closing Stock/Inventory The stocks/inventory shown in the balance sheet at the end of an accounting period, which become the opening stocks/inventory for the next accounting period.

Collar The simultaneous sale and purchase by one party of options for the same notional amount, term and dates, but at different strike rates, with offset of the respective premiums. See *Cylinder* (*Options*).

Collateral An alternative word for security, although sometimes taken as being security additional to the principal security.

Collecting Bank (Collection) Any bank (whether nominated by the principal or selected by the remitting bank) involved in the collection chain other than the remitting bank. Usually it is the presenting bank.

Collection (Trade Payments) The sending by a bank (remitting bank), on behalf of a seller of goods or services (principal), of documents to another bank (presenting bank) for them to be released to a buyer of those goods or services for either payment or the acceptance of a tenor draft/bill of exchange.
There are two types of collection:
- 'Clean' – where the only documents are financial documents, e.g., drafts or promissory notes.
- 'Documentary' – where the documents are commercial documents, e.g., bills of lading, with or without accompanying financial documents.

See also *Advances Against Collections, Collection Instruction, Collecting Bank, Inward Collection* and *Outward Collection*.

Collection Instruction/Collection Order The instructions to be followed by the banks involved in a collection, that accompany the documents.

Collection Period See *Average Credit Given*.

Commercial Paper (CP) Unsecured negotiable debt instruments issued by governments, highly rated financial institutions and **companies/corporations**. Includes USCP in the US, ECP in the Euromarket and SCP in the sterling market. See also *Euro Commercial Paper*.

Commodities Tradable goods having a physical form, e.g., oil and gas. They can be 'hard' such as precious metals, or 'soft' such as agricultural produce.

Commodity Derivatives Derivative contracts based on **commodities**.

Commodity Loans See *Produce Loans*.

Commodity Risk The exposure to adverse movements in the **market price** of commodities.

Common Stock/Ordinary Shares See *Ordinary Shares/Common Stock*.

Company/Corporation (Companies/Corporations) A business incorporated as a legal entity separate from that of its **shareholders/stockholders**, and usually with 'limited liability' (i.e., the shareholders/stockholders can only lose their investment including any uncalled **capital** and are not liable to third parties for the **debts** of the company/corporation), although their liability might alternatively be wholly or partially 'unlimited'. In some countries the term 'company' can also relate to **partnerships** and **sole traders**. See also *Board of Directors, Closed/Private Company/Corporation, Partly Paid Capital/Shares/Stock, Public/Open Company/Corporation* and *Quoted/Listed*.

Company Doctor Someone appointed to help sort out the problems of an ailing business.

Compensation Culture The belief that, whatever goes wrong, someone else must pay.

Complexity Risk Where something is so complex it may not be clearly understood and is more likely to be subject to error.

Compliance Ensuring that the trading and other activities of a business comply with regulatory and supervisory requirements.

Compound Interest Where **interest** is paid on both the **principal** amount and on the **interest** that has previously accumulated on that **principal** amount (and has been added to **principal**). See also *Flat Interest* and *Simple Interest*.

Concentration Risk Exposure to a high level of risk on any **instrument** or in any sector. An extension of concentration risk is that to a market which is dominated by only a small number of firms.

Conditions Precedent Conditions to be met before something can happen, e.g., the actions required of a borrower before a lender will advance funds. See also *Conditions Subsequent* and *Covenant*.

Conditions Subsequent Conditions to be met after an event, e.g., the actions required by a lender of the borrower after funds have been provided. See also *Conditions Precedent*, *Covenant* and *Negative Pledge*.

Confidential Invoice Discounting See *Invoice Discounting*.

Confirmed Documentary Letter of Credit Where a **confirming bank**, usually in the country of the **beneficiary**, adds to the letter of credit its confirmation that the **beneficiary** will be paid on presenting to the confirming bank the specified documents in good order. See also *Documentary Letter of Credit*.

Confirming Bank (Documentary Letter of Credit) At the request of the **issuing bank** a confirming bank undertakes that, on presentation to it or another **nominated bank** of the documents specified in the letter of credit in good order, the **beneficiary** will be paid.

Confirming House An institution which confirms an importer's order, thereby undertaking that the exporter will be paid. May also provide finance to importers.

Consideration A payment, whether in cash or by delivery of an **asset** or service.

Consolidated Accounts The combined financial statements of a **parent company** and its **subsidiaries**.

Consolidation Clause (Lending) A **term** in an agreement giving the lender the right to consolidate the security referred to therein with any other security charged in its favour by that borrower, usually providing cover for all present and future liabilities of the borrower (i.e., it provides 'continuing security').

Consortium Those joining together to share the risks and benefits of a transaction. Known as 'members' of the consortium. See also *Agent*, *Lead Bank/Manager*, *Majority Lenders* and *Syndicated Loan*.

Constitution See *By-laws/Articles of Association*.

Contango Where price is in direct relationship to the length of time. For example, where the price for delivery of a future is higher at six months than at three months. It is the opposite of **backwardation**.

Contingent Liability A **liability** which may or may not arise, and the amount of which may not be known. Wherever possible contingent liabilities should be identified and the maximum potential liability quantified. The fact that they are contingent does not mean that they are necessarily insignificant – and have often been of such magnitude as to cause the demise of a business. See also *Deferred Consideration*.

Contract A legally binding agreement between two or more **counterparties**.

Contract Guarantee See *Bond/Contract Guarantee*.

Contract Period (Forward Rate Agreement) See *Forward Rate Agreement*.

Controlling Interest A stake in a business sufficiently large to give the holder (or group of connected holders) control of its activities.

Contribution See *Gross Contribution*.

Convergence The converging of market and futures prices over the term of a **futures** contract.

Convertible Currencies Those freely exchangeable into other currencies in the international market, for example the US$ and sterling.

Convertible Bonds and Convertible Preference Shares These 'hybrids' pay a fixed rate of interest unless, on the occurrence of specified events, they are converted at the holder's option into **ordinary shares/common stock** in the issuing **company/ corporation**. They can be attractive to the issuer as the rate of **interest** is usually lower than that for bank borrowings or **bonds**, and may appeal to investors as there is usually a set 'conversion price' which may be lower than the **market price** at the conversion date. See also *Bonds, Preference Shares/ Prior-preferred Stock* and *Warrants*.

Corporation See *Company/Corporation*.

Correspondent Bank If a bank does not have a branch or **subsidiary** in another country it may ask a 'correspondent bank' to act on its behalf as necessary. The banks normally maintain **nostro** and **vostro** accounts with each other.

Cost and Freight (CFR) An **Incoterm**. The supplier is responsible for the cost of carriage to a named port of destination, export licence, duties and taxes and for insurance until loaded on board the vessel at the port of shipment.

Cost Insurance and Freight (CIF) An **Incoterm**. The supplier is responsible for the cost of carriage to a named port of destination, delivery on board the vessel, export licence, duties and taxes and insurance during the carriage.

Cost of Funds (Lending) The cost to the lender of obtaining the monies it then on-lends. See also *Associated Costs* and *Reserve Requirement/Asset Costs*.

Counter Indemnity (Bond/Contract Guarantee) The indemnity given by the principal (being the party requesting a bank or insurance company to issue a **bond/contract guarantee**) that they will reimburse the **guarantor** for claims made against them by the beneficiary under the bond/contract guarantee.

Counterparty (Counterparties) A party to a transaction, each party being a counterparty to every other party.

Counterparty/Credit Risk The risk that a **counterparty** will not honour their obligations. If the default occurs before the date when settlement of the underlying transaction is due the party who has been let down will be exposed to the 'replacement' risk of having to bear any costs of replacing or cancelling the deal – which are commonly less than the full amount of the transaction. A potentially greater threat is **settlement risk**, which arises when a party pays away cash or delivers assets before their counterparty is known to have performed their part of the deal. Settlement exposure is normally for the full amount of the transaction, and may exist during the course of a trading day (daylight exposure), or last overnight (overnight exposure) or longer.

Counterpurchase A form of **countertrade** involving two separate parallel contracts between the buyer and seller.

Countertrade The direct or indirect exchange of goods or services for other goods or services. See also *Barter, Buy-back, Counterpurchase, Offset* and *Switch*.

Country Risk See *Political and Country Risks*.

Coupon The annual **interest** rate paid on **bonds** and other **debt instruments**. **Bearer** bonds are issued with a set of 'coupons' that can be exchanged for interest payments at specified dates.

Coupon (Swap) See *Vanilla Swap*.

CP See *Commercial Paper*.

CPT See *Carriage Paid To*.

Covenant The overall creditworthiness of a party. Also an undertaking to act in a certain way, whether to do something (positive/affirmative covenant) or not to do something (negative covenant). See also *Conditions Subsequent* and *Negative Pledge*.

Crash A sudden substantial fall in **market values**.

Credit Derivatives Derivative contracts that transfer credit risk, e.g., on **loans** and **bonds**. In their simplest form the 'credit swap' provides for one of the **counterparties** to the contract to receive a cash payment from the other counterparty if the value of the 'reference debt' falls as a result of specified 'credit events'. An alternative is the 'total return swap', where the counterparty owning the reference debt exchanges the income from it with a counterparty who pays in return (say) **money market** rate plus or minus a margin.

Credit Given See *Average Credit Given*.

Credit Insurance Insurance cover against bad debts, subject to specified terms and conditions.

Credit Limit The maximum exposure a business is prepared to accept for any **counterparty**.

Credit Rating Measurement of the creditworthiness of governments, local authorities, banks, companies/corporations, other businesses and individuals. See *Rating Agencies*.

Credit Risk See *Counterparty/Credit Risk*.

Credit Taken See *Average Credit Taken*.

Creditors Those to whom you owe money (in their books you are a **debtor**). See also *Accounts Payable*.

Critical Dependencies Those factors that make all the difference to the success or failure of a business or project.

Cross-currency Swap See *Currency Swap*.

Cross-currency Basis Swap See *Currency Swap*.

Cross-default Clause A provision, for example in a borrowing agreement, whereby a default by a borrower under any other agreement is an event of default under the agreement containing the cross-default clause.

Cross Rate The 'indirect' rate of exchange between two currencies as calculated against a common third currency. See also *Exchange Rate*.

Cum Dividend When the purchaser of **shares/stock** has the right to receive the benefit of a recently declared **dividend**. See also *Ex Dividend*

Cumulative Preference Shares/Stock See *Preference Shares/Prior-preferred Stock*.

Currency Exchange Controls The regulations of a country that restrict foreign currency transactions. See also *Convertible Currencies* and *Floating Rate Currencies*.

Currency Exchange Rate Risk Even between major currencies substantial **exchange rate** movements may be experienced over relatively short periods of time. These can alter your **balance sheet** if you have **assets** or **liabilities** 'domiciled' in a currency other than that in which you prepare your accounts ('translation' or 'balance sheet' risk), and may affect your **profit and loss account** if the impact is on income or expenditure ('trading' or 'transaction' risk). There might also be longer-term strategic ('economic') consequences for the value of your business if, for example, rates of exchange settle at levels which fundamentally alter your competitiveness in international markets.

Currency Option A **derivative** contract giving the **buyer** the right, but not the obligation, to exchange a specified amount of one currency into another specified currency on or before a specified date at a specified rate of exchange (**strike price/rate**). The buyer of the contract pays a **premium** to its **writer** (seller). See also *Option*.

Currency Swap A **derivative** contract to exchange at an agreed future date **principal** amounts in two different currencies at a conversion rate agreed at the outset. During the term of the contract the parties exchange **interest**, on an agreed basis, calculated on the principal amounts. Currency swaps can be at **fixed rates** in both currencies, or a fixed rate in one currency and a variable/floating rate in the other ('cross-currency swap'), or floating rate in both currencies ('cross-currency basis swap'). Each **counterparty** is a **receiver** of interest in one currency and a payer of interest in the other, e.g., if counterparty A is receiver of floating rate dollars and payer of fixed rate sterling, then counterparty B will be the receiver of fixed rate sterling and payer of floating rate dollars. See also *Swap*.

Current Assets The cash and other **assets** of a business, e.g., **debtors/accounts receivable** and **inventory/stock** that should be capable of conversion into cash within 12 months. See also *Fixed Assets* and *Goodwill*.

Current Cost Accounting The preparation of business accounts based on replacement cost rather than depreciated costs as in conventional historical cost accounting. See also *Inflation Accounting*.

Current Liabilities Usually taken as being the **liabilities** of a business due for payment within 12 months. See also *Term Liabilities*.

Current Ratio (Working Capital Ratio) The ratio of **current assets** to **current liabilities**, which may indicate the solvency of a business.

Cylinder (Options) An **option** derivative contract combining two **European-style currency options** (one bought and one sold) at different **strike prices**. See *Collar*.

D/A See *Documents Against Acceptance*.

DAF See *Delivered at Frontier*.

Data Room When third party access has to be allowed to otherwise sensitive or confidential documents, viewing may be restricted to a 'data room' (often at a lawyer's office) where it can be ensured that, for example, unauthorized copies are not made.

Daylight Exposure See *Settlement Risk*.

Days of Grace Days allowed to the payer in which to make a payment after it becomes due.

DDP See *Delivered Duty Paid*.

Dead Cat Bounce When a share price falls rapidly then rallies briefly, often to fall again.

Dealer A party trading for their own account. See also *Broker*, *Broker-dealer* and *Market Maker*.

Debenture A debt instrument.

Debt What one party owes another. May also be a debt **instrument**, e.g., **bonds** and **notes**. See also *Creditor* and *Debtor*.

Debtors Those who owe you money (in their books you are a **creditor**). See also *Accounts Receivable*.

Decay (Option Derivative Contract) See *Time Value*.

Deed of Priority (Lending) An agreement prioritizing the rights of recourse to security between two or more lenders.

Deep Discount **Bonds** or other **instruments** issued at a substantial **discount** to their **par** value, and paying a low rate of **interest**. At **maturity** they are usually repaid at par. This can be especially attractive to investors in countries where the non-interest element (being the difference between **redemption value** and the discounted issue price) may be subject to more favourable taxation treatment than interest payments. Whilst the issuer receives less than face value at the outset there is a **cash flow** benefit to them in the reduced interest payments during the term of the instrument. See also *Discount Instruments* and *Zero Coupon*.

Default The failure to meet an obligation.

Deferred Consideration A payment due at a future date, typically being all or part of the purchase price of a business, the amount of which might depend upon subsequent performance and not be known at the outset. See also *Contingent Liability*.

Deferred Shares/Stocks Shares/stocks where no **dividends** are to be paid for a period of time.

Delivered Duty Paid (DDP) An **Incoterm**. The supplier is responsible for carriage and insurance to a named place (usually the buyer's premises) in the country of importation, and for any export and import licences, duties and taxes.

Delivered at Frontier (DAF) An **Incoterm**. The supplier is responsible for carriage, insurance, export licence, duties and taxes to a named place at a named frontier.

Delta The measure of change in the price of an **option premium** against a change in the price of the **underlying**.

Demand Loan A **loan** without a specified repayment date, where the lender can call for repayment on demand. See also *At Call*, *Overdraft* and *Term*.

Demurrage The costs incurred by delayed loading/unloading of goods in transit.

Deposit Money, or other **assets**, placed with one party by another, either as security for a transaction or to earn **interest**.

Deposit Margin Money, or other **assets**, provided by one or both parties to a transaction as protection to the **counterparty** for losses that might arise as a result of market movements. Often placed with a **clearing house** or other third party. May be subject to frequent, often daily, adjustment by top-up or withdrawal as **market prices** move. See also *Initial Margin* and *Variation Margin*.

Depository Receipts Tradable receipts given to investors in respect of foreign **securities** where the securities are being held on behalf of the investors by a local bank in the investors' country. The investors receive the income from the securities. See also *American Depository Receipts*.

Depreciation (Amortization of Fixed Assets) The reduction in the value of an **asset** in the books of a business to reflect its reduced worth over a period of time. It is a deduction from profits but is not a **cash flow** item. See also *Net Book Value*, *Reducing-balance Method* and *Straight-line Method*.

Derivatives Financial instruments based on underlying assets and used for managing risks and for **speculation**. See also *Commodity Derivatives, Credit Derivatives, Exchange Delivery Settlement Price, Exchange Traded, Forward Rate Agreements, Futures, Options, Over-the-counter, Swaps* and *Underlying*.

Differential (Forward Exchange Rate) See *Forward Exchange Rate*.

Dilution Where, for example, the percentage of **equity** in a **company/corporation** held by an existing **shareholder/stockholder** is reduced by the issue of new shares to third party shareholders. See also *Pre-emption Rights*.

Direct Costs See *Variable Costs*.

Director See *Board of Directors* and *Shadow Director*.

Discount The amount by which a price is below a specified base, e.g., below the **market price** or below **par**.

Discount Instruments **Debt instruments** issued at a **discount** to **par** (face value). See also *Deep Discount, Yield* and *Zero Coupon*.

Discount Rate (Present Value) The rate of **return** used in **present value** calculations. See also *Internal Rate of Return*.

Discount to Issue Price Where the **securities** of a new issue are trading in the market below the issue price.

Discounted Cash Flow See *Present Value*.

Discountee (Invoice Discounting) A business which sells its **accounts receivable** to an invoice discounting company (**discounter**) for an immediate cash payment (advance) under a confidential invoice discounting agreement. See also *Invoice Discounting*.

Discounter (Invoice Discounting Company) A finance company which buys the **accounts receivable** from the **discountee** under a confidential invoice discounting agreement See also *Invoice Discounting*.

Discounting (Accounts Receivable) See *Invoice Discounting*.

Discounting (Drafts/Bills of Exchange) The sale of an accepted **draft/bill of exchange** for an immediate cash payment. See also *Acceptance* and *Negotiation*.

Discovery Subject to jurisdiction, the right of a **counterparty** in a legal action to see the 'other side's' documents relevant to the case including internal records.

Disintermediation Where two parties deal directly with each other rather than through the intermediation of a bank, e.g., where a **company/corporation** issues a **bond** which is purchased by an investor (rather than where the investor lends money to a bank which, as a separate transaction, lends to a borrower). See also *Intermediation*.

Dividend A payment by a **company/corporation** to its **shareholders/stockholders** out of its profits. There may be one or more 'interim' dividends, and a 'final' dividend in respect of an **accounting period** Together they are the 'annual dividend'. See also *Scrip Dividend*.

Dividend Cover The number of times that a **company's/corporation's** earnings after tax cover its **dividend** payment.

Documentary Collection See *Collection*.

Documentary Letter of Credit An undertaking issued by a bank (**issuing bank**) at the request of its customer (**applicant**) to pay a third party (**beneficiary**) against presentation to the bank of specified documents evidencing compliance with the terms and conditions set out in the documentary letter of credit. See also *Advising Bank, Back-to-back, Confirmed, Confirming Bank, Irrevocable, Nominated Bank, Red Clause, Revocable, Revolving, Standby* and *Transferable*.

Documentation Risk The exposures resulting from errors or omissions in documents. See also *Jurisdiction Risk*.

Documents Against Acceptance (D/A) Where under a **collection** the documents are to be released to the **drawee** against their **acceptance** of a **tenor draft**. See also *Documents Against Payment*.

Documents Against Payment (D/P) Where under a **collection** the documents are to be released to the **drawee** against payment. 'Acceptance D/P' is where the **drawee** is required to accept a **tenor draft** but the documents are still not released until payment is made at maturity. See also *Documents Against Acceptance*.

Domestic Bonds Bonds issued to investors in the country and currency of the issuer, e.g., a sterling bond issued in London by a UK corporate. See also *Eurobonds and Foreign Bonds*.

Double Taxation Agreements Arrangements between countries whereby tax paid in one country can be wholly or partially offset against tax payable in the other country, by means of a 'tax credit'. See also *Withholding Taxes*.

D/P See *Documents Against Payment*.

Draft/Bill of Exchange An unconditional order in writing signed by the party which prepares it (**drawer**) requiring the party to whom it is addressed (**drawee**) to pay a stated amount to, or to the order of, a specified party (**payee**) or to bearer, either on demand or at a fixed or determinable future date (the **matu-**

rity or **due date**). See also *Acceptance, Accommodation Party, Bankers' Acceptance, Check/Cheque, Discounting, Endorser, Negotiation, Sight Draft* and *Tenor Draft*.

Draw Down (Lending) The taking of funds by a borrower under a **loan** or other agreement. There may be a lapse of time between the date the agreement is signed and the date funds are drawn down. It might, for example, be necessary for the borrower to first comply with a **condition precedent** such as the provision of security.

Drawee (Drafts) The party to whom a **draft/bill of exchange** is addressed.

Drawee (Collection) The buyer of the goods to whom presentation of the documents is made by the **presenting bank**. See also *Collection*.

Drawer (Drafts) The party which prepares and signs a **draft/bill of exchange**.

Dual Currency Notes **Debt instruments** where **interest** is paid in one currency but the **principal** amount is repaid in another currency.

Due Date The date on which a specified event is to take place, e.g., repayment of a **loan**. See also *Maturity Date* and *Settlement Date*.

Due Diligence The review of a business, commonly undertaken by bankers, accountants or lawyers on their own or a client's behalf. The areas covered and degree of detail will depend on circumstances, but might typically include finances, operations, markets, prospects, **assets**, **liabilities**, legal structure and management. See also *Short* and *Long Form Reports*.

Earnings at Risk A **modelling** technique used to quantify risk.

Earnings Per Share/Stock (Company/Corporation) Profit after tax and preference dividends ÷ number of **ordinary shares/common stocks** in issue.

EBIT Stands for 'earnings before **interest** paid and tax'. See *Trading Profit/Loss*.

Economic Risk (Currency) See *Currency Exchange Rate Risk*.

ECP See *Euro Commercial Paper*.

EDSP See *Exchange Delivery Settlement Price*.

Endorser (Indorser) A **payee** or any previous endorsee who signs the back of a **negotiable instrument** (e.g., **draft/bill of exchange**), and thereby becomes liable for its payment.

Equity The financial and legal interests of the owners in a business. Also, in law, that which is fair. See also *Ordinary Shares/Common Stock*, *Preference Shares/Prior-preferred Stock* and *Securities Exchanges*.

Equity Kicker See *Warrants*.

Equivalence The 'standardization' of different types of risk for comparison purposes.

Euro Commercial Paper (ECP) Short-term unsecured **bearer promissory notes** issued in US dollars and other major currencies by governments, financial institutions and large **companies/corporations** and mostly purchased by financial institutions and fund managers. They do not usually pay **interest** but are issued at a **discount** to **par** value and redeemed at par, and must be issued outside the country in whose currency they are denominated. See also *Commercial Paper*.

Eurobond A **bearer bond** sold internationally to investors outside of the country in whose currency the issue has been denominated. See also *Cedel*, *Domestic Bonds*, *Euroclear*, *Eurocurrency* and *Foreign Bonds*.

Euroclear A **Eurobond** settlement organization based in Brussels. See also *Cedel*.

Eurocurrency Any money which is held in countries other than the country of issue of that currency, e.g., US dollars deposited with a UK bank, or French francs deposited with a Japanese bank.

Euromarket The markets for **Eurocurrency instruments** such as **Eurobonds**.

Euro-notes Short-term unsecured promissory notes the issue of which is underwritten by banks within agreed limits.

European-style Option (Derivative Contract) An **option** that can only be exercised by the **buyer** on its **expiry date**, although an earlier **close out** may be possible. See also *American-style Option*.

Events of Default An event the occurrence of which is a breech of an agreement, e.g., a borrower not paying **interest** to a bank on the date specified in a **loan** agreement. See also *Letter of Waiver*.

Evergreen Facility A lending or other facility for a specific **term** which, at a pre-set frequency (and provided both the lender and the borrower agree at that time) can be renewed for its original term. For example, a three-year **revolving loan** might be reviewed by the lender and the borrower at the end of the first year. If both agree it will be renewed for a three-year term from the review date. In this example, a borrower would always have a minimum of two years' notice of the repayment date, but the commitment of the lender would never be longer than three years.

EXW See *Ex Works*.

Exceptional Items Items in the accounts of a business which arise from transactions within its normal activities, but are of a size or significance requiring specific disclosure if the accounts are to give a true and fair picture, e.g., an unusually high level of stock write-offs. Treatment may be subject to local accounting practice. See also *Extraordinary Items*.

Exchange Controls See *Currency Exchange Controls*.

Exchange Delivery Settlement Price (EDSP) The price for **settlement** at its **expiry** of an **exchange traded derivative** contract.

Ex Dividend Shares/stock purchased after the declaration of a **dividend,** where the buyer is not entitled to receive the dividend. See also *Cum Dividend.*

Exchange Rate The rate at which the currency of one country can be converted into the currency of another country. A currency may be **floating rate, fixed rate,** operate within 'exchange rate bands' against that of another country or 'crawl' on a specified basis (e.g., the domestic country's rate of inflation against that of a reference country). See also *Cross-currency Rate, Currency Exchange Controls, Convertible Currencies, Forward Exchange Rate,* and *Spot Rate.*

Exchange Rate Risk See *Currency Exchange Rate Risk.*

Exchange Traded A **derivative** contract that is bought or sold on a recognized exchange, e.g., CBOT **(Chicago Board of Trade)** and LIFFE **(London International Financial Futures Exchange).** See also *Over-the-counter.*

Exercise (Derivative Contract) The exercise by the **buyer** (holder) of its rights under an **option.**

Exercise Price/Rate See *Strike Price/Rate.*

Exotics Complex **derivative** contracts, as distinct from **vanilla** contracts.

Expiry Date For an **option** derivative contract the last date on which the **buyer** can exercise the option. See also *Maturity Date* and *Value Date.*

Extraordinary Items Those items in the accounts of a business which arise from transactions or events outside of its normal activities and are not expected to occur frequently, e.g., the closure of a business unit or the effects of an earthquake. Treatment may be subject to local accounting practice. **Earning per share,** and hence the **price to earnings ratio,** are normally calculated before extraordinary items. See also *Exceptional Items.*

Ex Works (EXW) An **Incoterm.** The buyer collects the goods from the supplier and is responsible for carriage and insurance.

Face Value See *Par.*

Factor The **finance company** which buys the **accounts receivable,** manages the **factorees** sales ledger and collects the **debts** under a **factoring** agreement.

Factoree The business which sells its **accounts receivable** to a factoring company **(factor)** for an immediate cash payment **(advance)** under a **factoring** agreement.

Factoring The sale by a business **(factoree)** of its **accounts receivable** to a **finance company (factor)** in return for an immediate cash payment **(advance)** within pre-set limits and with the **debtors** being aware of the sale of the **debts.** See also *Invoice Discounting.*

Fair Value (Option Derivative Contract) The premium loss writer's profit margin.

FAS See *Free Alongside Ship*.

FCA See *Free Carrier*.

Fees (Lending) Include:
- arrangement/negotiation – for arranging/negotiating the facility, normally payable no later than the date when a borrower signs the agreement and not refundable even if, for whatever reason, the facility is unused
- commitment – on the undrawn or otherwise unutilized portion of a facility, to reimburse the lender for any costs and for tying up its funds or limits
- annual ('management') – similar to an arrangement fee, but payable on the anniversaries (or at other agreed frequencies) throughout the term of the facility
- cancellation – where the borrower asks for the facility to be cancelled before its specified expiry date (thereby saving the borrower further annual, commitment and other fees)
- pre-payment – if the borrower repays all or part of the facility in advance of the **due dates**
- repayment – due on the repayment of a facility, and sometimes calculated as a percentage of the profits made by a borrower from using the facility for a specific purpose (e.g., the purchase of an asset subsequently sold for a profit)
- agency – to the **agent** bank in a **syndicated loan**, for the work it undertakes in that capacity.

See also *Participation Fee*.

Finance Company Normally a business that makes loans but, not being a bank, raises its finance in the **money market** rather than by taking deposits.

Firewall A barrier to unauthorized access to a computer system.

Fitch Investors' Service See *Rating Agencies*.

Fixed Assets The assets of a business that are not held for sale or used up in the production process e.g., land, buildings, **fixtures and fittings**. See also *Current Assets*, *Goodwill* and *Plant*.

Fixed Costs (Overheads) Those costs of a business that do not vary with the level of **sales/turnover**, e.g., usually including administrative salaries, rental/premises costs, lease and hire purchase payments, insurance premiums, professional fees and communication costs. *Depreciation* may be sold separately. See also *Variable Costs*.

Fixed Rate Currency A currency the **exchange rate** of which is fixed in relation to another (reference) currency. See also *Floating Rate Currency*.

Fixed Rate Interest Where the rate of **interest** on a borrowing, lending or deposit is fixed for its entire **term**. See also *Variable/Floating Rate Interest*.

Fixtures and Fittings Part of the **fixed** assets used by the business (e.g., office furniture) rather than being for sale, and often of relatively small value. See also *Plant*.

Flat Interest Where **interest** continues to be paid on the full initial amount of **principal** irrespective of any repayments. See also *Compound Interest* and *Simple Interest*.

Floating Rate Currency A currency the **exchange rate** of which is determined by the market. See also *Fixed Rate Currency*.

Floating Rate Interest See *Variable Rate Interest*.

Floor Price The lowest price a seller will accept. See also *Ceiling Price*.

Floor (Interest Rate) A form of **option** derivative giving the **buyer** the right, but not the obligation, to fix the rate of **interest** (the **strike rate**) for the entire term of a notional deposit. The buyer pays a **premium** to the **writer** and, if the option is exercised on any of the specified dates, is paid in cash an amount equal to the difference between the strike and the **market rate** that day (calculated on the notional deposit). See also *Cap* and *Collar*.

Flotation/floatation Commonly, the offering of **shares/stock** in a **company/corporation** to the public.

FOB See *Free on Board*.

Forced Sale When circumstances make it necessary to sell an **asset** as quickly as possible, even if **market prices** are depressed at that time.

Foreign Bonds Bonds issued in a country, and in the currency of that country, other than that in which the issuer is domiciled, e.g., a sterling bond issued in the UK by a non-UK issuer, known as a 'Bulldog' bond, or a US dollar bond issued in the USA by a non-USA issuer, known as a 'Yankee'. See also *Domestic Bonds* and *Eurobonds*.

Foreign Exchange Market The global network of those trading, **hedging** and **speculating** in currencies as principals **(dealers)** and as **brokers**.

FOREX Stands for 'foreign exchange'.

Forfaiting (à Forfait) The purchase for an immediate discounted cash payment of **tenor drafts/bills of exchange, promissory notes,** or other documents evidencing a sale and a deferred payment, without the purchaser having a right of recourse to the beneficiary or to any previous holders if payment is not received at **maturity**. The beneficiary who sells the **instrument** (e.g., a bill of exchange drawn on and accepted by an importer) is often an exporter and the purchaser (forfaiter) a bank or other financial institution. The instruments will typically have been accepted by a bank, financial institution or government department, guaranteeing that they will be paid (honoured) at maturity. See also *Acceptance* and *Avalising*.

Forward Contract (Currency) A commitment to exchange one foreign currency for another at a specified **exchange rate**, with the exchange taking place on either a specified future date or during a specified future period. Whereas a standard forward contract can only be utilized on a single fixed date an 'option dated forward contract' allows the exchange of currencies at any time between two agreed dates (the 'option period'), usually subject to two working days' notice. See also *Forward Exchange Rate, Settlement Risk* and *Spot Rate*.

Forward Exchange Rate The rate at which **counterparties** agree to exchange currencies at a future date. The forward rate will normally be quoted as a 'differential' against the **spot rate**. See also *Forward Contract* and *Spot Rate*.

Forward-forward A **term** facility starting at a future date e.g., where a bank agrees an **interest** rate today for a **loan** with a term of six months with **draw down** in three months' time (i.e., the loan is for a future (forward) period starting on a future (forward) date).

Forward Purchase (Project Finance) Where the provider of finance receives all or part of the output from the project to service and repay the **debt**.

Forward Rate Agreement (FRA) A **derivative** contract where two **counterparties** commit to respectively pay and receive an amount equivalent to the difference between:

- an agreed rate of **interest** (the 'FRA rate') and
- the interest rate available in the market on a specified future date (the 'settlement date'), based on a notional **loan** or deposit for a specified **term** (the 'contract period'). They are **over-the-counter** not **exchange traded** derivatives. By means of an FRA the **interest** rate can be fixed for a contract period that starts at a known future date (the 'settlement date') and ends on a known future date (the 'maturity date').

Forward Reversing Option (FRO) Also known as a 'Boston Option'. Combines a currency **forward contract** with a **European-style currency option**. This gives a contract to buy or sell one currency against another at a specified forward rate with the ability to reverse out the transaction by means of the option if it is more advantageous to exchange the currency at **spot rate** in the market.

FRA See *Forward Rate Agreement*.

FRA Rate See *Forward Rate Agreement*.

FRO See *Forward Reversing Option*.

Free Alongside Ship (FAS) An **Incoterm**. The supplier is responsible for carriage and insurance alongside a vessel at a named port.

Free Carrier (FCA) An **Incoterm**. The supplier is responsible for carriage and insurance until into the custody of a carrier named by the buyer at a named point, and for any export licence, duties and taxes.

Free Issue See *Capitalization Issue*.

Free on Board (FOB) An **Incoterm**. The supplier is responsible for carriage and insurance until on board a specified vessel at a named port, and for export licence, duties and taxes.

Funding Risk A business fails when it cannot pay its **debts**.

Fungibility When things are interchangeable, e.g., for trading purposes any US$100 bill is as good as any other US$100 bill, and any grain of rice of a specified type and quality is as good as another grain of rice of that type and quality.

Futures (Financial) **Exchange traded derivative** contracts, which commit the **counterparties** to respectively buy and sell a standard pre-set amount of a financial **instrument** at an agreed price at a specified future date. Being exchange traded, the size of the unit of trading, delivery dates and **tick** values are pre-set, and it will be necessary to buy whatever number of contracts is needed to match requirements.

Gamma The sensitivity of **delta** to small changes in the price of the **underlying**.

Gazelles Businesses (usually small) where, typically, revenues have increased by at least 20% in each of the previous four years.

Gearing/Leverage The accepted definitions of gearing and leverage can differ from country to country, and it is important to know which is being used. In general a highly-geared business is more dependent on borrowings/**debt** than a low-geared business which relies to a greater extent on **equity**. It is important to consider the nature of the business, and whether any borrowing/debt is being used to create future growth. The possible definitions include the following.

- Total gearing — Total **liabilities** ÷ **Net tangible assets**
- Net/capital gearing — Net borrowings ÷ Net tangible assets
- Gross gearing — Total borrowings ÷ Net tangible assets
- Operational gearing — Sales less **variable costs** ÷ **Trading profit**, or
  — Trading profit plus **fixed costs** ÷ Trading profit.

Gilts UK government **bonds**.

Going Concern Basis The assumption, usually in the context of financial accounts or projections, that a business will be able to continue to trade.

Going Down the Credit Curve Accepting greater risks to achieve increased potential returns.

Golden Hello Incentives given to attract key personnel to join a business.

Golden Handcuffs Incentives given to the key personnel of a business to encourage them to stay for a period of time.

Golden Handshake Payment to an employee when they depart from a business.

Goodwill The value of the name or reputation of a business or product (an **intangible asset**).

Grey Market See *Securities Exchanges*.

Green Shoe Option (Over Allocation Option) Named after The Green Shoe Manufacturing Company, Boston, where it was first used in a share offering. The managers of an issue can increase the number of shares to be sold, which may help support the market price and take-up of equity. If the market price is lower than the issue's offer price the managers can buy the extra shares in the market. If the market price is higher than the issue's offer price the managers exercise the option, requiring the issuers or sellers of the shares to provide the extra shares at the issue offer price.

Gross Contribution Sales less the **variable costs** of producing the goods or services sold. See also *Breakeven*, *Gross Profit/Loss*, *Net Profit/Loss* and *Trading Profit/Loss*.

Gross Profit/Loss Sales less costs of producing the goods or services sold. May differ from **gross contributions** by allowing for some of the fixed production costs (overheads).

Gross Profit Margin (Gross profit x 100) ÷ sales.

Guarantee (Contract) See *Bond/Contract Guarantee*.

Guarantees v Indemnities See *Indemnities v Guarantees*. See also *Bond/Contract Guarantee*.

Guarantor The bank, insurance company or other party which issues a guarantee.

HP See *Hire Purchase*.

Hard Currency The readily convertible currency of a financially strong and stable country.

Hedging (to Hedge) Taking action to reduce a risk in whole or in part, often by entering into an opposing transaction. It may be possible to obtain a perfect match of risks, but more often the available hedging instruments do not exactly offset the risks being hedged, leaving some exposure. See also *Basis Risk*, *Hedging Risk* and *Speculating*.

Hedging Risk Occurs when you fail to achieve a satisfactory hedge for your exposure, either because it could not be arranged or as the result of an error. You may also be exposed to **basis risk**.

Herstatt Risk The **settlement risk** on foreign exchange transactions is often referred to as Herstatt risk, named after the German bank which collapsed at a time when it had received the Deutschmark equivalent of US$ on trades within German banking hours but before it could make payments in settlement when New York opened for business. See also *Counterparty/Credit Risk*.

High-yield Bonds See *Junk Bonds*.

Hire Purchase Where the owner of an **asset** transfers its possession and the right to use that asset to a 'hirer'. Legal title (ownership) remains with the original owner throughout the term of the hire purchase contract, during which time the hirer makes regular payments to the owner (normally sufficient to cover cost of the asset and the owner's funding costs and profit margin). At the end of the contract term the hirer usually has the option of making a final (usually nominal) payment to the owner for the legal title to the asset. In practice, the hirer is paying for the asset whilst using it. See also *Leasing*.

Historical Cost Accounting See *Current Cost Accounting*.

Holder (Option Derivative Contract) See *Buyer*.

Holding Company A **company/corporation** which controls and may own a majority of **shares/stock** in one or more other companies/corporations.

Holiday A period of time when payments do not have to be made, e.g., contributions into a pension fund or installment repayments of a **loan**.

Hurdle Rate The rate of return below which you will not invest. See also *Capital Asset Pricing Model*, *Internal Rate of Return* and *Present Value*.

Hybrids See *Convertible Bonds and Convertible Preference Shares* and *Warrant*s.

ITM (Option Derivative Contract) See *In the Money*.

Implied Forward Rate (Futures Derivative Contract) The rate of **interest** the market expects to see on the delivery date for an interest rate **future**.

Incoterms Standard contract terms published by the International Chamber of Commerce which set out the respective responsibilities of a buyer and of a seller for goods in transit.

Indemnities v Guarantees (Subject to the Jurisdiction) Example: a guarantor A undertakes that if party B does not honour its obligations to party C, then A will do so. The guarantor has a secondary liability as this depends on the obligations of B to C and on B's default. With an indemnity A would be directly and primarily liable to C irrespective of the obligations of B to C or on B's default.

Index Swap See *Basis Swap*.

Indorser See *Endorser*.

Inflation Accounting Financial accounts that are adjusted for inflation. See also *Current Cost Accounting*.

Information Memorandum See *Syndicated Loan*.

Initial Margin The amount placed with the **clearing house** by both parties to an **exchange traded derivative** at the time of entering into the contract. Both parties pay the same initial margin, irrespective of whether they are buying or selling. See also *Standard Portfolio Analysis of Risk* and *Variation Margin*.

Insider Trading Using knowledge not in the public domain to trade at an advantage, which is a criminal offence in many jurisdictions. See also *Price-sensitive Information*.

Insolvency Where **debts** cannot be paid as they fall due. See also *Bankruptcy* and *Wrongful Trading*.

Instruments Commonly used to mean **securities**.

Intangible Assets 'Non-physical' assets of a business, e.g., goodwill and patents. See also *Current Assets*, *Fixed Assets* and *Goodwill*.

Interest Payment for the use of money, usually expressed as a percentage of the **principal**. The 'real interest rate' is the actual rate adjusted for the rate of inflation. Also a stake in something. See also *Compound Interest*, *Fixed Rate Interest*, *Flat Interest*, *Simple Interest* and *Variable/Floating Rate Interest*.

Interest Cover (Profits) Profit before **interest** and tax ÷ interest. If the cover is too low a business will be at risk from any fall in profits or increase in interest rates.

Interest Cover (Cash) Cash flow ÷ **interest** paid.

Interest Only (Lending) When **interest** is payable on a borrowing at specified intervals but repayments of **principal** have been deferred.

Interest Rate Cap See *Cap*.

Interest Rate Collar See *Collar*.

Interest Rate Floor See *Floor*.

Interest Rate Option A **derivative** contract giving the **buyer** the right, but not the obligation, to pay or to receive **interest** at an agreed rate (**strike rate**) on a notional **loan** or deposit for a specified term starting from a specified future date. The buyer of the contract pays a **premium** to its **writer** (seller). See also *Option*.

Interest Rate Risk If you are a borrower or a lender there will be a direct impact from changes in the rates of **interest** you pay or receive. This may be compounded by exchange rate risk if the amounts are in foreign currency.

Interest Rate Swap A **derivative** contract between two **counterparties** to exchange **interest** streams with different characteristics, e.g., **fixed rate** for **variable/floating rate**, on the same **principal** amount. See also *Margin Swap*, *Money Market Interest Rate Swap*, *Payer*, *Receiver*, *Rollover Dates*, *Swap*, *Swap Rate*, *Swaption*, *Term Interest Rate Swap* and *Vanilla Swap*.

Intermediation Where parties deal with a bank rather than directly with each other, e.g., where an investor lends money to a bank and that bank then lends money to a borrower (rather than a **company/corporation** issuing a **bond** which is purchased direct by an investor). See also *Disintermediation*.

Internal Rate of Return (IRR) The **discount rate** at which the net **present value** of the cash flows of an investment or project is nil. When considering the financial viability of investments the IRR should be equal to or greater than the rate of return required by the investor. See also *Capital Asset Pricing Model*, *Hurdle Rate*, *Present Value* and *Yield*.

International Swaps and Derivatives Association (ISDA) An organization whose documentation is one of the standards for **derivatives** contracts.

In The Money (Option Derivative Contract) An **option** with **intrinsic value**, i.e., the **strike price** is more advantageous to the **buyer** than the current **market rate** for the **underlying** (e.g., a **call option** where the strike price is below the market price, or a **put option** where the strike price is above the market price). See also *At the Money* and *Out of the Money*.

Intra-day Limit The limit set for any maximum exposure during a business day. See also *Settlement Risk*.

Intrinsic Value (Derivative Contracts) The **present value** of the amount by which an **option contract** is **in the money**. It is the difference in the buyer's favour between the **strike price** and the **market price** of the **underlying**. See also *Premium*.

Introduction Where the **shares/stock** in a **company/corporation** are already widely held by **shareholders/stockholders** they may be listed on a **securities exchange**, provided no new monies are thereby being raised. See also *Securities Exchanges*.

Inventory (Stock) The raw materials, work-in-progress and finished goods awaiting sale of a business.

Inventory Risk A variant of **market risk**, an example of which would be the exposure to a fall in value of **securities** held by a bank or other financial institution for trading purposes.

Inverse Yield Curve See *Yield Curve*.

Invoice A statement of goods or services provided, prepared by the seller and addressed to the buyer, specifying the amount to be paid in settlement and usually the date by which payment is to be made. See also *Pro Forma Invoice*.

Invoice Discounting The sale by a business (**discountee**) of its **accounts receivable** to a **finance company** (**discounter**) in return for an immediate cash payment (advance) within pre-set limits and without the **debtors** needing to know that the **debts** have been sold. See also *Factoring*.

Inward Collection (Collection) Where a presenting bank receives from another bank a **collection** for presentation to a buyer (**drawee**). See also *Outward Collection*.

Irrevocable Documentary Letter of Credit A credit that cannot be altered or cancelled by the **applicant** without the agreement of the **beneficiary**, the **issuing bank** and any **confirming bank**. Banks will only confirm irrevocable credits. See also *Documentary Letter of Credit* and *Revocable Documentary Letter of Credit*.

ISDA See the *International Swaps and Derivatives Association*.

Issued Capital/Shares/Stock That part of the **authorized capital/shares/stock** that has been issued to **shareholders/stockholders**. See also *Paid-up Capital/Shares/Stock* and *Partly Paid/Capital/Shares/Stock*.

Issuing Bank (Documentary Letter of Credit) The bank instructed by the **applicant** to issue the letter of credit in favour of the **beneficiary**. See also *Documentary Letter of Credit*.

ITM See *In the Money*.

Joint and Several Usually referred to in the context of guarantees given by two or more guarantors, and meaning that each guarantor is liable for the entire amount of the guarantee, not just for a *pro rata* (i.e., 'several') share of the guarantee. For example, if three guarantors are jointly and severally liable under a guarantee for US$9000,000 then each is liable for the entire $9000,000 not just for $3000,000. The beneficiary under the guarantee can usually decide how many and which guarantors to proceed against.

Junk Bonds Debt instruments issued by **companies/corporations** which either have no ratings from the recognized **rating agencies**, or are rated below 'investment grade'. In return for the potentially higher risk, the **bonds** pay a high rate of **interest** to investors, although they still usually cost the issuer less than borrowing from a bank (and may be more attractive than suffering **dilution** by issuing **shares/stock** to raise finance). Sometimes referred to as 'high-yield bonds' or 'non-investment grade bonds'.

Jurisdiction Risk It may be difficult or costly to obtain a satisfactory legal ruling or resolution of disputes in the country within whose jurisdiction contracts fall or your **counterparties** are based, and what happens in **insolvency** situations? Conversely, could a plaintiff take action against you in an overseas court where they have better prospects of success or of higher awards? Are your contracts even valid in the territories where you do business? The term 'exclusive jurisdiction' means that you can only take legal action in one specified country. 'Non-exclusive jurisdiction' means that whilst it would be the intention for legal actions to be taken in a specified country, each of the parties reserve the right to commence proceedings in another country. See also *Documentation Risk* and *Political and Country Risk*.

Large Exposure Policy Banks and other regulated financial institutions are required to limit their exposures to individual industry sectors, individual counterparties (and connected counterparties) and to that institution's **subsidiary** and **associated** companies. The limits are usually expressed as a percentage of the institution's capital base.

Lead Bank/Manager The bank or other institution with responsibility for organizing and coordinating a securities issue or financing. See also *Agent*, *Arranger* and *Syndicated Loan*.

Leasing A contract whereby a 'lessee' is entitled to use an **asset** owned by the 'lessor' on payment of a rental. There are two principal forms of lease.

- 'Finance (capital) leases', where the risks, rewards and duties (e.g. maintenance and insurance) of ownership of the asset (but not the legal title) are transferred by the lessor to the lessee. The depreciated fair value of the lessee's rights (net of obligations) must normally be shown on their **balance sheet** and the full cost of the asset and its funding is normally **amortized** over the **term** of the lease.
- 'Operating (service) leases', where the lessor depends on the residual value of the asset it receives back at the end of the lease (when it hopes to be able to sell or re-lease the asset) and often has asset maintenance or other obligations to the lessee. The asset is not shown on the lessee's balance sheet, although the rental payments are taken into the **profit and loss account**.

The lease may be based on **fixed** or **variable/floating interest** rate finance costs, there may be tax benefits to the lessor and, because the lessor is principally reliant on the asset as security, the lessee may be able to finance the acquisition of an asset more easily and cheaply than by borrowing the funds elsewhere for an outright purchase (e.g., the lessor may not need to undertake detailed **due diligence** into the lessee, and the lessee may avoid problems where the terms of their existing facilities with third parties restrict additional **debt**). With a 'lease purchase' part of the payments are allocated towards the purchase by the lessee of the asset. See also *Hire Purchase* and *Sale and Leaseback*.

Legal Risks See *Documentation Risk* and *Jurisdiction Risk*.

Lender's Option (Derivative Contract) An **interest rate put option** contract where the benefit to the **buyer** is that it has the right, but not the obligation, to receive a fixed amount of **interest**. See also *Borrower's Option*.

Letter of Comfort A written statement that may not have any practical legal effect, e.g., a letter to a bank by the **parent company** of a borrower saying that it intends to give the **subsidiary** financial support, but that this does not amount to a guarantee of the **debts** of that subsidiary. Said to have moral rather than legal force.

Letter of Credit See *Documentary Letter of Credit* and *Standby Credits*.

Letter of Variation A written agreement to variation of the **terms** of a contract.

Letter of Waiver (Lending) A written agreement by a lender to waive their rights arising from an **event of default** by the borrower. See also *Letter of Variation*.

Leverage See *Gearing*.

Leveraged Buy-out Where the purchaser of a business takes on a higher than usual level of **debt** to fund the acquisition. See also *Management Buy-in* and *Management Buy-out*.

Liabilities Debts and other obligations. See also *Asset*.

Liability Swaps (Interest Rate) Swaps where **interest** payments are exchanged. See also *Asset Swaps*.

LIBID See *London Inter-bank Bid Rate*.

LIBOR See *London Inter-bank Offered Rate*.

Lien A claim against the **assets** of a third party, which usually have to be in the possession or control of the claimant.

LIFFE See *London International Financial Futures and Options Exchange*.

Limited Liability See *Company/Corporation*.

Liquid Assets Cash and **assets** that are readily convertible into cash.

Liquid Market A market with the capacity to handle the necessary trading volume. See *Liquidity*.

Liquid Ratio Also known as 'acid test', 'quick ratio' or 'cash ratio', it is the ratio of **quick assets** to **current liabilities**. A key **liquidity** ratio indicating the extent to which a business could pay its **creditors** provided it was paid by its **debtors**.

Liquid Surplus/Deficit See *Net Current Assets*.

Liquidation The winding up of a **company/corporation** (which may or may not be insolvent) with the proceeds of the sale of its **assets** being used to pay its **debts**. Any surplus funds are then returned to the **shareholders/stockholders**. See also *Bankruptcy*, *Chapter 11* and *Insolvency*.

Liquidity The ease and extent to which something can be turned into cash or readily traded in reasonable volumes. Also the ability to meet **current liabilities**. See also *Liquid Market*.

Liquidity Risk Where a market does not have the capacity to handle, at least without significant adverse impact on the price, the volume of whatever a party is trying to buy or to sell at the time they want to deal. Also, an inability to meet debts when they fall due.

Listed See *Quoted*.

Loan The making available by a lender to a borrower of an agreed amount of money in a specified currency or currencies for repayment on demand or over an agreed **term** and with specified **interest**, **fee** and other costs. The terms of the loan are likely to be set out in some detail in a facility letter or a loan agreement. The lender may be a syndicate or a less formal 'club' of banks and other financial institutions. See also *At Call, Bridging Loan, Conditions Precedent,*

Conditions Subsequent, Covenant, Demand Loan, Loan to Value, Overdraft, Revolving Loan and *Syndicated Loan*.

Loan to Value (LTV) The ratio of the amount lent (or that which a lender is prepared to **advance**) against the value of security, e.g., at an LTV of 70% a bank would lend a maximum of £700,000 against security with a value of £1,000,000.

Locals Individual members of a **derivatives** exchange who are trading as **dealers** for their own account rather than as **brokers** for others.

Locked Box Where overseas customers are asked by an exporter to send payments to a post office box in their own or a convenient country, which a local bank is authorized to collect on the exporter's behalf.

Lock Out Agreement An undertaking usually given by the prospective vendor of a business or property to the prospective buyer, not to negotiate with any third parties for a specified period of time, giving the prospective buyer an opportunity to undertake **due diligence**.

London Inter-bank Bid Rate (LIBID) The rate of **interest** which creditworthy banks pay for funds in the interbank (Eurodollar) market, whether in dollars, sterling or other currencies. See also *London Inter-bank Offered Rate*.

London Inter-bank Offered Rate (LIBOR) The rate of **interest** at which creditworthy banks offer to lend funds in the interbank (Eurodollar) market, whether in dollars, sterling or other major currencies. LIMEAN is the mean of LIBOR and LIBID. See also *London Inter-bank Bid Rate*.

London International Financial Futures and Options Exchange (LIFFE) The derivatives exchange in the City of London (pronounced 'LIFE' not 'LIFFY').

Long To 'go long' is to hold something for future sale e.g., to have bought more of a security or a currency than you have sold. See also *Short*.

Long Form Report An in-depth analysis, typically undertaken by potential investors in a business. See also *Due Diligence* and *Short Form Report*.

Long Tail Risk Where a liability may not become apparent for, perhaps, many years, and cannot usually be previously quantified.

Long Term Often taken as meaning any period greater than one year (e.g., in financial accounts) but subject to various interpretations for different markets and purposes. See also *Medium Term* and *Short Term*.

LTV See *Loan to Value*.

MOF See *Multi-option Facility*.

Majority Lenders (Syndicated Facilities) Those providers of **syndicated loans** or other facilities whose participations when added together represent a specified minimum percentage of the whole, and whose consent may be sufficient for some decisions without that of other lenders. See also *Lead Bank/Manager* and *Agent*.

Management Buy-in (MBI) When a management team not already responsible for a business is put in to run it (often by the providers of **venture capital**) after it has been acquired. See also *Management Buy-out*.

Management Buy-out (MBO) The purchase of an existing business by all or part of its management team, often with the backing of a **venture capitalist**. See also *Management Buy-in*.

'Mareva' Injunction (Subject to Jurisdiction) A court order restraining a **debtor** from removing **assets** outside the jurisdiction of the court.

Margin Call See *Call*.

Margin Swap A **swap** contract involving a margin over an **interest** rate base.

Market Capitalization The value of a **company's/corporation's** entire **shares/stock** in the market.

Market Makers Members of an exchange who, subject to its rules, may be required to quote **bid** and **offer** prices at which they will trade in designated shares/stock or other **instruments**. See also *Broker-dealer* and *Securities Exchanges*.

Market Price/Rate/Value The price (e.g., for **securities**) or rate (e.g., for currencies) at which something can be traded in the market or by private treaty (usually between a willing buyer and a willing seller); alternatively, the most recent price/rate at which a trade was concluded. See also *Bid-offer Spread*, *Bid Price*, *Book Value*, *Ceiling Price*, *Floor Price*, *Forced Sale*, *Offer Price*, *Market Makers* and *Par*.

Market Risk The exposure to adverse change in the price or value of something traded or held as an investment. Where market risk is a factor, and especially in volatile markets, the practice of **marking to market** on a regular basis is an important discipline.

Marking to Market Using current **market prices** to calculate any profit or loss that has arisen from price movements since the last time you calculated the value of your **assets** or the cost of meeting your **liabilities**. See also *Market Risk*, *Settled to Market* and *Variation Margin*.

Maturity/Maturity Date/Expiry Date The expiry of a **term** e.g., when payment under a **tenor draft/bill of exchange** becomes due, although settlement might not take place immediately. For an **option** contract the last date on which the **buyer** can exercise the option. See also *Due Date*, *Forward Rate Agreement* (maturity date) and *Settlement Date*.

MBI See *Management Buy-in*.

MBO See *Management Buy-out*.

Medium Term For many purposes **short term** is taken as being up to one year and **long term** as over one year. Sometimes, however, periods of typically two to seven years are referred to as 'medium term' e.g., the **Eurobond** market.

Memorandum of Association See *Articles of Incorporation*.

Mezzanine Debt/Capital Debt where the payment of **interest** and repayment of **principal** has been subordinated to **senior debt** and which, in view of the higher risk, earns a higher return. The provider of mezzanine debt may receive equity **options, warrants** or other incentives for providing finance. Can also take the form of **preference shares/prior-preferred stock**. Called 'mezzanine' as it falls between senior debt and **ordinary shares/common stock**.

Middle Market Price The mean of **bid** and **offer** prices.

Models/Modelling A mathematical representation usually on a computer of, typically, an economy, market or financial product.

Modelling Risk That there may be deficiencies in the **models** upon which a computer or other program is dependent, e.g., for the pricing of a financial **instrument**.

Money Laundering The process whereby cash that originated from criminal activities is transferred into 'legitimate' forms.

Money Markets Markets for the issue or trading of **debt** with maturities of usually up to 12 months including, for example, **commercial paper, bankers' acceptances** and **certificates of deposit**. See also *Bond Markets, Capital Markets* and *Notes*.

Money Market Interest Rate Swap Where the **tenor** of the **swap** is up to one year. See also *Interest Rate Swap* and *Term Interest Rate Swap*.

Moody's Investors' Service See *Rating Agencies*.

Mortgage A debt **instrument** giving the lender (mortgagee) a charge over an **asset** (often **real property**) of the borrower (mortgagor) as security.

Multi-option Facility (MOF) Where a borrower has (usually) a committed **standby** line of credit from a bank or syndicate which it can fall back on if unable to raise the finance it needs from any uncommitted lines (i.e., those facilities for which terms have been agreed in principle but which the lender only offers if and when it wishes). There may be a **tender panel** for the uncommitted lines, or different tender panels for different uncommitted lines. Sometimes the committed line may be available without the borrower needing first to explore the uncommitted lines. So, alternatively, there may be only a range of uncommitted lines. The attraction to borrowers is that they can tailor the facility to their needs, and the banks providing committed lines often charge less on the basis that they may never be asked to actually put up any monies.

NAV See *Net Asset Value*.

NIF See *Note Issuance Facility*.

NPV See *Present Value.*

NASDAQ (National Association of Securities Dealers' Automated Quotation System) The US computerized system providing securities dealers and brokers with price quotations.

Negative Pledge (Lending) A covenant by a borrower not to allow any charge, mortgage, lien or other encumbrance on all or part of their assets.

Negotiable An instrument the ownership (title) of which can be transferred by simple delivery or by endorsement and delivery, e.g., certificates of deposit and drafts/bills of exchange.

Negotiation (Drafts/Bills of Exchange) The sale of a sight or tenor draft for an immediate cash payment, with the buyer usually retaining a right of recourse against its seller if the draft is not honoured. Strictly speaking a draft is negotiated before it has been accepted and discounted after it has been accepted. See also *Acceptance* and *Discounting.*

Net Asset Value (NAV) The total assets of a business less its total liabilities.

Net Book Value (Written Down Value) The cost of an asset less its depreciation, as shown in the balance sheet of a business. See also *Amortization* and *Depreciation.*

Net Current Assets (Liquidity Surplus/Deficit) Current assets less current liabilities. See *Working Capital.*

Net Present Value See *Present Value.*

Net Profit/Loss Trading profit/loss less interest. See also *Gross Contribution* and *Gross Profit/Loss.*

Net Profit Margin (Profit before interest and tax x 100) ÷ Sales.

Net Tangible Assets (Tangible Net Worth) Net current assets plus fixed and other assets less term liabilities. See also *Net Worth.*

Net Working Assets See *Quick Assets.*

Net Worth (Shareholders' Funds) The value of the 'owners' equity stake in a business, being the difference between the total assets and total liabilities on a balance sheet. Commonly considered to be the same as net tangible assets but might include intangible items such as goodwill.

Netting Agreements Provide for settlement between two or more counterparties of the net amounts due to each. Bilateral netting takes place directly between the counterparties, whilst multilateral netting settlements are usually made via a clearing house (which may assume the counterparty credit risks).

Nominal Value See *Par.*

Nominated Bank (Documentary Letter of Credit) The confirming or any other bank nominated to pay the **beneficiary**, or to accept or negotiate drafts under the credit. May be known as the 'paying' or 'accepting' bank. See also *Acceptance*, *Documentary Letter of Credit* and *Negotiation*.

Nominee The party holding **securities** or other **assets** in their own name for the beneficial (often undisclosed) **interests** of a third party.

Non-executive Director (Outside/Board Director) See *Board of Directors*.

Nostro Account The account of a bank with a bank overseas, in the currency of the overseas bank. See also *Correspondent Bank* and *Vostro Account*.

Note Issuance Facility (NIF) Where banks commit to provide a line of credit if an issue of short-term debt is not taken up in the market. See also *Revolving Underwriting Facility*.

Notes **Debt instruments** of shorter **term** than **bonds**, i.e., typically less than one year.

Noting If a **draft/bill of exchange** is not paid or accepted when presented to the **drawee**, a notary or other legal officer may be asked to re-present it and to 'note' any dishonour. A formal document known as a 'protest' may then be prepared by the notary/legal officer giving details of the draft and its dishonour, for the purposes of providing evidence acceptable in a court of law. See also *Acceptance*.

Novation The transfer of a contract to a new **counterparty** by cancellation of the original contract and its substitution by an otherwise identical contract between the new and the remaining original counterparty(s). As distinct from 'assignment', where the original contract remains in place but rights and obligations thereunder are transferred to a new counterparty.

Obligor A party with an obligation to do something (usually to pay money), e.g., the borrower of money from a bank is an obligor in respect of both the **interest** and repayment of the **debt**.

Off-balance-sheet A financing activity that does not impact on the **balance sheet**, e.g., **leasing** (operating leases).

Offer for Sale Where new **shares/stock** in a **company/corporation** are offered for subscription by the public at a fixed price by means of a **prospectus**. See also *Securities Exchanges*.

Offer for Sale by Tender An **offer for sale** but with the public being invited to bid for the **shares/stock** at prices above a specified minimum figure. See also *Securities Exchanges*.

Offer Price (Asking Price) The price at which something is offered for sale. See also *Bid Price*, *Bid-offer Spread* and *Market Price/Rate/Value*.

Offering Memorandum See *Prospectus*.

Offset (Countertrade) Where a buyer (importer), typically of military equipment, either provides components to be incorporated into the imported product/equipment (direct offset/co-production), or is provided by the seller (exporter) with new technology or a production role unrelated to the product/equipment being imported or even investment by the seller in job or wealth creation schemes for the buyer or buyer's country (indirect offset). See also *Countertrade*.

Offsetting Trade A new contract that is the reverse of an existing contract, and has the effect of closing out the former. See also *Close Out*.

Open Account Where goods or services are provided by their seller on the basis of trust that the buyer will subsequently pay for what it receives. See also *Payment in Advance/On Delivery*.

Open Company/Corporation See *Public/Open Company/Corporation*.

Open Outcry (Derivative/Commodity Exchanges) The process whereby, using their voices and hand signals, members of the exchange trading in a **pit** agree to buy and sell contracts.

Opening Creditors The creditors outstanding at the start of an **accounting period**, which were the **closing creditors** shown in the last **balance sheet**.

Opening Debtors The debtors outstanding at the start of an **accounting period**, which were the **closing debtors** shown in the last **balance sheet**.

Opening Stocks/Inventory The stocks/inventory at the start of an **accounting period**, which were the **closing stocks** shown in the last **balance sheet**.

Operating Profit/Loss See *Trading Profit*.

Operational Risk A potential 'catch-all' that includes human errors or defalcations, loss of documents and records, ineffective systems or controls and security breaches.

Opportunity Cost What is lost by not doing something else (e.g., by not investing elsewhere).

Option (Derivative Contract) A derivative contract giving the **buyer** (holder) the right, but not the obligation, to buy or to sell something (the **underlying**) at an agreed price (the **strike/exercise price/rate**) within a specified time limit. Options differ from other types of derivative in that the buyer has the right but not the obligation to exercise the contract. The other **counterparty**, called the **writer** (or seller) must perform their side of the contract if called upon to do so by the buyer. Settlement is for the difference between the strike price chosen at the outset by the buyer and the **market rate** on the date the contract is exercised. An option which is not exercised lapses on its **expiry date**. Options are both **exchange traded** and available **over-the-counter**. The buyer, in return for the advantage of being able to decide whether or not to exercise the contract, pays a fee called a **premium** to the writer of the contract. See also *Abandon, American-style, At the Money, Borrower's Option, Call Option, Cap, Collar, Currency Option, European-style, Fair Value, Floor, Forward Reversing Option, Interest Rate Option, In the Money, Intrinsic Value, Lender's Option, Maturity Date, Option Period, Out of the Money, Participating Forwards, Put Option, Reference Period, Straddle, Strangle, Time Value,* and *Value Date.*

Option (Shares/Stock/Equity) The right but not the obligation of the holder of the option to convert all or part of a debt into **equity** of a borrower, or otherwise for the holder to have the right but not the obligation to acquire equity at a future date. See also *Convertible Bonds and Convertible Preference Shares* and *Warrants.*

Option Dated Forward Contract See *Forward Contract (Currency).*

Option Period (Forward Contracts) See *Forward Contract (Currency).*

Option Period (Interest Rate Option) The period of time from the date the **option** contract is written until the **maturity date** of any **loan** or deposit it is being used to **hedge.** See also *Reference Period.*

Ordinary Shares/Common Stock The basic form of **equity** investment in a **company/corporation,** giving the **shareholders/stockholders** the right to be paid any **dividends** and usually to vote on specific matters. Shareholders/stockholders can normally sell their holdings to another investor at an agreed or **market price,** but otherwise have no right to any repayment of their investment unless the company/corporation is wound up. See also *Authorized/Issued/Capital/ Shares/Stock, Bankruptcy, Closed/Private Company/Corporation, Convertible Bonds and Convertible Preference Shares, Insolvency, Quoted/Listed, Preference Shares/Prior-preferred Stock, Public/Open Company/Corporation, Securities Exchanges, Stock* and *Warrants.*

OTC See *Over-the-counter.*

OTM (Option Derivative Contract) See *Out of the Money.*

Out of the Money (Option Derivative Contract) An **option** contract without **intrinsic value,** i.e., the **strike price** is less advantageous to the **buyer** than the current **market rate** for the **underlying.** See also *In the Money* and *At the Money.*

Outward Collection (Collection) Where a bank receives from its customer a **collection** to be sent to a **presenting bank** for presentation to the buyer **(drawee).** See also *Inward Collection.*

Over-the-counter (OTC – Derivative Contracts) **Derivative** contracts written to meet the specific needs of individual clients, such as businesses, banks or governments. They are usually provided by banks or other financial institutions. See also *Exchange Traded.*

Over-the-counter (OTC – Securities Markets) Where **securities** are bought and sold by means of telephone and computer links, instead of physically on the trading floor of a **securities exchange**.

Overdraft A flexible lending facility (secured or unsecured) provided by a bank where the borrower can borrow up to an agreed maximum amount (the limit) but is not required to do so. The **debt** can be repaid in whole or part at any time but the facility remains available for repeated utilization by the borrower up to the limit. The lender usually has the right to cancel the facility and call for repayment of the debt on demand. **Interest** is charged on the daily debit balance.

Overdrafts are of the following two types.

- Authorized – where the limit has been agreed in advance between the borrower and the bank.
- Unauthorized – where, whether by accident or the borrower's design, an account moves into debit without prior arrangement with the bank.

Some banks mark 'anticipatory limits' for customers, as a guide to their lending officers when faced with either a request for an overdraft/loan or an unauthorized excess. See also *At Call* and *Demand Loan*.

Overheads See *Fixed Costs*.

Overnight Exposure See *Counterparty/Credit Risk* and *Settlement Risk*.

Overtrading Can occur when a business tries to produce and sell too high a level of goods or services on the **asset/working capital** base it has available. A business that is overtrading may not be able to meet its obligations without further funding. See also *Bankruptcy*, *Insolvency*, *Liquidation* and *Undertrading*.

Paid-up Capital/Shares/Stock The amount of the **issued capital/shares/stock** of a **company/corporation** that has been paid for by **shareholders/stockholders**. See also *Partly Paid Capital/Shares/Stock*.

Paper Another word for **securities**.

Par The 'face' or 'nominal' value of a security or other **asset** and the amount on which any **interest coupon** is normally calculated. A **bond** issued at $100 is at par if its **market price** is $100. At $95 it would be 'below par', and at $105 'above par'. The par value of, for example **shares/stock** is chosen by the **company/corporation** at the time they are issued, and may bear little relationship to **market value**. A share with a par value of £1 could be trading at, say, £9. See also *Redemption Value*.

Parent Company A company/corporation which owns or controls a **subsidiary company**, may also be known as a **holding company**.

Participating Forward (Option) Where a **buyer** enters into both a **put** and a **call option** at the same **strike price** but for different amounts of the **underlying**, offsetting the **premiums** payable and receivable to achieve a zero cost.

Participation Fee (Lending Syndicate) The fee paid to the members of a **syndicated**

loan on the basis of their participation, usually due from the borrower on signature of the facility. See also *Fees (Lending)*.

Partly Paid Capital/Shares/Stock) Where the full price of the **capital/shares/stock** has not been paid, leaving the shareholders/stockholders liable for the uncalled amount. See also *Authorized* and *Issued Capital/Shares/Stock* and *Paid-up Capital/Shares/Stock*.

Partnership Where two or more individuals or entities are in business together. Depending on the jurisdiction all partners may be **jointly and severally** liable for all partnership debts or, alternatively, the 'general partners' may be jointly and severally liable whilst 'limited partners' are only liable to the extent of their investments.

Pawnbroking A lending based solely on the available security, without consideration by the lender of the inherent viability of the proposal underlying the borrowing.

Pay Back Period The period of time before an investment will be fully recovered from inward **cash flows**. See also *Present Value*.

Payee The named beneficiary in a **draft/bill of exchange** or other financial **instrument**.

Payer (Vanilla Swap) The party paying the fixed **interest** stream in a **vanilla swap**. Also known as the 'buyer'. See also *Receiver (Vanilla Swap)*.

Paying Bank (Documentary Letter of Credit) See *Nominated Bank*.

Payment Bond A **bond/contract guarantee** covering the supplier of goods or services in the event that the buyer fails to make payment of the contract amount when due.

Payment in Advance/on Delivery Where the buyer of goods or services pays for them, in whole or part, in advance or at the time of the seller delivering the goods or providing the service. See also *Open Account*.

PBIT Stands for 'profit before **interest** and tax'. See *Trading Profit/Loss*.

Performance Bond A **bond/contract guarantee** undertaking that the principal (being the seller/exporter who asks the bank or insurance company to issue the bond) will provide the goods or services as specified in a separate contract with the beneficiary (being the party in favour of whom the bond has been issued).

P/E Ratio See *Price to Earnings Ratio*.

Pit (Trading or Futures Pit) The area on the trading 'floor' of a **derivatives** or other exchange where the **brokers** and **dealers** buy and sell contracts through **open outcry**. There are different pits for different derivative contracts.

Placing Where new **shares/stock** in a **company/corporation** are offered to the private and institutional clients of a **broker**. See also *Securities Exchanges*.

Plant The machinery and equipment being part of the **fixed assets** of a business. See also *Fixtures and Fittings*.

Point 1% of value. See also *Basis Point*.

Poison Pill Tactic used by a **company/corporation** to defend itself against a hostile takeover by making it more expensive or otherwise less attractive for a prospective acquirer to proceed.

Political and Country Risks Exposure to the potentially negative impact of actions by national and supra-national governments, government agencies and the numerous bodies empowered to regulate trade or to set prices and industry standards. Their extensive armoury includes taxation, quotas, tariffs and other trade barriers, **currency exchange controls**, restrictions on foreign ownership and the repatriation of profits or **capital**, availability of grants and subsidies, setting **interest** rates, granting licenses and monopolies, nationalization, expropriation and restitution of assets to former owners. When dealing with an overseas business or with a foreign government (**sovereign risk**) it may also be necessary to consider the country's social and economic stability, its trading practices, customs and ethics, its commercial law, including **insolvency** situations, and the effectiveness of its legal system. There may be a limit to the amount of exposure that is acceptable in respect of any single country, making it necessary to mark 'country (credit) limits'. See also *Jurisdiction Risk*.

Pour Aval See *Avalising*.

Pre-emption Rights Any right of existing **shareholders/stockholders** to be offered the opportunity to buy new issues of shares/stock before they are offered to other potential investors, i.e., a right of first refusal. See also *Dilution*.

Preference Shares/Prior-preferred Stock The holders of preference shares/prior-preferred stock receive a **dividend** at a fixed rate irrespective of the profits of the business, unless these are insufficient for the payment of that dividend in whole or in part. If this happens some preference/preferred shares are 'cumulative', i.e., the fixed dividend will be paid when the **company/corporation** is able to do so, whilst others are 'non-cumulative', i.e., the dividend for that period is forfeited. The fixed dividend is paid before any dividend payment to holders of **ordinary shares/common stock**, and if the company/corporation is wound up, the preference/preferred **shareholders/stockholders** rank before the holders of ordinary shares/common stock for any repayment of their **capital**. Some preference/preferred shares/stock are 'participating', which means they receive a share of the profits of the company/corporation by way of a variable dividend in addition to the fixed dividend. Others are 'convertible' into ordinary shares/common stock on a specified basis, or 'redeemable' by the company/corporation on set terms. Preference/preferred shareholders/stockholders cannot normally vote at the meetings of the company/corporation. See also *Convertible Bonds* and *Convertible Preference Shares*.

Premium (Option Derivative Contracts) The cost of an **option**, paid by the **buyer** to the **writer**, comprising the **intrinsic value** and the **time value**. See also *Fair Value*.

Premium (Shares) See *Share Premium*.

Present Value Money invested today to earn **interest** will be worth more in the future (before any adjustment for the rate of inflation), i.e., its 'future value' will be greater by an amount equal to the interest earned. In the same way, money you will not receive or pay until a future date has a lesser 'present value'. The difference is the actual or notional amount of interest that would have been earned on the money if you had it available to invest today. For example, if you will receive US$100,000 in one year and could today have earned 5% per annum for an amount of that size put on deposit for 12 months, then the present value of the future US$100,000 is US$952,381. To calculate a present value multiply the future amount by $1 \div (1+i)^n$ where i (discount rate) is the rate of interest/return as a decimal, e.g., 5% is 0.05 and n the number of interest periods. Cash flows on an investment can be discounted back ('discounted cash flows') to give the 'net present value' (NPV). The 'discount rate' used is the investor's 'required rate of return' for the investment. An investor would usually require a positive NPV before investing. See also *Hurdle Rate*, *Internal Rate of Return*, *Pay Back Period* and *Yield*.

Presenting Bank (Collection) The bank which receives the documents via the **remitting bank** and contacts the **drawee** (buyer). See also *Collection*.

Price-sensitive Information Knowledge which could affect the price at which someone would be prepared to trade, e.g., in the **shares/stock** of a **public/open company/corporation**. See also *Insider Trading*.

Price to Earnings Ratio (P/E Ratio) Middle **market** price of an **ordinary share/common stock** ÷ **earnings per share/stock**. Shows the number of years it would take for the earnings per share/stock of the **company/corporation** at their current level to repay the cost of its purchase, and facilitates comparison between companies/corporations. Inverse of earnings yield. See also *Yield*.

Primary Market See *Securities Exchanges*.

Prime Banks Banks of good standing.

Prime Rate The rate of **interest** at which banks will lend to customers considered to be highly creditworthy.

Principal (Amount) The amount invested, deposited, lent or subject to an obligation.

Principal (Collection) The seller of the goods who asks the **remitting bank** to handle the **collection**.

Prior-preferred Stock See *Preference Shares*.

Private Company/Corporation See *Closed/Private Corporation/Company*.

Produce/Commodity Loans Borrowings by an importer against the security (pledge) of the goods it is buying. When the importer sells the goods the lender is repaid. Suitable for readily saleable goods, such as **commodities**, which can be held (and insured) in the bank's name.

Production Payments (Project Finance) Where the provider(s) of finance receives all or some of the output from the project to service and repay the **debt**. See also *Project Finance*.

Profit See *Contribution, Gross Profit, Trading Profit* and *Net Profit*.

Profit and Loss Account The record of the trading activities of a business over a specified period of time (the **accounting period**), usually ending on a **balance sheet date**. See also *Balance Sheet*.

Profit and Loss Reserve See *Reserve (Profit and Loss)*.

Pro Forma Invoice A quotation, in the format of an **invoice** issued by a prospective seller, inviting the prospective buyer to place an order. Often required where the buyer needs evidence of the terms of an intended purchase to obtain **exchange control** or import licences.

Project Finance The financing of a project where the servicing and repayment of the funding depends on the revenue stream or value of the completed project rather than principally on the **covenant** of the borrower or on a charge over **collateral** security.

Promissory Note A written and signed unconditional undertaking to pay a specified amount at a specified date, effectively an 'IOU'.

Proprietor (Sole) See *Sole Trader*.

Proprietory Trading Trading for own account not as a **broker** for clients. See also *Dealer*.

Prospectus (Offering Memorandum) A document issued to prospective investors, e.g., in **shares/stock**, giving details of the offering.

Protesting See *Noting*.

Provision (Lending) A reserve for bad debts. May be 'specific', relating to a particular lending or 'general', being a contingency against a portfolio of loans. There can be a difference in the tax treatment of specific and general provisions.

Proxy The giving by one party to another of authority to act on their behalf. **Shareholders/stockholders** who do not intend to be present at an **annual general meeting** are often encouraged by the directors of that **company/corporation** to complete a proxy in favour of the chairperson of the meeting, enabling their votes to be exercised on resolutions.

Public/Open Company/Corporation A **company/corporation** whose **securities** are listed on a **securities exchange** for purchase by the public. See also *Closed/Private Company/Corporation* and *Quoted/Listed*.

Public Offer Where new **securities** are offered for sale to the general public. See also *Securities Exchanges*.

Put Option (Derivative Contract) An **option** where the **buyer** has the right but not the obligation to sell a specified quantity of the **underlying** to the **writer** at an agreed price on or before a specified date. The buyer can benefit from a fall in the **market price** of the underlying. See also *Call Option*.

Puttable (Bonds) Where the investor can require the issuer to redeem the **bond** prior to its specified **maturity**.

Qualified (Auditors' Report) When an **auditors'** report refers to divergence(s) of the accounts from accounting practice, or to other reservations. See also *Clean (Auditors' Report)*.

Qualitative Factors that involve subjective judgement rather than numerical analysis, e.g., the quality of management or customer service. See also *Quantitative*.

Quantitative Factors that involve numerical analysis rather than subjective judgement, e.g., the **liquid ratio** or **gearing/leverage**. See also *Qualitative*.

Quick Assets (Net Working Assets) **Current** assets less stock of finished goods and raw materials and less work-in-progress.

Quick Asset Surplus/Deficit Quick assets less **current liabilities**.

Quick Ratio See *Liquid Ratio*.

Quotation The **bid** and **offer** prices given by one party to another, being those at which they are prepared to buy or sell. See also *Market Makers*.

Quoted/Listed Where a **company's/corporation's** securities (e.g., **shares/stock**) are listed on a **securities exchange** for purchase by the public following **flotation**. See also *Closed/Private, Public/Open Company/Corporation* and *Unquoted*.

RUFs See *Revolving Underwriting Facility*.

Ranking (Creditors) The relative seniority of **creditors** for repayment, especially if the **debtor** becomes insolvent. Can also refer to the seniority of charges taken by way of security against the assets of a business. See also *Bankruptcy, Insolvency* and *Senior Debt*.

Ratchet Where an increased reward (e.g., a greater **equity** stake in a business for its management) is offered if specified criteria are met.

Rating Agencies Organizations such as Standard & Poor's, Moody's and Fitch who prepare and publish credit evaluations, e.g., on the likelihood of default by the issuer of a **bond** in the timely payment of **interest** and repayment of **principal**.

Real Interest Rate See *Interest*.

Real Property/Realty/Real Estate Land, the buildings thereon and the rights to any assets thereunder or thereover.

Receivables See *Accounts Receivable*.

Receiver (Vanilla Swap) The party being paid the fixed **interest** stream in a **vanilla swap**. Also known as the 'seller'. See also *Payer (Vanilla Swap)*.

Red Clause Documentary Letter of Credit Allows the **beneficiary** to draw a percentage of the value of the credit from the **confirming** or other **nominated bank** in advance of any shipment, against an undertaking to use the monies for the underlying purposes of the credit. See also *Documentary Letter of Credit*.

Redemption Value The amount paid to the holders on redemption of **securities**, normally taken as meaning that they have been held to their specified **maturity date** when redemption will often be at **par**. See also *Yield*.

Reducing-balance Method (Depreciation) A method of **depreciation** where the annual depreciation is a constant **percentage** of the net book value of an asset at the start of each accounting period. The actual **amount** of depreciation therefore reduces each year, as the net book value on which the percentage is calculated is itself getting smaller as a result of each previous year's depreciation.

Reference Period (Interest Rate Options) The period of time between the date when the **option** can be exercised and the **maturity date** of any loan or deposit that the option is being used to **hedge**. See also *Option Period*.

Registered (Securities) Where ownership is evidenced by some form of registration, usually in the books of an issuer or of a 'registrar'. See also *Certificate* and *Bearer*.

Remitting Bank (Collection) The bank which at the principal's (seller's) request, forwards the documents to a bank **(presenting bank)** located conveniently for the **drawee** (buyer). See also *Collection*.

Replacement Risk See *Counterparty/Credit Risk*.

Repo See *Repurchase Agreement*.

Repurchase Agreement (RePO) A sale and repurchase agreement, typically involving tradable **securities** and sometimes **commodities**. The sale is for immediate cash settlement and the repurchase is at an agreed price. The repurchase may be set for a specific date or 'open', i.e., until a **counterparty** wishes to close out the transaction. The difference between the (lower) sale and the (higher) repurchase price is the profit to the counterparty who initially buys the securities. The seller raises cash in a liquid market at attractive rates, whilst the buyer has the securities as **collateral** (although they normally remain as an **asset** on the **balance sheet** of the seller together with the **liability** for the repurchase). A repo allows cash to be 'borrowed' against securities (even to finance the purchase of those securities) and, conversely, securities to be borrowed for cash (e.g., by a **dealer** with a **short** position it needs to cover). The repo market can be used by **central banks** as part of their management of **short-term interest** rates and the money supply and in some countries the repo rate is the key interest rate.

Reputational Risk Where the actions of a business damage its reputation, to the extent that it may lose sales or customers.

Reservation of Title See *Retention (Reservation) of Title.*

Reserve Asset Costs (Lending) See *Reserve Requirement/Asset Costs.*

Reserve (Capital) The **capital** surplus of a **company/corporation**, including any **share premium** and (unrealized) **asset** revaluation reserve, that is not normally available for distribution to **shareholders/stockholders** as **dividends**. See also *Reserve (Profit and Loss).*

Reserve (Profit and Loss) The accumulated profits of a **company/corporation** that have not been distributed as **dividends**. See also *Reserve (Capital).*

Reserve Requirement/Reserve Asset Costs The cost to a bank of any requirement of its government, **central bank** or other regulatory body for a percentage of its funds to be held as cash or as 'special deposits' with the government or central bank. See also *Associated Costs* and *Capital Adequacy Requirement.*

Retention Bond A **bond/contract guarantee** for the refund of retention monies paid by the beneficiary of the bond (being the buyer of the respective goods or services) if the principal (being the supplier of the goods or services who asks the bank or insurance company to issue the guarantee) fails to meet its post-completion contractural obligations. In return for the bond the beneficiary releases to the principal the retention monies it would otherwise continue to hold.

Retention (Reservation) of Title Where the seller of goods reserves the legal title to them (and sometimes for any other goods supplied to the same buyer) until they are paid for.

Return on Assets Profit before **interest** and tax ÷ **total assets**.

Return on Capital Employed (Profit before **interest** and tax × 100) ÷ average **capital employed**.

Return on Equity (Return to Shareholders) Profit before tax ÷ **net tangible assets**.

Return to Shareholders See *Return on Equity.*

Revocable Documentary Letter of Credit A letter of credit which can be altered or cancelled by the **issuing bank** without the agreement of the **beneficiary**, at any time prior to a payment or commitment to pay the beneficiary. Banks will not confirm revocable credits. See also *Documentary Letter of Credit* and *Irrevocable Documentary Letter of Credit*.

Revolving Documentary Letter of Credit A documentary letter of credit which remains available for repeated re-use over a specified period of time, although often subject to a maximum amount during any set period.

Revolving Loan A loan with a fixed upper limit but where a borrower can repeatedly draw down and repay in whole or part (subject to any specified term and minimum tranches).

Revolving Underwriting Facility (RUF) The underwriting of an issue of short-term notes. See also *Note Issuance Facility*.

Rho The measure of change in the price of an option premium against a change in interest rates.

Rights Issue When existing holders of ordinary shares/common stock are invited to subscribe for new shares/stock in a company/corporation *pro rata* to their existing holdings, and usually at a discount to current market price. See also *Capitalization/Scrip/Bonus Issue*.

Risk Asset Ratio See *Capital Adequacy Requirement*.

Rollover (Forward Contract) To extend a forward contract at its maturity.

Rollover Date (Interest) See *Variable/Floating Interest Rate*.

Rollover Dates (Interest Rate Swaps) The dates when the counterparties swap interest streams. See also *Swap* and *Interest Rate Swap*.

Rollover Period (Interest) See *Variable/Floating Interest Rate*.

Rule of 78 A method of apportioning regular payments, e.g., on a lease, between interest and capital over a term, with a bias towards interest in the early stages. The name derives from the total of the numbers 1 to 12.

Sale and Leaseback Where the owner of an asset transfers its legal title to a third party for (usually) a cash payment and, at the same time, enters into a lease with that third party allowing the original owner continued use of the asset on regular payment of a lease rental. Used where, for example, the owner of real property wishes to raise cash against the asset whilst continuing to occupy the property. See also *Buy-back Agreement, Leasing* and *Repurchase Agreement (Repo)*.

Scalpers Traders who only hold their market positions for usually up to a few minutes, but make their money by trading large volumes at small margins.

Scrip Dividend Where a dividend is paid in shares/stock not cash.

Scrip Issue See *Capitalization Issue*.

Secondary Market (After Market) See *Securities Exchanges*.

Secondary Market (Lending) The trading of their existing **loans** by banks.

Securities Commonly taken as meaning **capital market** and **debt instruments**, especially those traded on **securities exchanges**, (e.g., **shares/stock** and **bonds**). May also be regarded as including, for example, **drafts/bills of exchange** and **promissory notes**. Sometimes called 'paper'.

Securities Exchanges (Stock Exchanges) Regulated markets in which the **shares/stocks** and, as appropriate, **bonds** and **warrants** of **quoted/listed companies/corporations** (i.e., those whose shares/stocks are available to the public) may be bought and sold. The aim should be to provide **liquidity** for the **securities** in an orderly and fair market. When a company/corporation issues new shares/stock or bonds they are sold in the 'Primary Market' (where the proceeds go to the issuer). Once the issue has closed the shares/stock/bonds are subsequently traded in the 'secondary market' or 'after market' (where the proceeds go to the previous holder). There may be a **grey market** if new issue securities are bought or sold during the period between an offer closing and the date on which secondary trading starts. See also *Flotation/Floatation*, *Offer for Sale*, *Offer for Sale by Tender*, *Placing*, *Introduction* and *Public Offer*.

Securitization Where **assets**, or the benefits of assets, are repackaged by an 'originator' (e.g., a bank) into 'asset-backed' **debt securities** issued to investors. The assets typically comprise a portfolio of loans with similar characteristics but different sizes and creditworthiness, e.g., loans to individual borrowers by way of **mortgages** on residential properties or credit card receivables. The originator would continue to 'service' the loans, collecting **interest** and **capital** repayments from the individual borrowers which are used to fund the interest cost and redemption of the debit issued to investors (the originator is usually entitled to retain any surplus), i.e., the **cash flows** on the assets and on the debt issue differ. The originator is not liable for losses above any pre-set amount. To make the issue attractive to investors it may be necessary to 'enhance' the assets by, for example, their over-collateralization or partial cash-collateralization, an originator's limited-recourse guarantee or insurance cover for bad debts. The effect of securitization is to segment the risks and rewards between the originator and investors, whilst improving the issuer's **balance sheet** and providing access to funds from new sources (i.e., the investors) at a cost which may be below that at which an originator could otherwise obtain finance.

Security Risk Can any security be enforced, and under what circumstances or conditions? What is it really worth and does it bring with it any **liabilities**?

Seed Corn Capital/Start-up Capital Investment monies used to develop a new business or project often provided by **venture capitalists**.

Seller (of an Option Derivative Contract) See *Writer*.

Seller's Market When demand is high and sellers can take a tough line in negotiations. See also *Buyer's Market*.

Senior Debt **Debt** that ranks before other debt for repayment or security rights. See also *Mezzanine Debt/Capital*, *Ranking* and *Subordinated Debt*.

Sensitivity Analysis Calculation of the effects of one or more changes on other factors, e.g., how changing sales volumes affect the levels of **stock** and **accounts receivable**. See also *Stress Testing*.

Set-off The right of a **debtor** to set-off against monies they owe to a **creditor** any amounts owed to them by that creditor. It will be subject to the **terms** of any contracts between the parties and to applicable law, the latter being particularly relevant in **insolvency** situations.

Settled to Market Each **business day** every **derivative** contract outstanding on an exchange (i.e., those recorded as not having reached their **settlement date**) is settled to market. The contracts are **marked to market**. If the value of the contract has changed since the previous business day, the amount of that change is credited by the **clearing house** to one of the **counterparties** (in favour of whom the market has moved) and debited to the other (against whom the market has moved). This means that 'profits' and 'losses' are crystallized and paid every day. The daily payment is known as the **variation margin** and is in addition to the **initial margin**.

Settlement Date The date on which delivery of cash or other **assets** is made to complete a transaction. May be known as 'value date'. See also *Due Date*, *Maturity Date*, *Forward Rate Agreement* (settlement date) and *Settlement Risk*.

Settlement Date (Forward Rate Agreement) See *Forward Rate Agreement*.

Settlement Limit The limit set for **settlement risk** exposure to any **counterparty**.

Settlement Risk Arises when you pay away cash or deliver **assets** before your **counterparty** is known to have performed their part of the deal. The exposure is normally for the full amount of the transaction, and may exist during the course of a trading day (daylight exposure), or last overnight (overnight exposure) or longer. See also *Counterparty/Credit Risk*, *Herstatt Risk*, *Intra-day Limit* and *Settlement Limit*.

Severability Clause A condition in a document stating that if any of its individual **terms** or conditions become invalid the remaining terms and conditions remain valid.

Several See *Joint and Several*.

Shadow Director Someone other than a director of a **company/corporation** who is deemed to influence or control the actions of that business and may, for example, be held liable for third party losses if the company/corporation becomes insolvent. See also *Board of Directors* and *Insolvency*.

Share Premium The excess of the sale price of a **share/stock** over its **par** value, being part of the **capital reserve**.

Shareholders/Stockholders The holders of **shares/stock** in a **company/corporation**, who only get all or some of their investment back if they sell their shares/stock to someone else or if the company/corporation is wound up and there is a surplus after paying **creditors**. They are entitled to share in any **dividends** paid by the company/corporation and, usually, to receive information about the business and to vote on certain matters (e.g., the constitution of the **board of directors**). There may be different classes of shares/stock having different rights. See also *Ordinary Shares/Common Stock*.

Shareholders' Funds See *Net Worth*.

Shares/Stock See *Authorized/Issued Capital/Shares/Stock, Convertible Shares, Discount to Issue Price, Options, Ordinary Shares/Common Stock, Paid-up Capital/Shares/Stock, Partly Paid Capital/Shares/Stock, Preference Shares/Prior-preferred Stock, Quoted/Listed, Stock* and *Warrants*.

Ship's (Sea) Waybill An alternative shipping document to **bills of lading**. They are not negotiable nor do they constitute a document of title.

Short To 'go short' is to sell something you do not hold, e.g., to have sold more of a security or a currency than you have bought. See also *Long*.

Short Form Reports Usually an accountant's report in accordance with the requirements of a **securities exchange**. See also *Due Diligence* and *Long Form Reports*.

Short Term Often taken as meaning any period up to one year (e.g., in financial accounts), but subject to various interpretations for different markets and purposes. See also *Long Term* and *Medium Term*.

Sight Draft/Bill of Exchange A draft/bill of exchange payable on demand. See also *Tenor Draft/Bill of Exchange*.

Simple Interest Where **interest** is calculated on the outstanding **principal** amount, and normally paid to the lender/investor as it becomes due. See also *Compound Interest* and *Flat Interest*.

Softs Commodities such as grain, coffee and pork bellies.

Sole Trader/Proprietor An individual trading on their own for their own account.

Source and Application (Uses) of Funds A statement showing the movements of funds in a business over a given period, i.e., where they have come from and where they went. See also *Cash Flow*.

Sovereign Risk That the government of a country will default on its obligations. See also *Political and Country Risk*.

SPAN See *Standard Portfolio Analysis of Risk*.

Speculating (Speculation) Buying or selling something in the hope of profit from a favourable future change in the market. Speculation increases risk, as distinct from **hedging** where the objective is to reduce an existing exposure.

Speculator Someone who speculates.

Spot Rate (Currency) The rate at which currency is bought or sold with settlement (i.e., delivery of the currencies being exchanged) normally becoming due two business days later. See also *Forward Contract* and *Settlement Risk*.

Spread The difference between the **bid** and **offer** prices. See *Bid-offer Spread*.

Stag Someone who buys **securities**, e.g., at the time of a **flotation**, with the hope of making a profit by selling shortly thereafter.

Standard Portfolio Analysis of Risk (SPAN) The system for calculating the amount of the **initial margin** for an **exchange traded derivative**.

Standard and Poor's See *Rating Agencies*.

Standby Credits (Standby Letters of Credit) In countries where there are restrictions on banks issuing guarantees for their customers they may instead be able to provide standby letters of credit undertaking to pay a named beneficiary if the bank's customer defaults in respect of specified obligations. For all practical purposes a standby credit is a guarantee. See also *Documentary Letter of Credit* and *Bond/Contract Guarantee*.

Standby Facility A fall-back commitment, e.g., to lend money, which is not expected to be regularly (if ever) used. See also *Multi-option Facility*.

Start-up Capital See *Seed Corn Capital*.

Statement of Financial Position See *Balance Sheet*.

Stock The equity in a **company/corporation**, e.g., ordinary **shares/common stock** and **preference shares/prior-preferred stock** and sometimes considered to include **bonds**. Also, another word for **inventory** (i.e., the raw materials, work-in-progress and finished goods awaiting sale in a business). See also *Authorized Capital/Shares/Stock*.

Stock Dividend A dividend paid in the form of **shares/stock** in the **company/corporation** instead of in cash.

Stock Markets See *Securities Exchanges*.

Stocks (Shares) See *Shares/Stocks*.

Stock Turnover A ratio showing the number of days that **stock** (inventory) has been held by a business.

Stockholder See *Shareholders/Stockholders*.

Straddle (Option Derivative Contract) A **call** and a **put option** with the same **strike price, underlying** and exercise date. It is a gamble that the market **volatility** will be sufficient for one of the options to be sold back for sufficient gain to leave a profit after the upfront cost of both **premiums**.

Straight-line Method (Depreciation) A method of **depreciation** where the (usually) annual depreciation of an **asset** is its initial cost less its estimated residual value at the end of its forecast useful life, divided by the number of years of its forecast useful life. Once the amount of the annual depreciation has been calculated in this way it remains a constant.

Strangle (Option Derivative Contract) A **straddle** with different put and call exercise prices. See also *Call Option* and *Put Option*.

Strategic Risk (Currency) See *Currency Exchange Rate Risk*.

Stress Testing Subjecting projections to extreme changes, to see what happens. See also *Sensitivity Analysis* and *Value at Risk*.

Strike Price/Rate (Option Contract) The price at which the **buyer** of an **option** has the right to buy or sell the **underlying**. Also known as the 'Exercise Price/Rate'.

Strike Price (Offer for Sale by Tender) The price at which **shares/stock** are allotted. See also *Offer for Sale by Tender*.

Strike Rate See *Strike Price/Rate (Option Contract)*.

Strip (Bonds) Separating the entitlement to **coupons** from the right to be repaid **principal** with each component trading separately.

Stuffees Those you can usually rely upon to take what you offer, e.g., to take a participation in a **syndicated loan** if asked by the **lead bank/manager**.

Subordinated Debt Debt ranking for repayment in **liquidation** after other debt. See also *Mezzanine Debt/Capital* and *Senior Debt*.

Subsidiary Company/Corporation A **company/corporation** either controlled by another company/corporation or (in most countries) having at least 50% of its **equity** held by a **parent/holding company**. If it is 100% owned by another company/corporation it is a wholly owned subsidiary. See also *Associate Company*.

Substance Over Form Looking at the underlying transaction rather than the surface appearance, e.g., the accountancy treatment in some countries for **off-balance-sheet** transactions.

Swap (Basis) See *Basis Swap*.

Swap (Coupon) See *Vanilla Swap*.

Swap (Interest Rate) See *Interest Rate Swap*.

Swap (Vanilla) See *Vanilla Swap*.

Swap (Derivative Contract) Over-the-counter **derivative** contract where the **counterparties** commit to make and to receive payments, e.g., to swap **fixed** for **variable/floating rate interest** streams and/or to swap one currency for another currency at an agreed **exchange rate** at a specified future date. See also *Currency Swap* and *Interest Rate Swap*.

Swap Rate (Vanilla Swap) The **swap** rate is that for the **fixed rate**, e.g., 3.6%:3.4% means a **broker-dealer** would pay fixed **interest** at 3.4% to a **counterparty** who paid floating rate but would want to receive 3.6% fixed interest from a counterparty who wished to be paid **variable/floating rate**. For swaps in major currencies, such as the US dollar, the quote will be for a swap spread against a **benchmark interest** rate. The benchmark will be the rate of interest on whichever government **bond** with **maturity** nearest to that of the swap has the greatest **liquidity**, e.g., a swap spread of 40/45 means the broker-dealer wants to receive **interest** at a fixed rate of 45 **basis** points over the benchmark interest rate, but would only pay 40 basis points.

Swaption An **option** contract giving the buyer the right but not the obligation to enter into an **interest rate swap** (the **underlying**) at a future date.

Switch A virtually extinct form of **countertrade** where third party traders make use of bilateral trading accounts that are out of balance.

SWIFT The Society for Worldwide Interbank Financial Telecommunication which, amongst other activities, facilitates the electronic remittance of funds between its member banks.

SWOT Analysis An analysis of strengths, weaknesses, opportunities and threats, e.g., to a business.

Syndicated Loan A **loan** provided by two or more lenders on the same or similar terms and conditions and usually using a single facility agreement. A **lead bank/manager** is normally mandated by the borrower to arrange the loan, including finding and negotiating with the other lenders who participate in the facility (and who individually decide upon the extent of their participation subject to any minimum or maximum limits set by the lead bank). The lead bank usually sends out to prospective participants an 'information memorandum' containing a summary of the proposal, with full details following for those expressing interest. Some lenders may participate on an undisclosed sub-participation basis, with their identities unknown to the borrower. One of the lenders (usually the lead bank) acts as **agent**, coordinating the actions of the other lenders ('syndicate members') and administering the loan **draw downs, interest** payments, **capital** repayments and information flows. There may be provision for some decisions to be made solely by the **majority lenders**. The credit risk and capital requirements of the loan are spread amongst the members of the syndicate, whilst the borrower only has to initially negotiate with the lead bank and can often raise substantial amounts more easily and on better terms than by issue of **bonds** or other **debt instruments**.

Systemic Risk The supervisor's nightmare, where problems in one financial institution or market may cross over to others and to other countries, having a domino effect, potentially threatening chaos in the global financial markets.

Tangible Assets See *Assets*.

Tender Panel The members of the panel (usually banks or other financial institutions) bid competitively when a client wishes, for example, to issue **notes**. If the notes are not taken up by the tender panel then there is usually an **underwriting** panel behind them who are committed to taking them up at a previously agreed price.

Tenor A period of time.

Tenor Draft/Bill of Exchange Also known as a time, term or usance **draft/bill of exchange**. Although, strictly speaking, 'tenor' refers to any period of time for which a draft is drawn to run before it matures and could, therefore, apply to a draft payable at sight, it is commonly understood to mean a draft drawn payable for a specified period of time other than at sight. See also *Sight Draft*.

Term A provision within a contract or other agreement. Also, a period of time, e.g., the length of time before a **loan** has to be repaid. See also *At Call*.

Term Draft/Bill of Exchange See *Tenor Draft/Bill of Exchange*.

Term Interest Rate Swap Where the **tenor** of the **swap** is over one year. See also *Interest Rate Swap* and *Money Market Interest Rate Swap*.

Term Liabilities Usually taken as being the liabilities of a business due for payment after 12 months. See also *Current Liabilities*.

Theta The measure of change in the price of an **option premium** against a change in the time to **maturity** of the contract.

Ticks The minimum amounts by which prices for **exchange traded derivatives** can move, e.g., the unit of trading on **LIFFE** for a 3-month Eurodeutschmark **interest** rate **future** is DM1,000,000 and the tick size set by the exchange is 0.01%. The tick value is therefore, DM25 (as the contracts are for 3 months, i.e., DM1m x [0.01 ÷100] x [3 ÷12]).

Time Draft See *Tenor Draft*.

Time Value See *Present Value*.

Time Value (Option Derivative Contract) That part of the **premium** paid by the **buyer** of an **option** contract that represents the risk to the **writer**. Time value plus **intrinsic value** (and any additional profit margin to the writer) equals the premium. Time value has two components, as follows.
- The time to expiry of the option contract, as the risk to the writer that the **underlying** might cost more is greater the longer the contract has to run.
- The 'volatility' of the underlying. If the **market price** of the underlying normally shows little variation, then the risk of it costing more on the **expiry date** is less than for an unstable underlying, where there are potentially more occasions when the option might favour the buyer.

The value of an option is said to 'decay' over time, as the nearer the contract gets to its expiry date the less uncertainty there is and, hence, the smaller the time value.

Tombstone The advertisements in newspapers, etc, that are published as a matter of record, giving details of **securities** issues and other financial or business events, e.g., public issue of shares or a merger.

Total Assets Everything shown as an **asset** in the **balance sheet**, including **intangible** assets.

Total Return (on an Investment) The **interest/dividend** income plus/minus movement in **market value** (usually with interest/dividend reinvested). See also *Yield*.

Tracking Error If, for example, you are using a **derivative** based on an **index** to hedge a portfolio, you may need to weight the number of contracts, as the index is unlikely to be a perfect match to the portfolio (i.e., it will not exactly 'track' the portfolio). See also *Basis Risk*.

Trader Someone whose business is to buy and sell in the hope of profit, rather than buying to hold as an investment. See also *Broker*, *Broker-dealer* and *Dealer*.

Trading Profit/Loss (Operating Profit) Gross contribution/Gross profit/loss less **fixed** costs (overheads). Also known as **EBIT** and **PBIT**. See also *Breakeven* and *Net Profit/Loss*.

Trading Risk (Currency) See *Currency Exchange Rate Risk*.

Transaction Risk See *Currency Exchange Rate Risk*.

Tranche An instalment, e.g., a **loan** may be drawn down in tranches by the borrower.

Transfer Price The price at which goods and services are sold between members of a group, sometimes artificially adjusted to move profits from one company/ division or country to another.

Transferable Documentary Letter of Credit Where the benefit of the letter of credit can be transferred in whole or in part by the **beneficiary** named therein to another beneficiary(s), who is normally the actual supplier(s) of the goods. See also *Documentary Letter of Credit*.

Transit Insurance Sometimes taken out by either the buyer or seller of goods in case their counterparty, who should have arranged insurance cover, fails to do so (or when it might be difficult for a party to claim and obtain prompt settlement under the counterparty's insurance).

Translation Risk (Currency) See *Currency Exchange Rate Risk*.

Treasury Bills Debt instruments issued by governments in their local currency.

Turn See *Bid-offer Spread*.

Turnover Has different meanings in different countries, being, for example, another word for 'sales' and the number of times that something is sold or used and replaced in a given period.

USM See *Unlisted Securities Market*.

Ultra Vires Actions outside the given powers of authority. See also *Borrowing Powers*.

Uncommitted Lines of Credit See *Multi-option Facility*.

Underlying (Derivative Contracts) The asset or index to which the derivatives contract relates.

Undertrading Occurs when a business fails to achieve an adequate level of sales on its asset base. See also *Overtrading*.

Underwriters/Underwriting Where a third party, e.g., a bank, commits for a fee to purchase whatever is not sold to others, e.g., an underwriter of a share/stock issue will be obliged to buy those securities not taken up by other investors. Normally all or part of the commitment and part of the fee is passed on to 'subunderwriters'.

Unfair Calling Insurance Protects the principal (being the party who asks a bank or insurance company to issue a bond/contract guarantee) if they have to reimburse the guarantor under the counter indemnity if the beneficiary of the bond makes an unfair demand thereunder.

Uniform Customs and Practice Published by the International Chamber of Commerce, these guidelines are widely accepted as the basis for many aspects of international trade.

Unquoted Where companies'/corporations' shares/stock are not quoted/listed on a recognized securities exchange, although they may still be traded over the counter.

Usance Draft/Bill of Exchange See *Tenor Draft/Bill of Exchange*.

Usury Charging an exorbitant rate of interest.

VAR See *Value at Risk*.

Value at Risk (VAR) A model that calculates as a single number the maximum potential loss from price volatility, i.e., market risk, based on statistical analysis of historic movements/standard deviation. Assumes that the past may be a reasonable guide to the future, and that you know how long it might take to trade out of a position in an illiquid market.

Value Date See *Settlement Date*.

Value Date (Option Derivative Contract) The date on which the writer has to deliver the underlying or make payment to the buyer. For interest rate options the value date is the same date as the **expiry date**. For **currency options** the value date may be later than the expiry date (e.g., say two days may be allowed between the expiry and the value date for the writer to deliver the currency).

Vanilla Straightforward **derivative** contracts, as distinct from **exotics**.

Vanilla Swap Also known as a 'coupon swap'. An **interest rate swap** between **fixed** and **variable/floating** rates in the same currency. See also *Payer*, *Receiver*, *Swap*, and *Swap Rate*.

Variable Costs Those costs that vary with the level of **turnover**, e.g., materials and labour directly incurred in the manufacture of a product or provision of a service. May be referred to as 'direct costs'. Sometimes it is considered correct for a percentage of **fixed costs (overheads)** to be allocated to production costs as production overheads. See also *Fixed Costs*, *Gross Contribution*, *Gross Profit/Loss*, *Net Profit/Loss* and *Trading Profit*.

Variable/Floating Rate Interest Where the rate of **interest** on your borrowing, lending or deposit changes, either immediately or on rollover dates in line with any changes in a specified base. At a rollover date, which ends a 'rollover period', a new rate must be set for the next period (unless the borrowing or deposit is repaid), by which time rates could have moved up or down. See also *Fixed Rate Interest*.

Variation Margin The amount that changes hands between the two parties to a **derivative** contract, via the **clearing house**, when it is **settled to market** every **business day**. See also *Initial Margin* and *Marking to Market*.

Vega The measure of change in the price of an **option premium** against a change in **volatility**.

Venture Capital The availability and forms taken by venture capital vary from country to country, and may be provided by private individuals, financial institutions or large **companies/corporations**. The funds made available by venture capitalists are typically invested into potentially high-risk situations and **management buy-outs** or **buy-ins**. In addition to providing finance the venture capitalists can often offer good advice and valuable business introductions to the management of the business in which they are investing. A venture capitalist will hope to make a profit if the business is subsequently sold, or if its **shares/stock** are listed on a **securities exchange**, or if the business buys back the shares/stock. See also *Seed Corn Capital/Start-up Capital*.

Venture Capitalist A provider of **venture capital**.

Volatility The degree of variability in prices or returns.

Volatility (Option Derivative Contracts) See *Time Value*.

Vostro Account The account maintained by a bank for an overseas bank, in the currency of the bank maintaining the account. See also *Correspondent Bank* and *Nostro Account*.

Warrants (Subscription or Stock Purchase Warrants) Tradable **bearer instruments** that may be issued as a 'sweetener' or 'equity kicker' with **preference shares/prior-preferred stock, bonds** or other **debt**, giving the holder the right to buy **ordinary shares/common stock** or bonds in the future at a set price. The price is normally above the market price at the time the warrants are issued, and the warrants can be traded on a **securities exchange** separately from the shares or bonds with which they were issued. See also *Convertible Bonds* and *Convertible Preference Shares* and *Option (Shares/Stock)*.

Warranty/Maintenance Bond A **bond/contract guarantee** that the principal (being the supplier of goods or services who asks the bank or insurance company to issue the bond) will provide on-going warranty/maintenance support to the beneficiary of the bond (being the buyer of the goods or services) for a specified period of time.

Weighted Risk Asset Ratio See *Capital Adequacy Requirement*.

Withholding Taxes Tax deducted at source which a foreign investor may be able to reclaim if there is a **double taxation agreement**. When lending to overseas borrowers, banks often require them to bear any withholding tax burden on **interest** payments.

Without Prejudice A caveat written on documents where, for example, settlement of a dispute is being discussed but you do not wish the contents of the document to be used against you if agreement cannot be reached.

Working Capital Often considered to be the same as **net current assets**, i.e. **current assets** less **current liabilities**. A definition preferred by many is net current assets tied up directly in the **cash conversion cycle** which will differ from net current assets in excluding non-operational assets and liabilities.

Working Capital Ratio See *Current Ratio*.

Working Capital Turnover A ratio of sales to **working capital**, indicating the additional working capital a business might need to fund an increase in sales.

Writer (Option Derivative Contract) The party who is paid a **premium** by the **buyer** of the **option** and must perform their side of the contract if called upon to do so by the buyer. Also known as the 'seller'.

Written Down Value See *Net Book Value*.

Wrongful Trading If the **board of directors** allows an **insolvent company/corporation** to continue trading they may, subject to the jurisdiction, be considered guilty of wrongful or fraudulent trading and be potentially liable to **creditors** of the business for resultant **debts**. See also *Shadow Director*.

Yankee A **bond** denominated in US dollars and issued in the US by a non-US issuer.

Yield The return on an investment – definitions include the following.

- 'Coupon rate/nominal yield' – the annual **interest** rate as a percentage of the **par** value of a **debt instrument**.
- 'Discount yield' – the annualized return to an investor from a **discounted instrument** based on the **discount** as a percentage of **par** value for the period to **maturity**.
- 'Running/current/income/earnings/flat/interest yield' – the annual (e.g., **coupon** or **dividend**) income as a percentage of **market price**.
- 'Maturity yield' – the rate at which the total of future interest payments and the **redemption value** must be discounted to have a **present value** equal to the current **market price**.
- 'Reverse yield ratio' – is that of the yield on government **bonds** to that on **company/corporation shares/stock**.
- 'Gross redemption yield' – the annual income plus the capital gains or losses at redemption as a percentage of market value.

See also *Discounted Instruments*, *Internal Rate of Return*, *Present Value* and *Price to Earnings Ratio*.

Yield Curve The variation in **yields** against the **terms** to **maturity**. Normally the yield required by an investor on any **instrument** increases as the period to maturity lengthens because the risk over time is perceived to be greater (an ascending/positive yield curve), as distinct from an inverse/descending/negative yield curve where investors expect yields to fall.

Zero Coupon Non-interest-paying **bonds** and other **instruments** issued at a discount. At **maturity** they are usually repaid at **par**. See also *Deep Discount*.

Z Scores **Models** that use a range of weighted financial ratios to analyze a **company/corporation** and the likelihood of it getting into financial difficulties.

Index

acceptance credits 179
accounting dates 30
accounting ratios
  average credit given 34–5
  average credit taken 36
  average remuneration per
    employee 47
  breakeven analysis 42
  cash flow 47–8
  current liability to stock 38
  current ratio 32–4
  debt repayment 50
  depreciation 51
  fixed assets to net tangible assets
    45
  gearing 39–41
  gross profit margin 43
  interest cover 48–9
  liquid ratio 34
  net profit margin 42–3
  price to earnings (P/E) 50
  profit per employee 46
  return on assets 45
  return on capital employed 43–4
  return on equity 44
  sales per employee 46
  sales to assets 46
  sales to liquid surplus 46
  stock turnover 37
  working capital turnover 38
accounts 27–32
  asset valuations 28, 30
  assumptions used 28
  benchmarks 32
  and business plans 116
  capitalizing costs 28
  changes of accounting policy 27
  contingent liabilities 30–1
  discontinued operations 32
  identifying trends 28–9
  and mergers/acquisitions 31–2
  minority interests 32
  off-balance-sheet transactions 31
  pension/healthcare contributions
    30
  prepared in a foreign currency 29
acid test ratio 34
acquisitions/mergers 24, 31–2, 124–6
advance payment guarantees 97, 100
advances against collections 182
aggregation risk 189
air waybills 81
American options 192, 254
annual fees for loans 149
arrangement fees 149
asset swaps 229
asset-based financing 160–82
  acceptance credits 179
  advances against collections 182
  bill advances 182
  factoring 113, 163–70
  forfaiting 170–8
  invoice discounting 113, 161–3,
    166–70
  negotiating a bill of exchange/draft
    179–82
assets
  current assets 33
  fixed assets 45
  quick assets 34
  return on assets ratio 44–5
  valuation 28, 30
auditors' reports 29
avalising 105
average credit given ratio 34–5
average credit taken ratio 36
average remuneration per employee
  ratio 47

back-to-back letters of credit 80
backing-up data 13
bad debts contingency 62, 203
balance sheets 29
    and currency risk 239–40
    off-balance-sheet transactions 31
    post-balance-sheet events 27
    see also accounting ratios
banks
    and the business cycle 8
    drawing against uncleared funds
       117
    sources of capital 203
barter 106
basis swaps 233
bearer bonds 127
benchmarks 32, 134
bid bonds 96–7, 98
bill advances 182
bills of exchange 68, 85, 93–4,
    179–82
    notes and protesting 181–2
bills of lading 81, 82
BNY Financial Limited 160–1
bonds 113, 127–8
    country risk 129, 130–2
    grading system 135–6
    industry risk 129, 132–3
    issuer business risk 129, 133–5
bonds/contract guarantees 95–104
bonus issues 121
borrowing
    choosing a lender 140
    foreign currency 29, 201–2, 244–5
    information needs 123–4
    setting of interest rates 202–4
    syndicate lenders 140, 150
    see also lending; loan agreements
Boston options 255
brands 30
breakeven analysis 42
broker-dealers 186
budgets 118
business cycle 7–8

business plans 114–16
buy-back deals 107–8
buying a business 24

call options 191–2
cancellation fees 149
capital employed 44
capital gearing 40–1
capitalization issues 121
capitalizing costs 28
caps 225
carriage and insurance paid (CIP) 86
carriage paid to (CPT) 86
cash flow 47–8
    forecasts 116–19
    operating cash flow 49
CBOT (Chicago Board of Trade) 186
certificates of origin 84
CFR (cost and freight) 86
character and ability of borrowers
    52–3
Chicago Board of Trade (CBOT) 186
CIF (cost insurance and freight) 86
CIP (carriage and insurance paid) 86
class of borrowers 140–1
clean collections 87, 89
clearing houses 187
collars 227–9, 255–6
collection period ratio 35
collections 87–93, 94, 180
commitment fees 149
commodity derivatives 196
common stock 121
competition 5, 133–4
computers
    backing-up data 13
    and crime 7
concentration risk 190
conditional bond/guarantee 96
conditions precedent 150, 153–4
confidential invoice discounting 113,
    161–3, 166–70
confirmed letters of credit 79
contingent liabilities 30–1

contract guarantees 95–104
contract risk 10, 14
   due diligence 24–7
convertible shares 122
cost and freight (CFR) 86
cost insurance and freight (CIF) 86
costs
   capitalizing 28
   direct 119
   and environmental/safety
     legislation 8–9
   of funds 202–3
   and loan agreements 145, 149–50
   overheads 119
counterparty trading 6, 23–4, 188,
   189
counterpurchase 106–7
countertrade 105–9
   barter 106
   buy-back deals 107–8
   counterpurchase 106–7
   offset 108
   switch trading 108
country risk 6, 7
   and bond evaluation 129, 130–2
   credit insurance 62
   and legal risk 10–11
   political risk 6, 15–17, 130, 131
   terrorism 20
coupon swaps 229, 230, 231–2
covenants 152, 154–7
CPT (carriage paid to) 86
creative accounting 27
credit derivatives 196–7
credit insurance 62–5
credit rating agencies 128–36
   grading system 135–6
credit risk 189
credit swaps 196
creditors 36
criminal risk 6–7
cross-currency swaps 258
currency
   balance sheet translation risk

239–40
borrowing in foreign currency 29,
   201–2, 244–5
collars 255–6
deposit accounts 243–4
exchange controls 16, 244
forward contracts 246–9
futures 256–7
and inflation 8
invoicing in a foreign currency
   243–4
options 193, 249–55
participating forward 256
pricing sales 244
spot values 242–3
swaps 257–61
trading risk 241–2
current assets 33
current liabilities 33–4
current liability to stock ratio 38
current ratio 32–4
cylinder options 255

DAF (delivered at frontier) 86
daylight exposure 24, 189
DDP (delivered duty paid) 86
debt recovery services 63
debt repayment ratio 50
debtors 35
deferred payments 124
delivered at frontier (DAF) 86
delivered duty paid (DDP) 86
delivery risk 24
depreciation 51
derivatives
   commodity derivatives 196
   credit derivatives 196–7
   equity/index derivatives 194–6
   exchange traded 185, 186–8
   futures 190–1
   options 185, 191–3
   over the counter (OTC) 185,
     188–9
   risks associated with 189–90

swaps 189, 194
  uses 185
direct offset countertrades 108
directors 14
discontinued operations 32
discovery 11
dismissed employees 7
dividends 30, 121, 122
documentary collections 87, 88–9,
  94
documentary letters of credit 68–79,
  95, 180
  principal documents 81–5
  types of 79–81
documentation risk 10, 14
drafts 68, 85, 93–4, 179–82
  notes and protesting 181–2
due diligence 24–7

earn outs 31
earnings per share 50
earnings yield 50
economic risk 7–8, 130, 131–2
ECP (Euro commercial paper) 128
emotional pressures on lenders 57
employment legislation 16
environmental risk 8–9, 17
equity derivatives 194–6
equity funding 113, 120–3
  stock markets 113, 122–3
equity index swaps 195–6
equity options 194–5, 196
Euro commercial paper (ECP) 128
Eurobonds 127–8
Eurocurrency 128
Eurodollar futures 212
Euromark futures 212
Euronotes 128
European options 192, 254
ex works (EXW) 86
exchange controls 16, 244
exchange rates see currency
exchange traded derivatives 185,
  186–8

export credit agencies 109
expropriation of assets 17

factoring 113, 163–70
fair value adjustments 31
FAS (free alongside ship) 86
FCA (free carrier) 86
fees and loan agreements 145,
  149–50
financial risk analysis 9, 134–5
fixed assets 45
fixed assets to net tangible assets ratio
  45
fixed costs 119
fixed rate facilities 201, 205
floating rate facilities 201, 204–5
floating rate notes (FRNs) 128
floors 225–7
flotation of companies 123
FOB (free on board) 86
forecasting
  cash flow 116–19
  profit and loss 119–20
foreign exchange see currency
forfaiting 170–8
forward contracts 246–9
forward rate agreements (FRAs)
  205–11
forward reversing options 255
fraud 6, 59
free alongside ship (FAS) 86
free on board (FOB) 86
free carrier (FCA) 86
FRNs (floating rate notes) 128
fundamentals of risk management
  3–5
futures 190–1
  currency 256–7
  index 194–5, 196
  interest rate 212–19

gearing 39–41
golden handcuffs 31, 124

grading systems
  for bonds 135–6
  for lending 60–2
grants 16
grey markets 122
gross profit margin 43
guarantors 151

health and safety
  costs 8–9
  legislation 17
hedging risk 12
hire purchase agreements 113
holiday periods 144

income recognition 29
incoterms 85–6
index futures 194–5, 196
index options 194–5, 196
index swaps 195–6
indirect offset countertrades 108
industrial espionage 7
industry risk 17–18, 129, 132–3
inflation
  and interest rates 202
  and preparation of accounts 29
information risk 9–10
information technology (IT) 13
initial margin 187, 188
inspection certificate 85
insurance certificates 84
insurance of goods in transit 86
interest cover ratios 48–9
interest rates
  caps 225
  collars 227–9
  and economic management 16
  fixed rate facilities 201, 205
  floors 225–7
  forward rate agreements (FRAs)
    205–11
  futures 212–19
  and loan agreements 144, 146–9
  options 192, 219–24

setting of rates 202–4
swaps 229–35
variable (floating) rate facilities
  201, 204–5
International Swaps and Derivatives
  Association (ISDA) 188, 233
inventory risk 12
invoice discounting 113, 161–3,
  166–70
invoices 82–3
invoicing in a foreign currency 243–4
inward collections 88
irrevocable letters of credit 79
ISDA (International Swaps and
  Derivatives Association) 188, 233
issuer business risk 129, 133–5
IT (information technology) 13

joint ventures 24
jurisdiction risk 10, 158–9

leasing 113
legal risk 10–11, 190
lending 52–62
  amount of loan 53–4
  character and ability of borrowers
    52–3
  class of borrowers 140–1
  and due diligence 24–7, 57–8
  emotional pressures 57
  grading system 60–2
  personal guarantees 15
  problem accounts 59–62
  process 57–8
  provisions for bad debts 62, 203
  purpose of loan 53
  repayment 54–5
  rights of lenders 159–60
  risk vs reward 56
  security 11, 55–6
  setting of interest rates 202–4
  see also borrowing; loan
    agreements
letters of credit 68–79, 94, 180

principal documents 81–5
  types of 79–81
letters of variation 158
letters of waiver 158
leverage ratios 39–41
leveraged buy-outs 126
liabilities
  contingent 30–1
  current 33–4
liability swaps 229
LIBOR 203, 213
licences 16–17
LIFFE (London International
  Financial Futures Exchange)
  186
liquid ratio 34
liquid surplus/deficit 33
liquidity risk 12, 190
litigation 9, 11
loan agreements 138–60
  amount of loan 142–3
  class of borrower 140–1
  conditions precedent 150, 153–4
  covenants 152, 154–7
  definition of terms 157–8
  events of default 159
  fees and costs 145, 149–50
  guarantors 151
  holiday periods 144
  interest rates 144, 146–9
  legal jurisdiction 158–9
  letter of variation 158
  letter of waiver 158
  negative pledge 155
  purpose of loan 146
  repayment terms 143–6, 150
  representations 141–2
  revolving loans 144, 145
  security 150–3
  type of facility 142–3
  warranties 141–2
  see also borrowing; lending
lock-out agreements 124
London International Financial

Futures Exchange (LIFFE) 186

maintenance guarantees 97
management buy-ins (MBIs) 126
management buy-outs (MBOs)
  125–6, 168
margin system 187–8
market makers 186
market risk 12, 190
markets and business plans 115
marking to market 12, 187–8
MBIs (management buy-ins) 126
MBOs (management buy-outs)
  125–6, 168
medium-term notes (MTNs) 128
mergers 24, 31–2, 124–6
mezzanine debt 126
minority interests 32
money markets 113
monopolies 16–17
Moody's 128
MTNs (medium-term notes) 128

nationalization 17
NCM 63
negative pledges 155
negotiating a bill of exchange/draft
  179–82
net profit margin 42–3
noting and protesting 182

off-balance-sheet transactions 31
offset countertrades 108
on demand bond/guarantee 96
open accounts 65–6
open outcry 186
operating cash flow 49
operational gearing 41
operational risk 12–14, 190
opportunity costs 202
options 185, 191–3
  Boston options 255
  collars 255–6
  currency 193, 249–55

cylinder 255
equity 194–5, 196
forward reversing 255
index 194–5, 196
interest rate 192, 219–24
participating forward 256
straddles 254
strangles 254
ordinary shares 121
outward collections 88
over the counter (OTC) derivatives
185, 188–9
overheads 119
overnight risk 24, 189
overtrading 46, 113–14

P/E (price to earnings) ratio 50
participating forward 256
partnerships 14–15
patents 30
payment in advance/on delivery 66–8
payment guarantees 97, 101
performance guarantees 97, 99
personal guarantees 15
personal risk 14–15
political risk 6, 15–17, 130, 131
post-balance-sheet events 27
preference shares 121
price to earnings (P/E) ratio 50
pricing
    and currency risk 244
    and sales volume control 47–8
    transfer pricing 31
prior-preferred stock 121
problem loan accounts 59–62
product risk 17–18
profit and loss accounts 29
    see also accounting ratios
profit per employee ratio 46
profits
    and cash 113
    forecasts 119–20
    margins 42–3
progress payment guarantees 97

project finance 136–8
promissory notes 85
protesting and notes 181–2
provision for bad debts 62, 203
public relations 18–19
put options 192

quick assets 34
quick ratio 34
quotas 15

rating agencies 128–36
    grading system 135–6
ratio analysis see accounting ratios
red clause letters of credit 81
reducing-balance depreciation 51
registered bonds 127
repayment of loans 54–5, 143–6, 150
representations 141–2
reputational risk 19, 190
resources risk 19
restitution 17
restricted liability 14
restructuring programmes 60
retention guarantees 97
return on assets ratio 45
return on capital employed 43–4
return on equity 44
revaluation of assets 28
revocable letters of credit 79
revolving letters of credit 81
revolving loans 144, 145
rights issues 121
rights of lenders 159–60
risk management fundamentals 3–5

safety legislation 8–9
sales per employee ratio 46
sales to assets ratio 46
sales to liquid surplus ratio 46
sales volume control 47–8
scrip issues 121
securities exchanges 113, 122–3
security for loans 11, 55–6, 150–3
setting of interest rates 202–4

settlement risk 24, 189
shadow directors 14
shareholders 14, 120, 121
shipping documents 81
ship's waybill 81
short sterling futures 212
sight drafts 85, 93
sole traders 14, 15
sovereign risk 6
spot values 242–3
Standard & Poor's 129–32, 135–6
standard portfolio analysis of risk
    system (SPAN) 187
standby letters of credit 80, 95
stock markets 113, 122–3
stock purchase warrants 122
stock turnover ratio 37
straddles 254
straight-line depreciation 51
strangles 254
strategic alliances 5
subscription warrants 122
subsidies 16
swaps 189, 194
    credit 196
    currency 257–61
    equity index 195–6
    interest rate 229–35
    total return 196–7
switch trading 108
SWOT analysis 116
syndicate lenders 140, 150
systemic risk 24, 190

tariffs 15
taxation 15
technological risk 20
tender guarantees 96–7
tenor drafts 68, 93–4
term of deposits 202
terrorism 20
three-month sterling futures 212
ticks 187
total return swap 196–7
trade barriers 15

trade creditors 36
trade debtors 35
trade payments 65–109
    avalising 105
    bills of exchange 68, 85, 93–4,
        179–82
    bonds/contract guarantees 95–104
    collections 87–93, 94, 180
    contract guarantees 95–104
    countertrade 105–9
    documentary letters of credit
        68–79, 95, 180
        principal documents 81–5
        types of 79–81
    drafts 68, 85, 93–4, 179–82
    export credit agencies 109
    incoterms 85–6
    open accounts 65–6
    payment in advance/on delivery
        66–8
trading risk 241–2
transfer pricing 31
transferable letters of credit 79–80

uncommitted facility agreements
    142–3
undertrading 46
unlimited liability 14

valuation of assets 28, 30
vanilla swaps 229, 230, 231–2
variable costs 119
variable rate facilities 201, 204–5
variation margin 188
venture capital 126

warranties in loan agreements 141–2
warrants 122
warranty guarantees 97, 102
wars 20
waybills 81
working capital ratio 32–3
working capital turnover ratio 38

zero coupon bonds 127